RACIST AMERICA

RACIST AMERICA

Roots, Current Realities, and Future Reparations

Joe R. Feagin

Routledge
A member of the Taylor & Francis Group
New York and London

Published in 2000 by
Routledge
29 West 35th Street
New York, NY 10001

Published in Great Britain by
Routledge
11 New Fetter Lane
London EC4P 4EE

A member of the Taylor & Francis Group

10 9 8 7 6 5 4 3 2 1

Library of Congress Cataloging-in-Publication Data
Feagin, Joe R.
   Racist America : roots, current realities, and future
reparations / Joe R. Feagin
      p.   cm.
Includes bibliographical references and index.
ISBN 0-415-92531-2 (hb : alk. paper)
1. Afro-Americans—Civil rights. 2. Afro-Americans—Social conditions—1975– 3. Racism—United States. 4. Race
discrimination. 5. United Statse—Race relations.
6. Afro-Americans—Claims. I. Title.
E185.615.F387   2000
305.8'00973—dc21   99-054694

To Roy Brooks and Hernán Vera

contents

Racist America

Antiracist Theory and Strategy

Recently, the American Civil Liberties Union (ACLU) filed a lawsuit in federal court contending that a black father and his twelve-year-old son were victims of discriminatory police targeting of black motorists — what many African Americans call the infraction of "driving while black." According to the lawsuit, this decorated war veteran and his son were stopped twice by the state police within a half hour of crossing into Oklahoma on an interstate highway. When the black motorist disputed a white officer's claim that he had not signaled for a lane change, other officers were called in. The man and his son were put in a very hot patrol car, and their complaints were ignored while their car was vigorously searched for drugs, with parts of the floorboard being removed. The son, frightened and in tears, was questioned separately by the police with a snarling dog nearby. Nothing was found in the motorist's car. Harassed and humiliated, he and his son were finally allowed to go on their way. This account of police harassment is not unique. Indeed, one New Jersey dentist was stopped by the police more than one hundred times in a four-year period as he drove from home to office in his expensive car. The targeting of black Americans is common practice for many law enforcement agencies across the nation. A 1999 ACLU report reported racial profiling by police in two dozen states.[1]

Police harassment and brutality directed at black men, women, and children are as old as American society, dating back to the days of slavery and Jim Crow segregation. Such police actions across the nation today reveal important aspects of the racism dealt with in this book—the commonplace discriminatory practices of individual whites, the images of dangerous blacks dancing in white heads, the ideology legitimating antiblack images, and the white-dominated institutions that allow or encourage such practices.

In the United States racism is structured into the rhythms of everyday life. It is lived, concrete, advantageous for whites, and painful for those who are not white. Each major part of a black or white person's life is shaped by racism. Even a person's birth and parents are shaped by racism, since mate selection is limited by racist pressures against interracial marriage. Where one lives is often determined by the racist practices of landlords, bankers, and others in the real estate profession. The clothes one wears and what one has to eat are affected by access to resources that varies by position in the racist hierarchy. When one goes off to school, her or his education is shaped by contemporary racism—from the composition of the student body to the character of the curriculum. Where one goes to church is often shaped by racism, and it is likely that racism affects who one's political representatives are. Even getting sick, dying, and being buried may be influenced by racism. Every part of the life cycle, and most aspects of one's life, are shaped by the racism that is integral to the foundation of the United States.

One of the great tragedies today is the inability or unwillingness of most white Americans to see and understand this racist reality. Among whites, including white elites, there is a commonplace *denial* of personal, family, and group histories of racism. Most do not see themselves or their families as seriously implicated in white-on-black oppression, either in the distant past or in the present. Referring to themselves, most whites will say fervently, "I am not a racist." Referring to their ancestors, many will say something like "my family never benefited from owning slaves" or "my family never benefited from segregation." Assuming racial discrimination to be mostly a thing of the past, many whites will assert that African Americans are "paranoid" about racism and will often give them firm advice: Forget the past and move on, because "slavery happened hundreds of years ago."

Numerous white commentators and scholars have suggested that racism is no longer a serious problem in the United States. One recent analysis of white attitudes on public policy and racial matters concludes that "racism is not built-in to the American ethos," while another book boldly proclaims "the end of racism."[2] A leading survey analyst, Everett Ladd, has summed up this view saying, "So let's get on with it. America is one nation, defined by shared values. It denied those values tragically in slavery and Jim Crow. Most of us, of all backgrounds, now acknowledge this." He adds that today it is wrongheaded to "think or act as though the American family is in any legitimate way understood in racial terms."[3] Writing in a leading newspaper in the late 1990s, John Bunzel, a conservative former member of the U.S. Commission on Civil Rights, expressed a view common among whites: The nation should no longer use a term like "racism" because it is a "smear word" and creates "bitterness and polarization."[4] Such unwillingness to face current racist realities is not healthy for the present or future of the United States. It has been said that a major task for the residents of the former Communist nations of Eastern Europe is to forget the falsified past once taught them and to learn the hard facts about their oppressive past. In this process, old heroes often become villains, and old villains become heroes. One can say the same about white Americans and American history. Few mainstream media presentations or school textbooks provide full and accurate accounts of the history or current status of racist oppression in the United States.

The great scholar of the Africa diaspora, C. L. R. James, once argued strongly that the oppressive situation of African Americans is the number one problem of racism in the modern world. If the problem of racism cannot be solved in the United States, it cannot be solved anywhere.[5] In this book I focus on this critical case of white-on-black oppression in the United States. One reason for this is practical: given limited space, this focus means that I can dig deeper into the development, structure, processes, and likely future of one major case of racism. My decision is also theoretically motivated. I will show that white-on-black oppression is in several important respects the archetype of racial oppression in North America. For example, African Americans were the only racial group specifically singled out several times in the U.S. Constitution for subordination within the new nation. The leading theorist of the U.S. Constitution, James Madison, noted that from a white man's point of view "the case of the black race within our bosom . . . is the problem most baffling to the policy of our country."[6] A few decades later, white-on-black oppression would be central to the bloodiest war in U.S. history, the Civil War. Within American society, African Americans have been dominated and exploited in much larger numbers than has any other group. Over nearly four centuries, tens of millions of African Americans have had their labor and wealth regularly taken from them. In contrast to other groups, their original languages, cultures, and family ties were substantially obliterated by their being torn from Africa, and the oppression faced under slavery and segregation was extremely dehumanized, racialized, and systematic. No other racially oppressed group has been so central to the internal economic, political, and cultural structure and evolution of American society—or to the often obsessively racist ideology developed by white Americans over many generations. Thus, it is time to put white-on-black oppression fully at the center of a comprehensive study of the development, meaning, and reality of this nation.

In his book I develop an antiracist theory and analysis of the white-on-black oppression that is now nearly four centuries old. Theory is a set of ideas designed to make sense of the empirical and existential reality in and around us. Concepts delineating and probing racism need to be clear and honed by everyday experience, not framed from an ivory tower. Here I attempt to develop concepts, in language understandable to the nonspecialist, that can be used for an in-depth analysis of this racist society. These concepts are designed to help readers probe beneath the many defenses and myths about "race" to the often painful racist realities. They are useful in countering inaccurate assessments of the society's history and institutions. They can be used to reshape the socialization that hampers insight into the operation of this society. A critical theory of racism can help us better understand the racialized dimensions of lives.

We need an antiracist theory not only to explain the operation of the racist system but also to envision possibilities for change. Antiracist theory attempts to facilitate human agency, the movement of human actors to bring change in spite of oppression. Since at least the time of Karl Marx, antioppression analysts have viewed the relationship between structures of oppression and human agency as dialectical. Structures of domination shape everyday existence, but an insightful knowledge of these structures and their recurring contradictions can enable people to act forcefully to resist oppression. It is hard to be optimistic in times of great oppression, but some contradictions—especially everyday resistance by those oppressed—can provide a source of optimism because they suggest the possibilities of change.

Systemic racism is about everyday experience. People are born, live, and die within the racist system. Much recent empirical research has helped to unmask the workings of this system. My theoretical perspective is informed not only by the research of others but also by numerous field research projects that I and my colleagues have undertaken in recent years. These projects have entailed hundreds of in-depth interviews with African Americans in various walks of life about their daily encounters with racism. Staying in contact with the lived experience of seasoned veterans of racism enables an analyst to move beyond the mental construction of race to the concrete reality, daily trials, and accumulating burdens of everyday racism. Black Americans and other people of color often experience the world differently from white Americans, and this experience can be an important guide for conceptualizing the structures, processes, and future of U.S. racism. My colleagues and I have also spent much time interviewing more than three hundred white Americans on their views of black Americans and on issues of public policy. I draw on these interviews in my understanding of white perspectives and actions.

Currently, we have theoretical traditions that are well developed in regard to the systems of class and gender oppression. There is a well-developed Marxist tradition with its many important conceptual contributions. The Marxist tradition provides a powerful theory of oppression centered on such key concepts as class struggle, worker exploitation, and alienation. Marxism identifies the basic social forces undergirding class oppression, shows how human beings are alienated in class relations, and points toward activist remedies for oppression. Similarly, in feminist analysis there is a diverse and well-developed conceptual framework targeting key aspects of gendered oppression. Major approaches accent the social construction of sexuality, the world gender order, and the strategy of consciousness-raising. Feminist theorists have argued that at the heart of sexism is the material reality of reproduction and sexuality, the latter including how a woman is treated and viewed sexually and how she views herself. In both the Marxist and feminist traditions there are also well-developed theories of resistance and change.

In the case of racist oppression, however, we do not as yet have as strongly agreed-upon concepts and well-developed theoretical traditions as we have for gender and class oppression. Of course, numerous researchers, writers, and activists have focused their analytical and theoretical tools on American racism now for more than a century. In this book I draw heavily on the most important analysts, including Frederick Douglass, W. E. B. Du Bois, Oliver Cox, Kwame Ture, Anna Julia Cooper, Bob Blauner, and William O. Douglas, among others. Each of these analysts has probed various aspects of America's racist history and institutions, and some have tried to define basic concepts for the analysis of racism. Beginning more than a century ago, these scholars and activists began a paradigm shift in conceptualizing and analyzing racism and antiracism. As yet, however, there is no widely used term for this antioppression paradigm, and I propose that we choose the terms *antiracist theory* and *antiracist strategy* for this ever growing antioppression tradition.

Today, the dominant social science paradigm, seen in much mainstream scholarship on "race," still views racism as something tacked onto an otherwise healthy American society. One variant of this perspective portrays the problem as one of white bigots betraying egalitarian institutions—the theme developed so well by Gunnar Myrdal and his contemporary followers (see chapter 8). Another variant in the mainstream approach accents "intergroup relations" or "race relations," the array of intergroup relations and conflicts in this society, with whites seen as only one group among many others having more or less equal impact or power. As I will show in this book, however, the central problem is that, from the beginning, European American institutions were racially hierarchical, white supremacist, and undemocratic. For the most part, they remain so today.

Nicolaus Copernicus started a revolution in astronomy by putting the sun at the center of the solar system. Begun some time ago by Frederick Douglass and W. E. B. Du Bois, a revolution in the analysis of American racism is slowly developing, one that views the U.S. social system as imbedding racism *at its very core.* The conceptual framework developed in this book places the reality, development, and crises of systemic racism at the heart of U.S. history and society. I develop a theoretical framework centered on the concept of *systemic racism*, viewed as a centuries-old foundation of American society. Systemic racism includes the complex array of antiblack practices, the unjustly gained political-economic power of whites, the continuing economic and other resource inequalities along racial lines, and the white racist ideologies and attitudes created to maintain and rationalize white privilege and power. *Systemic* here means that the core racist realities are manifested in each of society's major parts. If you break a three-dimensional hologram into separate parts and shine a laser through any one part, you can project the whole three-dimensional image again from within that part. Like a hologram, each major part of U.S. society—the economy, politics, education, religion, the family—reflects the fundamental reality of systemic racism.

There is a tendency on the part of many Americans, especially white Americans, to see racism as an individual matter, as something only outspoken white bigots engage in. Yet racism is much more that an individual matter. It is both individual and systemic. Indeed, systemic racism is perpetuated by a broad social reproduction process that generates not only recurring patterns of discrimination within institutions and by individuals but also an alienating racist relationship—on the one hand, the racially oppressed, and on the other, the racial oppressors. These two groups are created by the racist system, and thus have different group interests. The former seeks to overthrow the system, while the latter seeks to maintain it. Thus, in dialectical fashion social oppression creates contradictions that can bring about change. The great inequality of resources across the color line periodically leads to subtle or overt resistance by black Americans and other Americans of color. It is part of the nature of being positioned as "white" to be an oppressor, and it is part of the nature of being positioned as "black" to resist oppression.

While racism directed at black Americans and other Americans of color is a core characteristic of U.S. society, it is not the only major type of institutionalized oppression. I do not claim here that an antiracist theory can explain everything about societal oppression in the United States. Indeed, I reject a reductionist analysis that tries to reduce all oppressions to one type of oppression, as has been tried in certain orthodox Marxist traditions. A pluralistic analysis of oppression is ultimately necessary. Indeed, class-structured capitalism, sexism, bureaucratic authoritarianism, and homophobia are all important parts of the webbed package of oppressions internal to U.S. society. I will note some aspects of other oppressions as they interact with racial oppression at various points in this book. Ultimately a comprehensive analysis of U.S. society will require an in-depth consideration of all these areas in regard to one another. Yet, in my view we need to analyze each arena of oppression much more thoroughly than we have done to this point and not move too quickly to attempts at a comprehensive all-oppressions analysis. This is certainly true for white-on-black oppression, which is still in the early to middle stages of the theoretical and empirical analysis necessary for a full comprehension of its harsh and abiding realities.

As we begin a new millennium, whites are a modest minority of the world's population and are gradually becoming a statistical minority in the United States. Today, whites constitute less than half the population of four of the nation's largest cities—New York, Los Angeles, Chicago, and Houston. They will soon make up less than half the population in large areas of the nation, including the largest states. Demographers forecast that if current trends continue whites will be a statistical minority in California by approximately the year 2002 and in Texas by approximately the year 2010. Sometime in the middle of the twenty-first century, whites will likely be a minority of the U.S. population. Over the next few decades this demographic change will likely bring great pressures for change in the racist practices and institutions in the United States. Moreover, as the world's peoples of color become more influential in international politics and economics, still other pressures will likely be put on the institutions of the United States to treat all people of color with greater fairness and justice.

It is now past time to take an international perspective on the systemic racism that plagues the United States. Adopting an international human rights perspective gives one a place from which to critically assess human rights, social justice, and racial equality in a powerful nation-state like the United States. As I will demonstrate in this book, there is a growing international view of what are the fundamental human rights, which include rights extending well beyond the civil rights ideally guaranteed by U.S. laws. Drawing on this international viewpoint, one can argue that each person is entitled to equal concern and treatment because they are human beings, not because they are members of a particular society or nation-state. According to the United Nation's 1948 Universal Declaration of Human Rights, which the U.S. government signed, basic human rights are rooted in the inherent dignity of each human being, are inalienable and universal, and are acquired at birth by "all members of the human family." This declaration asserts the principle of nondiscrimination and equality and lists three fundamental rights: life, liberty, and personal security. The right to a life free from racial alienation and racist oppression is clearly enunciated in international law and morality. Today, the United States stands judged by international human rights doctrine and law as still unjust and inegalitarian.

Lives are like symphonies, with a grand assortment of people having effects on how we grow and develop. I am indebted to my parents Frank and Hanna Feagin for showing me that respect for others was possible even as I grew up in a sea of blatant racism in the South. I am especially grateful to my friends Connie and

Preston Williams and Melvin and Zeta Sikes for teaching me, in ways small and large, what the black experience in America means in many of its complexities, pains, frustrations, and joys. I am also indebted to my graduate school professors Tom Pettigrew and Gordon Allport, who introduced me to the study of U.S. racism and showed me that ethical concerns can be part of social science.

In the preparation of this book, I relied on Hernán Vera, Sharon Rush, Roy Brooks, and Sidney Willhelm for their friendship and encouragement, for vital discussions, and for reviews of various chapters. I would also like to thank the following scholars for their willingness to read and discuss sections of this manuscript over an extended period of years: Nestor Rodriguez, Leland Saito, Karyn McKinney, Eileen O'Brien, Carla Edwards, Jim Button, Rodney Coates, Greg Squires, Ken Nunn, Mel Sikes, Karen Pyke, Earl Smith, Ray Allen, Christiana Otto, Joseph Rahme, T. R. Young, Michelle Dunlap, Hsiao-Chuan Hsia, Claire Jean Kim, Steve Rosenthal, Nancy DiThomaso, John Liu, Kerri Vitalo, Leslie Houts, Margaret Roinkin, Jessie Daniels, and Laurel Tripp. I would also like to express my gratitude to the many black men and women, now in seven different field studies, who have explained to my colleagues and me how systemic racism still operates in their everyday lives.

one

Systemic Racism
A Comprehensive Perspective

> We the people of the United States, in order to form a more perfect union, establish justice, insure domestic tranquility, provide for the common defense, promote the general welfare, and secure the blessings of liberty to ourselves and our posterity, do ordain and establish this Constitution for the United States of America. —Preamble, U.S. Constitution

> Culturally the Negro represents a paradox: Though he is an organic part of the nation, he is excluded by the entire tide and direction of American culture. . . . Therefore if, within the confines of its present culture, the nation ever seeks to purge itself of its color hate, it will find itself at war with itself, convulsed by a spasm of emotional and moral confusion. —Richard Wright, *Black Boy*

The year is 1787, the place Philadelphia. Fifty-five men are meeting in summer's heat to write a constitution for what will be called the "first democratic nation." These founders create a document so radical in breaking from monarchy and feudal institutions that it will be condemned and attacked in numerous European countries. These radicals are men of European origin, and most are well-off by the standards of their day. Significantly, at least 40 percent have been or are slave owners, and a significant proportion of the others profit to some degree as merchants, shippers, lawyers, and bankers from the trade in slaves, commerce in slave-produced agricultural products, or supplying provisions to slaveholders and slave-traders.[1] Moreover, the man who pressed hard for this convention and now chairs it, George Washington, is one of the richest men in the colonies because of the hundreds of black men, women, and children he has held in bondage. Washington and his colleagues create the first democratic nation, yet one for whites only. In the preamble to their bold document, the founders cite prominently "We the People," but this phrase does not encompass the fifth of the population that is enslaved.

Laying a Racist Foundation   Many historical analysts have portrayed slavery as a side matter at the 1787 Constitutional Convention. Slavery was central however, as a leading participant, James Madison, made clear in his important notes on the convention's debates. Madison accented how the convention was scissored across a north/south, slave/not-slave divide among the states.[2] The southern and northern regions were gradually diverging in their politicoeconomic frameworks. Slavery had once been of some, albeit greatly varying, importance in all states, but the northern states were moving away from chattel slavery as a part of their local economies, and some were seeing a growing abolitionist sentiment. Even so, many northern merchants, shippers, and consumers still depended on products produced by southern slave plantations, and many merchants sold goods to the plantations.

Debates Influenced by Slavery   While all delegates to the Constitutional Convention agreed that the new government should protect private property, and thus economic inequality, this elite had a right wing, a center, and a left wing. The small left wing, with its strong views on equality and popular revolution, was closest to the general population, and some of its members had dominated the writing of the Declaration of Independence. At the Constitutional Convention, however, the center and the right wing had more influence. The right wing included twenty-one delegates who desired some form of monarchy for the new nation. The left wing and center were able to successfully counter this desire for monarchy, for that seemed unacceptable to the majority of the population. In numerous provisions the final document was oriented to political liberty: there was agreement on rejecting religious tests for office and an established religion, on protecting freedom of debate in Congress, and on protecting citizens from arbitrary government. Even so, many right wing and center delegates at the convention were antidemocratic in their thinking, fearing "the masses." The left wing was unable to add a specific list of individual rights to the Constitution, and some states did not ratify the new document until their populations were persuaded that a democratic Bill of Rights would be added.[3]

The trade in, and enslavement of, people of African descent was an important and divisive issue for the convention. Most of these prominent, generally well-educated men accepted the view that people of African descent could be the chattel property of others—and not human beings with citizens' rights. At the heart of the Constitution was protection of the property and wealth of the affluent bourgeoisie in the new nation, including property in those enslaved. There was near unanimity on the idea, as delegate Gouverneur Morris (New York) put it, that property is the "main object of Society."[4] For the founders, freedom meant the protection of unequal accumulation of property, particularly property that could produce a profit in the emerging capitalist system. Certain political, economic, and racial interests were conjoined. This was not just a political gathering with the purpose of creating a major new bourgeois-democratic government; it was also a meeting to protect the racial and economic interests of men with substantial property and wealth in the colonies. As Herbert Aptheker has put it, the Constitution was a "bourgeois-democratic document for the governing of a slaveholder-capitalist republic."[5]

The harsh reality of slave conditions and the death-dealing slave trade hung over the Convention like a demonic specter. Slavery intruded on important debates, perhaps most centrally debates over representation in Congress. Northern and southern delegates vigorously argued the matter and reached the famous three-fifths compromise on counting slaves for the purpose of white representation. Article I speaks only of three groups in the new nation: "free persons," "Indians not taxed," and "all other persons." The "other" persons they had in mind were those enslaved, mostly those of African descent. Whether free or enslaved, African Americans were not to be citizens or voters, yet 60 percent of their number could be counted to enlarge white representation in the states. Interestingly, the earlier Articles of Confederation had used the term "white" in setting the formula for enumerating the population. The new Constitution made use of the Confederation's language in this regard but without the word "white."[6]

One delegate from Pennsylvania, James Wilson, questioned the three-fifths compromise; he did not see "on what principle the admission of blacks in the proportion of three-fifths could be explained. Are they admitted as Citizens? Then why are they not admitted on an equality with White Citizens? Are they admitted as property? Then why is not other property admitted into the computation?"[7] The answer, however, was clear. Enslaved blacks were to be counted as human beings only when it suited whites to do so. Otherwise, they were white property. These framers of the Constitution realized that they were divesting black people of their humanity. Soon after the convention, the *Federalist Papers* supported the compromise thus: "Let the case of the slaves be considered as it is in truth, a peculiar one. Let the compromising expedient of the Constitution be mutually adopted, which regards them as inhabitants, but as debased by servitude below the equal level of free inhabitants; which regards the slave as divested of two fifths of the man."[8]

The new nation formed by European Americans in the late eighteenth century was openly and officially viewed as a *white* republic. These founders sought to build a racially based republic in the face of monarchical opposition and against those people on the North American continent whom they defined as inferior and as problems. James Madison, who enslaved many black Americans himself, put it thus: "Next to the case of the black race within our bosom, that of the red on our borders is the problem most baffling to the policy of our country."[9]

The concerns of slaveholders would appear again and again in debates over taxation, the presidency, commerce, and other matters. For example, initially there were two days of debates over the importation of slaves into the colonies. Some members denounced the trade, while others vigorously defended it and argued that no Constitution would be accepted if the trade was not protected. In the end, a compromise was reached and placed in Article I, Section 9. This section allowed the brutal trade to continue until at least 1807.[10] Historian Donald Robinson concluded that "rarely, if ever in human history, has the institution of slavery formed so fundamental and so pervasive a part of the political community."[11]

At the convention a few delegates spoke critically of chattel slavery or the slave trade. George Mason, a prominent Virginia slaveholder, blamed the slave trade on the greed of British merchants. He noted the threat of slave uprisings and argued that slavery made poor whites lazy. As Mason saw it, "every master of slaves is born a petty tyrant." Strikingly, however, Mason did not mention slavery's impact on those in chains.[12] He and delegate Elbridge Gerry (Massachusetts) would later refuse to sign the document, in part because of its slavery provisions. Yet their objections were not moral but political. Mason feared that the continuing slave trade would make the new United States "more vulnerable" and less capable of defense.[13]

Not one of the fifty-five delegates advocated that the abolition of slavery should be an integral part of the new Constitution. On key votes most northern delegations voted with southern delegations, in part because the trade in slaves and slave-produced products was of economic benefit to many northern traders and merchants. At one point Luther Martin, a slaveholding delegate from Maryland, expressed the view that there should be a tax on those imported for enslavement. Representing the views of a state with a surplus of enslaved Africans, Martin sought to reduce the overseas slave trade. The South Carolina delegate John Rutledge, also a slaveholder, opposed the proposal and threatened secession if it were included; the "true question at present is whether the Southern States shall or shall not be parties to the Union," he explained. If the northern representatives consulted "their interest," Rutledge added, they should "not oppose the increase of slaves which will increase the commodities of which they will become carriers." Oliver Ellsworth, a Connecticut representative and later Chief Justice of the Supreme Court, supported this view, arguing that he did not want to debate the "wisdom of slavery" and felt that "what enriches a part enriches the whole" of the nation.[14]

In regard to a provision about extradition of criminals, Pierce Butler and Charles Pinckney, both of South Carolina, moved that fugitive slaves should be returned "like criminals" to their owners. Significantly, no delegate spoke about the oppressive conditions faced by runaway slaves. Instead, James Wilson argued only that such a requirement would put a financial burden on northern governments, while Roger Sherman (Connecticut) noted that he saw "no more propriety in the public seizing and surrendering a slave or servant, than a horse."[15]

The "Most Prominent Feature"   In one of the vigorous debates touching on slavery, the wealthy Gouverneur Morris noted cogently that "domestic slavery is the most prominent feature in the aristocratic countenance of the proposed

Constitution."[16] By the end of the summer of 1787 there were at least seven sections where the framers had the system of slavery in mind: (1) Article 1, Section 2, which counts slaves as three fifths of a person; (2) Article 1, Sections 2 and 9, which apportion taxes on the states using the three-fifths formula; (3) Article 1, Section 8, which gives Congress authority to suppress slave and other insurrections; (4) Article 1, Section 9, which prevents the slave trade from being abolished before 1808; (5) Article 1, Sections 9 and 10, which exempt goods made by slaves from export duties; (6) Article 4, Section 2, which requires the return of fugitive slaves; and (7) Article 4, Section 4, which stipulates that the federal government must help state governments put down domestic violence, including slave uprisings.[17]

The founders were aware of the oppressiveness and cruelty of the slavery from which they profited. In spite of their freedom to speak, read, and do business in the colonies, they and other whites often described their own sociopolitical condition as one of actual or potential "slavery." As F. Nwabueze Okoye has put it, "The allusions, similes, metaphors, and concrete images which they utilized reveal how profoundly and disturbingly chattel slavery was embedded in their consciousness. It was, in fact, their nightmare."[18] Many publications and pamphlets of the revolutionary period compared colonial conditions under the British king to slavery. As early as 1774, the ever influential George Washington noted the coming crisis over colonists' rights: "The crisis is arrived when we must assert our rights, or submit to every imposition, that can be heaped upon us, till custom and use shall make us tame and abject slaves, as the blacks we rule over with such arbitrary sway."[19] One Convention delegate, John Dickinson, expressed the common view: "*Those* who are *taxed* without their own consent, expressed by themselves or their representatives, are *slaves. We are taxed* without our own consent, expressed by ourselves or our representatives. *We* are therefore—SLAVES."[20] Dickinson, a farmer and lawyer, was at one time the largest slaveholder in Philadelphia. Dickinson, Washington, and other influential white leaders described slavery as creating people who would be cowardly, weak, degenerate, and inferior. From their viewpoint, only black Americans deserved to be kept and treated as slaves.

Generally, the founders viewed Americans from Africa as slaves by *natural law*. Conceptualized as inferior beings, these Africans were fit by nature for enslavement by whites. Natural law was also used to explain why the white male founders and their compatriots could subordinate two other large groups—white women and Native Americans. White women were not directly mentioned in the Constitution, and their legal rights under local and national laws were limited. In Article I of the Constitution, the section dealing with Congress regulating interstate and foreign commerce adds relations with "Indian tribes," indicating that indigenous peoples were not generally seen by the founders as part of their new nation. Until the mid- to late nineteenth century, indigenous societies were generally viewed as separate nations, with some whites advocating treaty making, land purchases, and the "civilizing" of Native Americans while others pressed for land theft, extermination, or removal of all Native Americans to the distant western areas of the new nation.[21]

A House Founded on Antiblack Racism   Antiblack racism is centrally about the lived experiences and interactions of black and white Americans. Historical events represent, reflect, and embed the tangible realities of everyday life—both the means of concrete oppression and the means of symbolizing and thinking about that domination. Every day in the United States a great number of politicians, columnists, teachers, lawyers, executives, and ordinary Americans cite the U.S. Constitution, and the founders' actions, as the underpinning and glory of U.S. society. The founders' decisions and understandings still shape the lives of all Americans in many different ways.

The "Agreement with Hell"   The U.S. Constitutional Convention, the first such in the democratic history of the modern world, laid a strong base for the new societal "house" called the United States. Yet from the beginning this house's foundation was fundamentally flawed. While most Americans have thought of this document and the sociopolitical structure it created as keeping the nation together, in fact this structure was created to maintain separation and oppression at the time and for the foreseeable future. The framers reinforced and legitimated a system of racist oppression that they thought would ensure that whites, especially white men of means, would rule for centuries to come.

The system they created was riddled with contradictions that have surfaced repeatedly over the course of U.S. history. By the 1830s and 1840s, for example, many black and white abolitionists were aggressively protesting slavery and the constitutional document undergirding it. Before this period there had been white antislavery advocates—black Americans, of course, had advocated abolition from the beginning—but large-scale action against the slavery system did not take place until the nineteenth century. At one 1843 meeting of the Massachusetts Anti-Slavery Society a resolution was adopted: "Resolved, that the Compact which exists between the North and the South is a 'covenant with death, and an agreement with hell'—involving both parties in atrocious criminality—and should be immediately annulled." At a gathering in Massachusetts on July 4, 1854, the eminent abolitionist, William Lloyd Garrison, burned a copy of the U.S. Constitution, uttering the words: "So perish all compromises with tyranny."[22]

The "Normality" of Slavery   Then, as now, this was not the prevailing view of the U.S. Constitution. Indeed, in the first two centuries of the new nation the majority of white Americans, in spite of the professed ethic of liberty, saw nothing wrong with the brutal subordination of black Americans or the driving away or killing of Native Americans. This was true for a great range of white Americans. Religious leaders like Cotton Mather, the famous Puritan, and William Penn, a Quaker and

founder of Pennsylvania, owned black Americans. The founder of American psy-
chiatry and perhaps the leading intellectual of his day, Dr. Benjamin Rush, owned
a black American. Men of politics like Thomas Jefferson, George Washington,
Alexander Hamilton, Patrick Henry, Benjamin Franklin, John Hancock, and Sam
Houston enslaved black Americans. Ten U.S. presidents (Washington, Jefferson,
James Madison, James Monroe, Andrew Jackson, John Tyler, James Polk, Zachary
Taylor, Andrew Johnson, and Ulysses S. Grant) at some point in their lives enslaved
African Americans.[23]

Many in the elites at the head of the new United States supported, or were not
uncomfortable with, the idea of a *permanent* slave society. Even as president,
Abraham Lincoln, often called the Great Emancipator, was willing to support a
constitutional amendment making slavery permanent in the existing southern
states if that would prevent a civil war. Such a projected proslavery amendment
was supported by many Republicans and was actually approved by both houses of
the U.S. Congress in early 1861.[24] Strikingly, from the 1780s to the Civil War period,
some slaveholders articulated grand visions of expanding the U.S. slavery system
across the globe.

Understanding the centrality and harsh realities of slavery leads to some tough
questions for today: How are we to regard the "founding fathers"? They are our
founding fathers, yet many were oppressors who made their living by killing, bru-
talizing, and exploiting other human beings. The combination of white freedom
and black enslavement seems radically contradictory. However, William Wiecek
notes that "the paradox dissolves when we recall that American slavery was racial.
White freedom was entirely compatible with black enslavement. African
Americans were, as the framers of Virginia's first Constitution determined, simply
not part of the Lockean body politic."[25] Indeed, the work of those enslaved brought
the wealth and leisure that whites, especially those in the ruling class, could use
to pursue their own liberty and freedom. Some recent analysts have argued that it
is unfair to judge early white leaders by contemporary standards. However, there
were strong opponents of slavery among whites at that time, including many white
antislavery advocates. The founders themselves sometimes exhibited guilt over
the system of slavery. James Madison himself argued that it would be wrong to
state openly in the Constitution the "idea that there could be property in men."[26]
As a result, the words *slave* and *slavery* do not appear in the document; euphemistic
terminology is used in the sections dealing with slavery.

Into the mid-nineteenth century, the majority of whites—in the elites and
among ordinary folk—either participated directly in slavery or in the trade around
slavery, or did not object to those who did so. The antihuman savagery called *slavery* was considered *normal* in what was then seen as a white republic. This point
must be understood well if one it to probe deeply into the origins, maintenance,
and persistence of racist patterns and institutions in North America. W. E. B. Du

Bois put this forcefully in summing up European colonialism in the Americas and elsewhere, saying, "There was no Nazi atrocity—concentration camps, wholesale maiming and murder, defilement of women and ghastly blasphemy of child-hood—which the Christian civilization of Europe had not long been practicing against colored folk in all parts of the world in the name of and for the defense of a Superior Race born to rule the world."[27]

A Continuing Foundation   European colonialism and imperialism eventually reached most of the globe and thus created a *global racist order*, which has had severe consequences for the world's peoples now for centuries. The U.S. Constitution, which embraced slavery and imbedded the global racist order in the United States, remains the nation's legal, political, and—to a substantial degree—moral foundation. Its openly racist provisions, though overridden by amendments, have not been deleted. At no point has a new Constitutional Convention been held to replace this document with one created by representatives of all the peo-ple, including the great majority of the population not represented at the 1787 Convention. Moreover, the racist spirit of the original document persists today. Even as they live in, and often maintain, a racist system, most white Americans still do not see slavery, legal segregation, or contemporary racism as part of the nation's foundation. At the most, the majority see racist institutions as something in the distant past, something tacked on to a great nation for a short time, and something nonsystemic. From their perspective the racism that may have once intruded into the American house has substantially been eradicated.

Toward a Theory of Systemic Racism

A Rich Conceptual Tradition   The black intellectual tradition is a rich source for developing a far more accurate and systemic view of this American house of racism. Drawing on the analyses of Frederick Douglass, W. E. B. Du Bois, Oliver Cox, Anna Julia Cooper, Kwame Ture, and Frantz Fanon, among others, I accent here a conceptual framework understanding American racism as centuries-long, deep-lying, institutionalized, and systemic. As I suggested in the introduction, *systemic racism* includes a diverse assortment of racist practices; the unjustly gained eco-nomic and political power of whites; the continuing resource inequalities; and the white-racist ideologies, attitudes, and institutions created to preserve white advan-tages and power. One can accurately describe the United States as a "total racist society" in which every major aspect of life is shaped to some degree by the core racist realities.

Frederick Douglass was one of the first U.S. analysts to develop a conceptual approach accenting *institutionalized* racism across many sectors of society. In 1881, speaking about the ubiquitous impact of racist prejudice and discrimination, he argued that "[i]n nearly every department of American life [black Americans] are confronted by this insidious influence. It fills the air. It meets them at the workshop and factory, when they apply for work. It meets them at the church, at the hotel, at the ballot-box, and worst of all, it meets them in the jury-box. . . . [the black American] has ceased to be a *slave of an individual*, but has in some sense become *the slave of society*."[28] No longer did a small group of slaveholders hold black Americans in chains; the *total racist society* held them in bondage. This broad conception of racism permeated Douglass's later speeches and writings. By the late 1800s, and early 1900s, drawing on the black experience and intellectual tradition, W. E. B. Du Bois was working from a conceptual perspective viewing U.S. society as pervaded by racism across major institutions. He was probably the first social scientist to analyze the emergence of the dominant idea of "whiteness" and of a white-racist order extending beyond the United States. Writing of the years around 1900, Du Bois argued, "White supremacy was all but world-wide. Africa was dead, India conquered, Japan isolated, and China prostrate. . . . The using of men for the benefit of masters is no new invention of modern Europe. . . . But Europe proposed to apply it on a scale and with an elaborateness of detail of which no former world ever dreamed."[29]

The first extended analysis of U.S. society as a system of racism was probably that of Oliver C. Cox, who provided in the 1940s a well-honed, book-length argument showing how the sustained labor exploitation of black Americans had created a centuries-old structure of racial classes. In the case of African Americans, the white elite decided "to proletarianize a whole people—that is to say, the whole people is looked upon as a class—whereas white proletarianization involves only a section of the white people."[30] By the 1960s a number of black activists and scholars were developing the institutional-racism perspective even further. For example, drawing on Du Bois and Fanon, Kwame Ture and Charles Hamilton demonstrated in some emipirical and theoretical detail the importance of institutionalized racism—the patterns of racism built into this society's major institutions, the discriminatory patterns and practices involving much more than the actions of scattered white bigots.[31] Moreover, by the late 1960s a few white scholars and analysts were also moving in the direction of accenting institutional racism.[32] These critical black and white analysts saw racism as much more than demons in white minds, for white racism entails a complex array of racialized relationships developed over many generations and imbedded in all major societal institutions.

Historically the social-science study of racial oppression has been identified by such terms as "intergroup relations" or "race relations." These somewhat ambiguous and euphemistic phrases are accented by many analysts who prefer to view an array of racial groups as more or less responsible for the U.S. "race problem." Such terminology, however, can allow the spotlight to be taken off the whites who have created and maintained the system of racism. Moreover, many white analysts have written about the "race problem" as "in" U.S. society. Yet, race relations—or, more accurately, *racist relations*—are not *in*, but rather *of* this society. In the American case systemic racism began with European colonists enriching themselves substantially at the expense of indigenous peoples and the Africans they imported for enslavement. This brutally executed enrichment was part of the new society's foundation, not something tacked onto an otherwise healthy and egalitarian system.

In the rest of this chapter we will examine briefly some key aspects of systemic racism, including: (1) the patterns of unjust impoverishment and unjust enrichment and their transmission over time; (2) the resulting vested group interests and the alienating racist relation; (3) the costs and burdens of racism; (4) the important role of white elites; (5) the rationalization of racial oppression in racist ideology; and (6) the resistance to racism.

Undeserved Impoverishment and Enrichment   Analyzing Europe's colonization of Africa, Du Bois demonstrated that extreme poverty and degradation in the African colonies was "a main cause of wealth and luxury in Europe. The results of this poverty were disease, ignorance, and crime. Yet these had to be represented as natural characteristics of backward peoples."[33] The unjust and brutal exploitation of African labor and land had long been downplayed in most historical accounts of European affluence. By bringing the unjust impoverishment of Africa back into the picture, Du Bois showed that this impoverishment was directly and centrally linked to European prosperity and affluence. A similar connection needs to be made between the immiseration and impoverishment of black Americans and the enrichment and prosperity of European Americans.

Several scholars, including Theodore Cross, Patricia Williams, Ian Ayres, and Richard Delgado, have suggested extending the idea of *unjust enrichment*, an idea taken from the Anglo-American legal tradition, to discuss the reality and consequences of racist oppression.[34] *Unjust enrichment* is an old legal term associated with relationships between individuals. One legal dictionary defines the concept as "circumstances which give rise to the obligation of restitution, that is, the receiving and retention of property, money, or benefits which in justice and equity belong to another."[35] This legal concept encompasses not only the receiving of benefits that justly belong to another but also the obligation to make restitution for that injustice. This idea can be extended beyond individual relationships envisioned in the traditional legal argument to the unjust theft of labor or resources by one group, such as white Americans, from another group, such as black Americans. I suggest here the parallel idea of *unjust impoverishment* to describe the conditions of those who suffer oppression. As we will see later in this book, for over fourteen generations the exploitation of African Americans has redistributed income and wealth earned by them to generations of white Americans, leaving the former relatively impoverished as a group and the latter relatively privileged and affluent as a group.

Racial Classes with Vested Group Interests   Understanding how this undeserved impoverishment and enrichment gets transmitted, reproduced, and institutionalized over generations of white and black Americans is an important step in developing an adequate conceptual framework. Black labor was used unjustly for building up the wealth of this white-dominated nation from the 1600s to at least the 1960s—the slavery and legal segregation periods (see chapter 2). Recall Oliver Cox's arguments that the sustained process of black labor exploitation created a structure with contending racial classes. Black Americans as a group were proletarianized to build up white profits and prosperity. Racial classes are the rungs on the racist ladder and thus have greatly divergent group interests.

Arising in Middle English, the word *interest* (literally "to be between") originally meant a title to or share in something. From the beginning this idea of interest has entailed social relations. A *group interest* can now be seen as a relation of being objectively concerned in something, of having a stake in something. Interests are outcomes likely to benefit the members of a particular class or group. Thus, whites are strong *stakeholders* in a centuries-old hierarchical structure of opportunities, wealth, and privileges that stems from a long history of exploitation and oppression. The interests of the white racial class have included not only a concrete interest in labor and other exploitation during the slavery and segregation periods, but also a concrete interest later on in maintaining the privileges inherited from one's ancestors.

The racial-class system, initially created by the white ruling class, provided benefits to most white Americans. From the seventeenth century onward, the farms and plantations run with enslaved laborers brought significant income and wealth to many white Americans, and not just to their particular owners. These enterprises multiplied economic development for white Americans well outside the farms' and plantations' immediate geographical areas (see chapter 2). As we will see shortly, ordinary whites for the most part bought into the identity of whiteness, thereby binding themselves to the white racial class.

Slavery's impact extended well beyond the economy. Each institutional arena in the new nation was controlled by whites and was closely linked to other major arenas. As we have seen, the new Constitution and its "democratic" political system were grounded in the racist thinking and practices of white men, many of whom had links to slavery. Those who dominated the economic system crafted the political system. Likewise the religious, legal, educational, and media systems were interlinked with the slavery economy and polity. Woven through each institutional area was a broad racist ideology—a set of principles and views—centered on rationalizing white-on-black domination and creating positive views of whiteness.

Alienated Racist Relations   Systemic racism involves recurring and unequal relationships between groups and individuals. At the macrolevel, large-scale institutions—with their white-controlled normative structures—routinely perpetuate racial subordination and inequalities. These institutions are created and recreated by routine actions at the microlevel by individuals. Philomena Essed has noted that individual acts of discrimination regularly activate whites' group power. Discriminatory practices express the collective interests of whites and regularly activate and sustain the underlying racial hierarchy.[36]

People do not experience "race" in the abstract but in concrete recurring relationships with one another. Individuals, whether they are the perpetrators of discrimination or the recipients of discrimination, are caught in a complex web of *alienating racist relations.* These socially imbedded racist relations distort what could be engaging and egalitarian relationships into alienated relationships. The system of racism categorizes and divides human beings from each other and thus severely impedes the development of common consciousness and solidarity. It fractures human nature by separating those defined and elevated as the "superior race" against those defined and subordinated as the "inferior race." As a result, life under a system of racism involves an ongoing struggle between racially defined human communities—one seeking to preserve its unjustly derived status and privileges and the other seeking to overthrow its oppression.[37]

The alienation of oppression extends to other areas. In the case of black Americans, that which should most be their own—control over life and work—is that which is most taken away from them by the system of racism. There is a parallel here to the alienation described by analysts of class and gender oppression. In Karl Marx's analysis of capitalism, the workers' labor, that which is most their own, is that which is most taken away from their control by the capitalist employer. The worker is separated from control over, and thus alienated from, his or her work. In addition, feminist theorists have shown that at the heart of a sexist society is an alienating reality of dehumanized sexuality. Women are separated by sexism from control over how their own sexuality is defined.[38] To lose significant control over one's own life choices, body definition, future, and even self is what subordination imposes. Thus, racial oppression forces a lifelong struggle by black Americans, as a group and as individuals, to attain their inalienable human rights. Dehumanization is systemic racism's psychological dynamic, and racialized roles are its social masks. Recurring exploitation, discrimination, and inequality constitute its structure, and patterns such as residential segregation are its spatial manifestations.[39]

In much theorizing about contemporary racial inequalities and conflicts, racial matters have been more or less reduced to issues of class, as in some Marxist work,[40] or to issues of socioeconomic status, as in the work of William Julius Wilson.[41] Many analysts have argued that racism is of declining importance in U.S. society.[42] These positions have been rigorously contested. Michael Omi and Howard Winant have shown with sustained evidence and argument that "race" cannot be reduced to ethnicity or class, but rather is an "autonomous field of social conflict, political organization and cultural/ideological meaning."[43]

However, even among those analysts who take contemporary racism seriously, such as Omi and Winant and Robert Miles,[44] there is in my judgement too much emphasis on the ideological construction of race or the formation of racial meanings and identities. While these are very important aspects of systemic racism—which I examine in detail in chapters 3 and 4—they are by no means the most important aspects. As is clear from the arguments above and the chapters that follow, the conceptual framework I accent is grounded in an understanding of the concrete advantages whites have gained, unjustly, over several centuries of slavery, segregation, and contemporary racism.

Systemic racism is not just about the construction of racial images, attitudes, and identities. It is even more centrally about the creation, development, and maintenance of white privilege, economic wealth, and sociopolitical power over nearly four centuries. It is about hierarchical interaction. The past and present worlds of racism include not only racist relations at work but also the racist relations that black Americans and other Americans of color encounter in trying to secure adequate housing, consumer goods, and public accommodations for themselves and their families. Racism reaches deeply into family lives, shaping who has personal relations with whom, and who gets married to whom. Racism shapes which groups have the best health, get the best medical care, and live the longest lives. As Cornel West has put it, "Categories are constructed. Scars and bruises are felt with human bodies, some of which end up in coffins. Death is not a construct."[45]

Undeserved Impoverishment and Undeserved Enrichment

The Wealth of a White Nation   Not long ago, Bob Dole, onetime Senate Majority Leader and presidential candidate, spoke in a television interview of "displaced" white men who must compete with black workers because of affirmative action. He said that he was not sure that "people in America" (presumably he meant whites) should now be paying a price for racial discrimination that occurred "before they were born." He was fairly candid about the past, saying, "We did discriminate. We did suppress people. It was wrong. Slavery was wrong." Yet Dole added that he was not sure any compensation for this damage was now due. Similarly, Representative Henry Hyde (R-Illinois), who served as chair of the House Judiciary Committee, has commented that the idea of collective guilt for slavery in the distant past "is an idea whose time has gone. I never owned a slave. I never oppressed anybody. I don't know that I should have to pay for someone who did generations before I was born."[46] This questioning of the relevance of the racist past for the present is commonplace among white Americans.

Sources of White Wealth: A Vignette   Consider four young children coming into the American colonies in the late seventeenth century. An African brother and sister are ripped from their homes and imported in chains into Virginia, the largest slaveholding colony. Their African names being ignored, they are renamed "negro

John" and "negro Mary" (no last name) by the white family that purchased them from a slave ship. This white (Smith) family has young twins, William and Priscilla. Their first and last names are those given to them by their parents, and they never wear chains. The enslaved children are seen as "black" by the Smith family, while the twins will live as "white."

What do these children and their descendants have to look forward to? Their experiences will be very different as a result of the system of racist oppression. William's and Priscilla's lives may be hard because of the physical environment, but they and their descendants will likely build lives with an array of personal choices and the passing down of significant social resources. As a girl and later as a woman, Priscilla will not have the same privileges as William, but her life is more likely to be economically supported and protected than Mary's. Indeed, John and Mary face a stark, often violent existence, with most of their lives determined by the whims of the slaveholder, who has stolen not only their labor but their lives. They will never see their families or home societies again. They can be radically separated at any time, a separation much less likely for William and Priscilla. From their and other slaves' labor some wealth will be generated for the Smith family and passed on to later generations. Unlike the white twins, John and Mary will not be allowed to read or write and will be forced to replace their African language with English. Where they eat and sleep will be largely determined by whites. As they grow older, major decisions about their personal and family relationships will be made by whites. Mary will face repeated sexual threats, coercion, and rape at the hands of male overseers and slaveholders, perhaps including William. Moreover, if John even looks at Priscilla the wrong way, he is likely to be punished severely.

If John and Mary are later allowed to have spouses and children, they will face a much greater infant mortality rate than whites. And their surviving children may well be taken from them, so that they and later generations may have great difficulty in keeping the full memory of their ancestors, a problem not faced by William and Priscilla. If John or Mary resist their oppression, they are likely to be whipped, put in chains, or have an iron bit put in their mouths. If John is rebellious or runs away too much, he may face castration. John and Mary will have to struggle very hard to keep their families together because the slaveholders can destroy them at any moment. Still, together with other black Americans, they build a culture of resistance carried from generation to generation in oral traditions. Moreover, for many more generations John's and Mary's descendants will suffer similarly severe conditions as the property of white families. Few if any of their descendants will see freedom until the 1860s.

The end of slavery does not end the large-scale oppression faced by John's and Mary's descendants. For four more generations after 1865 the near-slavery called legal or de facto segregation will confront them, but of course will not affect the descendants of William and Priscilla Smith. The later black generations will also be unable to build up resources and wealth; they will have their lives substantially determined by the white enforcers of comprehensive segregation. Where they can get a job, where they can live, whether and where they can go to school, and how they can travel will still be significantly determined by whites. Some may face brutal beatings or lynchings by whites, especially if they resist oppression. They will have inherited no wealth from many generations of enslaved ancestors, and they are unlikely to garner resources themselves to pass along to later generations. From the late 1600s to the 1960s, John and Mary and their descendants have been at an extreme economic, political, and social disadvantage compared to William and Priscilla Smith and their descendants. The lives of these black Americans have been shortened, their opportunities severely limited, their inherited resources all but nonexistent, and their families pressured by generations of well-organized racial oppression.

The desegregation era of the 1960s may renew hopes for major changes in the system of racism. But the changes bear a great price. For example, the parents of young black children will be forced to watch them be spit upon by howling mobs of whites seeking to stop school desegregation. Since the civil rights movement forced an end to legal segregation in the 1960s, John's and Mary's descendants have had more opportunity to control their lives and to garner some socioeconomic resources. Yet they have faced large-scale discrimination in employment, housing, and most other arenas of U.S. society because the 1960s' civil rights laws are largely unenforced. The descendants of William and Priscilla Smith have not faced such discrimination, nor have the many whites whose families came into the nation after the end of slavery or legal segregation. Over the many generations since the late 1600s, John's and Mary's descendants have usually been unable to build up the economic, educational, and cultural resources necessary to compete effectively with white individuals and the greater socioeconomic resources they typically enjoy. Most of William and Priscilla Smith's descendants, as the beneficiaries of the oppression of John and Mary's descendants, have more or less prospered.

From this vignette we can begin to see how racism is economically and systematically constructed. Unjust impoverishment for John and Mary and undeserved enrichment for William and Priscilla become bequeathed inheritances for many later generations. Undeserved impoverishment and enrichment are at the heart of colonial land theft and the brutal slavery system. Over time this ill-gotten gain has been used and invested by white colonizers and their descendants to construct a prosperous white-dominated nation. Today there is a general denial in the white population that black Americans have contributed much to American (or Western) development and civilization. This denial is part of contemporary white racist misunderstandings of the reality of the history of the West. However, the facts are clear: The slavery system provided much stimulus for economic development and generated critical surplus capital for the new nation. As we will see in chapter 2, without the enslaved labor of millions of black Americans, there might well not be a prosperous United States today.

Extorting More Resources: Legal Segregation   Once in place, oppressive institutions have demonstrated great social inertia. When the Civil War and the Thirteenth Amendment to the Constitution put an end to official slavery, systemic racism soon took the form of officially sanctioned segregation, the process that Douglass called blacks becoming "slaves of society." Like slavery, widespread segregation was implemented under the cover of law. Extensive Jim Crow segregation of free African Americans—in employment, housing, the justice system, and politics—was invented in the North in the 1700s and early 1800s. It was firmly in place there when southern elites adopted it. Significantly, the war and its aftermath created a national economy, with the South becoming ever more integrated into that economy. A national system of racist exploitation of black labor now parallelled the growth of a national economic system.[47]

The Thirteenth Amendment abolished slavery but did not abolish the new barriers faced by those formerly enslaved. After the Civil War the status of being a slave for an individual master was replaced by a condition of being a slave to white society, in both the North and South. Access to wealth-building property and other resources was for the most part not open to the technically "free" African Americans. In contrast, whites coming of age in the century between the end of slavery and the early 1960s—including recent immigrants—were generally able to accumulate family resources or individual opportunities, unfairly and very disproportionately, because there was little or no black competition for most critical resources and opportunities. As we will see in later chapters, these resources and opportunities included, among other things, decent-paying jobs, quality educations, good farm land, oil leases, airline routes, radio and television frequencies, and good housing areas. The new barriers of segregation were regularly enforced by individual and organized violence, including police brutality, and many house burnings, bombs, beatings, and lynchings.

Contemporary Racism: More Impoverishment and Enrichment   With the end of apartheid in the United States in the 1960s came some changes in the operation of systemic racism. For the first time African Americans had, at least in theory, access to many areas of the economy and the larger society that had been off limits to them for centuries. However, the political and legal changes of the contemporary era have by no means eradicated racism as the foundation of the American house. Since the 1960s racial oppression has persisted in widespread discrimination against African Americans—often in violation of civil rights laws. To make matters worse, these laws have for the most part been weakly enforced. Some continuing oppression of black Americans is more covert or subtle than in the past, and this can make racist practices difficult to see for those who are not the targets. Nonetheless, racism is still systemic and webbed across all sectors of society. Whites still dominate almost every major organization and most major resources, be they economic, political, educational, or legal. And official violence against African Americans can still be seen in recurring instances of police mal-practice and brutality.

In chapters 5 through 7 we will detail the character of this current oppression and exploitation of African Americans and its many advantages for whites. Here we can briefly note one example: like the legally segregated economy of the 1950s, the contemporary U.S. economy channels many black Americans into certain types of jobs and away from other employment. Many do not have access to good-paying jobs—or face unemployment—because of direct discrimination in the job market or because of the use of screening barriers by white employers that reflect the lack of access by these workers to adequate training or education. Not only are black workers often channeled into lower paying jobs, but the jobs they often hold service whites. Once again racial exploitation takes the form of transferring the benefits of the labor of blacks to whites. For centuries this transfer was done through slavery and segregation. Today, many low-wage service and unskilled menial jobs are held by African Americans or other people of color who service white managers, employers, or skilled workers. As Iris Young explains, "These jobs entail a transfer of energies whereby the servers enhance the status of those served."[48] In addition, even those black Americans who do secure good-paying jobs still face many other racist hurdles in workplaces. Employment discrimination has serious consequences that take the form of undeserved impoverishment for blacks and unfair enrichment for whites.

Today, the mechanisms of racial oppression and de facto segregation continue to operate in all major areas of U.S. society—a situation Supreme Court Justice William O. Douglas once described as "slavery unwilling to die."[49]

Social Reproduction: Transmitting Wealth and Privilege across Generations

How does prior wealth and privilege, however gained, translate into wealth and privilege for later generations? How is it reproduced from one generation to the next? And what are the main forms of sociocultural resources that are transmitted? More generally, how is the societal system of inequality reproduced as a whole? There is remarkably little discussion of these important issues, for any type of socioeconomic resources, in the social science literature. Yet, an intertemporal perspective on racial oppression is critical to a deep understanding of the devel-opment and structure of U.S. society.

Since this is a central argument of this book, let me elaborate this concept of *social reproduction*. For systemic racism to persist across many generations, it must reproduce the necessary socioeconomic conditions. These conditions include sub-stantial control by whites of major economic resources and posession of the political, police, and ideological power to dominate subordinated racial groups. Systemic racism is perpetuated by social processes that reproduce not only racial inequality but also the fundamental racist relation—on the one hand, the racially oppressed, and on the other, the racial oppressors. This alienated relationship, which undergirds the racial hierarchy, is reproduced across all areas of societal life, from one neighborhood to the next, from one city to the next, from one generation to the next.

The perpetuation of systemic racism requires an *intertemporal* reproducing of a variety of organizational structures and institutional and ideological processes. These structures and processes are critical to sustaining racial inequalities. Reproduced over time are racially structured institutions, such as the economic institutions that embed the exploitation of black labor and the legal and political institutions that protect that exploitation and extend oppression into other arenas of societal life.[50] Each new generation inherits the organizational structures that protect unjust enrichment and unjust impoverishment. Important too is the reproduction from one generation to the next of the ideological apparatus—the racist ideology and the concomitant set of racist attitudes—that rationalizes and legitimates racist oppression. We will examine this transmission process in detail in chapter 2.

By the 1700s the system of slavery was well-entrenched and profitable for whites, including slaveholders and those servicing or trading with slave plantations. After the initiation of this slavery system, the next step was its perpetuation and maintenance, not only in terms of meeting the internal requirements but also in terms of countering challenges to it. Much effort went into reinforcing, maintaining, and expanding this inhumane system. Numerous laws were passed, and courts were developed to sustain it. In addition, slave insurrections had to be protected against, so patrols and militias were created to police those enslaved. Slave breeding was expanded so that slaveholders did not have to rely on the international slave trade. The political system, including its founding documents, was shaped in response to the need to protect slavery. For many generations now this deeply imbedded system of racism has been regularly reproduced.

This social reproduction process may be hard to see because it is so much a part of everyday existence. It is a reproduction process that reproduces not only the specific aspects of systemic racism but U.S. society as a total racist society. Today most white Americans greatly underestimate the degree to which the nation is still such a total racist society. They not only underestimate the extent of their racial privileges but also the degree to which these privileges have been passed down from their predecessors through history. The social inheritance mechanisms are often deeply imbedded in the society and are disguised to make the intertemporal inheritance appear fair. Each new generation of whites has inherited an array of racial privileges. For example, over time the majority of whites inherit some economic resources—often in the form of house equity or family savings—or other resources such as job training or a good education. The vital resources inherited by whites are more than money; as Edward Ball, a slaveholder's descendant recently noted, "If we did not inherit money, or land, we received a great fund of cultural capital, including prestige, a chance at an education, self-esteem, a sense of place, mobility, even (in some cases) a flair for giving orders."[51] Ball adds that the creation of economic and cultural wealth in the slaveholding society has transmitted benefits not only to the descendants of slaveholders but to all white Americans.

Even poor immigrants who came to the United States from southern and eastern Europe in the early decades of the twentieth century were soon defined as "white." Although they faced some initial discrimination, they and their descendants benefited greatly from the far more extensive discrimination and segregation then restricting black Americans. Indeed, these new whites often participated in the discrimination that excluded black families from economic and housing opportunities. In a generation or two, they or their descendants were able to move up economically, politically, and socially. Not only do most whites now living benefit from the inheritance of economic and cultural wealth from ancestors who profited from slavery or legal segregation, but most also benefit from contemporary racist patterns—the job, housing, political, educational, and other discrimination that still gives them and their children advantages over black Americans. The racial inheritance comes whether or not the whites involved actively discriminate. While white Americans vary by class and gender in the scale of these privileges and ill-gotten wealth, most whites in all walks of life have benefited to some degree from white privilege (see chapter 6).

The Extraordinary Costs and Burdens of Racism   Unjustly gained wealth and privilege for whites is linked directly to undeserved immiseration for black Americans. This was true for many past generations, and it remains true for today's generations. Government reports regularly repeat the grim mortality and economic statistics: The average black person lives about six years less than the average white person. An average black family earns about 60 percent of the income of an average white family—and has only 10 percent of the economic wealth of an average white family.

Acts of oppression are not just immediately harmful; they often carry long-term effects. In the social science literature much has been made of the impact of historical racism on black families, subculture, or values, sometimes as part of a blame-the-victim perspective. More important, however, is the impact of systemic racism on the social, economic, political, and educational resources and opportunities available to black Americans for over fifteen generations. If the members of a group suffer serious bars to securing the resources necessary for achievement and mobility, this not only restricts their own achievements but also can shape the opportunities of descendants for generations to come.[52] When black men and women do not have significant access to inherited savings or resources such as a good education or important job skills because of blatant or subtle discrimination, they cannot prosper like privileged whites, and they and their descendants will likely retain a serious and long-lived disadvantage relative to whites.

The value of having money and other economic resources in hand is critical, for once a group is far ahead in terms of resources it is very difficult for another group without access to those resources, or even with modest new resources, to catch up, even over a substantial period of time. When entry to employment, education, or business is blocked by slavery, legal segregation, or widespread informal discrimination, African Americans have infinite entry costs. Even if these barriers are removed at a later point, and African Americans are finally allowed to enter once exclusively white societal arenas, they will likely enter with greater resource and operational problems, including higher personal or business costs, than whites who have not faced massive discrimination in the past or present (see chapter 6).

For African Americans systemic racism generally involves not only living with less in the way of social and economic resources but also enduring the consciousness that grows out of and reflects on oppressive conditions. Part of this consciousness is the pain in and of the "black" body created and maintained by the system of racism. In *Black Skin, White Masks* Frantz Fanon underscored how racism dehumanizes: "I am the slave not of the 'idea' that others have of me but of my own appearance. . . . Shame. Shame and self-contempt. Nausea. When people like me, they tell me it is in spite of my color. When they dislike me, they point out that it is not because of my color. Either way, I am locked into the infernal circle."[53] Antiblack racism is inscribed not only in society but in the body itself. Racism creates much distress and suffering.

Most theories about racial matters do not take seriously enough the existential perspective of the oppressed others, their experiential intelligence. When black men, women, and children speak of being black in a nation largely controlled by whites, they do not speak in abstract concepts learned from books, but rather voice their own encounters with whites. Take this recent account from an interview with a black woman, a dental assistant, who describes a black child's experience:

> [An] incident happened to my girlfriend's daughter about a month or so ago. She's in a Christian school. And the teacher told the kids that black, black children are born with their sin. And the little girl went home and she asked her mother, she said, "sit down," and told her mother. She said, "I just wish I was white." And she's only nine, she's nine. . . . And [the] little girl had said what the teacher had said, and she said, "Black people were born of sin, let's pray for the black people." And now the little girl is really scarred, but you

don't know how scarred . . . and that kind of stuff makes you angry. You take
a little child that doesn't know anything about prejudice, and this is the way
you plant it . . . in all these little white children's heads. . . .[54]

The white teacher in a religious elementary school appears to be drawing on one
of the oldest explanations of black inferiority, the apocryphal religious story of
Noah condemning his black son Ham's descendants to be the servants of whites
(see chapter 3).[55] We see here the operation of the racialized hierarchy of power—
the perhaps unthinking use of a white person's power to cause a black child and
the adults who love her much damage.

We see too that racism is a *lived* experience. It is about racist relations that recur
frequently in the lives of most black Americans. Whites generate much pain, frustration, stress, and anger. These are a few of racism's costs. We see the white-generated alienation of a black child from herself, and perhaps from her community.
Racism means that what should be most her own, the control of her self and identity, is what is often taken away. Also suggested in this account is the spreading
impact. Racist actions in the present become part of the collective experience, not
just fragments in the memory of one individual. In this case the negative impact
extends to the child's family and to other African Americans. In addition, the event
likely had a telling impact on white children in the class, thereby reinforcing their
sense of white superiority.

This account suggests that theories of racial oppression should take seriously
the life experiences and experiential intelligence of black Americans. They know
well the oppressive world that hits them in the face on a routine basis. This gives
them a well-developed knowledge base, from which they develop sophisticated,
and collective, understandings of everyday racism.

White Elites and Ordinary Whites: The Matter of Privilege   European and
European American elites began the large-scale exploitation of the labor of African
Americans and the land of Native Americans. Ever since, white elites have acted
aggressively to create or maintain the social, economic, and political organizations
and institutions, as well as ideologies, that reflect their interests. The actions of the
elites—originally composed of slaveholders, traders, and merchants, but later of
industrialists and other entrepreneurs—are critical for the creation and maintenance of the racist system of subjugation. White elites crafted and reworked the
system at each critical juncture in U.S. history, and they were central players in
its rationalization. We will examine these elites in detail in later chapters, but I
will underscore a few key points here. Significantly, the makeup of those drafting
the U.S. Constitution is similar to the demographic makeup of those in top positions in most sectors of U.S. society today. Since the 1780s, when the ruling elites
were 100 percent white and male in composition, there has been a modest decline

to a figure of about 95 to 100 percent today, with this percentage varying a little from one institutional sector to another.

The Psychological Wage of Whiteness   For several centuries now, most whites not in the elites have accepted the society's racist hierarchy, along with fewer socio-economic resources than the elites, because of their access to the privileges, opportunities, and cultural resources associated with being white and because they have bought heavily into the ideology of racism. White workers have accepted what W. E. B. Du Bois called the "public and psychological wage" of whiteness, instead of the greater economic wages they might have had if they had joined in strong organizations with black workers.[56] In the United States, unlike in numerous European capitalist countries, class consciousness among white workers has to a substantial degree been decentered by a racial consciousness (see chapter 6). This is probably a major reason why there has been less class polarization in the United States than in these European countries.

By the late seventeenth century many in the colonial elites were concerned about the resistance of white laborers and small farmers to elite rule. Critical to the development of the colonial economic system was the problem of labor. At first, the farmers who worked on a large scale made use of significant numbers of white laborers, the propertyless European immigrants who were often indentured servants. These white servants and laborers revolted a number of times against class oppression in the colonies. Sometimes they were joined by enslaved African Americans, as in Nathaniel Bacon's Rebellion in 1676, against elite administration of the colonies. Indeed, the possibility of biracial coalitions was a serious concern among the white elites; out of this fear was born, at least in part, the extension to propertyless whites of certain privileges and benefits of whiteness, as well as an extensive ideology rationalizing white superiority.[57] The creation of a system in which only African Americans could be enslaved was coupled with accenting racial solidarity across all white economic classes.

Just after the Civil War the elite-crafted social and ideological arrangements that deflected white workers' class consciousness were threatened by the new freedom for ordinary blacks and whites that emerged with the destruction of slavery and the implementation of more democratic governments in the South during Reconstruction. Once again there was the opportunity for a new era of the "ascendancy of the working classes."[58] On occasion, blacks and some whites joined again in protest and mutual-aid organizations, such as the militant farmers' organizations working for better farming conditions in the late nineteenth century (see chapter 6). It was not long, however, before the old elites in the South recovered their positions by aggressively persuading and buying off ordinary white farmers and workers with a renewed racist ideology that made whites of all classes feel superior, as well as by the use of violence against African Americans and some white activists. Ordinary whites often clung to the material rewards of working for white planters and the hope of becoming planters themselves some day.[59]

This history is important to understanding how systemic racism was perpetuated over time. Historically, it has often been the case that when white and black
(and other) workers have sought to organize against their capitalist oppressors, the
latter have used white supremacist arguments and efforts to break up worker organizations. Moreover, when white workers have sought to organize, white capitalists have sometimes used various workers of color—already hated by most white
workers—to break up that organization, thus furthering the racist views of white
workers. To a substantial degree, class oppression is obscured by the elites' use of
a racist ideology and by white workers' buying into that ideology and into the concrete advantages they see as stemming from it. Racial stratification is the core
stratification reality in part because it decentered class oppression in the thinking
and orientation of most white workers.

For the most part, white labor leaders in the union movements that expanded
across the United States from the mid-1800s to the 1960s collaborated in maintaining the system of black exclusion and white privilege. White union leaders
were often outspoken in their ideological racism and their commitment to exclu-
sionary barriers. While research is less comprehensive on the racial history of
women's rights movements, it is clear that white women were important in the
leadership and membership of abolitionist movements in the mid-nineteenth century. They often spoke out against the evils of slavery. However, once slavery was
abolished, and the movement for women's rights accelerated in the late nineteenth
and early twentieth centuries, many white leaders in this women's rights movement dismissed the concerns of black women and developed segregated interests
and organizations. According to Louise Newman's analysis, the majority of the
white leaders in this women's movement accepted white racial privileges and the
new racist theories of U.S. imperialism at the turn of the twentieth century with
little questioning.[60]

The Reality of White Unity   From at least the 1830s to the first decades of the 1900s
new European immigrant groups, especially those not initially considered to be
white—for example, the Irish and the Italians—by native-born whites, clamored
to be defined as white in the U.S. Whiteness has long been the goal for all those
who can squeeze into that category. We will examine this process in later chapters.

Charles Mills has accented the point that in the United States there has long
been a cross-class, cross-gender world of racial privilege and power in which all
whites participate. According to Mills, a common white racial identity has "generally determined the social world and loyalties, the lifeworld, of whites—whether
as citizens of the colonizing mother country, settlers, nonslaves, or beneficiaries
of the 'color bar' and the 'color line.'"[61] In later chapters we will observe the great
intensity of white identity and white-racist attitudes in many aspects of American
history and society. Consider here the issue of interracial marriage. For centuries
now the majority of whites, whatever their class position or gender, have been
united in opposition to the idea of a close relative marrying a black person. Today,

the majority of whites still seem more opposed to a close relative marrying a well-educated black professional than to the same relative marrying a less-educated white laborer. In contrast, there is no similar transracial world of workers in which all workers hold a strong and common class identity and loyalty across the racial line. Nor is there a transracial world of gender where all women (or all men) hold a strong common identity and loyalty across the color line. Historically, most white workers and most white women have been uninterested in building unity of identity and protest with, respectively, black workers or black women across the color line.

Rationalizing Racism

Creating a Dominant Ideology   Whites have not been content to exploit African Americans and then to admit candidly that such action is crass exploitation to their individual or group advantage. Instead, white Americans have developed a strong ideology defending their own privileges and conditions as meritorious and accenting the alleged inferiority and deficiencies of those being oppressed. A critical aspect of systemic racism is a racist ideology that defends whites' group position. As we will see in detail in chapter 3, a *racist ideology* is a socially imbedded set of beliefs that is widely accepted and critical to maintaining the subordination of black Americans and other people of color. One way to rationalize a racist hierarchy is to define "superior" groups who are "justifiably" dominant and "inferior" groups who "deserve" their lower place in society. Most Americans are indoctrinated in some version of this ideology from their early years. Once developed and imbedded in human minds a racist ideology becomes a concrete force in history.

Today, as in the past, the impoverishment and enrichment stemming from centuries of slavery, legal segregation, and contemporary racism are rationalized by an extensive system of myths, prejudices, and stereotypes. We have noted how the founders' myths about freedom and liberty coexisted with extreme subordination for black Americans. Elites are indispensable for this myth-making process, for they create or reformulate legitimizing beliefs through the mass media, schools, workplaces, legislatures, and churches. Oliver Cox noted that the major source of the racist ideology is the white elite that "orients the society on all significant questions. It could not exist in opposition to the wishes and ideology of this class."[62]

Early on, as we will document in subsequent chapters, the religious, political, and economic elites of the colonies and the new United States crafted new, or reframed existing, ideological rationalizations to defend the system of black subordination. These initially took the form of viewing Africans and African Americans (and Native Americans) in negative religious terms (as "unchristian" and "heathen") and negative cultural terms (as "uncivilized").

The Central Idea of Whiteness   In what was perhaps the first extended analysis of whiteness, a chapter in *Darkwater* (1920), W. E. B. Du Bois noted that "the discovery of personal whiteness among the world's people is a very modern thing. . . . The ancient world would have laughed at such a distinction . . . we have changed all that, and the world in a sudden, emotional conversion has discovered that it is white and by that token, wonderful!"[63] The early articulations of whiteness as a defense of white power and privilege came from slaveholders and others who sought to rationalize slavery. The generally darker skin (early called "black") of Africans was used by white slaveholders and other whites as a early marker of subordinated status. The skin color imagery was part of a larger conceptual framework among whites that viewed most aspects of "blackness" in negative terms. By the 1600s whiteness, in contrast, stood for "civilization" and "culture."[64]

According to Benjamin Franklin, one of the most liberal U.S. founders, the ideal of the virtuous American was grounded in whiteness. "[T]he number of purely white people in the world is proportionably very small," he said. "Why increase the sons of Africa, by planting them in America, where we have so fair an opportunity, by excluding all blacks and tawneys, of increasing the lovely white and red?"[65] Even the liberals among the founders, those opposed to importing more Africans, held antiblack images and saw their strong preferences for the "lovely white" as natural. Ideological racism includes strongly positive images of the white self as well as strongly negative images of the racial "others."

Aggressive Biological Racism   By the late eighteenth century a virulently racist framework was created, and it came to dominate most white views on "race" for the next two centuries. Images of "lovely whiteness" were soon wedded to a strong biological racism, a deterministic view that saw white Americans as the biologically and intellectually "superior race" and black Americans as the biologically and intellectually "inferior race." Influential men like Immanuel Kant in Europe and Thomas Jefferson in the United States lent their authority to the notion of a hierarchy of races (see chapter 3). The new biological racism developed by leading intellectuals in the late 1700s was spread by the newspapers, pamphlets, and pulpits of the day to the general population. Over the course of the nineteenth century this biological view of a hierarchy of races came to accompany older antiblack views accenting black inferiority in culture, religion, and civilization. As we will see in later chapters, by the early twentieth century the developing motion picture, radio, magazine, and television industries further accelerated the spread of racist attitudes toward and images of African Americans to all corners of U.S. society.

Today, many social scientists and popular analysts view racism as mainly about racial attitudes, as prejudices "directed at people because of their race."[66] They focus on the microlevel of the bigoted individual. Although this conventional perspective often recognizes some of the relational aspects of racism, it too frequently overlooks the point that the prejudices held by individuals are rooted firmly in an extensive *system* of racism. As Oliver Cox put it, "race prejudice is not an individual idiosyncrasy; it is a social attribute. Ordinarily the individual is born into it and accepts it unconsciously, like his language, without question."[67] Antiblack prejudices and stereotyping have been socially perpetuated as a way of stigmatizing black Americans "as inferior so that the exploitation of either the group itself or its resources or both may be justified."[68] Today, as in the past, antiblack attitudes are deeply imbedded in European American culture and are closely linked to the well-developed racist ideology that has dominated white society for centuries now. Taken together, all the images, attitudes, fictions, and notions that link to and buttress systemic racism constitute a broad white-racist worldview.

Resisting Systemic Racism   A comprehensive theory of systemic racism should encompass the dialectical idea that oppression creates the seeds of its destruction. Historical analysis indicates that racist oppression regularly breeds resistance. Racist structures heavily shape the lives of human beings, but when human agents gain solid knowledge about these structures of oppression, they can use that knowledge to rebel. As Michel Foucault once noted, power is more than an obligation on those who do not have it. Instead, it "invests them, is transmitted by them and through them; exerts pressure on them, just as they . . . resist the grip it has on them."[69]

The social process that reproduces systemic racism has major contradictions. One important contradiction is that subordinated groups like black Americans have for some time been allowed access to limited resources so that they can survive and be useful to the American economy. However, when they have secured some resources beyond subsistence, they have often increased their individual and collective resistance to oppression. Human beings have a unique ability to reflect on their own circumstances and to create, in association with others, a collective consciousness that can lead to change. Because black women and men have long been at the center of the racist system, their protest consciousness has perhaps the greatest potential for remaking or destroying that onerous system. Periodically, changes in the racist system have been forced by the antiracist consciousness and organizational efforts of African Americans. We see evidence of this in the many conspiracies to revolt, and periodic insurrections, of enslaved African Americans that took place between the mid-1600s and the 1850s (see chapter 8). In addition, in the decades before the Civil War hundreds of thousands of black and white (female and male) abolitionists organized actively against slavery. Continuing resistance could again be seen in the rise of the Niagara movement and the National Association for the Advancement of Colored People (NAACP) in the early 1900s, which built a strong tradition of legal action and educational efforts against racism (see chapter 8). These movements also laid the basis for the later civil rights movement that brought some changes in the operation of systemic racism by the 1960s and 1970s. Over their long and arduous history with racism, black Americans have created or participated in many resistance organizations, some of which are still working actively today.

From the beginning, black Americans have been the theorists of their own experiences with white racism, as they have made clear in a long history of antidiscrimination manifestos and protests. Encounters with discriminating whites are not just stressful for the targeted individual but also have a stressful impact on families and communities. These discriminatory encounters and countering responses to them are remembered and become a great store of collective memories that are passed on in black communities as needed. Out of their collective experience black Americans have created a culture of resistance, an oppositional culture that has been the underpinning for individual and group strategies to attack racist oppression.

In each period of overt struggle by black Americans against racism there has been a recurring ideological crisis for white Americans. The renewed development of antiracist perspectives by black leaders and other leaders of color are often viewed by white Americans, including elites, with alarm. Black protest against oppression has encompassed not only overt confrontation with the dominant group but also the development of a critical perspective on the surrounding racist world, an antiracist perspective generated from daily fighting domination. An antiracist framework of ideas is important for liberation struggles, as was articulated by black leaders from David Walker and Frederick Douglass to Dr. Martin Luther King, Jr. and Malcolm X. Nothing is a clearer thread running through the tapestry of U.S. history than recurring black struggles against oppression.

Conclusion   The United States can be seen in metaphorical terms as a house of racism, one with a politicoeconomic foundation firmly built during the first two centuries of colonial development. While many of the founders asserted in the Declaration of Independence and elsewhere that "all men are created equal," they did not mean what they said. Their egalitarian ethic was conditional and hypocritical, for it specifically excluded black Americans, indigenous peoples, and women. The real foundation was crafted to create wealth and privilege for those transplanted Europeans who stole the lands of the indigenous peoples and enslaved African labor. In this process these Europeans and European Americans came to define themselves and their society as "white."

Since this house of domination was created, it has periodically been remodeled and repainted. We observe some remodeling in the Reconstruction period after the Civil War and again during and after the 1950s and 1960s civil rights movement. When progressive changes have come in the racist system, white elites — with debate and divisions among themselves — have worked to make the least significant changes possible under conditions of mass protest and pressure. Never have the elites been interested in changes that would be substantial enough to build a new nonracist foundation for this society.

Thus, under pressure from black and white abolitionists, and reacting to the impact of the Civil War, the liberal wing of the nation's white leadership finally saw to it that slavery was abolished in the 1860s by an amendment to the U.S. Constitution. However, in spite of this constitutional eradication of slavery, no new constitutional convention was called so that a new governing document could be democratically written with the participation of all Americans, including those newly freed from slavery. Moreover, the elites created, North and South, a new system of near slavery called *segregation*. Whether formal or informal, this widespread segregation was racist and brutal, with catastrophic costs for most black men, women, and children. Every sector of U.S. society—the economy, politics and the law, education, and the mass media—was still run by and for whites, with the elites making most important decisions.

When black protest movements in the 1960s forced white leaders to again consider societal changes, the elites—again, with internal divisions—made modest changes in the system of racism. They passed some civil rights laws and issued important court decisions against formal segregation, but over the next decade or two they also saw to it that the enforcement of antidiscrimination decrees would mostly be weak. Significantly, antidiscrimination programs, from the 1960s civil rights laws to present-day affirmative action programs, have mostly been framed by elite white men. For the most part, the enforcement of these programs has also been under their auspices. Most such antidiscrimination programs have only been intended to be modest efforts designed to fit some black Americans, other people of color, and white women into the Procrustean bed of existing white-male-controlled institutions.

At no point in these reform periods was the group interest of black Americans for full liberation brought to the center of national political action. Repainting and remodeling the edifice of racism has not eliminated this system of oppression. To a substantial degree, white talk about "equality" and "liberty and justice for all" has remained a ruse and an illusion. In no institution anywhere in U.S. society has antiblack oppression by whites been eliminated root and branch. Over the course of American history neither the white elite nor most of its followers have attempted to dismantle the hierarchical system of racial oppression put into place by the founders. Indeed, few whites have ever envisaged the possibility of a truly democratic and egalitarian society. To accomplish that goal, white Americans would have to abandon their group interest in white privileges, redefine the goals of the nation, and rebuild its racist house from the foundation up—doubtless under great pressure from African Americans and other Americans of color.

two

Slavery Unwilling to Die
The Historical Development
of Systemic Racism

A Bloody Foundation: Genocide and Slavery   This nation was born in blood and violence against the racialized "others." This grim historical reality must be understood well if we are to comprehend contemporary racism and interracial relations. As the European colonists established permanent settlements in North America, they intentionally drove off or killed the indigenous inhabitants and took their land. These colonists enriched themselves in a process of genocide against the indigenous peoples.

   Attacking Native Americans   Article II of the United Nations Convention on the Prevention and Punishment of Genocide defines genocide as "acts committed with intent to destroy, in whole or in part, a national, ethnical, racial, or religious group." These acts specifically include "causing serious bodily or mental harm" and "deliberately inflicting on the group conditions of life calculated to bring about its physical destruction in whole or in part."[1] From the late 1400s to the first decades of the 1900s, the European colonizers and their descendants periodically and deliberately inflicted conditions of life that brought about the physical devastation, in whole or in part, of numerous indigenous societies across the Caribbean islands and North and South America. Indeed, the intentional attacks on indigenous peoples—and the effects of European diseases—are estimated to have cost as many as ninety to one hundred million casualties—the largest example of human destruction in recorded history.[2] The brutal and exploitative practices of whites were not aberrations; they were common practice in European colonialism.

The English colonists on the Atlantic coast relied on indigenous peoples to survive the first difficult years. Soon, however, these Europeans turned on the indigenous inhabitants. As early as 1637, a war with the Pequots in New England ended when whites massacred several hundred inhabitants of a village and sent the rest into slavery. The 1675–1676 King Philip's War with the Wampanoag society and its allies, precipitated by the actions of the colonists, resulted in substantial losses on both sides. The Native American leader, Metacom (known by the English as King Philip), was "captured, drawn, and quartered: his skull remained on view on a pole in Plymouth as late as 1700."[3] Again, the survivors were sold as slaves by European colonists who, ironically, saw themselves as a "civilized" people dealing with "savage" peoples. It is not well known that European colonists enslaved some Native Americans as part of their initial attempts to find exploitable labor. In the mid-eighteenth century about 5 percent of those enslaved in several of the North American colonies were Native American.

Recall James Madison's comment that the stereotyped "red race" was second only to the "black race" in the openly racist concerns of whites.[4] What should be done with these people who stood in the way of European lust for the land and riches of the Americas? Few European colonizers made an effort to understand the attempts of indigenous peoples to protect themselves from European invaders. While some leaders like Benjamin Franklin and Thomas Jefferson expressed admiration for Indian societies (even viewing them as "the white men of America"), most whites more than balanced their admiration with hostility and negative imagery.[5]

Until the middle decades of the nineteenth century the majority of Native American societies maintained a substantial degree of political and cultural autonomy. Europeans were frequently forced by the strength of Native American societies to negotiate with them for land and other resources. A process of gradual encroachment became the rule. Europeans would move into Native American lands (often violating treaties), Native Americans would respond with defensive violence, U.S. troops would put the rebellion down, and a new treaty securing much or all of the stolen land for whites would be made. There was at least a pretense of negotiation and legal treatymaking. However, by the 1830s—with President Andrew Jackson's decision to expel Cherokees and other Native American groups from the eastern states by force (the infamous "trail of tears" that cost at least 4,000 lives)—Native American societies increasingly faced a policy of overt displacement from white areas to western reservations or renewed attacks designed to eliminate whole societies. Even the pretense of legality was gradually disappearing. Indeed, by 1831 the Supreme Court was moving to redefine indigenous societies as "domestic dependent nations."[6]

The Losing Struggle for Social Independence   In the 1857 Dred Scott decision the U.S. Supreme Court showed that leading whites viewed the situations of Native Americans and African Americans as quite different. Indians, Chief Justice Roger B. Taney asserted, had "formed no part of the colonial communities, and never amalgamated with them in social connections or in government. But although they were uncivilized, they were yet a free and independent people, associated together in nations or tribes, and governed by their own laws. . . . But they may, without doubt, like the subjects of any other foreign Government, be naturalized by the authority of Congress, and become citizens of a State, and of the United States; and if an individual should leave his nation or tribe, and take up his abode among the white population, he would be entitled to all the rights and privileges which would belong to an emigrant from any other foreign people."[7] Whites, the judge asserted, had long viewed Native American groups as autonomous nations, though less civilized than whites. In contrast, in this decision about the status of an enslaved black American, the white judges viewed black Americans not as a nation to be negotiated with, but rather as "beings of an inferior order, and altogether unfit to associate with the white race, either in social or political relations; and so far inferior, that they had no rights which the white man was bound to respect."[8] Whites' racist views of indigenous societies often allowed for more independence, albeit as groups only beyond white borders and as individuals only if assimilated. Moreover, over the centuries each Native American society has confronted whites on its own turf, with much strength arising from the indigenous cultural and geographical resources. In contrast, those peoples taken from the diverse societies of Africa had to face their white oppressors on white turf, completely severed from their families and home societies.

Native Americans lost their ability to make treaties in 1871. Over the next several decades, federal government policies forced many of the remaining Native Americans onto federally supervised and segregated reservations. With some oscillation, federal policies allowed whites to take more Native American land and pressured Native Americans to assimilate to white ways. By 1890, with most forced onto reservations, the number of Native Americans in North America had decreased to only about 250,000, sharply down from an estimated fifteen million people when the Europeans arrived in the late 1400s. The brutal and bloody consequences of the European conquests do indeed fit the United Nations definition of genocide.

Slavery and Modern Capitalism   In the Spanish colonies in Mexico and South America, Native Americans were the major source of labor, and thus they were central to the internal development of these colonial societies. This was not true for the English colonies. As Benjamin Ringer notes, "except for the early days when trade with the Indian was important for the survival of the English settler, the

Indian played virtually no significant role in the internal functioning of the colonial society, but a crucial role in defining its frontier."[9] It was Africans who would play a central role in the functioning of colonial society. By the early 1700s people of African descent had become a major source of labor for the colonies, and the economic foundation for several centuries of undeserved enrichment for whites was firmly set in place.

The North American colonies developed two major modes of economic production. One type of production was the subsistence economy of small-scale farmers, who were either European immigrants or their descendants. Early on, the North American colonies became places to dump surplus peasants and workers displaced by the reorganization of agricultural economies in European societies. Alongside this subsistence farming economy was a profit-making commercial economy, much of which was rooted in the slave trade, slave plantations, and the commercial businesses essential to the burgeoning slavery economy. Slavery in the Americas was generally a commercial and market-centered operation, which distinguished it from slavery in the ancient world.[10]

With much farm land available for the new European immigrants coming into the colonies, it was frequently difficult for colonial entrepreneurs and development companies to secure enough white laborers, particularly for large-scale agriculture. At first, the larger landowners made use of white indentured servants, but it became clear that these laborers could be difficult to control. By the late seventeenth century the white elites were worried about periodic revolts from white laborers and small farmers. White indentured servants also worked off their terms of servitude and went into farming for themselves. The enslavement of African women, men, and children not only stemmed from a desire for profit but also from a concern with developing a scheme of social control that maintained bond-labor against the resistance of those enslaved. The color and cultural differences of Africans made them easier for whites to identity for purposes of enslavement and control.

The Legal Establishment of Slavery   The first Africans brought into the English colonies were bought by the Jamestown colonists from a Dutch ship in 1619. Laws firmly institutionalizing slavery were not put in place in the English colonies until the mid-seventeenth century. In the decades prior to that time some imported Africans were treated more like indentured servants than slaves. Some were able to work out from under their servitude. However, even in this early period those of African descent were by no means the social or legal equals of the Europeans. During the earliest decade, the 1620s, the Africans for whom we have records were often treated differently from the English colonists. For one thing, all African laborers and servants were brought in involuntarily, even if they were in some cases allowed to work out their servitude. Moreover, getting out of servitude usually meant converting to Christianity. As early as 1624, one court case made it clear that a "negro"—note the early naming of Africans and the lower case spelling—could testify in court only because he was a convert to Christianity. A "negro" status was already socially and legally inferior to a European colonist's status.[11] Forrest Wood has argued that Christianity in this colonial period, as later in U.S. history, was highly dogmatic, Eurocentric, and antiblack "in its ideology, organization, and practice."[12] As we see in this 1624 example, central to the Eurocentric viewpoint was the idea that every person must become a Christian in order to have any legal rights. Indeed, many apologists for the enslavement of African Americans, from the seventeenth century to the present day, have argued that one of the virtues of slavery was its bringing Christianity to those enslaved.

By the 1670s the lives of most people of African descent were severely restricted by the new laws legitimating and protecting slavery. The degradation of this slavery was clear. In one 1671 declaration Virginia's General Assembly put "sheep, horses, and cattle" in the same category as "negroes." Colonial laws early attempted to prevent black men and women from running away; there were barbaric laws encompassing the whipping, castration, or killing of rebellious slaves.[13] Slavery was much more than a system of coerced labor. Enslaved blacks were legally subjugated in or excluded from all societal institutions including the economic, legal, and political institutions. Slavery was a totalitarian system in which whites controlled the lives of black men, women, and children—a total racist society protecting white interests.

As we saw in chapter 1, in the 1770s and 1780s the white group interest in the slavery system was recognized in the defining political documents of the new nation. The Declaration of Independence, prepared mostly by the slaveholder Thomas Jefferson, originally contained language accusing the British king of pursuing slavery, of waging "cruel war against human nature itself, violating its most sacred rights of life and liberty in the persons of a distant people who never offended him, captivating them and carrying them into slavery in another hemisphere, or to incur miserable death in the transportation thither."[14] Such accusations against the king were hypocritical, since at least half the signatories to the Declaration, including Jefferson, were important slaveholders or involved in the slave trade. Moreover, because of pressure from slaveholding interests in the South and slave-trading interests in the North, this critique of slavery was omitted from the final version of the Declaration. Recall too that in 1787 the U.S. Constitution was made by elite white men, many of whom had strong ties to the entrenched system of black enslavement.

Mercantilism, Capitalism, and Slavery   While a number of factors played an important role in the expansion of commercial capitalism in the Americas, slavery was one of the most consequential. Between the early 1600s and the 1820s some eight million Africans were forced to come to the Americas, while in contrast only 850,000 European immigrants came during the same period. In many parts of the

Americas enslaved African labor was far more important than European labor in building up the wealth of the white enslavers. Involved in this economic growth was an array of European participants on both sides of the Atlantic, including slave-holders, slave traders and merchants, intellectuals, ministers, and political officials. The trade in enslaved Africans was begun by the Portuguese and the Spanish as they early developed overseas empires, but the English (by 1707 called the "British") and English American colonists soon joined in the barbaric trade in human beings.

During the seventeenth and eighteenth centuries international capitalism had developed and grown within a context of royal mercantilism. European colonies were seen by the mercantilists as designed to build up the economy of the mother country. The English colonies in North America were supposed to trade only with England and not to manufacture goods or engage in trade in competition with the mother country. By the second half of the eighteenth century the new commercial bourgeoisie on both sides of the Atlantic was pressing hard to get rid of these restraints on international trade. The struggle for American independence destroyed mercantilist domination of international trade and thereby greatly spurred that trade.[15]

A principal objective of the colonization of North America was to secure raw materials and markets for English goods. Once land was taken from indigenous societies, the colonizers' search for labor soon led to the preexisting African slave trade, which became critical to the exploitation of the land. The larger farms and plantations using enslaved Africans were generally profitable and produced a range of important agricultural products for the international market—sugar, tobacco, rice, indigo, and, by the late 1700s, cotton. At first, most such products were for wealthy Europeans, but gradually the middle and working classes of Europe were able to purchase these commodities or products made from them. The plantation owners, particularly with the emergence of "King Cotton," demanded ever larger numbers of workers, and the number of enslaved men, women, and children grew rapidly—from about sixty thousand in the early 1700s to about four million by the 1860s. By the 1770s about 40 percent of the population in southern areas was African American.[16] In the North there were also significant numbers of enslaved and free African Americans. In the late eighteenth century, African Americans reached their highest proportion of the population (about one-fifth), before or since, in the area soon to become the United States.

Variations in Plantation Capitalism   In important respects the variant of capitalism developing in southern agricultural areas was different from the capitalism developing in northern urban areas. While this agricultural capitalism was generally a profit-oriented system set within a world market, it was also a social structure in which dominant labor arrangements did not center on wage labor. In addition, the value system surrounding slavery in the southern and border states was closer in some ways to aristocratic feudalism than to urban capitalism. For most slaveholders in the South there was more to slavery than just profit making. As Jefferson and other leading slaveholders emphasized, an agricultural society was to be preferred to an urban society. In their view the gentleman's life necessitated owning black men, women, and children for social status as well as for profit.[17] One of the great ironies of the slavery system is the accent that these "gentlemen" and their "ladies" put on values such as chivalry and honor, even as they practiced barbarism.[18] The political economy of slavery was a blending of capitalism with persisting elements of feudalism.

In the decade preceding the Civil War, a quarter of the white families in southern and border states owned nearly four million black men, women, and children. Thus, a large number of white families were directly involved in slavery. It was these families, especially those who held the largest number of slaves on big farms and plantations, who were the most influential in controlling the regional economy and politics. An array of ordinary whites provided the infrastructure of the slavery system—providing transport, growing foodstuffs, policing slaves, running local government, and providing many of the skilled trades. The slaveholding oligarchy—all white men—maintained its hegemony over the nonslaveholding white majority not only by these critical economic ties but also by propagating an ideology of white supremacy and providing certain types of white privilege. Most whites accepted the reality of slavery because "it provided not only an escalator by which they might one day rise, but also a floor beneath which they could not fall." As long as this was the case, "a Southern white consensus in defense of the peculiar institution was more or less assured."[19]

What was the position of white women in this system? Whatever their class level, they were generally under the control of husbands and fathers. They clearly had far fewer rights than white men, and all suffered significantly from patriarchal oppression. Working-class women, the majority of southern white women, provided most of the household labor that supported male workers and farmers. Women in the affluent slaveholding families sometimes inherited slaves or controlled some of their husband's slaves. They played a direct role in maintaining the racist system. One prominent analysis notes that white "mistresses, even the kindest, commonly resorted to the whip to maintain order among people who were always supposed to be on call; among people who inevitably disappointed expectations; among people whose constant presence not merely as servants but as individuals with wills and passions of their own provided constant irritation along with constant, if indifferent, service."[20] There was some recorded discontent from these slaveholding women about their lives, but rarely did they oppose the slavery system that gave them their own version of white privilege.

Among social scientists there is some debate as to whether the southern system was capitalistic or just a unique enclave economy imbedded in a capitalistic market system.[21] However, both groups of scholars generally agree on two points that are important for our analysis: (1) the larger slaveholders were oriented to making profits off their enslaved laborers; and (2) these slaveholders oriented themselves to trading within a capitalistic world-market system. Whatever other social values they may have held, the larger plantation owners were also early capitalists. Slavery capitalism was a system of worker control no other capitalist system could match. Enslaved men and women had a larger share of the worth of their work taken from them than did wage workers because they were chattel property and at the mercy of their owners at all hours of the day.

The Structure of Slavery in the North   Many northern merchants and manufacturers were active in the slave trade or had economic ties to the slave plantations. At the time of the American Revolution, the slave trade was, in Lorenzo Greene's detailed analysis, the "very basis of the economic life of New England; about it revolved, and on it depended, most of [the region's] other industries."[22] Greene lists more than 160 prominent slaveholding families in the area. Slavery-linked businesses included those dealing in sugar, molasses, and rum, as well as those dealing with shipbuilding and shipping. Leading textile manufacturers were "active participants in the slave trade or active in commercial and industrial endeavors that were closely intertwined with the slave(ry) trade."[23] Indeed, some northern industrialists were strong supporters of southern slaveholders, and most others colluded in the slavery structure that buttressed their industries. In addition, northern manufactures, farmers, and professionals sometimes bought black laborers or servants for their families. Even some antislavery advocates, such as the respected Benjamin Franklin, had owned slaves at some point in their lives.

Significant numbers of black Americans were enslaved in some northern areas well into the 1800s. The colony of Massachusetts Bay had been the first to legalize slavery, and by the mid-1600s there were strict slavery laws throughout the northern colonies. By the 1720s more than a fifth of New York City's population was black, and most of these New Yorkers were enslaved. Indeed, New York City's famous Wall Street area was one of the first large colonial markets where whites bought and sold slaves. This savage business lasted in New York City until 1862, even after the Civil War had begun.[24]

White northerners sometimes responded to black attempts to break the bonds of slavery in the same way as white southerners—with barbaric brutality. In New York there was great fear of slave revolts. In 1712 there was a major slave revolt in New York City; in retaliation whites hung, starved, or roasted to death fifteen African Americans. In New York state, where slaves made up 7 percent of the population in 1786, even a partial emancipation statute was not passed until 1799—and that statute only freed enslaved children born after July 4, 1799 and then only when they reached their mid-twenties. All enslaved black Americans there did not become free until the 1850s. In Massachusetts, famous for its antislavery abolitionists, one attempt to abolish slavery failed in the state House of Representatives in 1767. Not until the 1780s did pressures from the white populace force the abolition of slavery in New England. Even then, it was not a recognition of black civil rights but pressure from white workers, who objected to competing with enslaved laborers, that played the major role in forcing slavery's abolition.[25] Moreover, in northern states where black workers and their families were emancipated, they faced Jim Crow segregation and regular discrimination in jobs, housing, and public accommodations. They also faced much racist mocking in newspapers and in public entertainments such as blackface minstrelsy. The early enslavement of black Americans in the North was indeed a "deeply engrained coding" that facilitated later patterns of segregation and other institutional racism.[26]

Most white northerners, including most religious leaders, did not support the immediate emancipation of enslaved African Americans in the South until the first battles of the Civil War made this expedient.[27] Prior to the Civil War many whites in all regions felt that slavery could not be abolished because of its economic importance. Indeed, into the 1850s much of the merchant class of the North was allied politically with the southern planter class. Not only did northern merchants and traders buy products from southern plantations, they also made up a substantial part of the Democratic party in the North, while southern elites dominated that party in the South.

Unjust Immiseration: The Terrible Costs for Africans and African Americans

The Barbarity of Slavery   Unjust enrichment for whites brought great immiseration for blacks. Considering the number of people killed or maimed in the process, and the scale and time involved, the enslavement of Africans is one of the most savage and barbaric aspects of European and American history. According to those enslaved, the slavery system was hellish and deadly beyond description and comprehension. Once captured, enslaved Africans were often taken to slave corrals or castles in Africa where they were chained, branded, and held for shipping abroad. Many died there in barbaric conditions. On the Atlantic voyage those enslaved were chained together in close quarters, again in death-dealing conditions. The horror of the Atlantic trade was summed up by one young African, who in his autobiography explained, "I was soon put down under the decks, and there I received such a salutation in my nostrils as I had never experienced in my life: so that with the loathsomeness of the stench, and crying together, I became so sick and low that I was not able to eat, nor had I the least desire to taste any thing. . . . On my refusing to eat, one of them held me fast by the hands, and laid me across, I think the windlass, and tied my feet, while the other flogged me severely. . . . One day, when we had a smooth sea and moderate wind, two of my wearied countrymen who were chained together (I was near them at the time), preferring death to such a life of misery, somehow made through the nettings and jumped into the sea."[28]

The conditions of those enslaved at the points of destination were also brutal and oppressive. William Wells Brown, the son of a white slaveowner and an enslaved black woman, reported on what happened to an assertive man named Randall. One day a white overseer, named Grove Cook, got three white friends to help him subdue Randall. As Brown explains, "He refused to go; whereupon he was attacked by the overseer and his companions, when he turned upon them, and laid them, one after another, prostrated on the ground. [One man] drew out his pistol, and fired at him, and brought him to the ground by a pistol ball. The others rushed upon him with their clubs, and beat him over the head and face, until they succeeded in tying him. He was taken to the barn, and tied to a beam. Cook gave him over one hundred lashes with a heavy cowhide, had him washed with salt and water, and left him tied during the day. The next day he was untied, and taken to a blacksmith's shop, and had a ball and chain attached to his leg."[29]

Brown recounts that this brave man was forced to work hard in the fields with the chain on him and that the slaveowner was pleased with the sadistic cruelty of his overseer. Brown observed numerous beatings and killings of black men and women by whites during years of enslavement. The extant narratives of those enslaved are replete with accounts of chains, mutilation, stocks, whippings, starvation, and imprisonment.[30]

The Rape of Enslaved Women   Once fully instituted, the arrangements of slavery became much more than a machine for generating economic wealth. They constituted a well-developed system for the social and sexual control of black men and women.[31] During slavery, and later under legal segregation, many African and African American women were raped by white men, including sailors, slavemasters, overseers, and employers. Under the American system of racism the children resulting from the coerced sexual relations were automatically classified as black, even though they had substantial European ancestry. Indeed, it is estimated today that at least three-quarters of "black" Americans have at least one white ancestor. No other racial or ethnic group's physical makeup has been so substantially determined by the sexual depredations of white men. Recently, Patricia Williams, a black law professor, has described the case of Austin Miller, the thirty-five-year-old white lawyer who bought her eleven-year-old great-great-grandmother, Sophie. By the time Sophie was twelve, Miller had made her pregnant with the child who was Williams's great-grandmother Mary. Sophie's child was taken from her and became a house servant to Miller's white children. Williams's great-great-grandfather was thus one of a large number of white men who were rapists of black women or molesters of black children.[32]

Most of the surviving narratives of enslaved black women have accounts—sometimes quite numerous—of sexual exploitation by white men. Take the case of an enslaved black woman named Celia. In 1850 a prosperous Missouri farmer, Robert Newsom, bought Celia, then a fourteen-year-old, and soon thereafter raped her.

Over the next five years, Newsom sexually attacked her numerous times, father-
ing two children by her. In the summer of 1855 Newsom came to Celia's cabin
one last time to rape her, she hit him with a stick, and he died from the blows. In
a travesty of justice, Celia was convicted in a Missouri court of the "crime" and
hung in late December 1855.[33] Black women were doubly oppressed by the institution of slavery; they had no redress for the brutal crimes committed against them.

Like Miller and Newsom, many of these oppressors were respectable men in
their communities. One of the most famous was Thomas Jefferson. In his forties
he coerced the enslaved teenager Sally Hemings into his bed. That he fathered at
least one child with her has now been confirmed by DNA testing, and it is pre-
sumed that he fathered several other children by her. Yet in his lifetime Jefferson
never admitted to this coercive relationship.[34] Until the DNA evidence showed
the reality of the relationship, most white historians and commentators denied
that Jefferson could have had children with an enslaved woman. The reason for
this denial doubtless lies in the fact that Jefferson is an American icon. As the first
professional biographer of Jefferson, James Parton, put it in 1874, "If Jefferson was
wrong, America is wrong. If America is right, Jefferson was right."[35]

One of the most oppressive aspects of American racism lies in this sexual thread,
which weaves itself through various manifestations of racism to the present. White
men have often raped African American women with impunity, especially during
the nation's first three centuries. Many white men developed a contradictory set
of attitudes that saw black women as human enough to be exotic objects of sexual
desire, yet as less than human in their rights to protection from sexual attack. Given
that most such men proclaimed themselves to be virtuous and religious, such sexual attitudes and actions contradicted their expressed morality. The tensions
between this image of themselves as virtuous and their sexualized feelings and
actions toward black women—often coupled with a denial at the conscious level
of these feelings—seem to have led to a projection of many white men's sexual
desires onto black men. As the historian Winthrop Jordan has argued, white men's
passion for black women was "not fully acceptable to the society or the self and
hence not readily admissible. Sexual desires could be effectively denied and the
accompanying anxiety and guilt in some measure assuaged, however, by imput-
ing them to others."[36]

Given this projection of white males' desires into black men, one can better
understand certain aspects of U.S. racism—the obsession of many white men (and
women) with the black man as a rapist (see chapter 4) and the extraordinarily brutal and often sexualized attacks on black men in thousands of lynchings and other
violent attacks (see below).

African Immiseration   Numerous African societies paid a heavy, often catastrophic, price for the Atlantic slave trade. For several centuries many of the African
continent's young people were ripped from its shores, thereby damaging the future

development of the continent. Millions of Africans were lost in the slave trade, so many that the use of the term *the black holocaust* seems appropriate for this savage process. An estimated ten million Africans survived the Atlantic crossings to the Americas, with many millions more killed or lost to deprivation and disease on the way, or back in Africa before embarkation. Estimates for the total number enslaved or killed in the attempt to enslave at all points in Africa and the Atlantic trade suggest a figure of at least twenty-eight million from the 1400s to slavery's abolition in most areas by the late 1800s.[37]

Over time, this Atlantic trade in human beings had serious negative effects on social institutions in parts of Africa, a destruction that greatly facilitated later European exploitation of that continent. Recall W. E. B. Du Bois's argument that African colonization is usually omitted or downplayed in mainstream histories of European development, wealth, and affluence. Yet any serious understanding of the development of European wealth must center on early and late African colonialism, for the labor and mineral resources of Africans were taken to help create that European prosperity. Similarly, much African immiseration is linked to the creation of white prosperity over the course of North American history.

A number of scholars and popular writers have accented the role of Africans in this Atlantic slave trade, sometimes in order to play down the European role.[38] Yet one must put the African participation in perspective. Europeans were not enslaved by Africans. And virtually all Africans enslaved in the Americas were taken from their continent by European traders or merchants and sold to Europeans in the Americas. This Atlantic trade in human beings began when European ships arrived seeking commerce with African societies whose economies were not centered in profit making from enslavement. As Europeans grew in power along the coast, African nations were played off against each other, just as European colonizers in the Americas played off one indigenous nation there against another. Significantly, the European intruders had some six hundred slave ports built for their bloody trade, and they themselves recorded at least three hundred battles with Africans as part of the enslavement process. Africans did not seek out this system. In some cases Africans were kidnapped directly by Europeans slavers. In numerous other cases African political leaders, who had often at first traded certain African goods for European goods, ran out of these items and, pressed by the European slavers, turned to trading people held in servitude.[39]

Certainly, some leaders at the top of the hierarchies of African societies worked with the European slavers to provide the human cargo the latter sought. Indeed, trading in slaves became addictive for some African leaders without other goods to trade to Europeans. Those who were traded as slaves often included temporary wards, such as children of the poor or widows (who were then in the care of African leaders), as well as those captured in battles with other societies. Apparently, most African leaders did not realize that those traded would become permanently enslaved as property without *any* human rights and would often be worked to death in just a few years. In numerous West African societies many of those held in involuntary servitude were treated more like wards or indentured servants than like the rights-less chattel property they became in the Americas. They were often part of a family unit, had some legal rights, and could marry, own property, and sometimes inherit from their masters.[40] It is also important to note that many Africans saw the Atlantic slave trade as a serious threat, even as a sickness, and local healing societies developed to fight it. There was also substantial violent resistance to the Atlantic slave trade by Africans.

A Distinctive Form of Slavery   The enslavement of Africans in the Americas was not only more extreme than slavery in most African societies but also more oppressive than slavery in ancient societies such as the Roman Empire. Unlike Roman slaves, American slaves were generally forbidden by law to read or write. In the Americas the Europeans applied slavery, as Du Bois reminds us, "on a scale and with an elaborateness of detail of which no former world ever dreamed. The imperial width of the thing—the heaven-defying audacity—makes its modern newness."[41] An essential feature of North American slavery was the denial of most human liberties. Slaves "could own nothing; they could make no contracts; they could hold no property; nor traffic in property; they could not hire out; they could not legally marry . . . they could not appeal from their master; they could be punished at will."[42] In North America human beings were reduced to the status of things to be bought and sold.

Even the English language was "made an instrument of domination and silencing; it was used to regulate and police access to authority and knowledge among colonized peoples."[43] Enslaved Africans were from many different societies, and they were forced to learn the language of their oppressors. This was probably the most forced of all adaptations to the English language. Voluntary immigrants to the United States have been allowed to retain much more of their home languages and have probably kept more of the home culture associated with those languages. In the destruction of African languages and their more or less complete replacement by a new language we see how extensive the system of antiblack racism is. Enforced adaptation to the English language not only marked the movement of early English colonizers across the lands of conquest, but also marks today—in attacks on black English and on Spanish—similar attempts to maintain white cultural dominance over those long subordinated.

Ill-Gotten Gains: Wealth and Prosperity from Slavery   The enslavement of Africans was not just the work of slave traders and adventurers. Nor was it something marginal to the economic interests of the elites on both sides of the Atlantic. Instead, slavery was a system created, supported, and financed by a very large number of the leading political, business, and intellectual figures of the day. We can, as an example, take just one major enterprise of the early eighteenth century, the famous British South Sea Company. This was an official company set up to transport enslaved Africans overseas. Stockholders in this company included the leading physical scientist Sir Isaac Newton, major authors like Jonathan Swift and Daniel Defoe, and the founder of the Bank of England, the Earl of Halifax. They also included most members of the House of Lords and of the House of Commons. Many aristocrats also held stock in the company.[44] Clearly, the leading men of Britain were directly and financially involved in the slave trade. Similarly, many leading Americans, including George Washington, Thomas Jefferson, Patrick Henry, George Mason, and James Madison, profited greatly from slavery or the slave trade. These men saw slavery as an honorable business activity.

Building the Wealth of Britain and Continental Europe   The British merchants of the eighteenth century recognized the centrality of slavery in building the wealth of their nation. For example, in the 1740s one business pamphleteer wrote about Britain's wealth this way:

> The most approved Judges of the Commercial Interests of these Kingdoms have ever been of the opinion that our West-India and African Trades are the most nationally beneficial of any we carry on. It is also allowed on all Hands, that the trade to Africa is the Branch which renders our American Colonies and Plantations so advantageous to Great Britain: that Traffic only affording our Planters a constant supply of Negro Servants for the Culture of their Lands in the Produce of Sugars, Tobacco, Rice, Rum, Cotton, Fustick, Pimento, and all other our Plantation Produce: so that the extensive Employment of our Shipping in, to, and from America, the great Brood of Seamen consequent thereupon, and the daily Bread of the most considerable Part of our British Manufactures, are owing primarily to the Labour of Negroes; who, as they were the first happy instruments of raising our Plantations: so their Labour only can support and preserve them, and render them still more and more profitable to their Mother-Kingdom. The Negroe-Trade therefore, and the natural consequences resulting from it, may be justly esteemed an inexhaustible Fund of Wealth and Naval Power to this Nation.[45]

This remarkable business summary accents the primary role of the "labour of Negroes" to British shipping and manufacturing, and thus to "inexhaustible fund of wealth" for that nation.

The economic trade generated by British and French plantations in the Americas was the source of much of the capital for the commercial and industrial revolutions of the two nations. British and French industry, shipping, naval and merchant marine development, banking, and insurance were significantly stimulated by or grounded in the labor of enslaved Africans in their respective colonies.[46] From the early 1700s to the mid-1800s a large proportion of the major agricultural exports in world trade were produced by enslaved Africans. British port cities became prosperous as centers for the trade in Africans and British industrial cities became prosperous because of the manufacturing of goods with cotton from slave plantations. Textiles manufacturing was the core industry of the Industrial Revolution, and most of the raw cotton was grown by enslaved laborers. Liverpool slave traders, Caribbean sugar planters, and Manchester manufacturers were major sources of circulating capital in the eighteenth and early nineteenth centuries. Circulating through banking and lending enterprises, the profits from international trade—much of it directly or indirectly related to the slave trade and the trade in slave-produced products—provided a substantial part of the large-scale investments in British industry in this period, growth that in turn led to many new technologies and products of the Industrial Revolution. These investments also spurred a rapid buildup of the financial and insurance industries.[47] Some of these powerful institutions have persisted to the present day. Barclay's Bank was founded with profits from the slave trade, and Lloyds of London prospered early on by insuring slave ships and their cargos.[48]

The most famous technological development of the period, James Watt's much-improved version of the steam engine developed during the 1760s, accelerated the industrial development of Europe and its far-flung colonies. Capital accumulated from the West Indies trade in slaves and slave-produced products directly bankrolled Watt's reworking of the steam engine. Numerous industries, such as the metallurgical industries—which made possible the manufacturing of chains for slaves as well as new machinery, bridges, and rails—and the important railroad industry, were significantly spurred by the profits generated from the trade in slaves, products of plantations, and food and manufacturing exports flowing from Britain back to the American plantations and to Africa. In turn, much additional economic activity was generated as these profits flowed into all forms of European and colonial consumption. Economic activity was stimulated even if the recipients of the income from the slave trade and plantations put it into land, coaches, or banks.[49]

Slaveholders were not the only beneficiaries of the slavery system; those who bought and sold products of plantations were also major beneficiaries. This latter group included merchants and consumers in many nations. In addition, many white workers in Britain and other parts of Europe owed their livelihoods directly or indirectly to the trade in slaves and plantation products.[50] It seems unlikely that British and other European economic development would have occurred when it did without the very substantial capital generated by the slavery system.

We should note some important political and cultural linkages to this burgeoning economic system. In the eighteenth and early nineteenth centuries the British parliament was dominated on many issues by those with economic interests in the slave trade, slave plantations, or commercial trade with the plantations.[51] In addition, in Britain and North America the revival of the arts—music, painting, sculptures, and essay writing—in this period was spurred in part by substantial funding from patrons made prosperous by various slavery enterprises. For example, some of George Friedrich Handel's oratorios and anthems were commissioned by an investor in slave plantations (the Duke of Chandos), and major libraries and art galleries were built by similar patrons.[52]

Slavery and Economic Development in the Americas   Coerced black laborers constituted the "founding stone of a new economic system . . . for the modern world."[53] It is unlikely that the American colonies and, later, the United States would have seen dramatic agricultural and industrial development in the eighteenth and nineteenth centuries without the blood and sweat of those enslaved. Much of the wealth generated between the early 1700s and the 1860s came from the slave trade and the labor of enslaved men, women, and children on plantations and in other profit-making enterprises. In the seventeenth century the famous triangular trade emerged between Europe, Africa, and the American colonies. Europe and America provided ships and some agricultural exports, while Africa provided the enslaved laborers. As Eric Williams has noted, sugar plantations in the West Indies "became the hub of the British Empire, of immense importance to the grandeur and prosperity of England," and it was the African laborers who made the West Indies the "most precious colonies ever recorded in the whole annals of imperialism."[54] Recent reviews of the evidence have concluded that the main economic bridge between Europe and the overseas colonies in this period was the slave-sugar complex.[55] The Caribbean plantations also spurred mainland development. Much of the oats, corn, flour, fish, lumber, soap, candles, and livestock exported by the continental colonies went to the West Indies plantations. In 1770 no less than *three-quarters* of all New England exports of foodstuffs went to the West Indian plantations or to Africa.[56] A substantial proportion of the wealth of the New England and Middle Atlantic colonies came from the nefarious trade with slave plantations in the southern colonies and the Caribbean.

From the early 1700s to the mid-1800s much of the surplus capital and wealth of North America came directly, or by means of economic multiplier effects, from the slave trade and slave plantations.[57] With the growing demand for textiles, U.S. cotton production expanded greatly between the 1790s and the beginning of the Civil War. Cotton was shipped to British and New England textile mills, greatly spurring the wheels of British, U.S., and international commerce. By the mid-nineteenth century New England cotton mills were the industrial leaders in value added, and second in number of employees, in the United States. Without slave labor it seems likely that there would have been no successful textile industry, and without the cotton textile industry—the first major U.S. industry—it is unclear how or when the United States would have become a major industrial power.[58]

In the first half of the nineteenth century many northern merchants, bankers, and shipping companies became, as Doulass North has noted, "closely tied to cotton. New York became both the center of the import trade and the financial center for the cotton trade."[59] Slave-grown cotton became ever more central to the U.S. economy and accounted for about half of all exports, and thus for a large share of the profits generated by exports.

In the North the profits from the cotton economy and from the sale of products to slave plantations stimulated the growth of investment in financial and insurance enterprises, other service industries, and various types of manufacturing concerns, as well as, by means of taxes, of investment in government infrastructure projects. Cotton-related activities were perhaps the most important source of economic expansion in the United States before the Civil War, and most of the cotton was grown by enslaved black Americans.[60] Their agricultural production undergirded national economic development. As Ronald Takaki has noted, "The income derived from the export of cotton set in motion the process of accelerated market and industrial development—the Market Revolution."[61]

Before the American revolution, trading in slaves was an honorable profession in northern ports, and after the revolution it was equally as honorable to trade in products made by slaves or in manufactured products traded to plantations. One biographer of the leading merchant, T. H. Perkins, concluded that there was not a New England "merchant of any prominence who was not then directly or indirectly involved in this trade."[62] As the nineteenth century progressed, the sons and grandsons of the earlier traders in slaves and slave-related products often became the captains of the textile and other major industries in the North. The business profits made off enslavement were thereby transmitted across generations.[63]

British and New England manufacturers' demand for cotton fueled the demand for more enslaved workers and for more Native American land. The leading cotton states—Mississippi, Alabama, and South Carolina—were carved out of Native American lands, and as the cotton system expanded westward, the lands of more indigenous societies were taken. Land was usually taken by force or threat of force.[64] By 1850 most of the nation's enslaved population was involved in cotton production. Labor was perhaps the most critical factor in American economic production in the eighteenth and nineteenth centuries, so any scarcity in workers slowed development. "Slave labor not only removed this scarcity, but also made possible the development of the industry that spurred economic growth."[65] In the decade before the Civil War the dollar value of those enslaved was estimated by one leading planter to be $2 billion—a figure then exceeding the total value of *all* northern factories.[66]

Not only did the southern agricultural system provide fiber for the textile mills of the North, but profits from the cotton trade also generated demand for western foodstuffs and northern manufactured products. And the coerced labor of black men, women, and children in southern agriculture built up profits that were used by many white slaveowners for luxurious living, for further investments in plantations and related enterprises, for deposits in banks, or for paying off bank loans. Such capital—and the related capital generated in the international trade in southern products—could be used or borrowed by merchants, shippers, railroad executives, and other industrialists in the North or South.[67]

The economic prosperity and industrial development of Western nations, including the United States, were grounded to a substantial degree in the slavery system. Ali Mazrui summarizes the point, saying that "one of the forces that fed into the industrial revolution was slave labor. Western production levels were transformed. But so were Western living standards, life expectancy, population growth, and the globalization of capitalism."[68] Indeed, even the educational system of the new nation was sometimes funded from profits off slavery or the slave trade. For example, the founders of Brown University in Rhode Island made some of their fortunes by building slave ships and investing in the slave trade.[69]

The Wealth of Powerful Slaveholders   In the century prior to the Civil War the slaveholding oligarchy of the southern and border states controlled a huge share of the resources and riches of the nation. By the early nineteenth century the slaveholders owned much of the nation's most productive land and much of the agricultural produce for export. They owned a large proportion of the nation's livestock, warehouses, plantation buildings, and processing mills, as well as large numbers of enslaved workers. As a result, the South was the most economically prosperous and politically powerful region from the mid-1700s to the 1850s.[70]

The theft of land and the enslavement of Africans became the foundation of prosperity for many white families. George Washington, the leading general, chair of the Constitutional Convention, and first president, was one of the wealthiest Americans. Owner of more than 36,000 acres in Virginia and Maryland, he held substantial securities in banks and land companies. By 1783 his own accounting showed 216 enslaved black Americans under his control, including those he held and those of his wife's estate; in their lifetimes he and his wife had enslaved many more. Reading Washington's careful records, one can see that Washington viewed black men, women, and children as "little more than economic units," like farm animals whose purpose was to bring him monetary profit.[71] Enslaved blacks made possible his luxurious lifestyle. As Fritz Hirchfeld has documented, "Slaves washed his linens, sewed his shirts, polished his boots, saddled his horse, chopped the wood for his fireplaces, powdered his wig, drove his carriage, cooked his meals, served his table, poured his wine, posted his letters, lit the lamps, swept the porch, looked after the guests, planted the flowers in his gardens, trimmed the hedges, dusted the furniture, cleaned the windows, made the beds, and performed the myriad domestic chores. . . ."[72] Though Washington said he was opposed to violent brutality against those enslaved, his actions contradicted his stated view. His overseers were allowed to use flogging, and he vigorously pursued runways. He could be severe in his punishment, as in the case of one black man sold to the West Indies plantations — unusually savage places known for enslaved laborers being worked to an early death. Exhibiting his inhumanity, Washington wrote to his broker that this black man was a "rogue and a runaway" and should be kept handcuffed.[73]

Similarly, the principal author of the Declaration of Independence, Thomas Jefferson, was considered very wealthy because he owned 10,000 acres of land and because, by the early 1800s, he held 185 African Americans in bondage. He owned several hundred black Americans over his lifetime. His often extravagant lifestyle was made possible by those he enslaved. While Jefferson was sometimes critical of slavery, he rarely freed any slaves. The man seen as a principal progenitor of American liberty, who penned the phrase "all men are created equal," was an unrepentant Virginia slaveholder. He fathered at least one child whom he kept as a slave, and he chased down his fugitive slaves and had them severely whipped.[74] Like many wealthy men in the South and the North, Washington and Jefferson gained their prosperity on the bloody backs of those black men, women, and children they enslaved.

Slaveholders and the American Government

Another Irony of the American Revolution   Without the capital and wealth generated by enslaved black Americans it is possible that there would not have been an American Revolution and, thus, a United States. One of history's great ironies is the fact that the Declaration of Independence's "all men are created equal" did not apply to African Americans, yet the American victory in the struggle against Great Britain was possible substantially because the wealth generated by the slavery system and its economic spinoffs was available to help finance and support the American Revolution. A significant proportion of the money amassed or borrowed to fight that revolution came, directly or indirectly, from capital generated by the plantations and the trade in slaves and slave-produced products.[75] Money borrowed from northern sources often had its ultimate origin in the slavery constellation, as did some of the money borrowed from overseas. France's involvement in the American Revolution was essential to its successful outcome, and, as Edmund Morgan has shown, the "single most valuable product with which to purchase assistance was tobacco, produced mainly by slave labor. . . . To a large degree it may be said that Americans bought their independence with slave labor."[76]

The political structure established after the revolution continued to reflect the elite interest in slavery and in controlling African Americans, whether enslaved or free. The mainstream view of the U.S. government sees it and its actions as set, from its first decades, in the context of democracy — as the result of competing group interests jockeying for position through democratic political mechanisms.

From this viewpoint, there is often a denial of the highly elitist and racialized character of the U.S. government.

A contrasting view sees the early U.S. state as very undemocratic and as central to the creation of systemic racism and to the formation of racial groups.[77] Historically, white male elites have worked through local and federal governments to create social institutions serving their interests. In the early development of the U.S. state, white women, African Americans, and Native Americans had no representation. The white male ruling class created a racialized state, which played a central role in defining who was "black" and "white" and what the benefits of being in each racial class were. For African Americans—and Native Americans forced onto reservations—this took the form of a police state. The standard dictionary definition of *police state* is "a political unit characterized by repressive governmental control of political, economic, and social life usually by an arbitrary exercise of power by police."[78] While the usual example of this is a totalitarian European government such as that of Nazi Germany, for most blacks police-state repression of their lives lasted, under slavery and later segregation, until the 1960s. Indeed, certain elements of this police state can still be seen in contemporary policing practices that unjustly target black men and women.

Slavery dominated U.S. politics in many ways between the making of the Constitution and the beginning of Civil War. The first U.S. president was a leading slaveholder, as were the third and fourth presidents. For fifty of the first sixty-four years of the new nation the president of the United States was a slave owner. The Speaker of the House was a slave owner for twenty-eight of the first thirty-five years of the nation's history, and before the Civil War the president pro tem of the Senate was usually a slaveholder.[79] The Chief Justices of the Supreme Court for most of the period up to the Civil War, John Marshall and Roger B. Taney, were slaveholders, as were numerous other members of that high court.

In the decades after the U.S. Constitution was put into place, the slavery system continued to shape legal and political decision making in fundamental ways, including the building of constitutional law in a series of federal court decisions such as *Dred Scott* (see chapter 3). For decades few major decisions made by the federal legislative and judicial branches went against the interests of the nation's slaveholding oligarchy, and foreign and domestic policies generally did not conflict with the interests of those centrally involved with the slavery system. George Washington's presidential administration even lent money to French planters in Haiti to put down a major slave uprising there. John Adams, his successor and not a slaveholder, took action to support the rebels, with an eye to U.S. influence in the area. Thomas Jefferson, another slaveholder and the third president, reversed Adams's policy and moved to support France's attempt to reconquer Haiti. Moreover, in the first half of the nineteenth century much U.S. territorial expansion, such as into areas of Mexico, was undergirded by the slaveholders' interest in additional land for yet more slave plantations.[80]

The slaveholding oligarchy was not seriously challenged until the middle of the nineteenth century. By the decade of the 1850s a major schism in the ruling class, that between southern planters and northern industrialists who had little economic interest in slavery, was becoming clear in battles over such issues as the expansion of slavery into western lands and over tariffs. Southern planters opposed tariffs on imports and pressed for expansion of the slaveholding system into new western areas, while northern immigrant farmers and allied railroad interests increasingly pressed to keep those lands available for immigrant farmers. Fearful of its economic and political future, the South's slaveholding oligarchy eventually moved to secede. The victory of the North in the subsequent Civil War marked the arrival of northern industrialists and merchants as a dominant force in the U.S. economy and government.[81]

The grip of slavery on the nation could be seen even as the southern states were seceding and the nation was moving to war. Recall that President Abraham Lincoln was willing to make major concessions to slaveholding interests to preserve the union. Certain members of the Republican Party talked with representatives of the southern planters and proposed a thirteenth amendment to the Constitution that would guarantee slavery in the South. Lincoln was willing to accept this amendment, even though it perpetuated enslavement. Yet the southern oligarchy rejected this compromise proposal, apparently because they thought they could win a war.[82]

Legal Segregation: Slavery Unwilling to Die

Terrorism by White Americans   After the Civil War, in the late 1860s and early 1870s, the Reconstruction period came to the South as a breath of fresh air. Federally enforced Reconstruction policies were precipitated by southern whites' unwillingness to make major changes in the treatment of freed slaves or to prevent the unrepentant leaders of the old Confederacy from again assuming autocratic power. A brief period of limited federal military occupation resulted. Prior to the 1860s black Americans had not generally been allowed to vote at any level of government. Now the Thirteenth, Fourteenth, and Fifteenth Amendments to the U.S. Constitution abolished slavery, asserted the civil rights of black Americans, and guaranteed black men (but not women) the right to vote. During the Reconstruction period black southerners made substantial political gains. New state constitutional conventions included black delegates, although in most states white southerners were predominant. For a time southern governments were mostly controlled by whites who had not been active leaders in the Confederacy, and black men and women gained a measure of personal and political freedom, although considerable racial segregation existed. These biracial state governments brought many needed progressive reforms to the South, including prison reform and public education.[83]

Today there is little recognition, in the mass media or in most history textbooks, of the scale and barbarousness of the *white terrorism* that brought an end to the often progressive Reconstruction governments and, with that, any hope for political or economic equality for black Americans. Sometimes, this southern terrorism even gets positive coverage. For instance, the early 1900s movie, *The Birth of a Nation*, now considered an American classic by movie experts, aggressively celebrates the very hostile and racist Ku Klux Klan view of the Reconstruction period. The recurring release of proslavery movies (for example, *Gone with the Wind* was rereleased in the late 1990s) signals how unconcerned the white majority is about the nation's sometimes savagely racist history.

What these U.S. movies should cover, but never have, is how the South's white elite, often with the collusion of presidents and northern elites, established an extensive terrorist campaign against the Reconstruction state governments and newly freed black southerners. A leading Confederate general, Nathan Bedford Forrest, was the first Grand Dragon of the newly created Ku Klux Klan, and no less a figure than General Robert E. Lee pledged his "invisible" support to the Klan. White terrorism destroyed the generally progressive southern state governments, and thousands of men, women, and children were severely beaten, killed, or raped by the Klan and similar white supremacist groups. For example, during the white riots in Memphis, Tennessee in 1866 and in Meridian, Mississippi in 1871, white mobs raped black women as they went on an antiblack rampage. The Confederacy lost the four-year war, but fought on as Stetson Kennedy notes, for "twelve more years—using every weapon at its disposal, including the ultimate one of mass terrorism—until the nation finally acceded to most of the Confederacy's modified war aims."[84]

After a few years of white terrorism, northern interest in the South waned. Northern leaders were not interested in punishing those who led the rebellion. The Hayes Compromise of 1877 removed the few remaining federal troops and eliminated much federal protection of black southerners. The leaders of the old Confederacy had won most of their basic goals. This conservative revolution ended most attempts to provide the newly freed slaves with economic help or restitution. Thus, Kennedy explains, black southerners were "sold back down the river into virtual enslavement, and all three of the new constitutional amendments—so far as blacks were concerned—were rendered dead letters for a century to come."[85] The Thirteenth, Fourteenth, and Fifteenth amendments gave black Americans citizenship rights, but most of these new rights were effectively denied by the southern legislatures, federal courts, or presidential or congressional action until the civil rights revolution of the 1950s. Whites in the North and the South joined once again in solidarity on behalf of the overarching white group interest.

The Continuing Badges and Disabilities of Slavery   In a dissenting opinion to the 1883 Civil Rights Cases, Justice John Marshall Harlan argued, "That there are burdens and disabilities which constitute badges of slavery and servitude, and that the power to enforce by appropriate legislation the Thirteenth Amendment may be exerted by legislation of a direct and primary character, for the eradication, not simply of the institution, but of its badges and incidents, are propositions which ought to be deemed indisputable."[86] Harlan was arguing that the federal government had a right to dismantle the lingering effects of slavery, not just slavery itself.

The end of slavery did not bring an end to the badges, burdens, or disabilities of slavery. Black men, women, and children were effectively reenslaved through the laws and informal practices of the southern and border states. The first laws took the form of the infamous Black Codes. Severely limiting the rights of the newly freed African Americans, these laws were in effect revisions of the old slave codes and expressed open defiance on the part of white leaders. To a substantial degree, the Reconstruction period was brought on by this defiance, and progressive reforms ensued. After the terrorism of white supremacist groups killed Reconstruction, conservative whites developed segregation laws with similarities to the Black Codes. Legal segregation was linked to the white elite's successful attempt to disenfranchise black voters and reassert the power of the Democratic Party against inroads made during Reconstruction by the Republican Party. Black citizens lost most of the political power they had gained during the years of Reconstruction. New elite-controlled, authoritarian political regimes dominated all the southern states, and these regimes worked with white planters and new southern industrialists to insure control of black workers in agriculture and industry.[87] By the early 1900s enforced racial segregation was the rule throughout the South.

A key Supreme Court decision, *Plessy v. Ferguson* (1896), involved the racial segregation of Louisiana railroad cars, which was challenged by a man whose ancestry was one-eighth African and seven-eighths European. The court's decision delivered a major blow to the idea of civic equality by upholding the legality of so-called separate but equal facilities for white and black Americans. Following the long tradition of white supremacist thinking, this all-white court reasoned, with just one dissenter, that racism was natural and that "legislation is powerless to eradicate racial instincts or to abolish distinctions based upon physical differences, and the attempt to do so can only result in accentuating the difficulties of the present situation. . . . If one race be inferior to the other socially, the Constitution of the United States cannot put them upon the same plane."[88] The racial privileges of whites as a group were again maintained. Justice John Marshall Harlan, the only dissenter, argued that "the arbitrary separation of citizens, on the basis of race, while they are on a public highway, is a badge of servitude wholly inconsistent with the civil freedom and the equality before the law established by the Constitution. It cannot be justified upon any legal grounds."[89] The long-term effect of *Plessy v. Ferguson* and similar court cases was to keep African Americans from equal access to the nation's major institutions.

By the early 1900s police-state conditions in the South shaped the lives of the 80 percent of African Americans who lived in that region. Most public facilities were segregated, including buses, water fountains, public toilets, parks, theaters, hospitals, colleges, churches, and even cemeteries. Black southerners were forcibly denied electoral influence. A severely racist etiquette was observed in most areas, forcing black men, women, and children to shuffle and wear masks of subordination before whites. Black men and women were usually referred to by their first names, not receiving the dignity that comes from using Mr., Mrs., or Miss with their last names. Whites commonly called black southerners "niggers" or "nigras." Segregation continued the total racist society environment. There were a thousand indignities beyond the laws, and the major means of escape—and that a partial escape—was migration to the North. The impact on African Americans was severe and costly; as Richard Wright describes eloquently in his autobiographical book, *Black Boy*, "I could not make subservience an automatic part of my behavior. I had to feel and think out each tiny item of racial experience in the light of the whole race problem, and to each item I brought the whole of my life. While standing before a white man I had to figure out how to perform each act and how to say each word. . . . I could not react as the world in which I lived expected me to. . . . I began to marvel at how smoothly the black boys acted out the roles that the white race had mapped out for them. Most of them were not conscious of living a special, separate, stunted way of life."[90]

Maintaining Segregation with Violence   White violence against black southerners undergirded the growing edifice of segregation. A central aspect of these new arrangements was the omnipresent lynching, usually of a black man thought to have spoken against, organized against, committed a crime against, or insulted his white oppressors. The accusation was often fictional or greatly exaggerated. Some 3,513 lynchings of black men and 76 of black women were recorded for the years 1882 to 1927, but many more did not get recorded. In addition, many other lynchings took place before and after that period. Between the Civil War and the 1990s, perhaps as many as 6,000 lynchings of black men and women have been perpetrated in the southern states and in certain areas of the northern and border states.[91]

Lynchings were savage events with a strongly ritualized character. One account from the 1940s involved a black man who was accused of trying to rape a white woman. A participant told the story of a white mob's actions to a social worker: "I ain't tellin' nobody just what we done to that nigger but we used a broken bottle just where it'd do the most damage, and any time you want to see a nigger ear all you gotta do is go to see old man Smith and ast him for a peep at one. . . . Yes, ma'am, we done things I never knowed could be done and things I certainly ain't mentionin' to no lady." After being cut, the black victim was doused in kerosene and burned, with the ending being that "the groanin' got lower and lower and finely it was just little gasps and then it wasn't nothin' a tall." After pulling him out of the fire, the white mob tied him to a tree, leaving him for his relatives to take down.[92] In most lynchings there was no trial. At the heart of this ritualized barbarism is concern that white supremacy must be maintained against all challenges, real or imaginary. It was expected that such terrorism would make local black residents afraid to challenge the mores of segregation. Many lynchings involved large turnouts by white men, women, and children who cheered the killings as part of a local community celebration. In many cases, as in this account, the black victims were brutally tortured, and pieces of their bodies were taken by whites as souvenirs. The sexual mutilations of many black victims, as well as the emotional accusations of rape against many victims signal yet again the importance of the sexual thread in U.S. racism. Such brutality underscores the deeply rooted, emotional character of much white-on-black oppression. This level of internalized racist thinking and emotion coupled with grisly rituals of extreme inhumanity is distinctive in the history of antiblack racism.

Segregation's Economic Impact   Segregation had a severe impact on the economic opportunities of black Americans. Economic servitude to whites was the rule. A key problem was disconnection from the means of production in an agricultural economy: the lack of good land. Once slavery was ended, black families were promised some productive land by federal officials. Those newly freed pressed for "forty acres and a mule" with which to begin a new life. Some federal generals initially gave confiscated Confederate lands to African Americans. The famous Special Field Order 15, issued by General William T. Sherman as he marched through the South, gave former slaves confiscated plantation lands. Soon more than 40,000 freed blacks were working large areas of farmland. Yet most of the new black farmers lost this land when the new president, Andrew Johnson, a southerner and slaveholder, overruled Sherman.[93] Property had to be protected, even if it belonged to slaveholders and traitors; yet again the common interest of white southerners and northerners in protecting unjustly gained resources was stronger than commitments to liberty and justice.

Only a small amount of land was parceled out by the Freedman's Bureau, the agency set up to assist black citizens. Black southerners were not eligible for public land given away by the first Homestead Act (1862), and by the time the Southern Homestead Act came to be (1866), they were unable to take full advantage of it because of widespread discrimination, intimidation, and violence against them. Those who were able to overcome these odds often found the land they secured to be poor for farming or lost it later on to white force or threats of force.[94] Black leaders like W. E. B. Du Bois argued that without some new resources there was no possibility of democracy: "To have given each one of the million Negro free families a forty-acre freehold would have made a basis of real democracy in the United States that might easily have transformed the modern world."[95]

After slavery came a period of renewed enrichment and capital accumulation by the larger white farmers and merchants in the southern and border states. They made their fortunes from the labor of theoretically free black laborers, tenant farmers, and sharecroppers. Booker T. Washington described the conditions that free blacks faced on the large farms and plantations as "a kind of slavery that is in one sense as bad as the slavery of antebellum days."[96] Whites reaped an ideological advantage as well. The new form of near enslavement meant that no one seemed responsible for the poverty of black Americans but themselves. In theory, tenant farmers and sharecroppers could sell their share of the crops, pay off debts, and buy their own land. Yet most were not able to make enough to escape the cycle of indebtedness to white landowners and merchants. Moreover, when large-scale industrialization finally came to the South by 1900, black workers were virtually excluded, except for the lowest-wage menial positions. Black men and women were still mostly employed in agriculture and in urban service jobs close in lineage to the house-slave jobs of the earlier period.[97]

Segregation in the North   Long before the Civil War, Jim Crow laws in the North enforced segregation in public transportation, hospitals, jails, schools, churches, and cemeteries. Jim Crow cars were first established on the railroads in Massachusetts. In northern cities whites enforced severe housing segregation. At one point or another in their histories all the states east of the Mississippi, and many of the western states, had some type of segregation laws. Into the 1930s not only the eleven southern states had segregation laws, but all the bordering states as well—from Delaware and Maryland to Missouri and Oklahoma. Some northern states like Kansas and Indiana had towns and cities with racial segregation statutes. Into the late 1940s numerous northern and western states, including Michigan, Colorado, Oregon, and California, had laws banning marriages between white and black Americans.[98] Beyond these laws, white northerners openly enforced racial segregation in housing and employment by informal means.

Patterns of Employment Segregation
Racist Barriers: 1910 to the 1930s   In 1910 more than 80 percent of black Americans, most of whom were descendants of those recently enslaved, still resided in the southern states. Most found themselves in agricultural areas with little or no access to productive farmland and facing segregation in most aspects of their lives. As a result, they began to migrate to the North in significant numbers. There, too, they met large-scale discrimination and exclusion.

In the North many southern migrants were concentrated in domestic and service positions; they were routinely excluded by employers and unions from bet-ter-paying jobs in expanding industrial settings. In addition, black workers were often displaced by new immigrant workers from southern and eastern Europe. Like the Irish workers before them, these immigrants sometimes forced black workers out of good jobs into lower-paying ones. When this overseas immigration was cut off in the 1920s, black workers were finally able to penetrate the industrial sector, but then primarily at the bottom.[99] Without the racist exclusion and dis-crimination perpetrated by employers and collaborated in by waves of European immigrants, the black Harlems and South Chicagos, Bob Blauner explains, "might have become solid working-class and middle-class communities with the economic and social resources to absorb and aid the incoming masses of Southerners."[100] This time the unjust impoverishment of blacks and enrichment of whites stemmed from white control over access to better-paying jobs and jobs with the potential for mobility. Here we see how whites who arrived in the United States after the slavery period—and their many descendants—benefited greatly from legal and informal segregation in employment. Once again, whites had more or less exclusive access to the economic, housing, and political resources that enabled them and their children to move up the socioeconomic ladder.

Clashes with whites became frequent as black workers and their families moved into northern cities. Whites sometimes used violence to enforce informal patterns of discrimination. During one white-generated riot in 1900 in New York, a mostly Irish police force encouraged whites to attack black men, women, and children. One of the most serious riots occurred in 1917 in East St. Louis. There white work-ers, viewing black immigrants from the South as a job threat, violently attacked a black community. Thirty-nine black residents and nine white attackers were killed. This was followed in 1919 by a string of white riots from Chicago to Charleston.[101] Opposition to black workers searching for jobs has been a recurring cause of antiblack violence. Black workers have periodically become scapegoats when a serious economic crisis threatens white livelihoods. They, as well as Asian, Latino, and Jewish Americans, have been singled out as targets of anger, even though they are not responsible for the employment or other economic problems of white work-ers. Acceptance of the dominant racist ideology has meant that many white work-ers have little understanding of how a capitalistic system operates against their own interests.

In the North and South, millions of white men, and a least a half million white women, belonged to the Ku Klux Klan or voted for its political candidates. During the years 1910 to 1930 numerous state and national politicians belonged to the Klan, and dozens of members of the Senate and House of Representatives were elected with the help of the Klan. Prior to becoming president, Warren G. Harding was closely tied to the Klan. And before he was a leading Supreme Court justice, Hugo Black had also been a member of the Klan.[102] Klan activities included large-scale marches and thousands of cross burnings, assaults, and lynchings in towns and cities across the nation—actions often knowingly winked at by local, state, and federal government officials.

The globalization of U.S. racism began in the late 1800s and the early 1900s. U.S. citizens, including government officials, often brought racist ideas and practices to other parts of the world. By 1900 the U.S. government created systems of white dominance in its colonies, including Cuba and the Philippines. During World War I the French government received a formal complaint from the U.S. military command that the French people were treating black American soldiers too well, and U.S. military authorities gave the French government instructions on how to treat black soldiers in discriminatory fashion.

Racist Barriers: The 1930s to the 1940s   During the 1930s most black men, women, and children still lived in the South's near slavery of segregation, a subjugation that did not allow the build-up of significant economic or educational resources for most black families. Segregation, with its racist etiquette, was very much in place. Though the Supreme Court in 1915 had begun to invalidate restrictions on black voters, most black southerners were not permitted to vote. Threats of violence and job loss were used to scare potential voters from the polls. In agricultural areas most black southerners worked as wage laborers, domestic workers, or sharecroppers. A modicum of economic and personal security could only come from being "associated with a white person of some status in the community."[103] In the North black workers likewise remained mostly in low-wage jobs as unskilled workers, domestics, and laborers.

During the Great Depression of the 1930s, unemployed whites frequently pushed black workers out of even menial jobs. Whites in Atlanta organized a "Black Shirts" organization under the slogan of "No Jobs for Niggers Until Every White Man Has a Job." By 1932 half of all black workers in cities were unemployed. Extreme hunger or starvation was often their lot. Less than one-fifth received relief aid from southern governments, and private charities sometimes refused to let unemployed blacks into soup lines.[104]

As federally funded employment programs began to put some black job seekers back to work and provide some economic support, black voters shifted from a solidly Republican vote in 1932 to a solidly Democratic vote in 1936. Nonetheless, black workers continued to suffer much discrimination from whites who administered New Deal agencies. In most federal relief programs blacks got lower wages than whites, were employed only as unskilled laborers, and were employed only after whites were. New Deal housing programs increased residential segregation of black families by restricting the new federally guaranteed home loans to homes in segregated areas and by locating public housing so that it would be segregated (see chapter 6). President Franklin Roosevelt and most of his advisors were even unwilling to press for antilynching legislation to get rid of this violent means of subordinating African Americans because they were afraid of losing the votes of white southerners in Congress.[105] The U.S. state was still openly racist and segregationist in its policies.

Racist Barriers: The Impact of Wars   One of the ironies of U.S. history is that much black economic progress has come during wartime. For example, during World War I the white immigration from Europe to the United States subsided, but workers were badly needed to produce war goods. Opportunities for employment in many formerly all-white, male job sectors were opened for black workers, as well as for white women. During World War II the demand for workers allowed black workers into some semiskilled and skilled blue-collar jobs for the first time. Similarly, the 1950s Korean War permitted expanded black employment in better-paying jobs. In each war period, overt barriers were lifted because many whites were more concerned with winning the war than with racist practices. Nonetheless, after the end of each war the employment situation of black men and women changed for the worse. For example, white veterans and other white workers poured into the cities after World War II, and most of the jobs that remained for the displaced (and other) black workers were menial and low-paying.[106]

During the Vietnam War in the 1960s there was again significant black mobility into better-paying jobs, with an assistance this time not only from that war and its associated prosperity but also from the renewed civil rights movement. In spite of this progress, however, black workers were farther behind whites in income, occupation, and unemployment than they had been in 1945. Thus, in 1962 black workers in the prime working-age group still had an unemployment rate *three times* that of whites.[107] While formal segregation laws were dismantled by the civil rights acts of the 1960s, large-scale informal discrimination and segregation persisted in most areas of society.

Black Workers Become a Surplus   Since the 1950s the United States has undergone significant economic changes. There is an increasing surplus of workers among those qualified for blue-collar jobs. As Sidney Willhelm has shown, increasing automation and overseas investments lie behind the harsh reality of growing unemployment, underemployment, or lower real wages for many American workers.[108] Black workers have been especially hard hit by these trends.

During the periods of slavery and legal segregation, there was usually a heavy demand among white farmers and other employers for black workers. Initially, black labor was coerced and imported because of a severe labor shortage in the American colonies, and black labor generally continued to be important to white employers during the long decades of formal segregation. The capitalistic labor market could not provide enough workers without this racialized coercion. Between the late 1800s and the 1940s many white workers moved off the farms into industrial labor. During most of that period black labor was still needed on many farms in southern and border states, and except in wartime white employers generally excluded blacks from the better-paying industrial jobs. White workers and their families gained substantial material advantages from these racist practices in the form of higher incomes and better jobs. Moreover, during strikes white employers frequently played black workers off against white workers, thereby damaging labor solidarity across the color line.

The mechanization that came to many farming areas after World War II as well as the industrialization associated with the war itself forced many black Americans off the farms and into industrial cities. By the 1950s and 1960s further automation had created a situation where many of the nation's black workers were no longer needed either in farming nor in some sectors of the industrial economy. Significantly, it was not until this labor surplus became a conspicuous economic reality in the 1960s that many white farmers and other white employers were finally willing to consider the abolition of the coercive arrangements of legal segregation. They no longer needed the large numbers of black workers upon which they had formerly depended heavily. A nation that had built much of its prosperity off the backs of black workers was gradually abandoning many of them to a life of unemployment or underemployment.[109] During the 1950s and 1960s, against a backdrop of employment and related problems, black Americans accelerated their organized protests against legal segregation. This civil rights movement encompassed many demonstrations, boycotts, and sit-ins. Thousands of African Americans and their white allies participated in these protests, which pressured the U.S. Congress to pass legislation prohibiting racial segregation and other forms of discrimination, as well as to establish modest job creation and training programs for victims of the increasingly automated economy.

Since the 1960s, as we will see in chapter 5, black Americans have continued to face not only direct discrimination in employment settings, but also the impact of past discrimination as it hampers their ability to compete fairly with white workers in an increasingly automated economy.

Conclusion　The United States was originally built as a white-racist republic. It was a principal part of the world racist order created by European colonialism and imperialism to enrich Europeans and impoverish indigenous peoples. The racist institutions established during the slavery period and undergirded by the U.S. Constitution have generated, enhanced, and reproduced the mobility or prosperity of white Americans for many generations. For more than a century after the abolition of slavery, the core reality of the United States has remained one of systemic racism. While some changes have occurred in U.S. racial patterns from time to time, since the late 1600s the continuities in the basic features of the system of antiblack racism seem more significant than most of these changes. The current U.S. racial situation is very much the legacy of black enslavement, and the badges and disabilities of slavery still lie heavily on black Americans.

This reality is recognized, albeit only occasionally, at the highest levels of the U.S. justice system. For example, in a pioneering 1968 Supreme Court case, *Jones v. Mayer*, the U.S. Supreme Court considered blatant housing discrimination and segregation in St. Louis. In that perceptive decision the majority of the court ruled that "[j]ust as the Black Codes, enacted after the Civil War to restrict the free exercise of those rights, were substitutes for the slave system, so the exclusion of Negroes from white communities became a substitute for the Black Codes. And when racial discrimination herds men into ghettos and makes their ability to buy property turn on the color of their skin, then it too is a relic of slavery."[110] For a brief period a majority of the white Supreme Court judges recognized that persisting racial discrimination and segregation were relics of the slavery system.

In a concurring opinion in this case, Justice William O. Douglas enumerated the ways in which persisting discrimination is connected in a direct line to slavery, proclaiming, "Some badges of slavery remain today. While the institution has been outlawed, it has remained in the minds and hearts of many white men. Cases which have come to this Court depict a spectacle of slavery unwilling to die. We have seen contrivances by States designed to thwart Negro voting. . . . Negroes have been excluded over and again from juries solely on account of their race . . . or have been forced to sit in segregated seats in courtrooms. . . . They have been made to attend segregated and inferior schools . . . or been denied entrance to colleges or graduate schools because of their color. . . . Negroes have been prosecuted for marrying whites. . . . They have been forced to live in segregated residential districts . . . and residents of white neighborhoods have denied them entrance. . . ."[111]

Since Douglas's retirement from the court in 1975, only a few of the white justices have had a similar understanding of racial matters. Douglas had some recognition of the fact that racial segregation, like slavery, was a masterful machine designed to protect white privileges and continue the unjust enrichment of the past.

Today, slavery's badges and disabilities persist because they are perpetuated by the racist practices of many whites. The numerous kinds of antiblack discrimination still found in all areas of the United States, which we will catalog in later chapters, do indeed represent a "spectacle of slavery unwilling to die."

three

Racist Ideology as a Social Force

Creating a Racist Ideology   The expansion of Europe from the 1400s to the early 1900s eventually brought colonial exploitation to more than 80 percent of the globe. The resulting savagery, exploitation, and resource inequalities were global, and they stemmed, as W. E. B. DuBois has noted, from letting a "single tradition of culture suddenly have thrust into its hands the power to bleed the world of its brawn and wealth, and the willingness to do this."[1] For the colonizing Europeans it was not enough to bleed the world of its labor and resources. The colonizers were not content to exploit indigenous peoples and view that exploitation simply as "might makes right." Instead, they vigorously justified what they had done for themselves and their descendants. Gradually, a broad racist ideology rationalized the oppression and thereby reduced its apparent moral cost for Europeans.

An ideology is a set of principles and views that embodies the basic interests of a particular social group. Typically, a broad ideology encompasses expressed attitudes and is constantly reflected in the talk and actions of everyday life. One need not know or accept the entire ideology for it to have an impact on thought or action. Thus, each person may participate only in certain fragments of an ideology. Ideologies are usually created by oppressors to cover what they do, and counterideologies are often developed by the oppressed in their struggle against domination.[2] In this chapter we examine a critical aspect of the social reproduction of systemic racism from one generation to the next. The perpetuation of systemic racism requires an intertemporal reproducing not only of racist institutions and structures but also of the ideological apparatus that buttresses them.

The early exploitative relationships that whites developed in regard to African Americans and Native Americans were quickly rationalized, and they became enduring racist relations. From the beginning, racism has been webbed into most arenas of American life, including places of work and residence, and activities as diverse as eating, procreating, and child rearing. Racist practices in these life worlds create, and are in turn shaped by, basic racist categories in the language and minds of Americans, especially white Americans. A racist ideology has overarching principles and beliefs that provide an umbrella for more specific racist attitudes, prejudices, and stereotypes. In this chapter we examine in detail the overarching racist ideology of the American past and present, with an emphasis on the role of white elites in framing and perpetuating an antiblack ideology. In chapter 4 we will look at the present day, and focus on an array of specific antiblack attitudes and images in the United States, with an emphasis on the views of ordinary white Americans. As we will see, however, both chapters 3 and 4 and their subject matters are closely connected.

Major ideological frameworks, including racist frameworks, are typically created, codified, and maintained by those at the top of a society, although this construction takes place in ongoing interaction with the views and practices of ordinary citizens. Those with the greater power have the greater ability to impose their own ideas on others. As Karl Marx and Friedrich Engels long ago pointed out, "the ideas of the ruling class are in every epoch the ruling ideas: i.e. the class, which is the ruling material force of society, is at the same time its ruling intellectual force."[3] Elites have dominated the creation, discussion, and dissemination of system-rationalizing ideas in business, the media, politics, education, churches, and government. While there is indeed much popularly generated racist imagery and discourse, even this is usually codified and embellished by the elites. As with most important ideas, if the elites had been opposed to the development of the racist ideology, they would have actively combated it, and it would likely have declined in importance. Thus, in his detailed analysis of the racist ideas and actions of presidents from George Washington to Bill Clinton, Kenneth O'Reilly has shown that conventional wisdom about presidents *following* a racist populace is wrongheaded. The historical evidence shows that most of the men who control U.S. political institutions have worked hard "to nurture and support the nation's racism."[4] Racist thought did not come accidentally to the United States. It was, and still is, actively developed and propagated.

The Emerging Antiblack Ideology: Early Views   For several centuries white ministers, business people, political leaders, academics, scientists, and media executives have developed and disseminated to all Americans a complex and variegated racist ideology that defends the theft of land and labor from Americans of color. The antiblack version of this ideology is the most developed; it has included a variety of religious, scientific, and psychosexual rationalizations for oppression. Although the ideology has been elaborated and changed somewhat over time, in all its variations it has operated to rationalize white power and privilege.

Positive Images of Africa: The Early Period   Negative images of Africans and African Americans are now so commonplace that one might think that non-Africans have always held such views. This is not the case. Early Judeo-Christian writings, including sections of the Bible, reveal that images of Africans were often positive in the Middle East. In what Christians call the Old Testament, African kingdoms are frequently portrayed as strong societies and as allies of Jewish kings.[5] Moreover, during the Greek and Roman periods Europeans generally attached far greater significance to Africans' learning, advanced culture, and nationality than to their physical characteristics. Africa and the Africans, from whom Greeks and Romans borrowed substantially for their own development, were seen in mostly positive terms. While individual Greeks or Romans did sometimes express negative views of Africans' physique or skin color, these views were never developed into a broad color consciousness viewing Africans as a greatly inferior species. Before the European slave trade began in the 1400s, the world had not seen a well-developed racist ideology.[6]

However, in the writings of early Christian leaders the idea of spiritual "darkness" was increasingly linked to concepts of sin, evil, and the devil. As Jan Pieterse tells us, "Origen, head of the catechetical school in Alexandria in the third century, introduced the allegorical theme of Egyptian darkness as against spiritual light."[7] Gradually over the next several centuries Christian leaders and their followers came to associate evil, the devil, and non-Christian religions with notions of spiritual darkness and blackness. This set the stage perhaps for the next step in European thinking, which gradually associated Africans with negative views of darkness and blackness. Even so, there was still significant diversity in European perspectives on Africa in the Middle Ages. African (Ethiopian) Christian groups were well regarded and present at European church councils in the early 1400s, and some African religious figures were viewed in a positive light by many European Christians.[8]

Negative Images of the Colonized   European colonialism changed this situation greatly for the worse. By the mid-1400s the Portuguese were sailing regularly to Africa and exporting Africans in chains. Ideas of European superiority were developed and fostered in the first imperialistic nations, Portugal and Spain, as they exploited the labor of, and took the resources of, many indigenous peoples. For a time, a few leading Catholic priests and theologians opposed the ruthless exploitation of indigenous populations, including the savage, often genocidal operations

of Spanish colonizers such as those led by Christopher Columbus against indigenous peoples in the Americas in the late fifteenth and early sixteenth centuries.
However, in a 1550 debate the important Spanish theologian Gaines de Sepulveda
argued that it was lawful to make war on and enslave indigenous populations
because of their heathen, sinful, and uncivilized natures, which obligated the latter to serve those (the Spanish) with the superior culture. Sepulveda represented
the dominant view and was perhaps the first European intellectual to defend the
barbarity of colonialism in such comprehensive cultural terms.[9]

The English soon followed in the imperialistic ways of the Spanish. Prior to the
English colonization of North America and much of the globe, some negative
ideas about non-English peoples overseas were already current in England, perhaps coming from other European explorers. For example, in 1611, a few years
before English colonists brought Africans into the Jamestown colony, William
Shakespeare's play *The Tempest* — set perhaps on the island of Bermuda — had featured the sinister figure of Caliban. Caliban is portrayed as the dark other, as a
"savage and deformed slave." His mother is said to be from Africa. Caliban is portrayed as physically threatening to Prospero, a European man of intellect. The
English had some negative images of certain cultural others before their overseas
conquests were well underway.[10]

"Christians" Versus the "Uncivilized Others"   From the 1600s to the 1800s English
and other European Protestants dominated the religious sc ne on the Atlantic coast
of North America, and their religious views incorporated notions of European superiority and non-European inferiority. The early English Protestants regarded themselves as Christian and civilized, but those they conquered as unchristian and savage. Religious and cultural imperialism accompanied economic imperialism.

Why were Europeans first to engage in large-scale imperialism and colonialism across the globe? One proposed reason points to the relative absence of mineral and agricultural resources in Europe. Another reason often suggested is that
Europeans had the shipbuilding and military technologies to expand and colo-
nize overseas. However, one other society, that of China, had developed the technological potential (for example, large sailing ships) for major overseas conquest
well before the Europeans, but had not engaged in such large-scale conquest.
Perhaps very important to the emergence of European imperialism was the early
development of a strong acquisitive ethic, an ethic coupled with a missionary zeal
convinced of the superiority of European civilization. This was early revealed in
the conflicts of European Christians with Islamic regions that controlled access
to spices and gold, land control that spurred European expansion across the oceans.
European colonialism involved more than the we/they ethnocentrism common
to many societies. In European colonialism, the we/they dichotomy becomes
greatly accentuated, and the cultural other becomes much more than a traditional
enemy. Europeans view themselves as culturally superior to all others. At the cen-

ter of European imperialism was a powerful drive to dominate the entire world, at whatever human cost, for economic and cultural gain.[11]

By the late 1400s and early 1500s the emerging bourgeoisie in northern and western European societies adhered increasingly and strongly to values of individual acquisitiveness, market capitalism, and colonial expansion. The ever-spreading acquisitiveness and rapaciousness of the north European bourgeoisie was reinforced by the values of certain Protestant religions to which they adhered. The individualistic Protestant ethic did not create capitalism, but it did foster certain values of capitalism, including a rather greedy individualism that contrasted with the more collectivistic values of the majority of the world's peoples. Thus, throughout the British colonial period, the bloody conquests overseas were regularly consecrated by Christian ministers. The acquisitiveness and plunder of European colonialism and imperialism were not deviations from the dominant value system of the emerging bourgeoisie, but rather were part of a religiously reinforced pattern of behavior that eventually encompassed most of the globe.[12]

Most of the new colonists from Europe saw themselves as Christian people of virtue and civilization. From the first century of American colonization these Europeans frequently portrayed themselves as "virtuous republicans." They did not, or should not, have the instinctual qualities of the "creatures of darkness," the black and red Calibans they saw in their stereotyped images. Europeans were rational, ascetic, self-governing, and sexually controlled, while the African and Native American others were irrational, uncivilized, instinctual, and uncontrolled.[13] The first non-Europeans with whom many European colonists came into contact were Native Americans. Rationalizing the often brutal destruction of Native American societies, European colonists developed early on some negative images of Native Americans. Native Americans were "uncivilized savages" to be killed off or pushed beyond the boundaries of European American society. Moreover, much white thinking about indigenous peoples in the first centuries alternated between great hostility, such as can be seen in the Declaration of Independence's complaint about "merciless Indian savages," and the paternalism seen in the image of a "noble savage" who was independent of the vices of Europeans. Novelists such as James Fenimore Cooper heralded what they saw as the diversity in character of the "native warrior of North America. In war, he is daring, boastful, cunning, ruthless . . . in peace, just, generous, hospitable, revengeful, superstitious, modest, and commonly chaste."[14]

In Europe and the Americas, an early and commonplace European or European American explanation for the exploitation and enslavement of other groups drew on an old religious myth based on the biblical story of Noah and his sons (Genesis 9–10), a myth that as we saw in chapter 1 can still be found among some white Christians today. This old story relates how a drunken Noah was encountered by three sons. Two of them, Shem and Japheth, did not look upon him but covered his nakedness. Noah's son, Ham, had looked but did not cover him. As a result, Ham's son Canaan was cursed by Noah and told that he would be the servant of his brethren. A later version of this religious myth views Ham as African and as suffering the divine punishment of his descendants being made servants to other peoples, the descendants of Ham's brothers. However, in the Christian Bible there is nothing about Ham's African characteristics. It was later, in the Talmudic and Midrashic (Jewish) religious tradition, that Ham (or Canaan) was said to have "darkened the faces of mankind," and thus was asserted to be father to the African peoples.[15]

This Ham myth was picked up in Christian communities by the 1500s, and the story was soon used by European colonists to justify the subjugation and enslavement of Africans and African Americans. A religious theory of black subordination and separation remained strong throughout the slavery and legal segregation periods. For centuries religious myths about people of African descent have been retold as part of the dominant ideological framework by members of white ruling elites, including ministers, business leaders, political officials, and judges, as well as by ordinary whites. For example, one of the most important Supreme Court cases in U.S. history, *Buchanan v. Warley* (1917), dealt with a housing segregation ordinance. Apparently alluding to these religious myths, white lawyers for the City of Louisville, Kentucky, argued, "It is shown by philosophy, experience, and legal decisions, to say nothing of Divine Writ, that . . . the races of the earth shall preserve their racial integrity by living socially by themselves."[16]

Early Color Coding: The Link to Slavery   In the early seventeenth century English American colonists first used terms like "Christians" for themselves and "negroes" for African Americans. The latter term referred to African descent and was not yet a designation for a distinctive "race." Nonetheless, the conceptualization was gradually moving in the direction of a full-fledged biologized racism, for the colonists were paying increasing attention to skin color and the purity of their ancestry ("blood").[17] As early as 1614, Reverend Samuel Purchas spoke of the "black Negroe" and the "whiter European."[18] Moreover, some were arguing for a God-ordained hierarchy of human beings; God had created, as a Boston slaveholder put it in 1701, "different degrees and orders of men."[19] It was already part of the nature of being defined as "black" to have to suffer discrimination and to develop resistance to that discrimination. One was only "black" in relationship to those self-defined as "white."

In the process of English colonialism and the African slave trade some of the world's lightest-skinned people came into contact with some of the world's darkest-skinned people. Gradually, color and other physical characteristics became central to an ideology rationalizing exploitation and oppression. In the prevailing European view, the *enslaved status* of most black Americans was fundamental: African Americans were inferior because they were enslaved, and they were enslaved because they were inferior. The expansion of enslavement and color typing developed side by side, with one reinforcing the other. By the late 1600s colonial accounts refer to the unusual "complexion" of the slaves as making an impression on the "white" mind. The term "white" was increasingly used alongside "Christian" and "English" by the colonists to distinguish themselves from "negroes," who had no role in naming themselves. By means of slavery European colonists had created a new group consisting of people from many different African societies, one sharply differentiated from whites in rights and privileges. Enslaved Africans became a major point of reference for the construction of the newly defined whiteness. In 1709 an English official noted in his diary that a Spaniard had petitioned the Massachusetts Council for his freedom and that a certain Captain Teat had alleged that "all of that [dark] Color were Slaves."[20] Darker skin color was then taken by whites as the visible badge of enslavement.

The controlling language in the new nation was that of the English colonists. They had power to shape the terminology used in interaction with one another and with those they oppressed. Increasingly, skin color was linked to older color meanings in English. In Old English, the word "black" meant sooted, while the word "white" meant to gleam brightly, as for a candle. In line with earlier Christian usage, the word "black" was used by the English colonists to describe sin, evil, and the devil.[21] Old Christian images of darkness and blackness as sinister were transferred to the darker-skinned peoples exploited in the system of slavery.

The European colonists, who were usually some shade of tan, brown, or pink in skin color, must have seen that Africans varied greatly in skin color, with the majority being some shade of brown. There was no obvious reason for the English to connect the longstanding religious images of evil and darkness with the skin color of Africans.[22] The attributing of whiteness or blackness to those who are mostly some shade of brown suggests there are deep emotional roots to the antiblack thinking and imaging of whites, an issue to which we will return shortly.

In the first century of North American slavery the antiblack ideology was becoming ever more developed and comprehensive. The emerging ideology increasingly focused not only on the blackness of the others but also on the whiteness of Europeans. Africans and African Americans were viewed as physically, aesthetically, morally, and mentally inferior to whites—differences that were regarded as more or less permanent. "Whiteness" was created in opposition to "blackness," in comparison to which it was not only different but quite superior. Indeed, from the seventeenth century forward black women, men, and children were "constructed as lazy, ignorant, lascivious, and criminal; Whites as industrious, knowledgeable, virtuous, and law-abiding."[23]

Significantly, the antiblack image was not "out there," but rather in the white mind and emotions. In their thinking and imaging, some whites went so far as to view the dark skin of Africans as a "natural infection" or as "pollution." A leading medical educator of the late 1700s, Dr. Benjamin Rush, thought the dark skin color of African Americans resulted from a type of leprosy that could be cured with medical treatment.[24]

The Legal Underpinning   At an early stage, the antiblack perspective of white Americans was imbedded by them in new legal and political institutions. By the 1670s slavery was enshrined in colonial laws defining Africans as chattel property. From that time to the Civil War much lawmaking, in the North and South, strongly supported the barbaric institution. Consider the central colony in the first century and a half of North American development—Virginia. In that area could be found 40 percent of all those then enslaved, as well as many of the prominent whites who were speaking out on issues of liberty.[25] Thomas Jefferson published the cases of Virginia's General Court for the years 1730 to 1772. More than half involved legal matters of concern to slaveholders, "such as testamentary disposition of slaves, creditors' rights in a debtor's slaves, warranty in the sale of slaves, life estates in and mortgages of slaves, dower in slaves, and entailed slaves."[26] From the 1600s to the mid-1800s many state and federal court cases and decisions revealed the centrality of slavery to the new nation.

The U.S. Constitution recognized the slave economy and implicitly incorporated an ideology of white supremacy in such provisions as the one that counted an African American as only "three-fifths" of a person. After the new nation was created, the unifying of growing numbers of immigrants from various European countries was done in part through the legal and political doctrines buttressing white privilege and superiority. In the first naturalization law in 1790, the new U.S. Congress made the earliest political statement on citizenship. Naturalization was restricted to "white persons." Whiteness thereby became an official government category; only European immigrants could qualify to become citizens of the new United States. The legal doctrines established by Congress and the courts helped to shape and unify the white consciousness, including that of the nation's leadership.[27]

Education and the Antiblack Ideology   From the colonial era to the present, educational institutions have been critical to the transmission of the racist ideology across many generations. Elites have long maintained power in part by controlling the processes of learning and knowledge dissemination through public, religious, and other private schooling. At an early point in colonial history, a New England minister, Samuel Hopkins, noted why whites see blacks negatively: "We have been used to look on them in a mean, contemptible light; and *our education* has filled us with *strong prejudices* against them, and led us to consider them, not as our brethren, or in any degree on a level with us; but as quite another species of animals, made only to serve us and our children; and as happy in bondage, as in any other state. . . ."[28] Since the first century of colonization, whites have learned racist prejudices and attitudes at school, as well as at home and church.

Over centuries of colonialism Europeans and European Americans have celebrated conquests by various means, including controlling how conquered peoples and their physical environments came to be named. Many areas around the
world, including "America," were given lasting names by Europeans from within
their own interpretive frames. By such naming, the conquerors made other
peoples' spaces into their places and claimed them for their own. The spatial
conquests of colonialism have long been celebrated in the form of slanted histories and Eurocentric holidays, collections, museums, and monuments. Today, to
use the names given by imperialists or to visit their museums is to participate, however unconsciously, in the lasting consequences of European colonialism and
imperialism. [29]

Emotional Underpinnings   From the seventeenth century to the present the ideology justifying antiblack oppression, while overtly cognitive and legally enshrined,
has had a strong emotional base. Antiblack attitudes and actions among whites
have long been linked to or supported by such emotions as hate, fear, guilt, and
repulsion. W. E. B. Du Bois suggested that color barriers are created not only out
of overt maliciousness but also by "unconscious acts and irrational reactions
unpierced by reason."[30]

For instance, many whites have been emotionally obsessed with what they term
"racial mixing." Strong and irrational emotions are evident in the taboos and laws
against interracial sex and marriage, which have long been considered to be
extremely "unnatural" and "abominable" by many whites. In 1662 the colony of
Virginia established the first law against interracial sex, and in 1691 a law against
interracial marriage was enforced by banishment. White Virginians, scholars have
noted, were very "disturbed by the racial intermingling, especially white-Negro
mixtures, and introduced laws to prevent what they saw as the 'abominable mixture and spurious issue' by penalizing whites who engaged in interracial sex."[31]
Mixed-ancestry Americans were viewed not only as inferior but also as degrading
what Benjamin Franklin called a "lovely" whiteness. As Franklin argued, white
"amalgamation with the other color produces a degradation to which no lover of
his country, no lover of excellence in the human character can innocently consent."[32] Like most whites of the eighteenth century, Franklin seems to have developed a deep fear of black Americans. A slaveholder for several decades, then a
leading abolitionist later in life, Franklin openly opposed slavery not because of
its inhumanity but because of its negative impact on the whiteness of the American
population.[33] Ironically and significantly, for most of American history it was white
men who were the most likely to cross the color line and force sex on black women.

Strong emotions are evident in the white violence that has long targeted black
Americans. While most of the bloodthirsty lynchings of black Americans took
place after the Civil War, they were preceded before that war by barbaric beatings,
rape, torture, and mutilation of Africans and African Americans on slave ships,

farms, and plantations. The early white notion that African Americans were "dangerous savages" and "degenerate beasts" played a role in rationalizing this violence. To deserve such treatment "the black man presumably had to be as vicious as the racists claimed; otherwise many whites would have had to accept an intolerable burden of guilt for perpetrating or tolerating the most horrendous cruelties and injustices."[34] After slavery, the racist ideology legitimated lynchings, whose sadistic character suggests deep and shared white emotions of guilt, hatred, and fear.

Fear is central to the ideology and attitudes woven through the system of antiblack oppression. Significantly, of the three large-scale systems of social oppression — racism, sexism, and classism — only racism involves the dominant group having a deep and often obsessively emotional fear (some term it "Negrophobia") of the subordinate group. This is not generally true for men, who dominate women in the system of sexism, nor is it true for the capitalists who exploit workers in the class-stratified capitalist system. The racist system of oppression is often very deeply rooted in the identity and emotions of white men, women, and children.

Why do many whites often react viscerally to the presence or image of the black body, and especially the bodies of black men? Joel Kovel has argued that many whites dislike and reject black bodies because they project onto them their own deep fears, which are often rooted in childhood. As they are socialized, young whites learn, directly and indirectly, consciously and unconsciously, that the dark otherness of black Americans symbolizes degradation, danger, sinfulness, or the unknown — imagery dating back to at least the seventeenth century and still present in white imaginings. Over the course of a lifetime antiblack impulses and actions are strongly shaped by the images in whites' unconscious minds. From this perspective, a primary reason for the intensely emotional character of the racist ideology is that many whites project onto the black out-group their own deep-lying inclinations and forbidden desires, which cannot be openly acknowledged.[35]

Developing an Explicit Ideology of "Race"   We/they ethnocentrism existed long before Europeans built their colonial empires, but a well-developed exploitative, and soon to be fully racist, ideology emerged only with European domination of peoples overseas. As Oliver Cox has noted, the modern racist ideology did not arise out of some "abstract, natural, immemorial feeling of mutual antipathy between groups," but rather grew out of the exploitative relationships of colonialism.[36] There are significant variations in the stereotyping and treatment of external groups across societies. Some societies, for example, do not develop the high level of xenophobia that others do. Historically, many indigenous societies showed a friendliness (xenophilia) toward Europeans when the latter first came into their areas. As it turned out, this friendly attitude was usually a serious mistake.

The ideology rationalizing exploitation did not develop all at once, but was elaborated as colonialism expanded around the globe. First, as we saw above, the "others" were viewed as religiously and culturally inferior. This brought an early accent on a hierarchy of inferior and superior groups. Later on, those oppressed were seen as distinctive "races" that were inferior in physical, biological, and intellectual terms to Europeans. A clearly delineated concept of "race" as a distinctive pseudobiological category was developed by northern Europeans and European Americans about the time of the American Revolution.

By the late 1700s these hierarchical relations were increasingly explained in overtly bioracial terms. This biological determinism read existing European prejudices back into human biology; then it read that biology as rationalizing social hierarchy. Those at the bottom were less than human; they were alleged to have smaller, and thus inferior, brains.[37] Reflecting on European imperialism in the late nineteenth and early twentieth centuries, Frantz Fanon stressed the point that this colonialism was about much more than labor or resource exploitation, for it involved broad social domination constructed in racist terms. European colonialism created the modern idea of "race" across the globe. "In the colonies the economic substructure is also a superstructure. The cause is the consequence; you are rich because you are white, you are white because you are rich."[38] This new racist ideology had three important elements: (1) an accent on physically and biologically distinctive categories called "races"; (2) an emphasis on "race" as the primary determinant of a group's essential personality and cultural traits; and (3) a hierarchy of superior and inferior racial groups.

Early White Leaders and Intellectuals   Audrey Smedley argues that "race was, from its inception, a folk classification, a product of popular beliefs about human differences that evolved from the sixteenth through the nineteenth centuries."[39] However, much of the effort to create an ideology accenting a hierarchy of races has come from the top. While most people tend to sort others into categories, it is typically the elites who codify and propagate strong versions of social categorization. From the beginning, European and American elites worked hard to defend imperialism and its many forms of oppression. By the mid- to late eighteenth century, white leaders were arguing that "negroes" were a biologically different species or "race" from Europeans. For example, in a lengthy book, *The History of Jamaica* (1774), prominent judge Edward Long, a slaveholder, argued that Africans were a "truly bestial" and different species. Long's influential book was published in the United States in 1788.[40]

America's prominent theorist of liberty, Thomas Jefferson, contended that black Americans were an inferior "race." In *Notes on the State of Virginia*, written in the late eighteenth century, Jefferson articulated what were the first developed arguments by an American intellectual for black inferiority. Blacks are said to be inferior to whites in reasoning, imagination, and beauty. Blacks are alleged to favor white beauty "as uniformly as is the preference of the Oranootan [Orangutan] for the black women over those of his own species."[41] Blacks are alleged to be more adventuresome than whites because they have a "want of forethought," to be unreflective, and—perhaps most amazing—to feel life's pain less than whites. Blacks are alleged to have produced no important thinkers, poets, musicians, or intellectuals. Improvement in black minds comes only when there is a "mixture with whites," which Jefferson argues "proves that their inferiority is not the effect merely of their condition of life."[42] Over his long lifetime Jefferson was an active slaveholder, even as he asserted from time to time that he disliked slavery. Among his famous words on the subject are those inscribed on the Jefferson Memorial in Washington, D. C.: "Nothing is more certainly written in the book of fate than that these people are to be free." Significantly, the critical words following this sentence are omitted on this monument: "Nor is it less certain that the two races, equally free, cannot live in the same government."[43]

Paul Finkelman has summed up Jefferson's fears, saying, "First, he hated what slavery did to whites. Second, he hated slavery because he feared it would lead to a rebellion that would destroy the society. Third, he hated slavery because it brought Africans to America and kept them there. He cared little for the fate or feelings of these Africans or their African American descendants, but he could not stand their presence in America. None of this hatred motivated him to do anything about the institution."[44] Numerous white Americans, then and since Jefferson's day, have feared that those in the "black race"—or people of color more generally—are growing so fast as to destroy a supposedly homogeneous white society.

The West's Moral Philosopher   During the eighteenth and nineteenth centuries white American leaders in business, politics, and the universities were greatly influenced by European intellectuals and writers, many of whom held openly antiblack views. Indeed, the major Western philosopher of the late eighteenth century, Immanuel Kant, produced the first developed theory of race in modern terms. Intellectuals have long viewed Kant as the leading moral philosopher of the West, a pure philosopher uncontaminated by racist thought. However, for decades Kant wrote and taught some of the first courses explicitly dealing with the geography and anthropology of race. At the heart of his influential thinking was an attempt to define humanity: "If there is any science man really needs, it is the one I teach, of how to fulfill properly that position in creation which is assigned to man, and from which he is able to learn what one must be in order to be a man."[45] For Kant, one must be *white* to be fully human, for "humanity exists in its greatest perfection in the white race."[46] During the 1770s Kant wrote of the hierarchy of "races of mankind," one of the uses of the idea of races in the sense of biologically distinct, hierarchical categories. In one document Kant delineated a hierarchy, with whites at the top:

STEM GENUS, white brunette
First race, very blond (northern Europe), of damp cold.

Second race, Copper-Red (America), of dry cold.
Third race, Black (Senegambia), of dry heat.
Fourth race, Olive-Yellow (Indians), of dry heat.[47]

For Kant the essence of humanity can best be seen in a white man like himself. At this early point, European philosophy and philosophical anthropology were grounded in ideas about the supremacy of the white race and Western civilization.

Scientific Racism   From the middle of the eighteenth century to the middle of the twentieth century, the physical and social sciences were regularly used to defend the oppression of Americans of color. Leading scientists developed a scientific view of black Americans and other peoples of color as innately and permanently inferior beings. Ideological racism is not something that comes only out of the margins of Western societies, but rather from their intellectual and cultural centers.

As early as the 1730s the Swedish botanist and taxonomist, Carolus Linneaus, distinguished four categories of human beings—black, white, red, and yellow. Though he did not explicitly use the idea of "race," he associated skin color with cultural traits—with whites being superior and blacks inferior.[48] Between the 1770s and the 1790s the prominent German anatomist and anthropologist, Johann Blumenbach, worked out a racial classification that became influential. At the top of his list of "races" were what Blumenbach called the "Caucasians" (Europeans), a term he coined because in his judgment the people of the Caucasus were the most beautiful of the European peoples. Lower on the list were the Mongolians (Asians), the Ethiopians (Africans), the Americans (Native Americans), and the Malays (Polynesians). "White" was viewed as the oldest color of mankind, and white had degenerated into the darker skin colors.[49]

The new scientific racism firmly encompassed the notion of a specific number of races with different physical characteristics, a belief that these characteristics were hereditary, and the notion of a natural hierarchy of inferior and superior races. In their broad sweep these racist ideas were not supported by careful scientific observations of all human societies but rather were buttressed with slanted reports gleaned by European missionaries, travelers, and sea captains from their experiences with selected non-European societies. Most scientists of the late eighteenth and early nineteenth centuries, while presenting themselves as objective observers, tried to marshal evidence for human differences that the white imperialists' perspective had already decided were important to highlight.[50]

The first edition of the *Encyclopedia Britannica* (1798) authoritatively asserted in its entry called "Negroes" that this "unhappy race" was a people of "idleness, treachery, revenge, cruelty, impudence, stealing, lying, debauchery, nastiness and intemperance." They were said to be "strangers to every sentiment of compassion" and were "an awful example of the corruption of man when left to himself."[51] Such hostile, grossly stereotyped, and highly racialized language underscores the emotional and psychosocial roots of Western racist ideology—this time codified in what soon became the most prestigious encyclopedia of the English-speaking world.

Celebrating and Expanding the Racist Ideology: The 1830s to the 1930s

The International Industry of Racist Ideology   By the mid-nineteenth century the propagation of racist thinking had become a major industry in Europe and the United States. From that period to the present day, thousands of articles and books have been written, as well as speeches given, as part of an ideological machine that constantly defends white supremacy and racial oppression—principally antiblack oppression.

Some analysts have distinguished a traditional ideology from a conservative ideology. In this typology a traditional ideology has a passive attachment to the social structures inherited from the past, while a conservative ideology goes beyond that to aggressively defend the status quo in response to challenges. A dominant ideology is often challenged, such as when those oppressed fight back (see chapter 8). When their interests have been challenged, white elites have attempted to deflect or destroy the challenges. The ruling elite must constantly combat insights into the real nature of the racist reality that its members have fostered and maintained. For example, during the mid-decades of the nineteenth century the growing antislavery movement in Britain and the United States spurred an elite reaction that was combative. An even more developed and formalized racist ideology was created in a vigorous attempt to defend slavery against abolitionism.[52]

Many U.S. and European intellectuals argued for white supremacy and African inferiority. For example, in his 1830 lectures the leading German philosopher G. W. F. Hegel spoke about the Negro as "natural man in his wild and untamed nature" and argued that there is "nothing remotely humanized in the Negro's character."[53] Black people were not human beings with a real history and consciousness. Hegel based his racist judgments on the reports of European colonizers and travelers. Drawing on similar sources, leading authors as diverse as Thomas Carlyle, William Makepeace Thackeray, and Charles Dickens defended racist ideas or the enslavement of Africans.[54]

Count Joseph Arthur de Gobineau, a French diplomat and perhaps the most influential racist thinker of the nineteenth century, argued that whites are "gifted with reflective energy, or rather with an energetic intelligence. . . . They have a remarkable, even extreme love of liberty, and are openly hostile to the formalism under which the Chinese are glad to vegetate, as well as the strict despotism which is the only way of governing the Negro."[55] In his extensive writings on the superiority of the "white race," Gobineau articulated a highly developed racist ideology. Once translated, his writings became influential in the United States and other countries across the globe. For example, after a visit with Gobineau, Richard Wagner, the prominent German composer, set up the Gobineau Society to propagate the notion of white supremacy.[56] Gobineau's ideas would later influence German Nazis.

Preeminent physical scientists accepted the idea of white supremacy. In the mid-nineteenth century the leading French anatomist Paul Broca, founder of the Society of Anthropology of Paris, broke important new ground in understanding how the human brain works. In addition, Broca was a leading racist thinker who devised a measure of head shape, the cephalic index, and argued that variations in human head shape were linked to significant differences among the races. For him black skin and wooly hair were associated with inferior intelligence, while white skin and straight hair were the "equipment of the highest groups."[57] While Broca later retracted these racist views, many other scientists and popular writers picked up on his idea of head form being linked to race and character.

Political Elites   In the United States distinguished lawyers, judges, and political leaders promoted scientific racism and its white-supremacist assumptions. Recall that in the first half of the nineteenth century whites with an interest in slavery dominated much of the political and legal system. This influence was conspicuous in the infamous *Dred Scott v. John F. A. Sandford* (1857) decision. Replying to the petition of an enslaved black American, a substantial majority of the Supreme Court ruled that Scott was *not* a citizen under the Constitution and had no rights. Chief Justice Roger Taney, a slaveholder, argued that African Americans "had for more than a century before [the U.S. Constitution] been regarded as beings of an inferior order, and altogether unfit to associate with the white race, either in social or political relations; and so far inferior, that they had no rights which the white man was bound to respect; and that the negro might justly and lawfully be reduced to slavery for his benefit. He was bought and sold, and treated as an ordinary article of merchandise and traffic, whenever a profit could be made by it. This opinion was at that time fixed and universal in the civilized portion of the white race."[58] The Dred Scott decision showed that the racist ideology was both elaborate and well established: all black Americans, whether slave or technically "free," were inferior beings with no rights, and white supremacy was the law of the land.

Senators and presidents played their role in articulating and spreading this ideology. President James Buchanan, a northerner, urged the nation to support the racist thinking of the Dred Scott decision. Moreover, several years before he became president, in his debate with Senator Stephen A. Douglas, Abraham Lincoln argued that the physical difference between the races was insuperable, saying, "I am not nor ever have been in favor of the social and political equality of the white and black races: that I am not nor ever have been in favor of making voters of the free negroes, or jurors, or qualifying them to hold office or having them to marry with white people. . . . I as much as any other man am in favor of the superior position being assigned to the white man."[59] Lincoln, soon to be called the "Great Emancipator," had made his white supremacist views clear, views later cited by southern officials in the 1960s struggle to protect legal segregation and still quoted by white supremacist groups today.

The end of slavery did not end the pervasiveness of the white-supremacist ideology. Many whites pressed for a system of legal segregation. In this effort they had the support of President Andrew Johnson, who in 1867 commented on what he called the "naked savages," saying, "It is vain to deny that they [African Americans] are an inferior race—very far inferior to the European variety. They have learned in slavery all that they know in civilization."[60]

White members of Congress used the new racist science to argue for the subordination of black Americans. In 1867, using scientific charts on hair, skull size, and other anatomical data, Representative James Brooks argued to Congress that the differences between black and white Americans were "essential, organic, throughout, from the crown of the head to the very sole of the feet. The negro is a different creature, with different brain and different structural organization."[61]

With the end of Reconstruction in 1877 came comprehensive and coercive racial segregation in the South. Distinguished judges, including those on the Supreme Court, played a key role in solidifying the extensive segregation of black Americans and in unifying white defenses of institutionalized racism. Recall that in *Plessy v. Ferguson* (1896) a nearly unanimous Supreme Court legitimated the fiction of "separate but equal" for black and white Americans in a case dealing with racially segregated railroad cars. This separate-but-equal fiction was legal for more than half a century, until the 1954 *Brown v. Board of Education of Topeka* decision and until broken down further by the civil rights laws of the 1960s. There was widespread agreement in the elites and in the general white population about the desirability of thorough and compulsory segregation for black men, women, and children. A reactionary segregationist ideology was taking firm hold of white America.

Even whites opposed to official segregation articulated a belief in white dominance. Justice John Marshall Harlan, the lone dissenter in *Plessy v. Ferguson*, noted in his opinion that "the white race deems itself to be the dominant race in this country. And so it is, in prestige, in achievements, in education, in wealth and in power. So, I doubt not, it will continue to be for all time, if it remains true to its great heritage and holds fast to the principles of constitutional liberty."[62] The white race, this opponent of government segregation noted, would probably dominate for all time. Two sentences later, Harlan added that "our Constitution is color-blind, and neither knows nor tolerates classes among citizens." Harlan was among the first to articulate the idealistic, and mythical, view that the Constitution is color-blind.

The open assertion of white supremacist views was commonplace for government officials in the nineteenth and early twentieth centuries. Given the increasing immigration in this period from non-European countries, these officials gave increasing attention to who was, or was not, "white." Between 1878 and 1923 a series of federal court cases decided that the following Americans were *not* white and thus were ineligible for citizenship: Chinese Americans, native Hawaiians, those half-Asian, those half-Indian, Burmese Americans, Japanese Americans, Filipino Americans, those three-quarters Filipino, and Korean Americans. They were placed, by whites, toward the black end of the white-to-black racial desirability continuum that has long been common in white minds (see chapter 7). Indeed, whiteness as a criterion for immigrants to become U.S. citizens was not officially changed until the 1952 Immigration and Nationality Act.[63]

Social Darwinism   In his momentous and influential writings Charles Darwin applied his important evolutionary idea of natural selection not only to animal development but also to the development of "races" of human beings. For example, he saw natural selection at work in the killing of the indigenous peoples of Australia by the British, wrote of blacks as a category between whites and gorillas, and spoke against social programs for the "weak" because they permitted the least desirable people to survive. The "civilized races" would eventually replace the "savage races throughout the world."[64]

During the late 1800s and early 1900s a perspective called "social Darwinism" developed the ideas of Darwin and argued aggressively that certain "inferior races" were less evolved, less human, and more apelike than the "superior races." Prominent social scientists like Herbert Spencer and William Graham Sumner argued that social life was a life-and-death struggle in which the best individuals would win out over inferior individuals. Sumner argued that wealthy Americans, who were almost entirely white at the time, were products of natural selection and essential to the advance of civilization.[65] Black Americans were seen by many of these openly racist analysts as a "degenerate race" whose alleged "immorality" was a racial trait.[66]

Significantly, some analysts consciously connected their racist doctrines with defenses of other forms of oppression, particularly sexism and class oppression. For example, in the late nineteenth century one American author, M. G. Delaney, vigorously argued that the races at the bottom of the ladder were inferior and female-dominated, while those at the top of the ladder were superior and male-dominated. Those in between had equality between the gender groups. From this perspective a strong patriarchal system was a clear sign of the "better races."[67]

By the late 1800s a eugenics movement was spreading among scientists and other intellectuals in Europe and the United States. Eugenicists accented the importance of breeding the "right" types of human groups. Britain's Sir Francis Galton argued for improving the superior race by human intervention. Like

Galton, U.S. eugenicists opposed "racial mixing" (or "miscegenation") because it destroyed racial purity. Allowing "unfit races" to survive would destroy the "superior race" of northern Europeans. Those from the lesser races, it was decided, should be sterilized or excluded from the nation.[68] Such views were not on the fringe, but had the weight of established scientists, leading politicians, and major business leaders. Thus, in 1893 Nathaniel S. Shaler, a prominent scientist and dean at Harvard University, argued that black Americans were inferior, uncivilized, and an "alien folk" with no place in the body politic. In social Darwinist fashion, he spoke of their eventual extinction under the processes of natural law.[69]

In the first decades of the twentieth century most social scientists and intellectuals accepted or advocated some form of scientific racism. Thus, in 1923 Carl Brigham, a Princeton University psychologist who would later play a central role in developing college entrance tests, argued pugnaciously for the intellectual inferiority of various racial groups, using data from new psychometric tests given during World War I to draftees. Low psychometric test scores by Italian and Russian immigrants, as well as by black Americans, were explained in terms of their "inferior racial stocks."[70]

Madison Grant, an influential intellectual of the early twentieth century, developed his racist ideas in *The Passing of the Great Race*.[71] In this book, which had four editions between 1916 and 1923, Grant wrote that new immigrant groups from southern and eastern Europe would interbreed and destroy the superior "Nordic race." In 1920 Lothrop Stoddard, a Harvard-educated lawyer and historian, wrote, in another influential book titled *The Rising Tide of Color: Against White World-Supremacy*, of the "overwhelming preponderance of the white race in the ordering of the world's affairs . . . the indisputable master of the planet."[72] Like many of his contemporaries, as well as many white commentators today (see below), Stoddard feared that in the future whites would be overwhelmed by large numbers of blacks and other people of color. Grant and Stoddard were influential among white scientists and administrators at major universities, as well as among celebrated white politicians.

More Politicians and Presidents   Scientific racism was used by white members of Congress to support passage of discriminatory congressional legislation, including the openly racist 1924 immigration law excluding most immigrants other than northern Europeans. In this period overtly racist ideas were advocated by all U.S. presidents. Former president Theodore Roosevelt liked some aspects of scientific racism and praised Grant's book for its "grasp of the facts our people need to realize."[73] President Woodrow Wilson was well-known as an advocate of the superiority of European civilization over all others, including those of Africa. As president, Wilson increased the racial segregation of the federal government. Significantly, no less a racist leader than Adolf Hitler would later report having been influenced by Wilson's writings.[74] (The term *racism* first appeared in a 1933

German book by Magnus Hirschfeld, who sought to counter the Nazi and other European racists' notion of a biologically determined hierarchy of races.[75])

In 1921 President Warren G. Harding, who had once been linked to the Ku Klux Klan, said he rejected any "suggestion of social equality" between blacks and whites, citing Stoddard's book as evidence the "race problem" was a global problem. Not long before he became president, Calvin Coolidge wrote in *Good Housekeeping* magazine, "Biological laws tell us that certain divergent people will not mix or blend. The Nordics propagate themselves successfully. With other races, the outcome shows deterioration on both sides."[76] Ideas of white supremacy and rigid segregation were openly advocated by white political leaders.

With the expansion of European and U.S. colonialism into Asia and Africa in the last half of the nineteenth century, some new emphases were added to the prevailing ideology. One new emphasis, which had earlier precedents, was that of "teleological racism" — the view that non-European peoples, including Africans, had been created as inferior so that they could serve, and be civilized by, whites. Perhaps the most famous statement of this view is Rudyard Kipling's 1899 poem, "The White Man's Burden" ("Take up the White Man's burden / Send forth the best ye breed"). From Kipling's perspective whites had a missionary obligation to help the "inferior races," those he termed in the poem as "half-devil, half-child."[77] These formulations of white racist ideology explained not only the character and conditions of those oppressed but also celebrated whites as civilized, Christian, powerful, and generous toward those conquered. Variations on this racist ideology have long rationalized the oppressive policies directed at peoples of color across the globe — to the present day.

Immigrants Becoming "White"   What the white elites have propagated as racist ideology the white majority has usually accepted. The transmission of the racist ideology from one social group to the next is a critical mechanism in the social reproduction of the system of racism. We noted previously how most ordinary whites had come to look at their social world in racist terms. They have accepted the psychological wage of whiteness and the racist ideology peddled by elites. As Oliver Cox once noted, "[W]e may take it as axiomatic that never in all the history of the world have poor people set and maintained the dominant social policy in a society."[78]

From the 1830s to the early 1900s millions of European immigrants bought into the racist ideology in order to gain white privileges. Take the case of the poor Irish immigrants who came in substantial numbers in the first decades of the nineteenth century. The Irish did not initially view themselves as "white," but rather identified with their country of origin. Once in the United States, however, they were taught in overt and subtle ways that they were white by the already established white ministers, priests, teachers, business people, newspaper editors, and political leaders with whom they interacted. They were pressured and manipulated by British

American elites and their own leaders into accepting the dominant ideology denigrating blackness and privileging whiteness.[79] Over the course of the nineteenth century most Irish immigrants, who themselves had been viewed by their British oppressors in Ireland as an "inferior race," came to envision themselves as white and deserving of white privileges in regard to jobs and living conditions. Coupled with this move to whiteness was active participation in efforts to drive black workers out of better-paying jobs in northern cities.

Moreover, recent historical studies have shown how other groups such as Italian and Jewish Americans came to define themselves as white (see chapter 7). Many European immigrant groups accepted a comfortable place in a socially constructed "white race" whose privileges included such things as greater personal liberty, better-paying jobs, and the right to vote. They actively discriminated against black Americans and developed antiblack prejudices. A common acceptance of racist thinking, such as that reflected in the blackface (minstrel) shows in the decades before and after 1900, created a "sense of popular whiteness among workers across lines of ethnicity, religion, and skill."[80]

Perpetuating and Developing the Racist Ideology: Contemporary America
Periodically, the racist ideology framed in the first two centuries of American development has shifted somewhat in its framing or emphases. Those in charge have dressed it up differently for changing social circumstances, though the underlying framework has remained much the same. Some new ideas have been added to deal with pressures for change from those oppressed, particularly ideas about government policy. After World War II, as we will see below, certain aspects of the dominant racist ideology were altered somewhat to fit the new circumstances of the 1950s and 1960s, during which black Americans increasingly challenged patterns of compulsory racial segregation.

Continuing Elite Control: The Mass Media   In recent decades white elites—especially white male elites—have continued to dominate the construction and transmission of new or refurbished ideas and images designed to buttress the system of racial inequality, and they have used ever more powerful means to accomplish their ends. The mass media now include not only the radio, movies, and print media used in the past, but television, music videos, satellite transmissions, and the Internet.

Today, for the most part, the mass media are still controlled by whites. Just under 90 percent of the news reporters, supervisors, and editors at newspapers and magazines across the United States are white. On television whites are overrepresented in managerial jobs, and as on-air reporters; they are greatly overrepresented as "experts" in the mass media. Americans of color have only a token presence in the choice and shaping of news reports and media entertainment.[81] The concentration of media control in a few corporations has increased dramatically in recent decades. As we move into the twenty-first century, fewer than two dozen corporations control much of the mass media, and that number is likely to decrease further. In addition, the mass media, especially television, are substantially supported by corporate advertisers, and directly or indirectly such advertisers have significant command over actual programming. Thus, information about racial matters is usually filtered and whitewashed through a variety of elite-controlled organizations. This filtering is not a coordinated conspiracy, but reflects the choices of many powerful whites socialized to the dominant value system in regard to racial issues.[82]

Looking for data and stories, reporters and journalists typically seek out established government, business, academic, and think-tank reports and experts. The right wing of the U.S. ruling class, a very large segment, has historically been the most committed to the racist ideology and has pressed for repression of protests against racial and other oppression. The liberal wing of the white elite is much smaller and often more attuned to popular movements; it has been willing to liberalize the society to some degree and to make some concessions to protesters for the sake of preserving the society. (The center of the elite has waffled between the two poles.) In the late 1960s and 1970s many experts consulted by top executives in government and the mass media came from think tanks usually espousing the views of those in the center or on the left of the ruling elite. Becoming very concerned about this, wealthy conservatives began in the 1970s to lavishly fund right-wing think tanks and to press aggressively conservative views of U.S. society on universities, politicians, and media owners. In recent years the right-wing think tanks—including the American Enterprise Institute, the Manhattan Institute, and the Heritage Foundation—have been very successful in getting their experts into mainstream discussions and debates. Working alongside a large group of other conservative intellectuals, media experts, and activists, these right-wing think tanks continue to be successful in an indoctrination campaign aimed at shaping public views on racial and other social issues.[83]

Most Americans now get their news from commercial television and radio programs. The largest single source is local news programming.[84] Using these local and national media, the white elites have the capability to mobilize mass consensus on elite-generated ideas and views; this consensus often provides an illusion of democracy. These elites encourage collective ignorance by allowing little systematic information critical of the existing social and political system to be circulated through the media to the general population. Not surprisingly, omnipresent entertainment programs and incessant consumer advertising are dominant features of television and some other mainstream media.

Given this reality, and the generally weak history and other social science courses in schools, most Americans are not well informed about many important aspects of U.S. society. For example, the *Washington Post* recently published the results of a survey of Americans on their political knowledge. Less than a quarter knew the names of both of their U.S. senators; four in ten could not even name the vice president.[85] Moreover, most Americans know little about U.S. history. In one survey, multiple-choice questions on American history were given to respondents. Most could not choose 1775 as the year the Revolutionary War started, nor could they pick the area where that war ended (Virginia). Similarly, a U.S. Department of Education survey of high school seniors found that six in ten lacked knowledge of simple historical facts.[86] Even those Americans who think they know about U.S. history often adhere to the many myths and misconceptions taught in school. As one major research study has shown, current high school textbooks communicate much in the way of inaccurate, distorted, and elliptical views of that history, particularly in regard to issues of racism and interracial conflict.[87] Thus, the dominant white elites continue to have the ability to persuade, to create confusion in, and to foster apathy in the general population.

With the national racial order firmly in place, most white Americans, from childhood on, come to adopt the views, assumptions, and proclivities of previous generations and established white authorities. In this manner the system of racism is reproduced from one generation of whites to the next.

A Shift Against Compulsory Segregation   As late as the 1940s, the majority in the white elites saw little reason to make major moves to deal with white-on-black oppression. But pressure for change was building. By the 1940s and 1950s black protests against discrimination were growing and having some impact on the image of the United States abroad. Racial segregation and protests against it were creating international problems for a U.S. government trying to fight a racist Nazi Germany and, after World War II, trying to contend with the Soviet Union for the allegiance of non-European nations around the globe. As early as 1952, U.S. Secretary of State Dean Acheson gave the U.S. Supreme Court a statement proclaiming that "the continuation of racial discrimination is a source of constant embarrassment to this government . . . and it jeopardizes the effective maintenance of our moral leadership of the free and democratic nations of the world."[88] And a U.S. attorney general commented on the Brown decision (see below) to the effect that racial segregation in schooling must be eradicated because it "furnishes grist for Communist propaganda mills."[89] Derrick Bell has thus suggested that historically white elites act to improve the conditions of black Americans only when whites can benefit.[90]

By the mid-1950s, and accelerating in the 1960s, the more liberal wing of the ruling class was pressing for a softening or rejection of the old blatantly racist images and for modest new group-based remedies such as school desegregation and affirmative action, aimed at integrating, albeit in one-way fashion, some men and women of color (and white women) into historically white-male-dominated employment settings. For a time, a more liberal approach rejecting Jim Crow segregation and accenting civil rights laws and affirmative action was successful in bringing some racial desegregation to the nation. From the mid-1950s to the early 1970s the federal courts became important in ordering desegregation in a variety of institutions. Reversing the earlier Supreme Court position in *Plessy v. Ferguson,* a more liberal high court handed down *Brown v. Board of Education* in 1954—a unanimous ruling that "in the field of public education the doctrine of 'separate but equal' has no place."[91] Group-based remedies were increasingly used to implement public school desegregation. Moreover, for a modest period of time the elite's liberal wing and center provided important support for black-led civil rights organizations through funding from key corporate executives and liberal foundations. In the face of black protests in the streets—and sustained by positive economic growth—some powerful executives in multinational corporations decided not only to provide the civil rights movement with funds but also to support political liberals in the Democratic Party in efforts to expand government efforts on antidiscrimination and social welfare programs.[92]

Increased Equality Rhetoric   From the 1960s onward the rhetoric of racial equality, or at least of an equality of opportunity, grew in volume among members of the white elite, including presidents and members of Congress. The black protests and rebellions of the 1950s and 1960s had an important effect in eradicating not only the system of the legal segregation but also most public defense of racial discrimination by the nation's white leadership. Since the late 1960s most leaders have proclaimed the rhetoric of racial and ethnic equality. For example, a major advisor of leading business and political officials, Harvard professor Samuel Huntington, has recently asserted in the influential policy journal *Foreign Affairs* that U.S. identity is now centered in a widely accepted "set of universal ideas and principles articulated in the founding documents by American leaders: liberty, equality, democracy, constitutionalism, liberalism, limited government, private enterprise." The supposed consensus on equality is asserted to be the "great source of national strength."[93]

It is significant too that by the late 1960s a handful of white leaders and their researchers were moved by the protests and upheaval of the period to reject current racist ideas and practices in even stronger terms. An example of this more radical perspective can be seen in the report of the 1968 Kerner Commission, established by President Lyndon B. Johnson to investigate black rioting in the cities. In a bold report this commission, most of whose members were white, concluded that the United States was "moving toward two societies, one black, one white—separate and unequal." The report further asserted that "[w]hite racism is essentially responsible for the explosive mixture which has been accumulating in our cities since the end of World War II."[94] However, this view, while accurate, was too radical for most white political leaders, and the report and its perspective were soon buried.

The structural dismantling of a large-scale system of compulsory segregation did require a new equality emphasis in the prevailing racial ideology. However, while the structural position of whites and blacks had changed somewhat, at least officially, most whites — in the elites and the general public — did not seem interested in giving up significant white power or privilege. Thus, the racist ideology was altered in some ways but continued to incorporate many of its old features, and it continued to rationalize white privilege — now under conditions of official desegregation. There had long been some fairness language in the prevailing ideology — for example, most whites thought blacks were treated fairly — but now notions of fairness and equality of opportunity were moved to the forefront. As we will see in the following section and in the next chapter the acceptance by the white elite and public of the principles of equal opportunity and desegregation in regard to schools, jobs, and public accommodations did *not* mean that most whites desired for the federal government to implement large-scale integration of these institutions.

A More Conservative Orientation: 1969 to the Present   Beginning around 1969, with the arrival of Richard Nixon's presidential administration, the rhetoric of equality was increasingly accompanied by a federal government backing off from its modest commitment to desegregation and enforcement of the new civil rights laws. At the local level, there was increased police repression of aggressive dissent in the black community, such as the illegal attacks on Black Panthers and other militant black groups by local police and FBI agents. The old racist images of dangerous black men and black welfare mothers were dusted off and emphasized by prominent white leaders who often spouted the rhetoric of equality at the same time. Moreover, the liberal wing of the white elite, which had provided some funding for the civil rights movement and other social movements of the 1960s, significantly reduced its support for these movements.[95]

By the mid-1970s the right wing of the ruling elite was accelerating its attack on the liberal thinking associated with the new civil rights laws. Since the 1970s a growing number of conservative organizations have worked aggressively in pressing Congress, the federal courts, and the private sector to eviscerate or eliminate antidiscrimination programs such as affirmative action efforts, as well as an array of other government social programs (see chapter 8 for more detail). This signaled the increasing influence on national policy of a more conservative Republican Party that represented, almost exclusively, the interests of white Americans. Moreover, even at the top of the Democratic Party there was also some shift to the right, which could be seen in the relatively modest antidiscrimination policies of the Jimmy Carter and Bill Clinton administrations.

The shift away from government action to remedy discrimination was associated with a reinvigoration of notions about inferior black intelligence and culture. In the 1970s, and increasingly in the 1980s and 1990s, numerous white journalists, politicians, and academics were critical of what they saw as too-liberal views in regard to black Americans and remedies for discrimination and defended arguments about black intellectual or cultural inferiority. In public policy discussions, increasingly led by white conservatives, there was a renewed emphasis on the view that only the individual, not the group, is protected from discrimination under U.S. law.

The federal courts provide an important example of this conservative shift. In the decades since the 1970s these courts have often ruled that group-remedy programs against racial discrimination violate the U.S. Constitution, which they assert only recognizes the rights of individuals, not groups. For instance, in 1989 a conservative Supreme Court handed down a major decision, *City of Richmond, Virginia v. J. A. Croson Co.*, which knocked down a local program designed to remedy past discrimination against black and other minority businesses.[96] The high court ruled in favor of a white-run construction company, the plaintiff, which argued that the municipal government had unconstitutionally set aside business for minority companies. The court ruled that the city of Richmond had not made a compelling case for racial discrimination, even though the defendant's statistics showed that in a city whose population was one-half black, less than 1 percent of the city government's business went to black-owned firms (see chapter 5). The philosophical argument against significant remedial action for racism was reiterated in Supreme Court cases in the 1990s.[97]

At many levels of U.S. society, including the federal courts, we have seen in the last few decades a renewed accent on viewing major social institutions as "color-blind." Recall Supreme Court justice John Marshall Harlan's view that the "Constitution is color-blind, and neither knows nor tolerates classes among citizens." At the time of that statement (1896), the overwhelming majority in the white elites at the local and national levels were making it very clear in their statements and deeds that the phrase "all men are created equal" did not apply to black Americans, other Americans of color, or white women. Harlan's color-blind view did not become a common perspective among white elites until the 1960s and 1970s. Since then, white adherents of the color-blind perspective in the elites and the general public have come to the forefront. They view blatant racial discrimination as rare and see U.S. institutions as basically healthy and color-blind. Indeed, many individual whites assert, disingenuously, that they "don't see race anymore, just individuals." Today, the color-blind ideology provides a veneer of liberality, which covers up continuing racist thought and practice that is often less overt and more disguised.

Still Arguing for Biological "Races"   For much of the nineteenth and twentieth centuries the standard view among whites, including those in the academic elite, of the difficult socioeconomic conditions faced by black Americans was that those conditions resulted from blacks' inferior biological and cultural heritage. By the

1940s a number of leading scientists were openly questioning conventional wisdom on biological racism, and by the 1960s many U.S. scientists had rejected the old biological determinism.

Still, as late as the 1980s, there were many physical scientists who accepted the idea of biological races. One 1980s survey found that 50 percent of physical anthropologists and 73 percent of animal behaviorists supported the idea that there were biologically differentiated "races" within the species *Homo sapiens*. In contrast, only 29 percent of cultural anthropologists, 40 percent of developmental psychologists, and 34 percent of sociologists surveyed also agreed that there were biological "races." The majority of scientists in the social science disciplines no longer accepted the traditional biological determinism, doubtless accepting the idea of the social construction of "race."[98]

Nonetheless, in recent years some social and behavioral scientists have joined with certain physical scientists to continue to press for the idea of biological races and to connect that idea to concerns over government social policies. Since the late 1960s several social scientists at leading universities, including Arthur Jensen and Richard Herrnstein, have continued to argue that racial-group differences in average scores on the so-called IQ tests reveal genetic differences in intelligence between black and white Americans. Their views have been influential, especially on white politicians and the white public. In 1969 the *Harvard Educational Review* lent its prestige to a long article by Jensen, a University of California professor. The arguments presented there and Jensen's later arguments in the next two decades have received much national attention, including major stories in *Time, Newsweek, U.S. News and World Report, Life*, and major newspapers. Jensen has argued that on the average blacks are born with less intelligence than whites, and that the "IQ" test data support this contention. In addition, he has suggested that high birth rates for black Americans could result in a lowering of the nation's overall intelligence level.[99]

Perhaps the most widely read example of biological determinism is a 1990s book, *The Bell Curve*, which to this point has sold more than a half million copies. As we move into the twenty-first century, it is still being cited and read. Like Jensen, the authors of *The Bell Curve*—the late Harvard University professor Richard Herrnstein and prominent author Charles Murray—argue that IQ test data show that black (and Latino) Americans are inferior in intelligence to whites. Though the authors have no training in genetics, they suggest that this supposed inferiority in intelligence results substantially from genetic differences. Thus, biological differences account to a substantial degree for racial inequalities. The fact that the book has sold many copies and has been widely debated in the media—in spite of the overwhelming evidence against its arguments—strongly suggests that biologically oriented racist thinking is still espoused by a large number of white Americans, including those who are well-educated. Indeed, Herrnstein and

Murray explicitly suggest that their views are *privately shared* by many well-educated whites, including those in the elite, who are unwilling to speak out publicly. This book was launched during a major press conference at the conservative American Enterprise Institute. This publicity insured that the book would get much national attention, while antiracist books have generally gotten far less media play.[100]

Racist arguments about contemporary intelligence levels are grounded in nearly four hundred years of viewing blacks as having an intelligence inferior to that of whites. Today, such views are much more than an academic matter. They have periodically been used by members of Congress and presidential advisors in the White House to argue against antidiscrimination and other government programs that benefit Americans of color. Given this elite activity, it is not surprising to find these views in the white public.

Cultural Racism   Another aspect of older racist views that can be found in new dress is the idea of what one might call "cultural racism"—the view that blacks have done less well than whites because of their allegedly deficient culture with its weak work ethic and family values. As early as the seventeenth century, black Americans were seen as inferior in civilization and morality to white colonists. These blaming-the-victim views have regularly been resuscitated among the white elites and passed along to ordinary Americans as a way of explaining the difficult socioeconomic conditions faced by black Americans.

The accent on inferior family and personal values among black Americans got a major boost in a 1960s government report called *The Negro Family*, which focused on social pathologies in black communities. Social scientist and later U.S. senator Daniel Patrick Moynihan explained "the deterioration of the fabric of Negro society" in terms of family problems and emphasized the "tangle" of pathology and crumbling social relations he saw in black communities.[101] Significantly, racist practices by whites were *not* mentioned as an important reason for any of these troubling social conditions. Similarly, in an influential 1975 book Nathan Glazer accented the "tangle of pathology in the ghetto" that in his view could not be explained by "anything as simple as lack of jobs or discrimination in available jobs." From Glazer's viewpoint neither rapid economic growth nor government affirmative action could benefit culturally impoverished blacks that he supposed were reluctant to do low-wage work.[102]

Since the 1970s leading magazines have published articles accenting some version of this perspective on what came to be called the black "underclass"; the perspective accents the allegedly deficient morality and lifestyle of many black Americans. Prominent author Ken Auletta wrote an influential set of *New Yorker* articles, later expanded in his book *The Underclass*. He accented the black underclass and its supposed immorality, family disorganization, and substandard work ethic.[103] A later article in the *Chronicle of Higher Education* surveyed the growing research on the underclass, noting that "the lives of the ghetto poor are marked by a dense fabric of what experts call 'social pathologies'—teenage pregnancies, out-of-wedlock births, single-parent families, poor educational achievement, chronic unemployment, welfare dependency, drug abuse, and crime—that, taken separately or together, seem impervious to change."[104] To the present day, similar stories designed to explain black problems in cultural terms regularly appear in the local and national media across the nation.

These social analysts generally blame the victims and do not deal seriously with the systemic racism that is central to explaining the poor economic conditions faced by many black Americans—or to explaining the racial discrimination faced by all black Americans. Sidney Willhelm notes the irony here succinctly. "After centuries of abuse," he explains, "the white majority repudiates the American minority for the very conditions [for which] it is itself to blame: poverty, ignorance, family disruption, filth, crime, disease, substandard housing, incompetence, lack of initiative. While assuring majestic prospects for acceptance, the nation removes the basic opportunities for achievement."[105] Moreover, much underclass theorizing barely disguises the racist fears, assumptions, and biases long held by white Americans. Anthony Farley has argued that poor black communities in the cities are often seen by whites as "urban Bantustans" that export race pleasure by displaying themselves as the negation of white middle-class culture. Whites can once again feel superior because of the negative view they hold of black culture and community. In addition, many whites see these urban areas as dark seductive places where they can go for forbidden pleasures such as drugs or prostitution.[106]

Asserting Innocence, Denying Racism   A rosy view of U.S. history has long been commonplace among whites at all class levels. Today, as in the past, there is a strong impulse to break the historical linkage between the genocidal and enslaving past and the conditions faced by Americans of color in the current period. An important aspect of the contemporary ideology buttressing systemic racism is the omnipresent notion of white innocence. Today, many whites deny the seriousness of antiblack racism in the past and present history of the United States (see chapter 4). In recent interviews with members of the white elite, Rhonda Levine and I have found that many see racism as having declined significantly in importance. For that reason they often argue that certain government action, such as affirmative action, is no longer needed as a remedy for discrimination.[107] Optimistic views of the decline of racism are common. A major *Newsweek* story asserted that "mercifully, America today is not the bitterly sundered dual society the [Kerner] riot commission grimly foresaw."[108] In such accounts white analysts accent the great progress they feel has been made by black men, women, and children in recent decades. Most whites seem to view whatever is left of racism in the society as only the "blatantly racist ideologies and practices of the extreme right."[109]

Recall from chapter 1 the comments once made by former Republican presidential candidate Bob Dole and Representative Henry Hyde. They indicate that they are not sure that whites should have to pay for past discrimination. Like other whites they try to break the connection between the racist past and the present, temporizing on the question of reparations for damages inflicted by whites during the periods of slavery and legal segregation.

Powerful white men like Dole and Hyde still control most U.S. organizations and institutions as the twenty-first century unfolds. Yet, many of them came of age in a pre-1970 U.S. society where the majority of whites still made overtly racist arguments for keeping black Americans in their subordinate "place." This was true for presidents Jimmy Carter, Ronald Reagan, George Bush, and Bill Clinton, as well as for key leaders in Congress such as Trent Lott (see chapter 8) and key federal judges. Many adults now over the age of forty spent at least a few years growing up in the openly racist and legally segregated society that was the United States prior to 1970. Elite or nonelite, young or old, few whites have ever had any serious reeducation aimed at reducing the blatant and subtle racist notions most were taught at an early age.

Sincere Fictions of the White Self: Romanticizing the Past   Associated with a rosy view of U.S. society and the assertion of white innocence is a romanticizing of the racist past. This romanticizing can be seen, for example, in the long history of Hollywood movies dealing with U.S. history. To this day, no mainstream movie has dealt thoroughly and honestly with the deeper realities of slavery, segregation, or modern racism. Hollywood movies dealing with racial matters have of course evolved since the early 1900s. In a famous 1915 movie, *The Birth of a Nation*, pioneering filmmaker D. W. Griffith used cinematic advances to spread a viciously racist image of black southerners during the Reconstruction period. In this epic, black Americans are portrayed as savages, corrupt legislators, and uneducated officials. In contrast, white southerners are shown as gracious, brave, and honest. There is no hint that in the Civil War white southerners were fighting for one of history's most brutal political and social systems. If we move to the 1930s to the 1950s, we see yet more racist images of black Americans in classic movies like *Gone with the Wind*, the latter still treasured by many whites and reissued in the late 1990s. The images of black Americans are not as vicious as in *The Birth of a Nation*, but they include highly stereotyped black figures such as a black "mammy" and obsequious male slaves. Most whites are still gallant, gracious, or brave figures, and there is no hint of something being wrong with a society grounded in a bloody slavery system. Once again we see here the sincere fictions of the white self.[110] *Gone with the Wind* is but one of many such portraits. Between the 1920s and the 1940s more than seventy-five films portrayed the Old South. As Cedric Robinson notes, virtually all of these presented an image of slavery as a "natural, necessary, and generally benevolent institution."[111] By the 1930s almost all of the national media's accounts touching on the history of racism were highly romanticized and sanitized.

Moreover, other movies made since the early decades of the twentieth century have often portrayed Africans as savages and whites as saviors, such as in the old Tarzan movies still shown in the United States and across the globe. (The same is true for the old cowboy-and-Indian movies, with Native Americans portrayed as the savages.) Moreover, even today, a "wild Africa" image is often portrayed by media producers as they accent Africa's distinctive animals and savannahs much more than its history or peoples.

More recent movies dealing with the racial history of the United States, such as *Glory* (1989) and *Amistad* (1997), have portrayed black Americans in a substantially less stereotyped and much more humane light. While the most recent movies touching on racial issues have occasionally presented a white person as villainous, such images are usually more than balanced by those of whites who are honorable or heroic. We mostly see strongly positive stereotypes of whites—as good, civilized, and the central heroes even in stories that are mostly about blacks. As Hernán Vera and Andrew Gordon have put it, "The portrayal of whites in *Birth of a Nation* is almost identical to their portrayal in *Glory* and in *Amistad*. What we have found in our analysis is a persistence across time in representations of the ideal white American self, which is constructed as powerful, brave, cordial, kind, firm, good-looking, and generous: a natural-born leader."[112] In these recent movies there is no serious indication that the broader white-controlled society was ever grounded in a pervasive system of racism. A thorough unromanticized movie on the significance, venality, and human destruction of slavery and segregation has yet to be made by white directors at mainstream movie studios.

In recent years numerous writers and journalists have written accounts of U.S. history designed to preserve the white sense of innocence and of inculpability for the genocide, slavery, and segregation so central to that history. For example, in the best-selling book *The End of Racism* (1995) journalist Dinesh D'Souza, an Asian American whose work has been supported by white conservatives, has argued not only that antiblack racism has come to an end but also that the historical background of white oppression of black Americans has been misperceived. In his view the enslavement of black Americans had some very good features. "Slavery proved to be the transmission belt that nevertheless brought Africans into the orbit of modern civilization and Western freedom," D'Souza claims. As he sees it, "slavery was an institution that was terrible to endure for slaves, but it left the *descendants* of slaves better off in America."[113] Similarly, in a book attacking the idea of racial equality, former *Time* journalist William Henry, a Pulitzer Prize winner, argued that the European conquests were successful in dispersing superior cultures among inferior cultures, which were forced to accommodate.[114] Many white defenders

of slavery have articulated this Eurocentric view from the earliest days of colonialism in North America. Such arguments do not take seriously the bloody and
barbaric character of slavery and the slave trade. There is no discussion here of the
many millions of Africans who died in the European-controlled Atlantic slave trade
nor of the severe destruction of African societies by that trade and later European
imperialism (see chapter 2).

The extreme oppressiveness of American slavery is thus not taken seriously by
many white Americans. Not surprisingly perhaps, brochures circulated by some
southern state governments still provide a distorted view of U.S. history. One South
Carolina brochure provided to visitors at the state's travel centers has a two-page
history of the state from the 1500s to the present, with not a single mention of slaves
or slavery there.[115] Slavery had been central to the state's economy for a long period
of time. There are frequent if vague allusions to the enslavement of black
Americans in much common discourse. People often speak of being "masters" or
"slaves" in everyday comments. In white high schools and colleges across the land
there are slave auctions to raise money for various causes, sometimes advertised
with posters showing a black person in chains. In addition, white children have
been observed playing a game of master and slaves with puppets or other objects.
The insult here to black Americans is similar to the insult to Jewish Americans
that comes from those who make light of the Nazi death camps.

A Whitewashed Worldview   This antiblack ideology links in so many ways to so
much of white thought and behavior that we might speak of it as a broad worldview. Seen comprehensively, all the mental images, prejudiced attitudes, stereotypes, fictions, racist explanations, and rationalizations that link to systemic racism
make up a white racist worldview, one deeply imbedded in the dominant culture
and institutions. The U.S. system of racism is not just something that affects black
Americans and other Americans of color, for it is central to the lives of white
Americans as well. It determines how whites think about themselves, about their
ideals, and about their nation.

We saw earlier how European immigrants to the United States in the early 1900s
came to accept this worldview and its implicit assumption that being "American"
means being white. This has not changed much in the intervening years. Today
the term "American" still means "white"—at least for the majority of white
Americans, and probably for most people across the globe. One can pick up most
newspapers or news magazines and find "American" or "Americans" used in a way
that clearly accents *white* Americans. Take this sentence from a news writer in a
Florida newspaper: "The American Public isn't giving government or police
officers the blind trust it once did."[116] Clearly, "American" here means "white
American," for the majority of blacks have never blindly trusted the police.

One research analysis recently examined all the articles in sixty-five major
English-language newspapers for a six-month period and estimated that there were

thousands of references to "black Americans" or "African Americans" in the articles. However, in the same newspapers there were *only forty-six* mentions of "white Americans."[117] In almost every case these mentions by newspaper writers occurred in connection with "black Americans," "blacks," or "African Americans." (The exceptions were three cases in which "white Americans" was used in connection with "Native Americans" or "Korean Americans.") A similar pattern was found for major magazines. Not once was the term "white Americans" used alone in an article; if used, it was always used in relation to another racial category. The same study examined how congressional candidates were described in news articles in the two weeks prior to the November 1998 elections. In every case white congressional candidates were *not* described as "white," but black congressional candidates were always noted as being "black."[118] In the United States blackness is usually salient and noted, while whiteness generally goes unmentioned, except when reference is specifically made to white connections to other racial groups.

Being "American" still means, in the minds of many people, including editors and writers in the media, being white. This need not be a conscious process. For several centuries most whites have probably not seen the routines of their everyday lives as framed in white. "Race" is often not visible when one is at the top of the social hierarchy. Today, major social institutions, those originally created by whites centuries ago, are still dominated by whites. Yet from the white standpoint they are not white, just *normal* and *customary*. They are not seen for what they actually are—whitewashed institutions reflecting in many of their aspects the history, privileges, norms, values, and interests of white Americans. When whites live in these customary arrangements, they need not think in overtly racist terms. Nonetheless, when whites move into settings where they must confront people of color in the United States or elsewhere, they usually foreground their whiteness, whether consciously or unconsciously.

The sense of white entitlement is passed along in subtle ways. Edward Ball, a descendant of one of South Carolina's prominent slaveholding families, has underscored the sense of privilege and superiority passed along from slave plantation days to whites today. He notes that "inwardly the plantations lived on. In childhood, I remember feeling an intangible sense of worth that might be linked to the old days. Part of the feeling came from the normal encouragements of parents who wanted their children to rise, an equal part came from an awareness that long ago our family had lived like lords, and that world could still be divided into the pedigreed and the rootless."[119] This sense of superiority becomes part of the "woodwork" of whitewashed institutions.

Fear of a Multiracial, Multicultural Future   Recall the racist writers like Lothrop Stoddard who in the 1910s and 1920s openly feared that whites were becoming a minority in the United States and across the globe. Today, many white analysts still see Western civilization as under threat from groups that are not white or

European. Racist thinking is more than rationalizing oppression, for it also represents a defensive response, a fear of losing power to Americans of color. In recent years many advocates of white superiority have directed their attacks at the values or cultures of new immigrants of color coming to the United States, as well as at black Americans. In one recent interview study elite numerous white men openly expressed some fear of the growth of Americans of color in the United States, seeing Western civilization as under threat.[120]

We observe examples of this fear among U.S. politicians and intellectuals. For example, in several speeches and articles Patrick Buchanan, a perennial candidate for the Republican presidential nomination, has argued that "our Judeo-Christian values are going to be preserved and our Western heritage is going to be handed down to future generations and not dumped on some landfill called multiculturalism."[121] Once again, we see the linkage between religion and a strong sense of European supremacy. We also see a concern for the reproduction of the white-dominated system from current to future generations. In addition, Buchanan told one interviewer that "if we had to take a million immigrants in, say, Zulus next year or Englishmen, and put them in Virginia, what group would be easier to assimilate and would cause less problems for the people of Virginia? There is nothing wrong with us sitting down and arguing that issue that we are a European country, [an] English-speaking country."[122] The Zulus, who are Africans, seem to represent in his mind the specter of strange or savage hordes who would not assimilate well into the nation. Ironically, Africans have been in the nation longer than Buchanan's Irish ancestors, and Virginia has been home to African Americans for nearly four centuries.

Similarly, *Forbes* editor Peter Brimelow lays out white fears for Western civilization in a book, *Alien Nation*. For him, "the American nation has always had a specific ethnic core. And that core has been white." Back in the 1950s, he argues, most Americans "looked like me. That is, they were of European stock. And in those days, they had another name for this thing dismissed so contemptuously as 'the racial hegemony of white Americans.' They called it 'America.'"[123] Apparently, the concern here is for reinvigorating the old mechanisms for the reproduction of white privilege and dominance, which are viewed as being threatened by "alien" peoples that are not white. A more liberal commentator, historian Arthur Schlesinger, Jr., also views the challenges to the United States as serious. In his view multiculturalism is now the dominant viewpoint in the United States, especially in educational institutions, and that viewpoint entails "an astonishing repudiation" of the idea of "a unifying American identity." Schlesinger is concerned about what he calls the great "assault on the Western tradition" by the "tribalism" called multiculturalism.[124] Recently, influential Harvard professor Samuel Huntington has noted that "[i]f multiculturalism prevails and if the consensus on liberal democracy disintegrates, the United States could join the Soviet Union on the ash heap of history."[125] Great concern for Western cultural supremacy is evident in the views of leading white editors, scholars, and politicians. Nonetheless, multiculturalism is not dominant in the United States as yet.

Conclusion   The systemic racism that is still part of the base of U.S. society is interwoven with a strong racist ideology that has been partially reframed at various points in U.S. history, but which has remained a well-institutionalized set of beliefs, attitudes, and concepts defending white-on-black oppression. Until the late 1940s commitment to a white supremacist view of the world was proud, openly held, and aggressive. Most whites in the United States and Europe, led by elites, took pride in forthrightly professing their racist perspectives on other peoples and their racist rationalizations for Western imperialistic adventures. Brutal discrimination and overt exploitation were routinely advocated. Indeed, white domination of the globe was "seen as proof of white racial superiority."[126]

Beginning in the late 1940s, however, the open expression of a white supremacist ideology was made more difficult by a growing American awareness of actions of the racist regime in Nazi Germany. In addition, by the 1950s and 1960s growing black civil rights protests against U.S. racism—with their counterideology of black liberation (see chapter 8)—and the U.S. struggle with the Soviet Union made the open expression of a white supremacist ideology less acceptable. The dominant racist ideology changed slowly to reflect these new conditions, with a new accent on equality of opportunity and some support for moderate programs to break down the nation's segregated institutions. Still, as we have seen, many aspects of the old racist ideology were dressed up in a new guise, and they persist, with some barnacle-like additions, to the present day. From the beginning, the age-old idea of the superiority of white (Western) culture and institutions has been the most basic idea in the dominant ideology rationalizing oppression.

Control over a society's ideas and discourse includes control over its central metaphors. It is the powerful who usually decide what the dominant images and metaphors are, and thus what is or is not seen as valid and true. Metaphors are integral to most conceptual frameworks. As George Lakoff and Mark Johnson have noted, "In all aspects of life . . . we define our reality in terms of metaphors and then proceed to act on the basis of the metaphors. We draw inference, set goals, make commitments, and execute plans, all on the basis of how we in part structure our experience, consciously and unconsciously, by means of metaphor."[127]

For some time now, most whites have viewed the last few centuries of societal development in terms of a broad imagery equating "human progress" with Western civilization. We hear or see phrases like "Western civilization is an engine generating great progress for the world" or "Africans have only seen real advancement because of their contacts with Western civilization." Western imperialism's bringing of "civilization" or "democracy" to other peoples is made to appear as an engine of great progress, with mostly good results. However, this equating of "progress" with European civilization conceals the devastating consequences of imperialism and colonialism. The actual reality was—and often still is—brutal, bloody, oppressive, or genocidal in consequence for those colonized. When whites speak of Western civilization as equivalent to great human progress, they are talking about the creation of social systems that do not take into serious consideration the interests and views of the indigenous or enslaved peoples whose resources were ripped from them, whose societies were destroyed, and whose lives were cut short. Images of Western civilization, like the racist ideologies of which they are often part, are too often used to paper over the sordid realities of Western colonialism and imperialism.

four

Contemporary Racial Attitudes and Images
White Americans

At a late 1990s town meeting on racial issues in Akron, Ohio, a white college student admitted to the audience that he was fearful of black men who were not well-dressed. President Bill Clinton, who was moderating the discussion, said to the student, "That's a pretty gutsy thing for you to admit. Do you think that's because of television crime shows, or because of your personal experience?" The white student said it was *not* from his own experience but from things he had heard.[1]

For whites, specific antiblack images, prejudices, and stereotypes are part of a broader ideological structure of racialized thinking, a thought system accenting white superiority and black inferiority. As we saw in the last chapter, from the first decades of this nation, a white-racist ideology was developed, nurtured, and propagated by white elites. The attitudes associated with this broad ideology have changed in some ways over the centuries, but they are still reflective of overt or covert white-racist thinking. The elite-fostered ideology provides a racial overview of the world. It organizes and makes coherent the diverse prejudices and stereotypes of both elites and ordinary whites, which in their turn buttress the ideology, undergird white privilege, and generate discriminatory practices.[2]

The persistence of antiblack attitudes, images, and emotions over several centuries is much more than a matter of scattered bigots acting on their prejudiced notions and feelings; they are the continuing legacy of the material and ideological frameworks of slavery and segregation. The "everyday-ness" of contemporary prejudices and stereotypes among whites means that they are present in many situations of intergroup contact and often get translated into alienated racist relations — that is, into relationships of white-on-black discrimination. Thus, we see yet another important aspect of the social reproduction and transmission of the racist system. The perpetuation of systemic racism requires an intertemporal reproducing not only of racist institutions and structures but also of the ideological apparatus, which includes the racist ideology and its accompanying racist attitudes and images.

Racial Prejudice and Stereotyping   Too often the realities of individual racial prejudice and stereotyping have been disconnected from this larger framework of racist ideology and from the practices of racism. We should keep in mind how prejudice and stereotyping are part of a much larger social and cultural scaffolding. Antiblack prejudice and stereotyping are part of an expansive ideology of racism and are thus rooted in the defense of white power and privilege. As Herbert Blumer put it, prejudice is "rooted in a sense of group position."[3] Racial prejudice has been defined as antipathy toward a racial other based on a faulty generalization. Such prejudice can be directed toward a group as a whole, or toward an individual as a member of that group.[4] Typically, racial prejudice has both an emotional and a cognitive dimension. It can include a negative feeling about the racial out-group as well as a negative belief. The cognitive aspect is often termed a *stereotype*. As false or exaggerated generalizations, stereotypes commonly serve as rationalizers of racist behavior. Stereotypes are more than ideas in the head, for they often encompass negative visual images.

Today racist thinking and feeling attach great significance to skin color, which remains a badge of oppression for black Americans. This persistence is a clear example of the legacy of the past, of the marks and burdens of a "slavery unwilling to die." While many whites now reject, at least publicly or on a conscious level, a blatantly biologized racism, they still hold without misgiving many of the negative conceptions and images of black men and women that have been long associated with a biologized racism accenting "inferior races." Racist attitudes tend to distort a group's origins, physical appearance, values, or culture. In the case of white views of black Americans, we see how general principles and ideas of the broad racist ideology get imbedded in specific attitudes. In regard to ideas about origin, for example, during the first two centuries of slave importation whites regarded Africans and African Americans as foreign, uncivilized, and unchristian. While some aspects of this older view have disappeared, other aspects of it can currently be found in a variety of white notions and images that center on the alleged savagery of black men. Today, black men are often viewed by whites as deviant, dangerous, or violent. In regard to appearance, black men and women are still thought to have a distinctive and, for many whites, undesirable or ugly appearance. They are often seen as lazy, criminal, or immoral. We will examine some of these recurring images below.

Racist attitudes and images are revealed and reproduced constantly in the everyday discourse and writings of whites at all class levels. Seeing black Americans in negative terms and viewing whites in positive terms are perspectives shaped by elite indoctrination, such as through the mass media, but they also constitute the way most ordinary whites regularly communicate with each another about racial matters. These ideas are perpetuated over generations by means of everyday communication. Racist attitudes and images are constantly available to virtually all whites, including the young, by means of presentations in daily discourse, as well as in the media, through the writings of intellectuals, and in the speeches of politicians and business leaders (see chapter 3). Such attitudes and images are adapted and used as the situation warrants, and they vary in expression or impact depending on the situation and the persons involved. Over centuries now, they have had a severely negative impact on their targets (see chapter 6). Racist ways of thinking and feeling can be conscious and directly stimulative of discriminatory action, or they can be unconscious and implicit in that action. Moreover, most racial prejudice not only portrays the racial others negatively but also imbeds a learned predisposition to act in a negative way toward the others. In this manner, racist attitudes commonly link to discriminatory practices.

Racist Images and Attitudes, Past and Present: A Brief Overview   Historical data on white images of and attitudes toward black Americans suggest that for centuries the overwhelming majority of whites have been openly and unapologetically racist. While there were no national opinion surveys before the 1930s, we can infer strongly racist attitudes from the omnipresent and unreservedly racist letters, speeches, actions, jokes, popular entertainments, and organizations of the slavery and legal segregation eras.

For example, in the decades before the Civil War there was a dramatic increase in popularly expressed racism, including racist images, attitudes, and invectives. One place this is seen is in the growing popularity, especially among white workers, of whites-in-blackface minstrel shows. In front of large crowds, composed mostly of white working-class men, white performers made up in blackface did musical numbers and other comedy skits on the stage. Extreme caricatures and mimicking of black Americans were centerpieces of these shows, which featured a reinvigorated vocabulary of racist epithets (such as "coon" and "buck"), a mocking of black English, and a portrayal of fantasies and fictions held in white heads (for example, the white-male fantasy of the oversexed black woman). By presenting blackness in such negative terms, the virtues of whiteness were highlighted for everyone present. It was implied that whites were smart, courageous, and civilized, because blacks were presented as dumb, cowardly, deviant, oversexed, and uncivilized. The shows were very popular with white workers, including the new immigrants then seeking definition as "white." Moreover, they were also eagerly attended by many members of the elite, including presidents John Tyler (at his inauguration) and Abraham Lincoln.[5] These mocking public entertainments continued well into the 1900s.

The Recent Past   National opinion surveys in the 1930s showed strong white support for overtly racist or segregationist views. For example, a late 1930s Roper poll reported that eight in ten respondents thought that blacks should be kept out of white residential areas. In the late 1940s a Gallup poll found that 43 percent of those polled thought there should be segregated trains and buses. The majority opposed whites and blacks living and working together in the armed forces. (This strong opposition was expressed just before President Harry Truman boldly desegregated the U.S. armed forces.) A 1944 National Opinion Research Center (NORC) survey found that 51 percent of the respondents thought "white people should have the first chance at any kind of job." Just under half those polled thought local restaurants should not serve both blacks and whites, and a similar proportion said they would not like having a black nurse in a hospital.[6] These national surveys probably included some Americans of color—the data are not reported by racial group—so it is likely that an even larger proportion of whites than of the total sample supported enforced racial segregation in restaurants, hospitals, housing, workplaces, and the armed forces.

By the 1960s the support for legal Jim Crow segregation was waning, though whites' negative views of blacks were still strong. In a 1963 Harris poll a majority of whites nationwide said they agreed with several negative statements about black Americans: they "tend to have less ambition," "smell different," and "have looser morals." Four in ten whites thought that blacks "have less native intelligence," and more than one-third thought that blacks "breed crime." In the 1960s, the era when many contemporary white leaders received their early socialization, a majority of whites still expressed some openly and blatantly racist prejudices and stereotypes. Nonetheless, attitudes toward equal opportunity and public desegregation—at least in principle—were changing, for 57 percent of the white respondents said they approved of a federal voting rights laws, and 62 percent said they approved a fair employment practices law. Still, in 1963 white attitudes about certain personal contacts with blacks were quite negative. Half said they would object to a black family moving next door, and 84 percent were opposed to a close friend or relative marrying a black person.[7] Another Harris poll in 1966 found a similar level of racist stereotyping among whites, as well as continuing majority opposition to blacks moving into historically white neighborhoods.[8]

The White Majority Today   Much has been made in recent decades of the reduction among whites in certain negative attitudes toward black Americans. Some longitudinal data show that whites have become less likely to give openly racist and segregationist answers to pollsters and survey researchers than they did in earlier decades. For example, one 1942 survey found that only 47 percent of whites thought blacks were "as intelligent as white people," a proportion that increased to 77 percent by 1968.[9] Indeed, some researchers and journalists have taken this to mean that a majority of the white population is today no longer significantly racist in its attitudes, opinions, and images of black Americans.[10] This is not the case. A significant decrease in some overtly expressed segregationist or other blatantly racist attitudes does not necessarily mean that most white Americans are no longer substantially racist in their thinking about or imaging of black Americans. The decrease, in this case, may be from a very extreme level of racist thought and hostile imaging to a still serious magnitude. In addition, as we will see below, some research indicates many white men and women are less than forthcoming about their racial attitudes when asked brief questions in opinion surveys.

If one looks at responses to recent surveys, many whites still reveal themselves as, to some degree, openly racist to strangers (pollsters). They still express openly negative attitudes of black Americans. For example, a national survey by the Anti-Defamation League (ADL) asked whites whether they agreed with one or more of eight antiblack views and stereotypes. Evaluating a list of eight antiblack statements (for example, blacks "have less native intelligence than people of other races"), three-quarters of whites agreed with one or more of these stereotypical statements. Significantly, the majority (55 percent) agreed with two or more, and 30 percent agreed with four or more.[11] Other survey research studies have also found a substantial level of acceptance by whites of some negative thinking about black Americans.[12]

In addition to admissions about racist stereotyping, many whites still admit to pollsters that they hold other negative views and ideas in regard to black Americans. I analyzed white responses to five items in a recent NORC survey: (1) Do you think there should be laws against marriages between blacks and whites? (15 percent said yes); (2) White people have a right to keep blacks out of their neighborhoods if they want to, and blacks should respect that right (16 percent agreed); (3) Blacks shouldn't push themselves where they are not wanted (43 percent agreed); (4) One law says that a homeowner can decide for himself whom to sell his house to, even if he prefers not to sell to blacks (35 percent approved of this law); (5) Do you think blacks get more attention from government than they deserve? (18 percent said "much more").[13] Taking the five items together, the majority (59 percent) of these white respondents took an essentially antiblack position on at least one item. These overview analyses suggest that a majority of whites still harbor some negative attitudes toward, or negative images of, blacks.

Moreover, the usually brief character of a survey question may not tap the deeper views of many white respondents on racial matters. Some number of whites are likely to conceal their racist views in brief conversations with strangers in order to appear socially acceptable. Several studies have found that white respondents often alter their overt comments on racial matters so as to appear less prejudiced or unprejudiced.[14] Research by Eduardo Bonilla-Silva on white students at three major university campuses is also suggestive; this researcher found that attitudes expressed on short-answer survey items were often different from those expressed to similar questions requiring more detailed commentary. For example, on a brief survey item 80 percent of the 451 responding students said they approved of marriages between blacks and whites. However, when a smaller group of comparable students were interviewed in depth this figure dropped to about one-third. (Ninety percent of this smaller group had shown approval on the survey question.) When given more time to explain their views, the majority of white students expressed some reservations about marriage across the color line. A similar pattern was found for a question about affirmative action. Whites frequently used a variety of hedging phrases (for example, "I agree and disagree") to disguise or play down their negative views.[15] The in-depth interviews strongly indicated that a majority of well-educated whites still hold significantly negative attitudes on issues like racial intermarriage.

Seen from this perspective, the apparent decrease in certain antiblack images, prejudices, and stereotypes among whites from the 1930s to the present may reflect to some degree an increased concern for appearance and social acceptability. Clearly, it is less socially acceptable to publicly avow strong racist attitudes, so many whites may reserve most of their blatantly racist comments for the private spheres of home, locker room, and bar. This does not mean, however, that these hoary racist views are no longer of consequence for black Americans or for the larger society.

Antiblack Attitudes and Images: Some Specific Examples   The specific attitudes that whites hold toward themselves and toward black Americans often take the form of, on the one hand, a model of white merit and superior morality and, on the other, an "antimodel" of black deficiency, danger, and threat. The positive model encompasses a range of sincere fictions about the white self, such as the images of white innocence and nobility discussed in chapter 3. The antimodel encompasses a range of images and attitudes, including the often inherited views of black men and women as lazy workers, criminals, dumb athletes, or welfare cheaters.[16]

Attributions of Laziness   Specific representations of black Americans are critical parts of the package of white racism. One particularly strong and age-old representation is that of black laziness. The Protestant ethic, with its accent on individual acquisitiveness, was important for early European entrepreneurs and colonists. Enslaved Africans who resisted the very long hours of work typically imposed on them were judged by this ethic to be "lazy," even though these work-ers did much of the hard work that lay behind white prosperity. The same white attitudes about black laziness persisted during the system of formal segregation, although once again a disproportionate amount of the hardest work in local economies was done by the much maligned black workers.

Descending through many twists and turns of U.S. history, the racist image of lazy black men and women is still commonplace today. A recent NORC national survey asked whites to evaluate on a scale just how work-oriented blacks are. Only a small percentage, 16 percent, ranked blacks at the hardworking end; just under half put blacks at the lazy end of the spectrum.[17] Such views are also manifested in the omnipresent white comments on lazy black welfare recipients. Notions of laziness are so strong as to overcome countering evidence. Researchers Justin Lewis and Sut Jhally had white subjects watch "The Cosby Show," a popular television show from the 1980s and 1990s that is still seen in reruns across the globe. Whites generally liked the black Huxtable family portrayed on the show, yet many processed the images in a way that fit in with preexisting attitudes. They saw the success of the Huxtables as evidence that any black person could succeed if he or she would just work harder. As Lewis and Jhally conclude about white views, "The Huxtables proved that black people can succeed; yet in so doing they also prove the inferiority of black people in general (who have, in comparison with whites, failed)."[18]

Some sociopsychological research indicates that those with strong stereotypes of an out-group often attribute negative behavior by members of that out-group to its alleged group characteristics ("That's the way they are"). However, when they see positive actions or accomplishments by individuals in the out-group, they often attribute that to the uniqueness of the situation rather than to group characteris-tics. They will argue in the latter case that the person is an exception to the group, that they had a special advantage or luck, that anyone in the situation could have done well, or that it took exceptional motivation and effort to overcome the under-lying disabilities of the group. This is a common way that whites respond to the actions of black Americans. They tend to view negative actions by black Americans as tied to the group, to its biology or culture, while positive achievements are fre-quently linked to individual or situational aspects of the case at hand—and not to the values of black families and communities.[19]

Negative Images of Black Women   African American women have been targets for racist stereotyping for centuries. Reviewing U.S. history, Patricia Hill Collins has noted that "portraying African-American women as stereotypical mammies, matriarchs, welfare recipients, and hot mommas has been essential to the politi-cal economy of domination fostering Black women's oppression."[20] One chronic image, reproduced on the packaging of commercial products and in reissued movies like *Gone with the Wind*, is the Aunt Jemima image, that of the corpulent "mammy" borrowed from the racist past. In American and European culture the images of black women are often intense and visual. For many decades highly stereotyped and caricatured images of black women (and men) were very common in popular art, ads, movies, television, and on postcards.[21] Even today, "mammy" dolls and black female and male figurines with exaggerated physical features such as big lips, or in silly poses, can be found in antique shops across the United States and Europe. Racist dolls and figurines are still popular with some white Americans. Indeed, they are still manufactured and can be found for sale not only in the United States but in various other countries across the globe, including Spain and Japan.

A recurring stereotype found among many whites in all classes is that of the large, black welfare family with a woman in charge—often a corpulent woman. This is a popular example of the underclass imagery of black Americans that we examined as part of the contemporary social ideology propagated by certain intellectuals (see chapter 3). A CBS News/*New York Times* poll found that the majority of those questioned thought that *most* poor people were black and that *most* welfare recipients were black.[22] Yet the reality is different. At the time of that survey in the mid-1990s less than half the families receiving Aid to Families with Dependent Children (AFDC—commonly called "welfare") were black; the majority were white or Latino. The same survey found that negative views of people on welfare were associated with the belief that most people on welfare are black. This linking of welfare views to antiblack thinking has characterized the attitudes of whites since at least the late 1960s.[23] A major source of these antipoor stereotypes, once again, seems to be the mass media. In his research Martin Gilens has shown that network television and news magazines exaggerate greatly the black presence among the nation's poor. Among those pictured as poor in photos on television and in news magazines, more than six in ten were black Americans, yet blacks are just 27 percent of the poor.[24] In the United States the negative use of apparently class-typed imagery and language—such as negative images of the poor, those on welfare, or the underclass—is often just a covert way of expressing antiblack ideas.

Black women face yet other forms of gendered racism—the double burden of suffering prejudice and stereotyping because they *are* black and female. One example is the negative imaging of black women as "jungle bunnies." Recent interviews with black women have found that some report this type of stereotyping in encounters with white men.[25] As we have noted previously, since at least the seventeenth century, this white (especially white male) stereotype has accented black women's allegedly exotic sexuality. In her research Diane Roberts has shown how white notions of blackness have been loaded with sexuality. European books, beginning in the 1600s, often portrayed black women and men naked, and with exaggerated sexual organs. "The white world drew the black woman's body as excessively and flagrantly sexual, quite different from the emerging ideology of purity and modesty which defined the white woman's body," Roberts tells us.[26] Influenced by and perpetuating such images, some white men during the days of slavery and segregation sought out, molested, or raped black women. Today, some white men still seek out black women as exotic sex objects. In this manner, racism is regularly inscribed in the bodies of black women. Once again, public views and attitudes are closely linked to the racist ideology honed by scientists, writers, and other intellectuals.

Even preferences for body type are racialized in a manner biased against black women. From the seventeenth to the twenty-first century not only white politicians, explorers, and missionaries, but also those whites developing the sciences of medicine, biology, and ethnography and those developing the mass media have set white skin and body type as the standard for aesthetic superiority. For centuries white men have been the standard for male handsomeness, as well as masculinity and manly virtue. White women—in recent decades, especially those who are fair-haired and slender—have long been the standard for female beauty in the United States. As one black woman recently put it in an interview, "I went through a long, long time thinking I was like the ugliest thing on the earth. . . . It's so hard to get a sense of self in this country, in this society, where . . . every role of femininity looks like a Barbie doll."[27]

Images of Black Men   Another common white stereotype is that of the dangerous black man. This seems to be a staple of white thinking, including the thinking of white leaders and intellectuals speaking or writing about the black "underclass." A majority of whites seem to view the generic street criminal as a black man, an example of which can be seen in the town meeting incident noted in the opening of this chapter.[28] As we saw in chapter 3, during the first centuries of American development, whites constructed a view of enslaved black men as dangerous "beasts," a stereotyped view that has rationalized much discrimination over the centuries, including bloody lynchings. The beastlike image was then, as now, put into words, but it was also held at a deeper, more visceral level. As with black women, the bodies of black men are culturally stigmatized and routinely trigger antiblack stereotypes in white minds.

Racist images of and fears about black men can be found at all levels of white society. Members of the elite not only play a role in creating and maintaining common racist images, they of course buy into some or all of the images. Take the example of Dwight D. Eisenhower, a leading general who served as president during the 1950s. While President Eisenhower did not publicly advocate the inferiority of black Americans, he did speak in racially stereotyped terms in private. Earl Warren, then chief justice of the U.S. Supreme Court, reported that Eisenhower told him at a 1954 dinner that white southerners opposed to school desegregation were "not bad people. All they are concerned about is to see that their sweet little girls are not required to sit in school alongside some big overgrown Negroes."[29] White stereotyping of black boys and men often exaggerates their size or other physical characteristics. To describe ordinary school boys as "big overgrown Negroes" is reminiscent of the scary images of black men some white parents have used to discipline their children (see below). President Eisenhower did not mention the painful, often severe impact of the violent white opposition to school desegregation on the lives of little black boys and girls, and their parents.

As a result of these common stereotyped images, many whites have fearful reactions to a black man encountered in public settings such as on streets, in public transport, and in elevators. In my interview studies, numerous black men have reported aversive reactions taken by white women and men when they are walking the streets of U.S. towns and cities. Many whites lock their car doors, cross streets, or take other defensive precautions when a black man is near. Some conservative commentators have asserted that this defensive action is "rational discrimination" because of the high black crime rate.[30] These commentators, like many ordinary whites, seem to assume that the majority of criminals who violently attack whites are black. But this is not the case. Federal surveys of white victims of violent crime have found that about 17 percent of these attackers are black, while about three-quarters are white.[31] Most violent crime affecting whites is carried out by *white criminals*. Yet most whites do not take similar precautions when they are in the presence of those whites—disproportionately white men—who perpetrate most of the violent crimes suffered by whites. The reason for this is that they do not see themselves as being in the presence of someone likely to commit a violent crime when they are around those socially defined as white.

The emotionally freighted images of black men are often crafted in white minds in childhood. Many are gained in family settings. In the past and in the present, some white parents have threatened disobedient children with fearful images of black bogeymen coming to get them. In an interview conducted by one of my graduate students, a retired clerical worker described her mother's method of discipline: "'The niggers would come in the night and steal us away and use us for their pleasure,' that's what my mother told us. What an awful thing to do, don't you think, frightening little children like that. . . . I think she must have done that to make us behave. It worked; she scared us to death. The first time I ever saw a colored person I just about had hysterics."[32] The racist image here was translated into action.

Today, perhaps the major source of the negative images of black Americans is the mass media. Eight in ten Americans watch local news at least four nights a week. Local news programs, now the major source of information for a majority of Americans, often accent violent crime. One study of fifty-six cities found that crime was the subject of one-third of all local news programming.[33] In addition, a late-1990s study of local news in Los Angeles found that while violent crimes got extensive coverage, nonviolent crimes such as fraud and embezzlement got virtually none. The stories about violent crime mentioning a suspect featured blacks in a much higher proportion than their arrest rate indicates would be accurate.[34] In addition, a study of Chicago's major television stations found that blacks accused of crimes were much more likely to be shown in mug shots or still photos with no name appearing on the screen, while white defendants were more likely to be named when they were shown; accused whites were thus more likely to keep their personal identities. Black defendants were much more likely than whites accused of crimes to be photographed with the police holding or grappling with them — which probably signals to viewers that they are more dangerous. Perhaps most seriously, on these local news shows whites got much more coverage (a ratio of fourteen to one) as "good Samaritans" than blacks, who make up a percentage of the Chicago population not much less than that of whites. Apparently, the antimodel was so firmly in place that it was difficult for local media reporters and editors to visualize black Americans doing good in the community.[35] Numerous other research studies have shown a similar bias in news reporting on blacks and crime. Again and again, whites are overrepresented as victims of crime, while black Americans and other people of color are overrepresented among those said to be perpetrators of crime.[36]

When the mass media play up violent crime and mention black men in an unfair way, these criminal acts come to be linked in the white mind with black men, or black Americans generally. One Los Angeles study found that showing white, Asian, and Latino subjects who were political liberals some local crime news videos increased their punitiveness in regard to criminals — much more when they were shown black perpetrators than when they were shown white perpetrators of crime.[37] The stereotyped images of black men in the media have an impact on ordinary Americans.

In addition to local media elites, powerful whites in the national elite have played a role in perpetuating these stereotypes, sometimes intentionally. In the 1988 presidential campaign, some of George Bush's campaign officials developed a campaign to scare white voters. They picked William Horton, a black man convicted of raping a white woman, for one media campaign. They renamed him "Willie" Horton and made use of a scary photo taken when Horton was ill and unshaven. This photo image of a disheveled Horton was widely used by Republicans in efforts to create concern or fear in white voters about the supposed leniency of the opposing political party on crime issues. Significantly, the campaign ads did not feature white-male rapists, although most rapists who attack white women are indeed white men.[38] Once again we see the deep thread of sexualized racism. Moreover, as the fearful image of black men as criminals targeting whites has become ever more exaggerated and influential, many whites repeat it, including those in the white leadership. For example, in 1992 Ron Paul, a member of the

U.S. Congress from 1977 to 1984 and from 1997 onward, wrote in his *Survival Report* about black men in Washington, D.C., "I think we can safely assume that 95 percent of the black males are semi-criminal or entirely criminal."[39] White elites not only shape and manipulate a broad racist ideology but also reinforce and circulate specific racist images and stereotypes as well.

Images of Drugs and Deviance   Many, if not most whites seem to think that the majority of the poor, the homeless, drug users, and drug dealers are black Americans. This is yet another aspect of the black underclass mythology often parroted by whites. Generally speaking, the mass media exaggerate the role of blacks in poverty, homelessness, drug use, and drug crime, which contributes yet again to distorted images in white minds.

In fact, black youth are *less likely* than white youth to use marijuana or cocaine, smoke cigarettes, or drink alcohol. And rates of drug abuse (and child abuse) are higher for single-parent white families than for similar black families.[40] White and other nonblack Americans account for seven out of eight illegal drug users. However, in spite of these facts, black Americans have become the national symbols of drug abusers and dealers. This stereotyped imagery affects white actions in serious ways. For example, black drug users are disproportionately targeted by the police; three-quarters of those sentenced to prison for drug possession are black.[41] In contrast, white drug crime gets much less police surveillance, even though a substantial majority of drug dealers are white and even though there is much drug selling and use on predominantly white college campuses and in white suburban areas.

Images of Black Athletes   Many whites seem to assume that they are not racist because they cheer for black athletes on their favorite sports teams. They may also feel that U.S. society is no longer racist because black players are common on college and professional football and basketball teams. However, some research suggests that black male athletes are seen by whites as less intelligent and more animal-like than white male athletes. James Rada studied televised pro football games during the 1992 season on several major networks. In his sample of comments by on-air announcers, black athletes got most of the positive comments relating to physical characteristics or talents (82 percent versus 18 percent for whites). In regard to comments on cognitive abilities and intelligence, white athletes got 72 percent of the positive comments, compared to just 28 percent for black players. In addition, 100 percent of the comments of sympathy for players were made for white players. Of eighteen negative comments on the cognitive abilities of the athletes, all were directed at African Americans, as were all eleven commentaries that used animal or inanimate terminology. On-air commentaries also tended to portray white players in more friendly and intimate terms than black players.[42]

Again black men were portrayed as less intelligent and more animal-like than whites, while white men were shown as the "thinking men" on the field. While the whites in this study were on-air media commentators, it seems likely that their stereotyped views of black physical prowess and intelligence are shared by many white men who watch this sports programming.

Exaggerating the Black Demographic Presence   The focus on black men and women as physically dominant, deviant, or dangerous in the media and in various legislative and other public discussions appears to create in the white mind the impression that there are more blacks in society than there actually are. President Eisenhower's "big overgrown Negroes" image seems to extend to exaggerations about the black population. For example, conducting a survey of college students, Tom Steiger found that the students tend to overestimate the size and proportion of the black population in the United States. In a survey of 398 mostly white students, the median estimate given by the students was that 25 percent of the U.S. population was black. And one 1990s national survey found that white respondents estimated the black proportion of the U.S. population to be about 24 percent, and the Asian and Latino proportion to be 26 percent, of the nation.[43] The guessed proportions were at the time approximately double the actual proportions. In his research Charles Gallagher has explored the reasons for white overestimations of the black population. In interviews with whites he found that a major source of exaggerated estimations is the media. Whites who watch a lot of sports programs see many black athletes and conclude that the nation has a high percentage of African Americans. Some whites were also found to exaggerate the black presence because blacks seem "too vocal" about issues such as civil rights in the media. Even more important is the impact of local news. The constant barrage of stories about black criminals in the local news gives most whites, as well as many other Americans, the impression that the nation has a much larger black population than it does. In addition, the media's images largely go unchallenged. Most whites do not get information from other sources that counters the media distortions. [44]

Mocking Black Americans   Today, many white Americans reveal their negative views and images in the ways they mock or joke about black Americans. Sometimes this mocking is overtly racist, such as in the many antiblack jokes told, often by white men, across the nation on any given day. Among friends in the workplace, at a bar, or at home many whites tell stories that mock alleged black mannerisms, morals, or speech. Apparently, few other whites object when friends or relatives do so. Typical of racist jokes is the one told back in the 1970s by Earl Butz, a former university dean and then U.S. secretary of agriculture. Joking about what the Republican party could offer to African Americans, he joked that all a black man wants is loose shoes, warm toilet facilities, and sex.[45] For many whites at all class levels, ridiculing black Americans or other Americans of color in joking commentaries is commonplace and, it would appear, considered to be innocuous.

Associated with this racist joking is the mocking of black speech that many whites engage in when discussing black Americans. What whites believe to be a black way of speaking is mocked through imitative language. This is done at all levels of white society. For example, on March 14, 1970, President Richard Nixon and Vice President Spiro Agnew performed a piano duet at an elite Gridiron Club dinner. This came after several of those attending tried to create humor about Nixon's racial policies. After a series of jokes and comments about Nixon's "southern strategy" (the Republican political strategy to win back the South by making special appeals to white voters) by various luminaries on the program, Nixon and Agnew sat down at two pianos. Nixon asked Agnew, "What about this 'southern strategy' we hear so often?" In counterpoint fashion Agnew answered in mock black dialect, "Yes Suh, Mr. President, ah agree with you completely on yoah southern strategy." Nixon then played the favorite songs of three Democratic presidents, while Agnew drowned him out with a rendition of "Dixie." The almost entirely white audience of the Washington, D.C., elite reportedly laughed loudly and enjoyed the presidential performance.[46]

In recent years the vicious mocking of black Americans' language and culture seems to be spreading. On the Internet, for instance, whites with computer literacy have recently developed at least two dozen websites that feature crude, hostile, and racist parodies of what these whites consider to be black speech. For example, here is the opening of a mocking translation of a speech by Socrates: "How ya' gots felt, O dudes o' Athens, a hearin' de speeches o' mah accusers." Such mocking of black speech is frequently linked on these sites to a broad range of racist stereotypes, jokes, and images. For instance, the site with the mocking Socrates speech lists events at a fictional "Ebonic Olympic Games": the "torching of the Olympic City" and the "Gang Colors Parade."[47] Antiblack websites like these spread racist images around the globe; indeed, there is at least one antiblack site in the Russian language. The Internet's anonymity and loose connectedness allow the spread of racist ideas and opinions that are no longer acceptable to express in public settings to millions of people around the globe, particularly to the young people who are most likely to surf the Internet.

Less severe mocking of black speech has become so commonplace that many whites probably do not think of it as harmful. A white columnist for an Arizona newspaper wrote a satirical column on the junk mail that comes promising that "You have won 21 million dollars." The columnist wrote, "From what I've seen on the TV about past winners, they prefer if you meet the camera crew fresh out of the shower and shouting, 'Lawdy, Lawdy, Lawdy.' Hey, no problem. We'll definitely be home, waiting behind the door in our bath towels and practicing our best Hattie McDaniel delivery."[48] These "lawdy" comments make sense to readers because they draw on previous mocking of black speech by whites — in this case the exaggerated and contrived dialogue of the 1939 movie *Gone with the Wind*. While it is not entirely clear what this journalist had in mind, for many whites ordinary black people are thought to talk like they do in the old racist movies. Whatever its intention, such mocking perpetuates stereotypes of blacks as odd, silly, or uncultured.

In the movies, on television, and in newspaper and magazine columns, well-educated whites are often those who mock or ridicule black language and behavior. Moreover, in Hollywood films the "good guys" often speak prestige versions of the English language, while those portrayed as "bad guys," including black Americans and other Americans of color, often speak some negatively stigmatized version of English. Some cartoon movies have made use of mock black English accents for certain animals appearing in the movies. In this manner language is mapped onto a particular group, as part of an aural stereotyping process, and the old racist understandings are perpetuated in new forms. Anthropologist Jane Hill has studied mock Spanish, which is also common in the United States. Otherwise monolingual whites use made-up terms such as *no problemo, el cheapo,* and *hasty banana,* and phrases like *hasta la vista, baby.* Mock Spanish can be found on billboards and in movies, gift shops, and boardrooms. Such ridicule reveals an underlying stereotyping of Latinos among whites who might reject openly racist practices. Mocking speech is seen as more justifiable.[49] Ridicule of Mexican American and African American language or speech is racist because it has meaning only if one knows the underlying racist stereotypes and images. While it may appear harmless, this mocking enables whites to support traditional hierarchies of racial privilege and degradation without seeming to be racist in the old-fashioned, blatant sense.

White attacks on variants of Latino and black English are not just concerned with language. Instead, they show, as Rosina Lippi-Green has noted, a "general unwillingness to accept the speakers of that language and the social choices they have made as viable and functional. . . . We are ashamed of them, and because they are part of us, we are ashamed of ourselves."[50] Language mocking and subordination are not about standards for speaking as much as they are about determining that some people are not worth listening to and treating as equals.

Imbedded Racist Images: The Case of Language   There are other important examples of antiblack understandings in the English language and its everyday usage. Culture shapes language, and language fosters or facilitates many aspects of thought. The concepts and categories learned as children shape how we experience the world around us, and these concepts and categories—including stereotypes and prejudices—are usually delineated in sets of words and phrases. When racially coded language is embedded in white minds, it and its associated concepts often guide everyday thinking and behavior.

Today, antiblack racism is deeply imbedded in spoken and written English. Many whites still use epithets like "nigger," "coon," or "pickaninny," especially in private settings with friends and relatives. Diehard segregationists use terms like "boy" for a black man. And some whites persist in using other diminutive terms, such as replacing the name William with "Willie." While in recent decades there has been a decline in white use of openly racist terms, at least in public, a variety of terms used in the media and the everyday conversations of whites have hidden racial meanings. For many whites terms like *gangs, ghetto, slum, the poor, the economically disadvantaged, welfare recipients, violent criminals,* and *drug pushers* symbolize black Americans (and sometimes other people of color). A white person, including a media commentator, can use these terms to target or denigrate black Americans but still appear unprejudiced, at least to other whites.

Even in cases where certain color words and phrases were not crafted as intentionally racist, they can reinforce antiblack thinking. There are many phrases in English that use "black" and "white." Some may be racial in origin, but many seem linked to the old European tradition that associates negative concepts such as evil and the devil with darkness and blackness, and positive concepts such as purity and goodness with whiteness (see chapter 3). The conceptual framework underlying these words and phrases accents black in negative ways and white in positive ways. In a standard dictionary entry the adjective "black" is listed as having these meanings, in addition to color: dirty, soiled, wicked, sinister, connected with magic, gloomy, calamitous, marked with disaster, sullen, grim, and distorted. In contrast, the adjective "white" has these meanings, in addition to color: marked by upright fairness, free of blemish, innocent, not intended to cause harm, fortunate, favorable, and ardent.

The negative tone of many phrases using "black" can be seen in the following: to do a black deed; to be a black sheep; to tell a black lie; to indulge in the black arts (magic); to blacken one's name; to blackball someone; to be blackhearted; to have a black outlook; to be a blackguard (scoundrel); to have a Black Monday; to be on a black list; to give a black mark; to be blackmailed; and to be a black day. In contrast, we have the following: to be a white knight; to tell a white lie; to white list; to be the white hope; to be free, white, and twenty-one; and to say "that's very white of you." Moreover, in older novels and movies the "good guys" often wear white hats, while the "bad guys" often wear black hats. In Christian depictions, angels are often portrayed as white and devils as black.[51] While the white-black distinctions in English are much older than antiblack racism, they have, at the least, subtly reinforced dichotomous or antiblack thinking. Indeed, we noted in a previous chapter how people of English and African origin, who are in fact mostly shades of brown or tan, came to be labeled by English Americans in the stark terms of "black" and "white."

In addition, black Americans are frequently described by whites, in everyday speech and writing, in ways that do suggest the subordinate position of the former. There is, for example, the commonplace *denial of black agency*. Positive achievements of whites may be put in the active tense, while those of blacks may be put in the passive tense. Thus, Thomas Greefield reports visiting Thomas Jefferson's Virginia plantation, where he was told by his guide, who was referring to doors that had operated since 1809 without need of repair, that "Mr. Jefferson designed these doors," and also that "the doors were installed in 1809." Thus, the enslaved Africans who put up the well-crafted doors remained anonymous in the passive tense.[52] Only recently have tours at, and written brochures about, some slave plantations begun to give attention to the agency of enslaved workers. Moreover, today in many organizations a black man or woman who gets a very good job or position often is said by whites to have gotten it through affirmative action and not because of merit. In other cases, there is a *playing down of black agency*. Whites may recognize that blacks have achieved something, but run it down as flawed. For example, many whites have disparaged the innovative music often flowing from black communities, such as jazz in the early decades of the twentieth century or rap music in recent decades. There is also the strategy of viewing a black achievement as an *anomaly*. Success is something blacks do achieve—such as the Huxtables on "The Cosby Show"—but it is an exception to the rule.[53]

Toni Morrison has suggested an even deeper point—that black Americans function in many ways as a key metaphor and referent for white Americans in public discourse and in literature.[54] Black Americans often seem to be an overt or hidden referent for white thought and action. We have seen previously how black Americans constitute a major reference point for whites—in crafting the Constitution, in the Civil War period, in creating wealth and prosperity, in presidential politics, and in structuring cities. In later chapters we observe black Americans as a key referent in many areas of contemporary life—in debates over schools, the criminal justice system, welfare programs, housing and urban development, and political representation. We noted previously the black referent in public discourse about gangs, the poor, and criminals. Moreover, subtle use of the black referent extends to the definition of what is "American." Mass media writers often use the term "American" in a way that assumes whiteness and implicitly excludes blackness.

White Emotions, White Rage   Recall the point made by W. E. B. Du Bois about racist barriers being created by "unconscious acts and irrational reactions unpierced by reason." White thinking about racial matters is often rooted in deeplying emotions. As we have seen previously, for centuries many whites have been obsessed with blackness and have seen black people as not only inferior but also fearful and dangerous. Whites have often been particularly emotional about such matters as interracial sex and marriage. However, the level of white emotional involvement in racist thinking and action varies considerably both on an individual basis and in regard to the issue.

Take the comments in this anonymous hate letter I recently received, apparently from a white man. The writer of the letter is familiar with extreme white supremacist thinking and activities. The letter attacked a brief quote from me in a New Jersey newspaper article about current trends in racial discrimination and conflict. Handwritten on a New Jersey city's superintendent of schools stationery, the letter read in part as follows:

> So we should give privileges to placate filthy dirty subhuman coons, your nuts. Never! Never! I'm telling you. . . . Whites such as myself are just itching to take to the streets and exterminate every dirty nigger ape as well as every white nigger loving commie dog (such as your self). [O. J.] Simpson is the catalyst that will finally awaken the latent, dormant nigger hatred extant in this county. There will be no compromise, no quarter given. . . . First we elect Buchanan types, next suspend habeus corpis. Third disenfranchise and resegregate niggers. Then either deportation or extermination. Sound familiar? You white liberal swine are cancers even worse that filthy coons. When the reckoning comes, it will be curtains for them too. The only good nigger is a dead nigger. [Signed] WHITE RAGE.[55]

Judging from the letterhead and the vocabulary (if not the spelling and punctuation), this letter seems to be from a well-educated white person. We see here the old white images of black people as dirty and subhuman. We observe too the concern with "nigger-loving" whites who betray white racist concerns. This type of racist venom extends beyond crude racist epithets and images to the goal of racial extermination. Perhaps most clear in this kind of diatribe is the high level of *emotion*. Racist attitudes are about much more than cognitive interpretations of racial others.

While the letter is phrased in extreme racist terminology, some themes in it have been articulated, if in somewhat more restrained language, by many other whites—both those in the general public and those in the elites. As I have shown earlier, racist images and attitudes are strongly held by whites in the elites, although they often try to conceal their attitudes by not expressing them in public. They are sometimes less careful in private. Terrel Bell, Ronald Reagan's secretary of education, reports that in the 1980s midlevel aides in the White House and other government agencies made blatantly racist comments and told racist jokes. Some in the White House referred to Dr. Martin Luther King, Jr., as "Martin Lucifer Coon" and referred to the Arab peoples as "sand niggers." Moreover, because he supported the enforcement of civil rights laws, Bell was often sarcastically called Comrade Bell. These racist perspectives in house were often accompanied by antiblack actions in public, including the weakening of civil rights laws.[56] Moreover, from time to time some in the elite air their views openly. In the early 1990s Marge Schott, the owner of the Cincinnati Reds baseball team, reportedly remarked to an employee, "I'd rather have a trained monkey working for me than a nigger." She was also reported to have called some black baseball players "million-dollar niggers." Such barbed language may suggest not just cognitive stereotypes but strong and deep-seated emotions.[57]

Denying Discrimination and Racism: The White Public   In chapter 3 we examined how in recent years the white elites have generally played down persisting racism and accented instead the image of a just society where equality of opportunity is the reality. These broad themes in the current incarnation of the racist ideology provide the umbrella for everyday discourse. Not surprisingly, national surveys indicate that today a majority of white Americans see equality of opportunity as the societal reality. They more or less agree with the elite view. Included in this perspective is the idea that discrimination is no longer widespread and that black Americans who complain of it are paranoid or confused. There is a common saying among whites that a black person is "playing the race card," a comment generally used to suggest that that person is making an illegitimate demand because antiblack racism is no longer thought of as a serious obstacle in the United States.

Denying the Reality of Discrimination   Soon after the 1960s civil rights movement declined in intensity, most whites were moving toward the view that racial discrimination is no longer an important problem for the nation. In a 1976 survey, for example, most (71 percent) whites agreed that "blacks and other minorities no longer face unfair employment conditions. In fact they are favored in many training and job programs." A meager 12 percent of whites agreed with the statement that "discrimination affects all black people. The only way to handle it is for blacks to organize together and demand rights for all."[58] In a 1980 survey respondents were asked, "How much discrimination do you feel there is against blacks and other minorities in any area of life that limits their chances to get ahead?"[59] Just over half of blacks replied "a lot," compared to only a quarter of whites. In these surveys only a minority of whites viewed discrimination as a major hurdle.

In more recent surveys, black and white Americans still differ dramatically in how they view discrimination. A 1990 NORC survey question asked why blacks have worse jobs, income, and housing than whites. Choosing among alternative explanations, two-thirds of black respondents said that it was "mainly due to discrimination," compared to only 35 percent of whites.[60] Similarly, in a mid-1990s Pennsylvania survey researchers found that eight in ten black respondents thought inequality in jobs, housing, and income stemmed mostly from discrimination, while the majority of whites viewed this inequality as resulting from blacks' lack of motivation. Respondents were asked whether the quality of life for black Americans had gotten better in the last decade. Nearly six in ten whites said it had gotten better, compared to less than a third of black respondents.[61] Recent national polls have shown the same pattern. A 1997 ABC/*Washington Post* poll found that only 17 percent of the white respondents felt there was a lot of racial discrimination, compared to nearly half the blacks polled. In addition, several other surveys have found that on questions dealing with specific institutional areas such as housing, education, and jobs less than a majority of whites believe that blacks currently face discrimination.[62]

Several recent surveys have found that many whites think blacks are as well off as or are better off than whites in regard to education, health care, and jobs. For example, a Massachusetts survey found a majority of the white respondents saying that African Americans, Asian Americans, and Latino Americans now have *equality* in life chances with whites.[63] However, government statistical data indicate that such views are very much in error. Perhaps because of erroneous or misleading media reports, most whites do not understand just how much worse off blacks actually are than whites in most areas of political and economic life.[64]

"I Am Not a Racist": Denying Individual Racism   Clearly, a majority of whites do not see the United States as a nation that has a problem of serious and widespread racial discrimination. Apparently, most whites also do not view themselves as significantly racist in thought or action, often asserting "I am not a racist." In recent years many whites have also made such statements as "my family never owned slaves" or "my family did not segregate lunch counters." Many will say to black Americans something like, "Slavery happened hundreds of years ago — get over it." They do not know, or pretend they do not, that official slavery ended less than 140 years or so prior to their statements. In addition, whites making such assertions usually do not admit that they and their families have benefited greatly from slavery, segregation, and present-day discrimination.

Many whites seem to mix negative views of black Americans with images of white innocence, thereby giving specific expression to elements of a broader racial ideology. Take this example of a white college student's reply to a question about her first experience with black Americans, in this case children: "I switched from a private school which had no blacks to a public school, and I was thrown in the middle of a bunch of apes, no I'm just kidding. . . . And I don't know, my parents have always instilled in me that blacks aren't equal, because we are from [the Deep South]." In her interview she continues in this vein, making several negative comments about African Americans. Then at the end of her interview, she adds, "I don't consider myself racist. I, when I think of the word racist, I think of KKK, people in white robes burning black people on crosses and stuff, or I think of the Skinheads or some exaggerated form of racism."[65] We see here the imaging of the white self in positive terms.

It seems that most whites can assert that they are "not racist" because they see racism as something that *other* whites do. That is, they know other whites who are much more racist in thought or action than they are, and thus they see themselves as already beyond that racism. Jerome Culp has said, "To many white people, not being racist means having less racial animosity than their parents (something almost all can at least claim); having less racial animosity than someone they know (something all can claim); or not belonging to a white supremacist group. . . . For many white people, unless they believe overwhelmingly in the inferiority of black people, they are not collaborators with racism and are not racist."[66] As we saw in white views of athletes and actors on "The Cosby Show," many whites hold some more or less positive images of selected black men or women. However, these usually superficial positive views reduce the ability of whites to see their own culpability in personal and institutional racism. Indeed, many a white person has a false consciousness that occurs when a white "believes he or she is identifying with a person of color, but in fact is doing so only in a slight, superficial way."[67] It is possible to hold that black Americans can be good entertainers, musicians, or sports figures, yet also believe that most are inferior to whites in character, morality, or intelligence.

Historical changes in racism have also been misperceived by whites. When the legal segregation era came to an end with the passage of civil rights laws in the 1960s, most whites apparently concluded that serious racism was being rapidly extinguished. Today, most whites, like the young woman interviewed above, seem to view what racism remains as a matter of isolated Klan-type bigotry and not as a system of racism cutting across U.S. institutions. As a result, they do not see their own racism. Moreover, the level at which racist attitudes are held can vary in degree of consciousness. Psychologist Patricia Devine has suggested that whites who reject overtly prejudiced views can still hold less consciously prejudiced thoughts that stem from prior socialization. For many whites this attitudinal racism is a persisting bad habit that keeps coming up in everyday thought and behavior. One reason for this is the fact that human beings are characterized by automatic information processing, which involves the unintentional activation of previously socialized attitudes such as racist stereotypes and prejudices.[68] Racist attitudes can thus be conscious, half-conscious, or even subconscious.

White Views on Government Action against Discrimination   If antiblack discrimination is no longer regarded as a serious problem, then it is not surprising that most whites see less need, or no need, for strong antidiscrimination efforts by governments. From this perspective blacks pressing for continuing or enhanced antidiscrimination programs, such as aggressive affirmative action, are seen as making illegitimate demands. David Wellman has suggested that "the concrete problem facing white people is how to come to grips with the demands made by blacks while at the same time *avoiding* the possibility of institutional change and reorganization that might affect them."[69]

Symbolic and Laissez-Faire Racism   Some researchers have described a contemporary white perspective called *symbolic racism*. Whites often combine the notion of declining or eradicated blatant racism with the idea that blacks are making illegitimate demands for societal changes. As these researchers see the current situation, a majority of whites have shifted away from old-fashioned racist ideas and have accepted modest desegregation while strongly resisting aggressive government action for large-scale desegregation. This symbolic racism is grounded in white resistance to substantial changes in the status quo. Central to white concerns is a fear whites have of losing status and power because of black attempts to bring change. Deep-lying antiblack views—especially views of blacks violating traditional American work values—are still present, but white resentment of pressures for substantial change is central to the current racist ideology.[70] This symbolic racism perspective has been criticized by some scholars as playing down old-fashioned racism, when the latter still exists among whites and is directly connected to negative views of programs to eradicate discrimination.

Lawrence Bobo, James Kluegel, and Ryan Smith have suggested a more historical approach. Since the 1950s, and shaped by structural changes in the society, they say white attitudes have shifted from an accent on strict segregation and overt bigotry to "laissez-faire racism," by which they mean whites' continuing stereotyping of blacks and blaming of blacks for their problems. Roughly in line with, but probably lagging somewhat, the elite responses described in chapter 3, most ordinary whites have given up a commitment to compulsory racial segregation. Yet, also in line with the elite, they still strive to maintain white privilege and position. Survey data since the 1960s indicate a substantial discrepancy between white views on the *principle* of desegregation versus whites views on the *implementation* of desegregation by government. While surveys in the mid-1960s indicated that nearly two-thirds of whites accepted integrated schooling in principle, just 38 percent accepted a role for government in pressing for more integration. By the mid-1980s white support for the principle of school integration had grown to 93 percent, while endorsement of government intervention had declined to 26 percent.[71] The survey data indicate similar discrepancies in white views of job and housing integration. Acceptance of the principle of racial integration does not mean that whites wish to see government intervene aggressively, or to personally have more contact with blacks. Whites maintain a positive sense of self and their claims to greater privileges and resources while fending off what whites see as illegitimate black demands for a fair share of those resources.

Views on Affirmative Action   Affirmative action is a major example of a remedial program to deal with racial discrimination. Yet most whites, including most white leaders, have been opposed to *aggressive* affirmative action since at least the 1970s. In one 1977 survey of mostly white and male local and national leaders in business, farming, unions, the media, and academia, *most* were overwhelmingly opposed to affirmative-action quotas for black Americans in school admissions and jobs. Only 10 to 22 percent of the several leadership groups favored strong remedial quotas.[72] In addition, the overwhelming majority of these elites thought that equality of opportunity, not equality of results, was the best way to eradicate disparities. The white public seems to share this view. Earlier we noted mid-1970s surveys suggesting that the white majority views blacks as no longer facing serious job discrimination and expresses opposition to an expanded effort for civil rights.

Recent data show the same pattern: more than half of whites do not believe that government or private agencies should be making aggressive remedial efforts on behalf of black Americans or other Americans of color. In an ABC News/*Washington Post* survey only a quarter of whites thought minorities should receive some preferences in jobs and college admissions.[73] And a late-1990s Gallup poll found that 70 percent of Republicans, a heavily white group, felt the federal government should not make special efforts to help Americans of color, because they should help themselves.[74] A majority of whites took the same position in a late-1990s survey in Massachusetts.[75] Most national surveys have shown the same pattern of white opposition to strong programs with special preferences or quotas as a means of aggressively remedying past discrimination. (Milder remedial programs may sometimes be acceptable.) Indeed, today many whites believe that they are likely to be the victims of governmental policies helping black Americans. One recent Pennsylvania survey asked a question as to how likely it would be that a white worker might lose a job or a promotion to a less qualified black worker. Most black respondents (57 percent) thought this was unlikely, while most whites (80 percent) thought it was likely.[76] National polls using such a question have gotten similar responses: The majority of whites seem convinced that antiwhite discrimination is now commonplace.

White elites have periodically expended substantial effort to shape the public's views of remedial programs. In chapter 3 we discussed how elite perspectives on antidiscrimination programs and related public policies generally shifted in a more conservative direction in the two decades after the 1960s. Moreover, researcher Robert Entman has examined trends in mass media reports of the controversy over affirmative action that recurred periodically in the 1980s and 1990s. He found significant peaking in media attention to affirmative action during the years 1987, 1991, and 1995—years that preceded presidential elections. This pattern suggests elite manipulation of the affirmative action issue for political purposes. The media elites and their white-collar employees tended to present the issue of affirmative action in white-framed ways or in terms of national controversy, using such phrases as the "tide of white anger" or the "growing white backlash." Entman concludes that "journalists, it seems, built their frame on claims by elite sources with an interest in promoting the impression of white arousal, filtered through the conflict norm that shapes story construction."[77] The media attention accelerated concerns about affirmative action in the white public.

Related to opposition to strong affirmative action programs is the old individualistic ethic, especially the blame-the-victim version. Recall the historical importance of the individualistic (work) ethic from our previous discussion of racist ide-ology. Today, as in the past, many whites comment about the problems of blacks with such statements as, "Why can't they be like us?" The notion here is that if "they" will work harder and improve their personal and family values, then the normal assimilation processes will enable them to have greater socioeconomic mobility. One recent survey asked whether respondents agreed with this statement: "The Irish, Italians, and many other groups overcame prejudice and worked their way up, African-Americans and other minorities should do the same without any special help from the government." Most whites (69 percent) agreed.[78] Most seem to perceive the black experience in terms of an individualistic mobility model. Black Americans, from this viewpoint, are little different from white immigrant groups, such as the southern and eastern European immigrants of the early 1900s. Like those immigrants, who are seem as having encountered discrimination, black Americans should be able to work themselves up the social ladder. If they do not make it, it is mostly their own fault.

Imaging the White Self   As we saw clearly in previous chapters, the racist ideas and attitudes of white Americans encompass *much more* than their antiblack views. Among these racist attitudes are positive views of white superiority and merit. Generally, the broad white-racist ideology sees white history as meritorious. Indeed, in the United States, group merit and individual merit are judged by standards created by the white majority. In chapter 3 we noted the images of white superi-ority and virtue in many Hollywood films. From the first years of moviemaking to the present, when racial matters have been portrayed, whites as a group have almost always been portrayed as morally superior, intellectually superior, or otherwise meritorious. In these movies—including more recent television movies—there may be a few white individuals who are racist bigots, but the society as a whole is not portrayed as racist. Some white person is typically a central hero, even in movies mostly about black Americans (for example, *Glory*).

Among elites and in the general public, whites have developed numerous sin-cere fictions that reproduce aspects of the broad racist ideology at an everyday level. Such fictions may describe whites as "not racist" and as "good people" even as the same whites take part in racist actions or express racist ideas. This moral privileg-ing of whiteness may be conscious or it can be half-conscious or unconscious. Ruth Frankenberg found evidence of this unconsciousness in her research on white women: whiteness, she noted, is "difficult for white people to name. . . . Those who are securely housed within its borders usually do not examine it."[79] The sense of whiteness is often hidden deeply in individual psyches and practices. Being white, one might say, means rarely or never having to think about it. Whiteness is the national norm, and thus the white majority's views, practices, and culture are generally seen as normal.

Examining commentaries on racial inequality written by white students, Joyce King found that most were "unaware of how their own subjective identities reflect an uncritical identification with the existing social order." Only one student out of fifty-seven linked persisting racial inequality to the larger system of racial oppression.[80] Thus, while whites get many substantial advantages from systemic racism, they do pay a subtle and hidden price. This may include a lack of conscious awareness about certain critical aspects of social reality. Many have an uncritical mind that accepts the existing racial order with little questioning.

Perhaps most amazing is that a majority of whites today do not see the centuries of slavery and segregation as bringing whites substantial socioeconomic benefit. One survey found that nearly two-thirds of white respondents did *not* think that whites as a group had benefited from past and present discrimination against black Americans. Nor did they think whites should take significant action to remedy continuing discrimination.[81] Moreover, as we have seen, many whites have asserted their innocence with a torrent of comments such as "my family never owned slaves." This white guiltlessness is professed at all class levels, even by presidential candidates. Clearly, much work has gone into reframing the American history of racial oppression so that white Americans can appear blameless for the brutality and carnage they and their ancestors created.

Fostering and Learning Racist Attitudes

The Role of Elites   In chapter 3 we examined how elites have fostered a racist ideology rationalizing the realities of unjust impoverishment and enrichment. This effort is a major source of the racist ideology and its associated attitudes that are held in the nonelite part of the white population. Through various means the white elites have manipulated ordinary white Americans to accept the racist ideology and its component parts. Moreover, after the elements of an era's racist ideology and structural arrangements are in place, ordinary whites need less manipulation, for they generally understand what is in their group interest. Indeed, groups of ordinary people often generate new permutations on old racist ideas, innovations that in their turn reinforce and reproduce the racist ideology.

The often hidden power of the elite works through propagating the racist ideology and its associated beliefs and images by means of the mass media and the educational system, as well as in workplaces and churches. Increasingly, the mass media are as important as family or school in creating and propagating racist images and attitudes. In opening this chapter we saw a U.S. president interacting with a white man who saw black men in negative terms. While the president did mention a major source of the image — the mass media — he did not stop to consider why this image is so negative, nor did he comment on its harmful repercussions for black men. For centuries newspapers, magazines, advertisements, and other media have played an important part not only in generating a broad white-racist ideology but also specific negative images that are the daily product of that ideology.

In the century after the Civil War stereotyped images were aggressively circulated in the new commercial advertising. As Marimba Ani has noted, "Black faces were used to sell everything from tooth paste to pancakes. Distorted images appeared on boxes and tubes, and even on vaudeville stages, to make white people laugh."[82] Some of these images, like the aforementioned Aunt Jemima stereotype, are still found on certain consumer goods sold in the United States and across the globe, though in the United States most such images have been altered to appear less stereotypical. In marketing goods and attracting consumers the mass media generally do not confront, but rather reinforce, existing racist beliefs. Consumerism is based not only on consumption of material goods but also on the consumption of images, which have long included stereotypes of black Americans. Moreover, with the emergence of Hollywood and moviemaking on a large scale in the first decades of the twentieth century, the negative images of black Americans and other Americans of color were reinforced in millions of American minds.

The Role of Conformity   Some analysts have viewed racial prejudice as a sort of demon in an individual, as a type of psychological abnormality. Frustration-aggression and authoritarian-personality theories of prejudice focus on the externalization function of prejudice—the transfer of a person's internal psychological problems to an external object, such as a racial other, as a solution for an internal psychological problem. From this viewpoint, those whites who are racially prejudiced are "sick" individuals. There are certainly some whites who fit this interpretation, some of whom belong to racist extremist groups. However, much social science research indicates that social *conformity* is a much more important factor in shaping the prejudices of a majority of people, including a majority of whites. Most whites accept their social contexts and hold to prejudices taught at home and school or through the mass media.[83]

The white self is constantly shaped through interaction with other people; it develops in response to recognition from relevant others. Much learning about white superiority and black inferiority comes from informal lessons learned as whites grow up and mature, as children at home and school and as adults socializing with relatives and friends. White images of black Americans and other people of color are typically passed along family lines of communication. Social conformity to the views of important relatives and friends is a central source of routinized racist thinking and emotion. Most racial prejudices are not the result of individual pathologies but reflect shared social definitions. In this way prejudices function as a means of social adjustment to the views of an important ingroup. In general, scholars have noted, "our most private thoughts and feelings arise out of a constant feedback and flow-through of the thoughts and feelings of others who have influenced us. Our individuality is decidedly a part of a collective movement. That movement has feedback at its root."[84] Thus, negative images of blacks are old and deep in white communities; they become part of the evolving white self.

Some psychological research indicates that people often do not think through what they are doing in everyday behavior but proceed as if they are on automatic pilot; they tend to operate in line with a thoroughly routinized script learned from their social context.[85] Given that racist images, attitudes, and inclinations are well-learned processes that are imbedded in individual and collective memories, much racist behavior on the part of whites thus has an automatic, routinized character.

For most white Americans the earliest socialization in racist attitudes begins in the family. A recent CBS poll of high school students found that 52 percent of those whose parents made overtly racist comments admitted that they too had made such comments.[86] Recall the dramatic example of socialization reported by a retired clerical worker: "'The niggers would come in the night and steal us away and use us for their pleasure,' that's what my mother told us." Another example is from an interview conducted with a white father, a businessperson who reveals strong emotions. Responding to a hypothetical question about an adult child dating a black person, he replies, "I'd be sick to my stomach. I would feel like, that I failed along the way. . . . I'd feel like I probably failed as a father, if that was to happen. And it's something that I could never accept. . . . It would truly be a problem in my family because I could never handle that, and I don't know what would happen because I couldn't handle that, ever."[87] This man's comments signal more than negative images of the out-group; they point to his view of his white self and to how he sees being a father. The comments highlight the family context of such ideas; also evident is the substantial emotion being expressed. While perhaps more strongly stated than some, his views are in line with the interracial dating and marriage views expressed by many whites. For example, one national survey found the majority of whites saying they would have a negative reaction if a close relative married a black person.[88]

Mainstream theories of the cognitive development of children stress that they do not form clear ideas on racial matters until they are at least five or six years old. Until that time, egocentricity is said to be the child's natural state.[89] However, a recent study of young white children in a preschool setting found that even three-to-four-year-olds interact with children of other racial groups using clear and often sophisticated understandings of racist ideas and epithets (for example, "nigger"). White children used such ideas and terms to define themselves as white and to exclude or exert power over other children. This study also found that many white adults, including parents, do not know about or deny the racist language or activities of their children.[90] Even as whites socialize children in racist thought, emotions, and practices, they often deny to themselves and others what they are doing.

While most children are initially socialized into racist thinking in family groups, they also learn subtle and blatant racist ideas and images from peer groups and from children's books and school books. Children's (and adults') views of racial others are heavily shaped by certain television programs and movies, even movies that are specially designed for children, and by some of the child-oriented presentations in theme parks and museums. While these racial understandings are given by society to each individual, each person constructs and reconstructs them in everyday interactions. The racist ideology and attitudes carried in white minds are an encoding that likely began with parents but has evolved through contacts with many other people over a lifetime.

White Isolation and Its Consequences   Recent research shows that all U.S. cities have a high degree of residential segregation (see chapter 5). Whites are substantially segregated not only from blacks but also from most other Americans of color. Residential segregation is a basic part of the social process whereby systemic racism is reproduced from one generation to the next. Residential segregation breeds significant social and mental isolation; the absence of equal-status experiences with black families in neighborhoods contributes materially to white unfamiliarity with black Americans. In Chicago, several *New York Times* journalists did important field research on the impact of residential segregation in regard to cross-racial attitudes. They interviewed Chicagoans in two adjacent working-class suburbs, one predominantly white and one predominantly black. Whites were found to be very isolated and mostly living out their lives "without ever getting to know a black person." In both communities there were fears and suspicions of the other group. However, the *source* of these fears varied significantly. The black suburbanites were "fearful because much of their contact with white people was negative," while "whites were fearful because they had little or no contact" with similar black Chicagoans.[91]

Because of the racial demography and ecology of everyday life, the majority of blacks spend much more time interacting with whites than the majority of whites spend interacting with blacks. Most black Americans work, shop, or travel with large numbers of white Americans, whereas relatively few whites do the same with large numbers of black men and women. White views of blacks are not likely to be grounded in numerous equal-status contacts with blacks. The sense of white superiority is reinforced by the continuing process in which whites live separated from black Americans or other Americans of color. White isolation and lack of contact feeds negative stereotyping, and there is little chance to unlearn inherited antiblack attitudes.

Some psychological studies show that whites who are asked to describe a black person often see fewer descriptive aspects of that person than when they are asked to describe a white person. This has been called a bias toward out-group homogeneity. Members of an in-group tend to see the people in their group in more complex and differentiated terms than they see people in an out-group. Isolation increases bonding and conformity to the norms of the in-group. Moreover, the stronger one's attachment to the in-group, the greater the likelihood of prejudice against out-groups.[92] The process of attitudinal development in segregated communities provides yet another example of the social reproduction of racism.

Activating Antiblack Prejudices and Stereotypes   Racist prejudices and stereotypes are serious not just in themselves, but because they motivate actions implementing and reinforcing the racial hierarchy. Whites vary in how important their racist prejudices are in their thinking and practices. Some are so overtly racist in their thinking and emotions that they are completely taken over by their internalized racism. They may join openly white supremacist groups and target African Americans and other people of color for violence. In significant contrast, some whites recognize their own racist upbringing and proclivities and join groups openly working against racism.

Social science research reveals, as one might expect, a link between racial attitudes and discriminatory actions. One review of twenty-three different research studies concluded that there was a significant but moderate relationship between expressed racist attitudes and acts of discrimination.[93] However, the correlations between expressed prejudice and discrimination are not as strong as one might expect. One likely reason is that many people hide their prejudices from researchers. Indeed, experimental studies by social psychologists working in laboratories and in the field have found much more antiblack discrimination than they should have found if the unprejudiced views whites often express in polls and surveys were their real views.[94]

Racist thought or action is often precipitated by some type of visual or verbal cue. Perhaps the most common cue is the black body itself. When whites perceive someone to fit their internalized criteria for blackness—which can be skin color, other physical characteristics, or speech—their minds may generate negative attitudes or images, and they may act according to those internalized attitudes or images. Some social psychologists have suggested that there are four possible responses to a racial cue. Some whites do not automatically activate an antiblack stereotype when they encounter a black person. They activate a positive image and generally act in antiracist ways. Another group of whites react routinely and *consciously* to such cues with an overtly negative evaluation and actively express their negative views in discriminatory action. For a third group of whites, their negative evaluations are also activated in response to racial cues, but they are not aware of these negative reactions in a phenomenological sense. They act on the racist views but only *unconsciously*. Yet another group of whites is like the previous one, but they are aware of the negative evaluations and will try to counter them, albeit to varying degrees. Sometimes this countering is because of a personal distaste for the racist reaction, but in other cases it may be only a desire to be seen as socially acceptable to important others. [95]

Perhaps it would be more accurate to see these four groups of responses as over-lapping rather than as separate. Depending on the time in a person's life, or on the social situation, a given individual may react to socioracial cues in different ways. Under certain circumstances, many whites who hold strong racist prejudices and stereotypes will not act on them out of concern for social acceptability. According to researchers Bridget Dunton and Russell Fazio, "a conscious desire to project a nonprejudiced image and a willingness to refrain from actions that might provoke dispute with or about Blacks are not restricted to individuals with positive racial attitudes."[96] In contrast, many whites with strong racist views will express their neg-ative views in settings where they do not feel social pressures to act in nonracist ways. Thus, location and context are important in the expression of racist thought and actions. The reaction to racial cues will also depend on what stereotypes are triggered. Many racist stereotypes are so deeply imbedded in white consciousness (such as the dangerous-black-man image) that even whites with relatively low lev-els of racial stereotyping and prejudice may have difficulty in recognizing the role such stereotypes play in their everyday lives.

Conclusion   Racist attitudes and images are central to the operation of systemic racism in the contemporary United States. They can be seen as everyday expres-sions of the overarching white racist ideology that undergirds the nation. An array of racist prejudices and stereotyped images lie behind much discriminatory action taken by whites (and other nonblacks) against blacks. Among whites these atti-tudes are reinforced and perpetuated by millions of taken-for-granted comments, stories, and actions that target black Americans every day.

White racist images and attitudes do not stop at U.S. borders. At any given moment, white Americans working overseas are telling antiblack stories to people around the globe or television stations across the globe are playing racist American movies, such as *Gone With the Wind* or the old Tarzan and cowboy-and-Indian classics. U.S. media corporations have long played a major role in circulating racist images and attitudes overseas. These corporations dominate much of the world's mass media. Thus, one recent analysis found that a fifth of Western Europe's news broadcasts are based in U.S. sources, as are half of Europe's entertainment pro-grams other than sports. In addition, many people around the world get their infor-mation and entertainment from U.S. movies, syndicated television programs, and videos, as well as directly from the U.S. armed forces radio and television broad-casts. Various cable channels also reach around the globe. In the mid-1990s the MTV channel alone reached no fewer than 210 million households in seventy countries.[97]

As a result, the U.S. media are one of the most important forces shaping racist stereotyping around the world, including negative images of black Americans. Antiblack images are common in many countries. Relatively soon, if it has not already happened, much of the world's population will hold antiblack attitudes, and the curse of U.S.–generated racism will follow African Americans wherever they travel. In a recent study by Hsiao-Chuan Hsia, fifteen rural Taiwanese who had never been to the United States were interviewed. While the Taiwanese respondents sometimes realized that the U.S. media were engaged in stereotyping, most still accepted racist views of black Americans.[98] They generally thought that black Americans were self-destructive, dirty, lazy, unintelligent, criminal, violent, and ugly. The researcher found that these negative images were usually gleaned from U.S. television shows, movies, and music videos that the respondents had seen in Taiwan. Drawing on recent interviews with Latino immigrants from Central America, sociologist Nestor Rodriguez has also concluded that the U.S. mass media are creating negative views of black Americans in that area. "I have traveled to Guatemala and seen theaters showing the same violent, racist movies we show here," he says. "When I asked one migrant in Houston why some migrants have antiblack attitudes, he responded that they first learn about blacks from U.S. movies."[99] Similarly, a research study of foreign-born and U.S.–born Latinas in Houston found that the former had even more negative attitudes toward black Americans than did the latter. Such data suggest that the foreign-born bring negative views of black Americans from their countries of origin.[100]

Antiblack images and attitudes are often carried by Asian, Latino, and other recent immigrants to the United States. They become the basis for negative attitudes toward and negative interactions with black Americans—from the first days of contact. From this experience, black Americans in their turn are likely to develop negative views of Asians and Latinos. Thus, the negative attitudes of Asian or Latino immigrants toward African Americans—and the negative attitudes of African Americans toward Asian or Latino Americans—are part of the much larger system of white-managed racism, which these groups had no role in initiating.

five

Racial Oppression in Everyday Practice

The Heart of Systemic Racism: Discriminatory Practices   To many white observers racial oppression no longer seems important because it is no longer a matter of legal segregation. Racism seems to be gone or declining because there are at least a few African Americans in numerous professional or managerial positions in many historically white institutions. However, one can recognize the modest changes in white racist domination in the United States without downplaying the strong relationship between being black and being a target of serious racial discrimination. In one way or another, all black Americans continue to suffer discrimination because white domination of black Americans and other people of color remains a major organizing principle for group life in the United States. The racial hierarchy is supported by a range of dominant-group prejudices and stereotypes, yet it is perpetuated most centrally by the discrimination carried out by many whites on a recurring basis. Age-old patterns of racial inequality—of unjust enrichment and unjust impoverishment—are reproduced by the daily routines of antiblack discrimination.

Changing Models of Discrimination   Mainstream social scientists have often examined the paired ideas of racial prejudice and racial discrimination. The explicit model has typically been one of individual bigots acting out their attitudes in discriminatory ways.[1] In recent decades, however, some scholars have argued for a different emphasis in looking at prejudice and discrimination. They prefer to accent the *institutional* and *societal* racism that surrounds individual acts of discrimination.

In its origin, this institutional racism viewpoint comes from a long line of black scholars and activists, going back at least to the mid-1800s. As I underscored in chapter 1, thinkers like Frederick Douglass and W. E. B. Du Bois long ago put white society and its societal institutions at the center of serious analysis of racism. The 1960s civil rights movement brought a renewed emphasis among black intellectuals and activists on the social and institutional contexts of individual acts of discrimination.[2] For a time the pressure of the civil rights movement also enabled black activists, black intellectuals, and other black Americans to get their perceptive views on white racism—honed in considerable personal and group experience—into mainstream discussions of racial issues.

While in recent years numerous mainstream white scholars have moved away from a critical institutional-racism perspective, it remains the most important approach to understanding the U.S. system of racism. Today, black Americans experience discrimination not just as the actions of individual white bigots in one social arena, but rather as everyday, recurring actions of white actors across many of life's arenas—actions that are backed by a multifaceted and powerful system of white privilege. While all discrimination is carried out by individuals, the social context is very important, for that is where the beliefs, norms, and proclivities perpetuating racism are institutionalized. Individual acts of discrimination activate the underlying hierarchical relations of power in which whites generally dominate blacks.[3]

Since the 1960s, it is interesting to note that the international attack on all forms of discrimination has accelerated. The United Nations International Convention on the Elimination of All Forms of Racial Discrimination, implemented in 1969, defines discrimination as "any distinction, exclusion, restriction or preference based on race, colour, descent or national or ethnic origin which has the purpose or effect of nullifying or impairing the recognition, enjoyment or exercise, on an equal footing, of human rights and fundamental freedoms." This broad view accents not only distinctions on the basis of racial grouping, but also restrictions, preferences, and exclusion aimed at impairing human rights. It underscores the costs associated with being the target of discrimination. In another passage, the Convention adds that the "existence of racial barriers is repugnant to the ideals of any human society."[4]

The Social Context of Racist Practice   Contemporary patterns of discrimination are grounded in the benefits that whites have historically secured. All forms of racial discrimination transmit the legacy of the past, that of slavery and legal segregation. Today discriminatory practices reproduce and reinforce the unjust impoverishment and enrichment of the past. Discrimination also reflects and perpetuates the age-old racist ideology, with its associated array of antiblack images and attitudes. When blacks encounter whites in a broad array of contemporary settings, they often meet negative beliefs about their abilities, values, and orientations. Racial barriers persist today because a substantial majority of whites harbor antiblack sentiments, images, and beliefs and because a large minority are very negative in their perspectives. When most whites interact with black Americans at work, in restaurants, on the street, at school, or in the media they tend to think about the latter, either consciously or unconsciously, in terms of racist stereotypes inherited from the past and constantly reiterated and reinforced in the present.

As we observed in chapter 4, the translation of antiblack attitudes into actual discrimination is shaped not only by these attitudes but also by subjective norms, such as what other people might think, and by perceived behavioral controls, such as what the response to discrimination will be. Most discrimination is thereby con-textualized.[5] Routinized discrimination in housing, employment, politics, and public accommodations is carried out by whites acting alone or in groups. Whites are usually implementing shared racist attitudes and norms of their families and other important social networks. The social norms guiding discrimination can be formal or legal, but most today are unwritten and informal. Moreover, much antiblack action is not sporadic but is carried out repeatedly and routinely by numerous dominant-group members influenced by the norms of their social networks. Whites have the power to discriminate as individuals, but much of their power to harm comes from membership in traditionally white networks and organizations.

Everyday Racism: Subtle, Covert, and Blatant   The character of discrimination varies. Whites may actively persecute blacks, or they may engage in an array of avoidance behaviors. Discrimination can be self-consciously motivated, or it can be half-conscious or unconscious and deeply imbedded in an actor's core beliefs. At the level of everyday interaction with black Americans, most whites can create racial tensions and barriers even without conscious awareness they are doing so. Examples of this include when white men lock their car doors as a black man walks by on the street or when white women step out or pull their purses close to them when a black man comes into an elevator they are on. Stereotyped images of black men as criminals probably motivate this and similar types of defensive action. Such practices represent, according to Philomena Essed, the "integration of racism into everyday situations."[6] Systemic racism is thus a system of oppression made up of many thousands of everyday acts of mistreatment of black Americans by white Americans, incidents that range from the subtle and hard to observe to the blatant and easy to notice. These acts of mistreatment can be nonverbal or verbal, nonvi-olent or violent. Moreover, many racist actions that crash in on everyday life are, from the victim's viewpoint, unpredictable and sporadic. Such actions are com-monplace, recurring, and cumulative in their negative impact. They are, as one retired black American in her eighties put it, "little murders" that happen every day.[7]

In a specific setting, such as an employment setting, a white person in authority may select another white person over an equally or better qualified black person because of a preconceived notion that whites are more competent or because of discomfort with people perceived as somehow different. This latter type of subtle discrimination includes, in John Calmore's words, "the unconscious failure to extend to a minority the same recognition of humanity, and hence the same sympathy and care, given as a matter of course to one's own group." The selectivity results "often unconsciously — from our tendency to sympathize most readily with those who seem most like ourselves."[8] Yet oppression is not less serious because it is more subtle.

The racist system is made even more complex by its reinforcement in many other aspects of the everyday behavior of white Americans. When whites make racist comments to other whites, or when they think or say racist things when watching television by themselves or with their families, they also reinforce and maintain the white-racist system, even though no blacks are present. Racism is systemic because it infiltrates most aspects of life.

Who Does the Discriminating?   Antiblack discrimination comes from all levels and categories of white Americans. Most whites are involved in some way in creating, reinforcing, or maintaining, the racist reality of U.S. society. Depending on the situation and the opportunity to discriminate, very large numbers of whites can and do discriminate. Judging from the housing audit studies cited below, perhaps half of all whites are inclined to discriminate in some fashion, whether subtly or blatantly, in situations where they have housing to rent or sell to black individuals or families. It may well be that whites discriminate at similarly high levels in other major institutional arenas.

There are actively antiracist whites scattered across the nation. They consistently and regularly speak out against white racism, even to the point of risking personal injury, friendships, and jobs. However, in regard to racist practice, most whites seem to fall into three other categories of action. One large group of whites regularly engage in overtly racist behavior; some of these whites are greatly consumed by their racist hatreds, as can be seen in lynchings and hate crimes. A second, much larger, group of whites discriminate against blacks in a variety of ways, as the occasion arises, but they frequently discriminate in less overt or more subtle ways and may often not be consciously aware of their discrimination. A third group of whites are consistently bystanders, engaging in less direct discrimination but knowingly providing support for those who do. Whites in the latter two groups often reject the type of blatant discrimination in which some in the first group engage, and may speak out against it, even as they themselves are engaging in more subtle or covert types of discrimination. Most whites in these three groups routinely think in white-oriented terms when choosing mates, neighborhoods, schools, and business partners. The racist system is thereby reinforced in daily interactions among whites. A sense of white superiority, however dim, seems to be part of the consciousness of most whites, including those who are relatively liberal on racial matters.

Interestingly, when issues of racism are discussed in the mass media, it is often working-class whites, the Archie Bunkers of television fame, who get tagged as the serious racists by the news and other media programs. Blue-collar violence against black Americans often does get significant news attention. Yet elite and middle-class whites are less frequently the focus of attention in media discussions of racial problems, and media discussions of discrimination that do involve a few middle class or elite discriminators usually avoid making connections to broader issues of systemic racism. Indeed, most elite and middle class whites vigorously deny that they are racist

The portrait of discriminatory practice that emerges from research is quite different. Judging from hundreds of interviews that I and my colleagues have conducted with black and white Americans over the last decade, as well as from numerous other field studies of discrimination in housing, employment, and public accommodations cited later in this chapter, the majority of whites who do the serious discriminating are those with some power to bring harm, such as white employers, managers, teachers, social workers, real estate agents, lenders, landlords and apartment managers, and police officers.[9] Middle-income and upper-income men and women are heavily implicated in racial oppression, though it is likely that in most major institutional areas, such as corporate promotions and urban policing, white men account for the lion's share of discriminatory actions. Generally speaking, these middle-income and upper-income whites are the ones in a position to most significantly affect black lives. Certainly, whites with less social or economic power also discriminate against black Americans in all income categories. Blue-collar employees frequently harass black workers in the workplace, and blue-collar bigots may yell racist epithets or hurl beer cans at a black man, woman, or child on the street. And working-class whites do seem to predominate as perpetrators in violent attacks on blacks in public places.

Given the right circumstances, most whites in all income groups have the ability to put black Americans "in their place," to frustrate or sabotage their lives for racist reasons. However, the patterns of discrimination vary. Many in the employer class, for instance, may be most interested in the exploitation of black workers, whose lowest-paid members constitute a reserve army of workers. In contrast, those in the white working and middle classes may be more concerned about housing or educational competition with black Americans, and they appear to be the most likely to discriminate in these latter areas.

Facing Lifetimes of Racial Discrimination   Whether subtle, covert, or blatant, racist practices are commonplace and recurring in a great variety of settings, ranging from public accommodations to educational facilities, business arenas, workplaces, and neighborhoods. How frequent is the discrimination faced by black Americans? What forms does this discrimination take? We do not yet have full answers to these questions, but recent surveys are helpful.

Researchers Nancy Krieger and Stephen Sidney gave some 2,000 black respondents a list of seven settings, such as the workplace, where one can face discrimination. Seventy percent of the female and 84 percent of the male respondents reported encountering discrimination in at least one area. The majority reported discrimination in at least three settings.[10] Similarly, a survey in the Detroit area asked black respondents about facing discrimination in six situations. Thirty-two percent reported discrimination recently in at least one of the situations, and four in ten reported facing at least one form of discrimination frequently. In addition, a recent Gallup survey inquired of black respondents if they had experienced discrimination in five areas (work, dining out, shopping, with police, in public transportation) during the last month. Just under half reported discrimination in one or more of these areas, including 70 percent of black men under the age of 35.[11] Many black Americans frequently face racist barriers in an array of societal arenas.

Even these substantial data are likely to be serious underestimates of the frequency of racist obstacles. Short survey questions do not explore the great range of discrimination faced by black Americans in everyday life. Indeed, survey research on the black experience with discrimination is relatively recent and remarkably limited. Survey questions are usually brief and customarily deal with only a few of the many types of racial mistreatment in the society. Indeed, a few survey researchers have suggested that more detailed questioning would reveal a more substantial portrait of discrimination.[12]

There are other reasons why the existing survey data do not adequately describe the reality of everyday racism. Most black and white Americans are taught as children to focus on individual reasons for personal barriers or failures. Most are taught that blaming others, however legitimate that may seem, is generally not appropriate. The reasoning behind such socialization seems to be that a system-blame orientation makes a person seem weak to those she or he respects. Some black Americans who suffer from discrimination may thus feel that talking too much about racist barriers suggests that they as individuals are not capable of dealing with these difficulties. However, this reluctance to report to survey researchers some of the discrimination they experience does not mean that the discrimination is not harmful in the respondent's life.

In addition, the terminology used in most surveys leads to underestimates. The term "discrimination" itself is used by some black Americans only for very serious abuse by whites. Lesser forms of mistreatment, because they are so commonplace, may not be characterized as discrimination. For example, a young black college professor recently explained to me that he does not ordinarily think of certain everyday examples of differential treatment—such as white cashiers not putting money in his hand because they do not want to touch a black person—as "racial discrimination." It is the more serious incidents of racism that he would recall if asked a question by a pollster about having encountered racial discrimination recently. Racial obstacles are so much a part of black lives that they generally become a part of the societal woodwork. This "everydayness" of racist barriers means that for many black Americans a survey researcher's brief question about discrimination will bring quickly to mind primarily the more serious incidents that stay at the front of the mind—and sometimes not the many intrusions of more subtle racism that occur in one's life. A failure to recall some incidents with whites when questioned briefly does not mean these encounters are of little consequence. In order to survive in a racist society, black Americans cannot attend consciously to all the racist incidents that intrude on their lives. The personal and family cost of too-close attention to much discrimination is too great.

To my knowledge, there is no research on the frequency of the incidents and events of discrimination faced by individual black Americans over their lifetimes. In a few exploratory interviews with black respondents, I have asked a question about frequency and gotten large estimates in response. For example, I asked a retired printer from New York City how often he has faced discrimination over the course of his life. After some careful reflection, this man estimated that he confronts at least 250 significant incidents of discrimination from whites each year, if he only includes the incidents that he consciously notices and records. Blatant and subtle mistreatment by white clerks in stores and restaurants are examples he had in mind. Judging from my own field studies using in-depth interviews with black Americans, this man's experience seems representative. Over the course of a lifetime, a typical black man or woman likely faces *thousands* of instances of blatant, covert, or subtle discrimination at the hands of whites. Today, this omnipresent and routinized discrimination remains a key mechanism in the social reproduction of systemic racism.

Patterns of Discrimination in Political and Legal Institutions   For centuries now, the state, local, and federal governments have been proactive in protecting and expanding the system of racial oppression. As we have seen in previous chapters, government actions have generally favored the interests of white Americans. Thus, government programs historically provided much access to land and many other valuable resources exclusively to white Americans. Coupled with this "affirmative action" for whites, governments created and reinforced patterns of exclusion targeting black Americans and other Americans of color. Over centuries the white-dominated legislative, executive, and judicial branches of local, state, and federal governments upheld slavery and legal segregation. Governments have usually represented white interests.

Discrimination in Voting and Representation   In 1915 the U.S. Supreme Court finally began to knock down state segregation laws that severely discriminated against black voters. Over the decades since, black voters have been allowed back into the southern political system. Yet, increases in political representation in the South and the North have come slowly. In 1945, Adam Clayton Powell, Jr., elected from New York, became only the fourth black American to serve as a member of Congress in the twentieth century. The 1960s civil rights movement forced major legislative changes, including passage of the 1965 Voting Rights Act. By the 1970s, in part because of enforcement of this act, several million black citizens were again voting in the South. As a result, the number of black elected officials has increased from a few dozen in the mid-1960s to several thousand today.

Nonetheless, in many areas black voters are still unable to elect black officials in representative numbers; and, where they are able to elect some representatives, the latter are often unable to make their voices heard in white-dominated legislative bodies. Researchers have identified an array of blocking strategies used by white officials to reduce black representation: gerrymandering political districts, changing elective offices into appointive offices, adding new qualifications for office, purging voter-registration rolls, suddenly changing the location of polling places, creating difficult registration procedures, and using numerous other strategies to dilute the black vote. One dilution strategy consists of intentionally setting up or continuing at-large electoral systems, instead of utilizing elections by smaller districts. The purpose is to enable white voters, who dominate the larger political unit, to determine who will be the political representatives in that unit. Research data on local and state elections indicate that, taken together, these strategies have significantly reduced black political power in many areas.[13]

African Americans and other Americans of color have had difficulty even in getting white opinion makers and policymakers to take their proposals for increased political representation seriously. For example, during the mid-1990s President Bill Clinton attempted to nominate Lani Guinier, a leading scholar on political rights issues, to be an assistant attorney general. White conservatives attacked her scholarly views on increasing political democracy by using the racist stereotype of black "welfare queens." Guinier was smeared with the label of "quota queen" by white commentators, even though her proposals for political reform were well thought out and workable, and several had been made by other leading experts. For instance, to deal with the problem of a lack of black political influence in areas where there are significant numbers of black voters who, because they are a statistical minority, are regularly outvoted by whites, Guinier suggested a procedure called "cumulative voting." In this procedure, which has been tried in several cities,

each voter gets a number of votes equal to the number of positions open on a legislative body. Thus, where there are six positions open on a commission, each voter
gets six votes and may give all votes to one candidate or distribute them across several candidates. This strategy allows black voters to concentrate their votes and,
often, to elect at least one black candidate in districts where otherwise black representatives would not be elected. Reform strategies aimed at increasing black
input into the political system were rejected without even a fair hearing, and
Clinton withdrew Guinier's nomination.[14]

Since 1800 many political campaigns at the local, state, and federal levels have
been riddled with racial issues. Numerous recent campaigns by members of the
Republican and Democratic parties have made use of appeals, blatant or subtle,
to white voters. Recall Richard Nixon's "southern strategy," which was designed
to attract white southerners from the Democratic Party to the Republican Party.
Recall too the use of stereotypes of black men as rapists in George Bush's 1988 presidential campaign. In recent years, indeed, it appears that some key members of
the Republican Party (see chapters 4 and 8) have decided that the party should
become primarily a party for white Americans, with at best token appeals to the
political interests of black Americans. Since at least the late 1960s the Republican
Party has shown little interest in the civil rights issues of great concern to most
black voters. While the Democratic Party has seen far more participation by black
Americans in its deliberations and stated policies, since the 1980s its white elected
officials have also failed to increase the input of black Americans into state and
national policymaking to a truly representative level. Today, more than 130 years
after African Americans officially gained access to the political process by means
of the post–Civil War amendments to the Constitution, the promises of fair political representation and policy input remain to be fulfilled.

Discrimination in the "Justice" System   We saw earlier the critical role of the
Supreme Court in maintaining white dominance in such cases as *Dred Scott v.
Sanford*, which upheld slavery and the degradation of black Americans, and *Plessy
v. Ferguson*, which legitimated segregation after the Civil War. This is the historical legacy. Today, whites still benefit greatly from a legal system of their own making, one that favors the broad interests of whites as a group. It is not sufficient, as
the founders made clear in their criticisms of British rule, for there only to be equality in access to the law. There must be fair representation in the creation of laws.
This is not yet a reality in the United States. At the top of the legal system black
Americans make up less than two percent of the officials, including state attorney
generals, district attorneys, leading civil and criminal lawyers, and the judges in
major state and federal courts. Other Americans of color are also greatly under-
represented. Given the fact that a greatly disproportionate share of decision makers at the top of the system are white, it is not surprising that white assumptions
and interests routinely predominate. The assumptions of those whites still in con-

trol include (1) the idea that racial inequality is no longer a serious societal problem needing significant government intervention and redress, and (2) the notion that the legal system currently operates in a generally fair and nonracist fashion.

Consider the major Supreme Court case discussed briefly in chapter 3, *City of Richmond, Virginia v. J. A. Croson Co.* (1989).[15] In that case a white-run construction company argued that a city of Richmond program setting aside business for black and other minority companies was unconstitutional. Knocking down the set-aside program, a majority of the Supreme Court agreed and ruled the city had not made a compelling case for the program and had not demonstrated the continuing reality of racial discrimination. However, city officials had shown that, in a city whose population was half black, less than one percent (0.67 percent) of city business went to black firms. The high court also dismissed the testimony of numerous city officials—including council members, a former mayor, and the city manager—to the effect that legal segregation had for many decades been the rule in the city and that racial discrimination in construction contracting was still commonplace. Arguments that large-scale racial discrepancies in business development indicated a high probability of racist practices by white businesses were rejected by the high court's white majority.

Justice Sandra Day O'Connor, writing for the plurality, did note "the sorry history of both private and public discrimination in this country" and recognized the reality of "past societal discrimination." Yet she accented the "past," not the present, and described societal discrimination as "amorphous" and having no clear link to the present-day reality of black business conditions in contemporary Richmond. As one legal critic has put it, the use of the term "amorphous" here means that for the court's white majority societal discrimination is "something sporadic, erratic, and diffuse—something that leaves no clearly demarcated traces and produces no readily ascertainable direct effects."[16] Yet the traces of past discrimination in any U.S. city, as the data in this chapter demonstrate, are major, evident, and anything but sporadic. Once again, whites in power sought to deny the long centuries of slavery, segregation, and modern racism.

In addition, the white majority in the Croson case bought into the old racist idea that the problems of black Americans are the result of their own values and choices: "There are numerous explanations for this dearth of minority participation [in construction businesses], including . . . black and white career and entrepreneurial choices. Blacks may be disproportionately attracted to industries other than construction."[17] Here the majority suggests that black Americans—who have much experience as construction workers—do not go into construction contracting businesses just because of personal preferences. In making such a quaint argument the judges provided *no* evidence. Indeed, they made the racist assumption that black Americans are less economically rational than whites—that is, that they do not like to make money or do not like to prosper economically. Such a notion of disparate rationality is, as Martin Katz puts it, "racist and without any evidentiary basis."[18]

In a stinging dissent, the court's only black justice up to that point in U.S. history (1989), Justice Thurgood Marshall, concluded that "a majority of this Court signals that it regards racial discrimination as largely a phenomenon of the past, and that government bodies need no longer preoccupy themselves with rectifying racial injustice. I, however, do not believe this Nation is anywhere close to eradicating racial discrimination or its vestiges."[19] The idea of eradication, he noted, represents "wishful thinking" on the part of these white justices.

The legal scholar Jerome Culp has probed for the deeper assumptions lying behind these Supreme Court arguments. One assumption, which he views as white supremacist, is that "the interests of black Americans are not considered important enough to be examined or put into the constitutional calculus—the interest blindness assumption."[20] White group interests again took precedence over black group interests. The interests and concerns of black Americans in cities like Richmond are not hard to discover. Most black Americans there and elsewhere report racial discrimination in many areas of their lives, including the employment and business arenas, and seek to end that discrimination. They strongly support aggressive affirmative action and set-aside programs seeking to remedy past and present discrimination. From everyday experience most also know the justice system to be racially biased.[21]

Police Malpractice   The nation's racial hierarchy is routinely supported and reproduced by the actions of a broad array of government agents. White police officers have historically played, and still play, a major role in the violent repression of black Americans, including those who seek to protest racism. The data on police violence in U.S. history are chilling. For example, in the years 1920–1932 substantially *more than half* of all African Americans killed by whites were killed by police officers. In addition, police were often implicated in the six thousand lynchings of black men and women from the 1870s to the 1960s. In recent decades, police harassment and violence have been openly resisted by black Americans. Analysis of black community riots for the years 1943 to 1972 indicates that the immediate precipitating event of many uprisings was the killing or harassment of black men by white officers. Rioters openly protested this practice.[22] This reaction to police harassment can also be seen in more recent rioting by black citizens, such as in Los Angeles and Miami in the 1980s and 1990s.

In spite of some improvements in policing since the 1970s, police violence and mistreatment have continued to oppress black communities. A Gallup survey found that over half the African Americans polled thought most police officers viewed African Americans as criminal suspects and would be likely to arrest the wrong person for a crime. In addition, a quarter of black men indicated they had been harassed by the police when driving through white areas.[23] In a 1990 survey of 1,901 Los Angeles residents, half the black respondents felt there was a fair amount of police brutality there, twice the percentage of the white respondents.[24] A recent Gallup survey asked if black respondents had faced discrimination from the police in the last month. Fifteen percent of all the respondents, and 34 percent of the young men, reported problems with the police.[25] Unquestionably, young black men are frequently targeted for harassment by the police.

Since 1994 the U.S. government has been legally required to collect data on police brutality. However, the conservative Congresses in power after that date have failed to appropriate money to collect these important data. One social science study suggests what such data might show. Analyzing 130 police-brutality accounts in several cities across the nation, Kim Lersch discovered that the targets of this type of police malpractice are *almost always* black or Latino. The latter made up 97 percent of the victims of police brutality. Yet the overwhelming majority (93 percent) of officers involved in these incidents were white.[26] Police brutality mainly involves white-on-black or white-on-Latino violence. Moreover, it appears that white elites in many cities sometimes use or allow police harassment in order to keep black residents "in their place." Some police harassment and brutality targeting Americans of color seem to be linked to maintaining de facto housing segregation. Since the days of slavery, being "out of place" has been potentially dangerous for black Americans, especially black men. If black men are found in historically white residential areas, they still run the risk of harassment by the public or private police forces there.

This type of differential policing is sometimes defended as so-called statistical, or rational, discrimination. Many law enforcement agencies engage in the practice of screening by visual racial markers. In a recent account from a black flight attendant we see the impact of this stereotyped policing. The woman was waiting to fly on personal business in Denver's Stapleton airport. According to the account, a white man approached her and "asked if he could search her purse and luggage. She refused because she did not believe the man was a law enforcement officer. He shoved her against a wall. Two other men approached, showed badges and searched her forcibly."[27] Nothing was found, but the officers broke her finger in the process. Under the U.S. Constitution citizens have a right to be secure from unreasonable search and seizure. An officer must have a reasonable suspicion to stop someone. The "reasonable" suspicion in this case seemed to be based mainly on the woman's skin color.

Highway stops by various police agencies reveal a similar type of racial profiling. As in the Oklahoma case mentioned in the introduction, many law enforcement agencies screen and stop motorists according to their racial characteristics—what many black Americans call the offense of "driving while black" (DWB). For several years, in Florida's Volusia county, sheriff's deputies stopped drivers on a major highway searching for drugs. Most of those stopped were black or Latino, although only five percent of the drivers on that highway were black or Latino.

The sheriff's office contended that blacks and Latinos are more likely to be drug couriers. Police officers have been documented stopping mostly black and Latino motorists on suspicion of having drugs in several other states, including Mississippi, New Jersey, and Pennsylvania. Some government officials have openly admitted that racial profiling is police policy. Since many whites are predisposed to see blacks and Latinos as criminals, this stop-and-search pattern is not surprising and has engendered little protest from whites. However, in spite of their popularity, no government agency has shown the drug courier profiles to be valid.[28] Indeed, the majority of drug couriers are likely to be white, as are most drug users and pushers. Such unnecessary screening has led to police shootings of black motorists and pedestrians in numerous U.S. cities.

All types of law enforcement agencies have engaged in this racial profiling. For example, one study of body searches by U.S. customs officials found that 43 percent of all those searched were black or Latino.[29] In June 1999, President Bill Clinton made a strong statement that racial profiling by federal agencies was "wrong" and "destructive" and ordered law enforcement agencies to collect data on the extent of racial and gender profiling. However, it remains to be seen if such scrutiny will reduce this official discrimination.[30]

More Court Discrimination   Racial discrimination extends beyond policing to the court system. Few judges in the criminal justice system are black, and most white judges appear to have little understanding of the lives of the black Americans—mostly working-class or poor people—that they often face; they do not come from the same community or socioeconomic backgrounds as the black defendants in their courtrooms. Not surprisingly, some white judges thus discriminate against those in the courtroom. One New Haven, Connecticut, study of 1118 local arrests did a statistical analysis of bail-related variables and found that "after controlling for eleven variables relating to the severity of the alleged offense, bail amounts set for black male defendants [by judges] were 35 percent higher than those set for their white male counterparts."[31] In contrast, the researchers found that local bond dealers charged significantly lower bonding rates for black defendants than for whites. The bond dealers set their rates based on experience with defendants fleeing from prosecution, and the probability of flight was greater for whites than blacks. The researchers concluded that this is strong evidence of discrimination in bail setting in the justice system, saying, "Judges could have reduced bail amounts for minority males without incurring flight risks higher than those deemed acceptable for white male defendants."[32]

There is other evidence of racial discrimination. For example, there is differential punishment for two types of cocaine use. One criminal lawyer has recently explained, "Powder cocaine is a drug of the affluent suburbs, while crack is used and sold in the inner cities. Since 1986, people convicted in federal court of possessing just five grams of crack cocaine . . . face a mandatory sentence of at least five years in prison—and when you get five years of federal time, you do almost all of it. But those caught with powder cocaine must be in possession of 500 grams to get the same five-year sentence. . . . And day after day, black men are moved out of their homes and communities to serve stiffer sentences than their white, powder-using counterparts."[33] There has been no change in these laws in spite of evidence they are discriminatory. Moreover, while illegal drug use is as common among white men as among black men, black men are far more likely than white men to be arrested for drug crimes.[34] This is one major reason why there are unnecessarily large numbers of black men in jails and prisons.

During the 1990s some 350 Americans were put to death. And in the late 1990s there were about 3,300 people on death row across the country. Institutional discrimination is evident in the application of the death penalty in the past and the present. For example, between 1908 and 1962 *all* those put to death for rape in the state of Virginia were black, even though 45 percent of those convicted for rape were white. Between 1930 and 1967 black men made up 89 percent of all those executed for rape across the nation. For several decades it has been the case that, although white victims and black victims of murder are about equal in number, it is mostly those who kill whites who get sentenced to death. Killers of black people are much less likely to be sentenced to death. Moreover, one recent Philadelphia study found that black defendants were four times as likely as white defendants to get the death penalty for murder, even when aggravating factors were taken into account. Across the nation, 42 percent of those on death row are black, although blacks are just 12 percent of the population.[35] Racism is not just in the minds of whites; it also results in differential punishment.

Significantly, those who decide on pursuing the death penalty in this criminal injustice system, the district attorneys and similar state officials, are overwhelmingly white. For example, in 1998, only 22 (1.2 percent) of 1,838 such government officials were black. Whites overwhelmingly control who lives and who dies after committing murder. Moreover, in many areas of the country black jurors are knocked out of jury pools by the use of peremptory challenges by prosecutors, in clear violation of a Supreme Court decision requiring race-neutral reasons for such exclusion. White district attorneys desire this exclusion for racial reasons, as one training video for Philadelphia prosecutors makes clear. "Let's face it," the video says, "the blacks from low-income areas are less likely to convict. There's a resentment to law enforcement."[36] Those potential jurors who might disagree with the views and judgments of white authorities are thereby excluded from participation in the workings of the justice system.

Violence against African Americans

The Long History   For several centuries whites have used much brutal violence—from chains and whippings to lynchings and other mob violence—to keep African Americans racially subordinated. From the 1620s to the 1960s, violent acts

by whites acting individually and collectively were a recurring part of this subordination. Violent practices were engaged in not only by ordinary whites but also
by members of the elites, including leading slaveholders such as Thomas Jefferson,
George Washington, and James Madison. After the Civil War, many whites were
fearful of newly freed black Americans and engaged in large-scale violence to create and maintain the system of enforced segregation. The emerging system of legal
segregation was often enforced with private and police violence. Indeed, into the
late 1990s some southerners still serving in the U.S. Congress had earlier been outspoken advocates of the violence-enforced system of American apartheid.

Today, many whites exhibit naïveté or willing ignorance about this brutal history of enforced segregation and violence. For example, one white caller to a radio
talk show assessing public reaction to a jury's decision that athlete O. J. Simpson
was not guilty of murder suggested half-jokingly that whites should riot over this
verdict. The talk-show host and subsequent callers concluded that, of course,
"white people don't riot."[37] These whites, once again, show great ignorance of U.S.
history. Virtually all racial riots in U.S. cities from the 1840s to the 1930s—and there
were many—were characterized by whites attacking or killing African Americans.
In the decades just before the Civil War, whites rioted against free black workers
a dozen times in the cities of the North. In 1863, during the Civil War, many white
workers in New York City rioted for days over draft laws and the use of black workers to break a local strike. In that rioting at least one hundred people, including
numerous black Americans, were killed—the largest number for any riot in U.S.
history. Moreover, the decades after the Civil War saw many killings of black men,
women, and children at the hands of white mobs, including lynchings and terrorist attacks by Klan-type groups. Sometimes entire black communities—such as
Rosewood, Florida—were destroyed, with their residents driven out or killed.

In the early 1900s there were many more riots by whites targeting African
Americans. There was a major riot in East St. Louis in 1917. Whites workers, upset
about job competition from black workers, rioted and killed 39 black residents.
There were seven major riots by whites in 1919—in Longview, Texas; Phillips
County, Arkansas; Washington, D.C.; Chicago, Illinois; Knoxville, Tennessee;
and Omaha, Nebraska. The growing competition between black and white workers was often an underlying factor in this white rioting, and the all-white police
forces often took the side of white rioters. Mob violence targeted black communities over the next several decades. As late as the 1960s, white mob violence against
nonviolent civil rights demonstrators could be seen regularly on television.[38]

Recent White Violence   Attacks on black Americans are still part of the U.S. landscape. The number of racially-motivated crimes ("hate crimes") has increased in
the last two decades. Thousands of attacks on black Americans and other
Americans of color were reported each year in the 1990s. Some incidents have
involved the scrawling of racist graffiti on homes and cars or aggressive verbal

harassment of pedestrians or coworkers, while other attacks were more violent. For example, an Iowa doctor had a firebomb thrown through his window during the night, and the word "nigger" was scratched into his car's paint. A Texas family was hit with eggs and their car was set on fire just outside their home. In the spring of 1990 a group of white youths killed a black youth, Yusuf Hawkins, in New York's Bensonhurst area simply because the attackers thought he should not have been in their area. There have been numerous assaults and killings of this type across the nation.[39]

Some attacks are group lynchings. In 1987 one small Ku Klux Klan group was found responsible by a court in the lynching of a black man, Michael Donald, in Mobile, Alabama. More recently, in June 1998, a black man, James Byrd, Jr., was walking down a Jasper, Texas, road. Three white men, with tattoos suggesting ties to white-supremacist groups, beat him savagely, tied him to a pickup, and dragged him along a road until his head and arms were severed. One man reportedly said to the others, "We're starting *The Turner Diaries* early," referring to violence by white supremacists in that racist novel (see below). The girlfriend of one of the men said that, while she knew he was a member of the Aryan Brotherhood and did not like blacks, she did not see him as a racist.[40] This lynching was not just an isolated incident. Indeed, it brought to national attention the larger social context of antiblack violence. After the lynching a Ku Klux Klan group held a rally for the white supremacist cause in Jasper. In addition, this area of Texas is known to be white supremacist territory. A white militia group has a training facility in the county, and a few Christian Identity churches are in nearby towns.[41] The Jasper lynching triggered copycat crimes in at least two other cities, Belleville, Illinois, and Slidell, Louisiana, where several white men in cars reportedly attacked and injured black men.

The Jasper lynching and similar attacks on black men and women, as well as such attacks on other Americans of color, are most often carried out by working-class whites. Yet the responses of some elite and middle-class whites to the Jasper lynching revealed a certain indifference to these crimes. For example, the first *New York Times* article on the Jasper lynching was buried on page 16; the bloody lynching did not rise to the level of a front page story. In addition, one *New York Times* article spent considerable space on the problems of the black victim himself, describing his alcoholism and unemployment—as if such things mattered in assessing the meaning of his Klan-type lynching.[42]

Vicious harassment of black men and women remains all too common in the United States. A few months before the Jasper lynching, the ABC news program "20/20" recounted the harrowing story of Roy Smith, a longtime resident of a Colorado town. Smith, a black man, was attacked, beaten, and terrorized for several years by white residents. At one point, several whites strung him up by his feet in his cabin. Yet the local sheriff's department did not investigate the attacks and ignored his complaints, even listing him as "Nigger Roy" in their computer. Smith eventually had to file a lawsuit against the sheriff's department and won a major judgment against them.[43]

White supremacist groups have threatened larger-scale violence against black Americans and other Americans of color. The 1995 bombing of an Oklahoma City federal building by antigovernment activists who were white supremacists killed 169 people. A few months later, several bomb plots were uncovered, one targeting the Southern Poverty Law Center in Montgomery (an anti-Klan organization) and two others targeting federal buildings in Spokane and Austin.[44] Many antigovernment militia and white supremacist groups are made up of white (Christian) men who are angry about current social and economic conditions in the United States. When white workers face economic difficulties, many of them have turned to standard scapegoats as explanations—to blacks, Jews, or new immigrants as the villains behind their problems. One influential writer is William Pierce, a physicist and author of the racist *Turner Diaries* (1978). The widely circulated book describes a fictional uprising against the federal government by armed white supremacist revolutionaries who blow up a federal building. The book is popular in some militia and supremacist groups and is reported to have been read by Timothy McVeigh, the man convicted of the Oklahoma City bombing.[45]

In recent years members of the white militia and supremacy groups have reportedly stockpiled weapons and explosives, and have prepared bombing ventures. As we move into the twenty-first century there are hundreds of Klan, neo-Nazi, skinhead, and other white supremacist groups. An estimated two hundred thousand whites are active or passive supporters of such groups.[46] Significantly, little law enforcement activity seems to be directed at restricting the development of these openly racist and often violence-oriented organizations.

The Spatial Basis of Systemic Racism: Housing Segregation

Creating Segregated Neighborhoods   If we view the layout and activities of a typical city from a few hundred feet above the streets, the spatial structure of modern residential apartheid can be seen. For the most part blacks live separately from whites, and the latter are often separated from other Americans of color as well. Moreover, if we look closely, we can see whites and blacks moving about their daily routines, but we will likely find that blacks are more likely to cross the racial/territorial boundaries of towns and cities than whites. On the average, blacks spend much more time interacting with whites than whites spend interacting with blacks. There is a clear racial demography and topography to U.S. towns and cities.

Several research studies have shown that all metropolitan areas in both the North and the South have a high degree of racial segregation. Between 1980 and 1990 there were only small decreases in the level of white-black segregation in thirty major metropolitan areas, less change than there was for the decade from 1970 to

1980. Researchers have calculated indices of segregation for these cities and estimated that, on the average, two-thirds of the black residents of the southern metropolitan areas and more than three-quarters of those in northern metropolitan
areas would have to move from their present residential areas if one wished to create proportional desegregation in housing arrangements by redistributing the black
population in these areas. The high level of residential segregation from whites
characterizes all groups of black Americans, including those in the middle class.[47]

Slavery Unwilling to Die   The roots of this residential segregation are centuries
deep. Systemic racism has long involved control of space and territory. There is
today a town in the panhandle of Florida where the housing is segregated across
the proverbial railroad tracks, and the black area is still termed the "Quarters," a
name lingering from slavery days. There are numerous other mostly black areas
in various towns and cities that carry names given to them during the eras of slavery, Reconstruction, or legal segregation. Since the 1600s, being defined as "black"
has meant limitations on where one can work, live, and travel. During the centuries of slavery, most of those enslaved were separated in slave quarters, and their
spatial movements were controlled by law and violence. After slavery, southern
elites created an extensive system of segregation, following the lead of northern
states. Before the Civil War, the Jim Crow laws in the North enforced separate
housing areas at a time when southern cities had no comparable segregation (those
enslaved often lived near the residences of slavemasters).[48] Firmly in place by the
early 1900s, the rigid segregation of blacks from whites in housing and many other
institutional areas could be seen in all parts of the nation.

Today, housing segregation provides empirical evidence of the impact of past
and present oppression on African Americans. In the residential segregation of
black and white Americans we see what the Supreme Court, in a pathbreaking
1968 decision, *Jones v. Alfred H. Mayer Co.*, called "a relic of slavery." Ruling on
a housing discrimination case in St. Louis, the majority of this court argued that
current discrimination is a long-term consequence of slavery, saying that "this
Court recognized long ago that, whatever else they may have encompassed, the
badges and incidents of slavery — its 'burdens and disabilities'—included restraints
upon 'those fundamental rights which are the essence of civil freedom, namely,
the same right . . . to inherit, purchase, lease, sell and convey property, as is enjoyed
by white citizens.'"[49] The court further reasoned that the Thirteenth Amendment
abolishing slavery was intended to eradicate the badges and disabilities of slavery:
"If Congress cannot say that being a free man means at least this much, then the
Thirteenth Amendment made a promise the Nation cannot keep."[50] In a concurring opinion, Justice William O. Douglas used even stronger language, saying,
"the true curse of slavery is not what it did to the black man, but what it has done
to the white man. For the existence of the institution produced the notion that the
white man was of superior character, intelligence, and morality. . . . Some badges

of slavery remain today. While the institution has been outlawed, it has remained in the minds and hearts of many white men. Cases which have come to this Court depict a spectacle of slavery unwilling to die."[51] Douglas then listed the many kinds of discrimination still faced by African Americans (see chapter 2). For a brief period in its long history, the Supreme Court dug into the workings of systemic racism.

Systemic racism is maintained by social inheritance mechanisms that transmit wealth and privilege over the generations. Each generation of whites inherits a large-scale array of racial privileges, including the ability to enter residential areas and job settings reserved more or less for whites—and thereby the ability to build up family wealth in the form of housing equity. In parallel with the social transmission of white privileges is the transmission of racist barriers for black Americans.

Housing Discrimination Today   For the first 350 years of colonial and U.S. development, residential segregation was often legally imposed on black Americans. After the 1968 Civil Rights Act went into effect, this residential segregation became more informal, as it remains today. One factor maintaining this segregation is the array of racist images and attitudes held in many white minds. Many whites get fearful when the black percentage of the population reaches a modest level. Research has shown that, when a predominantly white residential area becomes more than about eight percent black, some whites will consider moving out. As the percentage reaches about 20 percent in what was once an all-white or nearly all-white residential neighborhood, many whites will not consider moving into such an area, and it will often become a mostly black or nonwhite community. It is estimated that just one in twenty U.S. neighborhoods is both racially diverse *and* stable. The rest are segregated or are diverse but unstable and in the process of becoming more segregated.[52] Segregation is enforced by the open hostility of white homeowners, occasional violence against black families, and whites deciding not to move into already integrated areas, as well as by the racial steering and related discriminatory practices found in the real estate industry.

Housing discrimination cuts across a variety of institutions and includes a range of white discriminators—landlords, homeowners, bankers, realtors, and government officials. Research studies suggest that many whites in each group will discriminate under certain circumstances. One major reason for segregated housing is the continuing discrimination by rental housing owners, managers, and real estate salespeople. In the last decade a number of audit studies, using white and black testers (and sometimes Asian and Latino testers), have demonstrated that racial barriers in housing are commonplace. For example, one major federal research project did 3,800 test audits in two dozen metropolitan areas. The researchers estimated that black renters faced discriminatory treatment by landlords about 53 percent of the time, while black homeseekers faced discriminatory treatment by real estate salespeople about 59 percent of the time.[53] In addition, four 1995 to 1997 audit studies conducted in Fresno, San Antonio, New Orleans, and Montgomery by local housing groups found even higher rates of racist barriers for black renters, who, when they went to look for places to rent faced discrimination between 61 and 77 percent of the time, depending on the city. Moreover, a recent Washington, D.C., audit study found that black testers seeking to buy a home faced racist barriers one-third of the time, a figure that increased to fifty percent in some D.C. suburbs.[54]

One should note that these percentages are likely to be low estimates of the range of housing discrimination faced by black Americans. The housing testers usually do not advance to later stages of renting or buying, where additional antiblack discrimination might occur. Moreover, many applicants for housing are steered away from predominantly white areas and into mixed or all black areas, a type of avoidance discrimination which they may not even be aware of. One white rationalization for housing segregation is that "blacks prefer to live with their kind." The audit data raise serious questions about this old notion. In fact, black man and women often try to improve their housing situations by seeking an apartment or home in traditionally white or newly integrated areas, yet run into entrenched opposition. Indeed, a survey of black, white, Latino, and Asian groups in Los Angeles found that black respondents were the most open to living in integrated neighborhoods and did not express opposition to other groups. In contrast, those in the white group, as well as in the Latino and Asian groups, ranked black families as the least preferred neighbors.[55]

Insurance Agents and Lenders   Many white-run insurance and banking businesses create subtle or blatant housing barriers for black Americans, as well as for other Americans of color. A recent study used black, Latino, and white testers, who presented themselves as homeowners seeking insurance to three major insurance companies' offices in nine cities. The researchers found the overall rate of racial discrimination to be 53 percent—ranging from 32 percent in Memphis to 83 percent in Chicago—in regard to such things as insurance coverage and price. They found that being white increased insurance options and saved money.[56] The process of unjust enrichment and advantage continues in many housing-related institutions.

For many years federal government regulations openly fostered racial discrimination in lending. Only since the 1960s have federal regulations sought to ban lending discrimination. For example, the 1968 Civil Rights Act and the Equal Credit Opportunity Act prohibit mortgage discrimination. Nonetheless, recent research documents continued, widespread discrimination by banking institutions against black Americans and other people of color who seek mortgages or loans. One report by the federal Office of Thrift Supervision found that across the nation black loan applicants are rejected by savings and loan associations at twice the rate as whites. A Federal Reserve Board study of more than six million bank mortgages found that 34 percent of black applications were rejected, compared to only 14 percent of white applications.[57] Such studies have been criticized by some in the lending industry for not considering the income or credit records of the applicants rejected. However, other major studies have controlled for factors such as income and credit records that supposedly account for racial differentials in loans, yet they have still found "racial differences in denial rates across all markets and for all loan types."[58] The higher loan rejection rates for black applicants frequently seem to be the result of lenders assuming that borrowers must fit the image of an ideal white family seeking to buy in white, middle-class residential areas. Most black families cannot fit that image and may suffer discrimination as a result.[59]

One Los Angeles study discovered that black buyers seeking homes in traditionally white residential areas regularly faced discrimination by lenders and appraisers, such as "stringent scrutiny of past credit problems, disappointing appraisals and a reluctance on the part of private mortgage insurers to provide the insurance that lenders demand."[60] A leading housing expert, John Yinger, has reviewed several studies showing an array of discriminatory strategies used by lenders in urban areas. These discriminatory strategies include requiring of blacks (but not of whites) credit checks and other documentation prior to appointments with bankers, more restrictive qualification standards, and higher escrow and reserve account contributions. Whites are more likely to get waivers and constructive advice than similar black applicants for loans.[61]

Some lending discrimination appears to be motivated by a concern for what are termed "sound business practices," and thus does not appear to be intentionally antiblack. Lenders and property insurers frequently refuse to provide services—or provide services on unfavorable terms—for people seeking to buy older homes in areas where the valuations are lower. These homes are often in neighborhoods whose residents are black. Such lending practices can have a very negative impact on black homebuyers. As housing expert Gregory Squires has noted, "many of those underwriters and sales agents who follow these rules really do believe they are acting on the basis of sound business practice. In fact, many of these same individuals are simultaneously working on a range of reinvestment activities in efforts to counter the long-term and current effects of their industries' practices. Obviously, racism went into the formulation of such rules, and these industries no doubt have as many racists as any other. But such institutionalized practices, with severely discriminatory effects, are often carried out by people who simply are not thinking about race."[62] The routinization of racism in housing decisions is such that some whites who practice it may not be aware of it.

Black Americans have seldom been consulted by the white-run insurance companies and banking organizations that determine the rules favoring white homeseekers. Indeed, the willingness to employ blacks varies significantly across banks and other lending organizations. Recent research on five metropolitan areas indicates that lenders' workforce composition affects the loan approval rate: as the percentage of black administrators and professionals increases, the loan approval rate for black applicants also increases. When employees from traditionally excluded communities are included in the lenders' workplace, the knowledge of those communities and their applicants' situations among white decision makers there also expands. It appears that the better that knowledge is, the less common are the racial barriers.[63]

There are a variety of local, state, and federal government programs that have a negative impact on black residents of cities. One Dallas report found that homes in black residential areas were much more likely to be torn down by the city's Urban Rehabilitation Standards Board than similar homes in predominantly white areas. A city audit found that the board had often failed to notify black property owners of impending demolitions.[64] Using a variety of urban redevelopment approaches, white politicians and business leaders in many cities have tried to rebuild their cities, and in the process have often further segregated black families and destroyed older black communities. Since the 1950s urban redevelopment projects have taken black neighborhoods and converted them into business districts or gentrified residential areas mostly for affluent whites. Over the last few decades some capital has flowed back into some central city areas for construction of new commercial and housing projects. Older housing has been renovated to accommodate the white professional or managerial families wishing to return to central cities. Those whites moving back commonly demand neighborhood services and housing amenities comparable in quality to what they or their parents have had in the suburbs—and they usually get them. The surrounding areas occupied by working-class residents, frequently people of color, often have less than adequate public services and may become a prime target for redevelopment. In this way the disinvestment/investment process has a resegregating impact. The differentiation of racial groups is pushed to the logical extreme of making black residents of the central cities outsiders in what was once their own space.[65]

In the United States there is no national watchdog organization that proactively and aggressively seeks and punishes housing discrimination. When complaints are brought by victims of housing discrimination, they often get no redress for there is mostly weak enforcement of antidiscrimination laws. In most residential areas white landlords and real estate salespeople can discriminate more or less with impunity. One housing expert has estimated that of the twenty thousand fair housing complaints filed each year in the late 1990s less than one-third of these, perhaps six thousand, are resolved in a way that is satisfactory for the complainant.[66] Even these resolutions usually do not involve stiff penalties for the discriminators, penalties that might act to discourage future discrimination. Moreover, if one considers the millions of housing discrimination incidents that occur each year, probably not more than one case in every seven hundred is resolved to the satisfaction of the target of the discrimination.

Discrimination in Employment   Residential segregation makes possible, or strongly reinforces, numerous other types of racial exclusion, discrimination, and subordination. When residential segregation is extensive, job segregation tends to follow. Since World War II, racial polarization in U.S. cities has increased with the movement of white middle-income families to the suburbs—leaving behind a mostly working-class and poor population in many central cities. This suburban migration is stimulated by the investment decisions of large corporations, banks, and developers and has usually been assisted by federal subsidies for home mortgages and roads. Much employment has decentralized, and many suburbs have growing numbers of jobs for their often mostly white populations. The creation of better-paying jobs a long way from the central cities makes it difficult for many black Americans and other Americans of color to have reasonable access to new types of employment. This residential and job redistribution contributes to the racial polarization of metropolitan areas.[67]

As we saw in chapter 2, the exploited labor of enslaved black men, women, and children was critical to the creation of prosperity and development in the United States, including the building up of wealth and privilege for many white families over many generations. When slavery gave way to the near slavery of segregation, little changed in regard to the possibility of building up family wealth. Black labor was again exploited in white homes, factories, stores, and construction projects. Today, this exploitation remains an essential aspect of the tangible reality of oppression. Black labor is still exploited, and black workers still experience differential treatment in their attempts to secure their families' everyday needs and to build up heritable wealth. Sociologist William Julius Wilson has argued that the dominant group seeks "to control scarce resources either by eliminating or neutralizing subordinate racial members as competitors or by exploiting their labor."[68] Similarly, the black legal scholar Derrick Bell has concluded that a major function of discrimination today is "to facilitate the exploitation of black labor, to deny us access to benefits and opportunities that otherwise would be available, and to blame all the manifestations of exclusion-bred despair on the asserted inferiority of the victims."[69]

Today in the United States there is much evidence of widespread employment discrimination; each year a great many lawsuits are filed charging racial discrimination against white employers, and tens of thousands of employment discrimination complaints are filed annually with state agencies and the federal Equal Employment Opportunity Commission (EEOC). Not surprisingly, thus, recent surveys of black workers have found that they report high levels of discrimination. One major study of more than a thousand black workers found that about 60 percent reported racist barriers in their workplaces in the last year.[70] This pattern can be seen in other surveys as well. A 1997 Gallup survey found that one in five among the black respondents reported workplace discrimination in just the previous month.[71]

Discrimination in Hiring   Some differential treatment occurs at the point of hiring, while other mistreatment is encountered later on in the workplace itself. Many top corporate executives and their subordinate managers make little or no serious effort to recruit and hire black employees, especially in higher-level white-collar positions. Research studies using government records have found that many companies hire far fewer workers of color than some other comparable companies drawing from the *same* labor pools, a result suggesting routinized discrimination.[72] In addition, the U.S. Department of Labor Federal Contract Compliance Programs office examined 4,179 companies as of 1994. They found three-quarters to be violating federal regulations by not recruiting widely, by openly discriminating in hiring, or by not having an affirmative action plan.[73] These are companies that voluntarily do business with the federal government and agree, at least on paper, to abide by regulations mandating affirmative action efforts to remedy past and present patterns of discrimination.

In the hiring process, black workers are less likely to obtain jobs than whites with equivalent credentials. Several studies have shown that, when white and black applicants are both interviewed, proportionally more white applicants get job offers. Between 1989 and 1992 several studies of employment discrimination in semiskilled, entry-level jobs were conducted by the Fair Employment Council (FEC) of Washington, D.C., and the Urban Institute (UI). Using pairs of white and black testers, the researchers sent them to file job applications and to seek to be interviewed. Black testers faced discrimination at the interview or job-offer stage about 20 percent of the time in the FEC study (in the Washington, D.C., area) and about 38 percent of the time in the UI study (in Chicago and Washington, D.C.).[74] In the FEC study the white testers received substantially more positive comments in the interview setting, such as "you are just what we are looking for," than did the black testers. In addition, 47 percent of the white applicants who were interviewed got a job offer, compared to just 11 percent of the black applicants.[75]

In the view of many white employers only certain groups of workers are seen as acceptable, and individuals are judged by their group characteristics. White employers often argue that they choose white over black workers because they feel whites are as a group more productive, and they may defend such choices by recourse to the recurring notion that it is "rational" discrimination. However, the workers they deem unacceptable, such as black workers, are often just as qualified as those whites who are chosen.

One major study jointly sponsored by the Russell Sage Foundation and the Ford Foundation examined the situation of black workers and other workers of color in four large cities—Atlanta, Boston, Detroit, and Los Angeles. The researchers found that the movement of jobs from central cities to suburban areas by employers had a serious impact on black employment in the cities. This is a common research finding. However, this study also found that racial motivations were intertwined with this economic restructuring. Some employers seemed to intentionally choose workplace locations inaccessible to black workers. In Boston and Los Angeles surveys found that employers were more likely to express a desire to move away from neighborhoods with increasing numbers of black families than from other neighborhoods. The spatial mismatch of jobs in many cities, it appears, is often linked to an intentional movement away from black populations by investors.[76]

Moreover, numerous employers admitted that their hiring decisions involved stereotypes about the personality traits, attitudes, and behaviors of black workers and other workers of color. The researchers found that white employers held stereotyped images that white male and female workers perform better than black workers or other workers of color. Employers often rejected skilled black workers because of racial stereotypes. They had a mindset that black (and Latino) workers were best fit for lower-paying menial jobs regardless of their skills; black workers were often not considered for more skilled positions. Drawing on racial stereotypes, retail employers often tried to match white clerks with white customers. And in Boston researchers found that some employers preferred recent immigrants as employees even though black workers were better educated and lived closer to these workplaces. Research in Atlanta and Los Angeles also found that white men were usually supervised by white managers and supervisors; few workers of color, especially women of color, were hired to supervise white men. Not surprisingly, this major national study concluded that U.S. employment institutions are "still highly racialized at the ground level."[77]

Private employment agencies today control much of the applicant flow into white-collar jobs. The FEC study noted above found that "screening out 'undesirable' applicants is one of the services many employment agencies provide to their client firms."[78] In that study black testers posing as job applicants faced discrimination at private employment agencies about two-thirds of the time. Moreover, one recent Los Angeles study of employment conducted focus groups with whites, blacks, and other people of color. All groups recognized the important role of employment agencies and organizations in securing jobs. However, black workers were more likely to use public employment agencies, while whites were more likely to use private resources such as college placement offices. In black workers' experience, many private agencies seem oriented to white workers. In addition, the black workers in this study spoke extensively about discrimination and about being steered into low-wage jobs. Black workers and other workers of color spoke about "never being contacted again after submitting an application for jobs for which they were overqualified and being given misleading information by supervisors about how to obtain promotions."[79]

Racial barriers in hiring affect blacks at all class levels. Those who are well educated are at least as likely as the less well educated to report hiring and other workplace discrimination. One Los Angeles study of a thousand black workers found that about 80 percent of those with a college degree and almost all of those with a graduate-level education reported facing workplace discrimination, compared to just under half of those with less than a high school education. This study also found that a majority of highly educated Asian and Latino workers reported workplace discrimination.[80] Educational achievement brought *more* discrimination, probably because of the increased number of whites that better-educated Americans of color often work with. Even in liberal Hollywood there is much reported discrimination against black actors, directors, and writers. This is true despite the fact that African Americans make up a quarter of moviegoing audiences. Apart from the occasional feature movie centered around token stars like Whoopi Goldberg and Denzel Washington, most of Hollywood's productions employ few black Americans or other Americans of color in significant roles. Moreover, very few black Americans have received one of Hollywood's major achievement awards.[81]

Job Tracking and the Lack of Job Mobility   Racial oppression encompasses the exploitative relationship that enables white employers to take more of the value of the labor of workers of color than of comparable white workers. Today, as in the past, some white employers have paid black workers less because they are black. They do this directly, or they do it by segregating black workers into certain job categories and setting the pay for these categories lower than for predominantly white job classifications. The Marxist tradition has accented the way in which capitalist employers take part of the value of workers' labor for their own purposes — thus not paying workers for the full value of their work. That theft of labor is a major source of capitalists' profit. Similarly, white employers have the power, because of institutionalized discrimination, to take additional value from black workers and other workers of color. White employers can thus superexploit workers of color. This continuing exploitation of black workers not only helps to maintain income and wealth inequality across the color line but also is critical to the reproduction of the entire system of racism over long periods of time.

Present-day employers benefit from the lower wages they sometimes pay to black workers for the same work as white workers, as well as from divisions created between black and white workers that reduce the likelihood of cross-racial organization. Some of these divisions can be seen in job tracking and job segregation, which are still commonplace. A majority of black men still are employed in unskilled, semiskilled, service, or other relatively low-paid blue-collar jobs or in professional and managerial jobs disproportionately servicing black clients or consumers, or they are unemployed or in part-time employment. Black women tend to be concentrated in service jobs, other unskilled blue collar jobs, professional and managerial jobs oriented to black clients and consumers, or moderate-wage clerical jobs. They too face major unemployment and underemployment problems.

Barriers to promotions and advancement are common in many organizations. Black managerial employees in large corporations often find promotion avenues restricted. One field study in Chicago conducted seventy-six interviews with top black executives in major corporations. Most were found to be ghettoized in jobs oriented to civil rights, affirmative action, or serving black communities. Most had reached an early plateau in their corporate careers and had little chance to move further up the corporate ladders. Not surprisingly, many black workers at all job levels report discrimination in promotions.[82]

Discrimination in promotions, assignments, and career enhancement has been reported for black military personnel. A recent major survey of 40,000 U.S. military personnel—including enlisted members and officers—found that 18 percent of the black personnel had faced racial discrimination in regard to their assignments or their career just during the last year. (The proportion would likely be much larger if reported for their entire careers.) In addition, another Pentagon survey of black officers found that a recurring complaint was that they did not get the same quality of mentoring as white officers. Officers of color were also less likely to be brought into the informal social networks that often provide the critical information necessary for doing well on the promotion ladder. For many black officers this lack of mentoring and lesser access to networks can restrict their ability to take advantage of career-enhancing assignments, and this in turn reduces their ability to be competitive with whites for continuing promotions up the military job ladder. A lack of mentoring is a serious problem for many black employees in historically white organizations in both the public and the private sectors.[83]

In certain professional sports, where there are many black players and merit is easily demonstrated, there is still racial discrimination and informal segregation. One study of 1,455 National Football League players found segregation by position, with whites disproportionately represented at quarterback, kicker, and offensive line positions, and players of color, mainly blacks, disproportionately represented at defensive back, running back, and wide receiver positions. This differential placement may be discrimination by NFL coaches, or it could be the effect of discrimination by coaches and others at earlier levels of play, such as college, that is carried over. The study also found that white players averaged about four percent more salary than players of color. Other research studies have revealed more substantial salary differentials between black and white basketball players.[84]

Moreover, as we noted previously, a major problem facing black workers concentrated in blue-collar jobs is their abandonment by capitalists who repeatedly restructure the economy to meet the goal of ever-renewed profit. Many jobs, especially the less-skilled, are being moved overseas by capitalist investors seeking low-wage labor and less government regulation. Many of the employers who dominate the U.S. economy no longer need as much black labor as they once did. By their overseas and other investment strategies they have created high unemployment and underemployment for many black workers and some other workers of color. In a type of economic triage, black workers can be dispensed with whenever this is necessary for the profitability of capitalism.[85]

Cycles of relative prosperity in the U.S. economy should not mislead us. Even when most media pundits describe the U.S. economy as "very good," a great many workers—especially black workers and other workers of color—are unemployed, or underemployed in low-wage or part-time jobs. If the economy turns sour, as it periodically does, many black workers face even worse conditions. When they are no longer needed, the less-skilled black workers are kept as a "reserve army," in a condition of painful poverty and unemployment, or in the prison-industrial complex, until they may be needed again. It is significant that at no point in the decades since the 1960s has any major business organization or government agency, including the U.S. Congress, shown concern for the plight of black workers and other workers of color in the form of large-scale job training or job creation programs.

A Hostile Workplace   When black workers do get hired, then they often face differential treatment in the workplace. For example, the overwhelming majority of employment complaints made to the Equal Employment Opportunity Commission (EEOC) on racial and ethnic grounds are for barriers beyond the hiring stage. There are several major types of barriers. Sometimes, white male workers are given better access than black (or white female) workers to job assignments and training programs that enable them to climb the employment ladder. In addition, in some workplaces black workers face more disciplinary actions. One study of postal workers in a northern city found that black workers were twice as likely to be fired as white workers—even after controls for job tenure, job title, union protection, absenteeism, and disciplinary actions were factored in.[86]

Recent research in other government settings has found that black employees and other employees of color face a variety of discriminatory incidents. For example, the aforementioned survey of 40,000 military personnel found that three quarters of the black military personnel had faced offensive racial encounters during the last twelve months. In that period 52 percent had been told offensive racist jokes or stories; 49 percent had suffered unwelcome attempts to draw them into offensive discussions of race; 46 percent had endured acts of racial condescension; 37 percent had encountered hostile racial stares; 28 percent had endured racist comments or epithets; 23 percent had been excluded from social activities because of race; and 20 percent had been confronted with racist periodicals or other materials. Smaller percentages of these black military personnel had faced very severe incidents. Nine percent were threatened with retaliation if they did not go along with racially offensive actions against them, and six percent had been physically threatened or intimidated because of their race. Not only did they report discrimination in the military workplace, a large percentage (69 percent) of these black enlisted people and officers also reported racial harassment or discrimination from people in the civilian community.[87]

A number of recent reports have indicated a hostile work climate at major corporations. In various workplaces, many whites who do hiring and promotion harbor the deep stereotypes (for example, "blacks are not hardworking") noted previously, racist views that make these whites less comfortable with—and less likely to promote—black employees. Because of these negative images, and positive in-group images, whites are more comfortable with, and thus inclined to favor, other whites.[88] In many employment settings whites often use overtly marginalizing and categorizing language and looks. Black employees may, periodically or routinely, be categorized and marginalized as "you people" or "one of them." The U.S. Third Circuit Court of Appeals ruled in one case that such categorizing phrases were enough to prove that a workplace had a racially hostile climate.[89]

In 1996 the *New York Times* revealed that some top executives at Texaco, an international oil company and the nation's fourteenth-largest corporation, had met in 1994 to discuss a discrimination lawsuit filed by black employees.[90] According to a tape of the meeting, the white executives did not take the discrimination complaints seriously and discussed destroying important documents. Black employees were termed "black jelly beans" who all agree with this "diversity thing" and who "seem to be stuck to the bottom of the bag." The executives may have used the word "nigger," though this has been denied. One executive says on the tape that he is "still having trouble with Hanukkah, and now I have Kwanzaa" (the African American winter festival).[91]

Moreover, in an affidavit filed with the lawsuit, a white manager in a midwestern office of Texaco reported to his boss, a senior executive in Texas, about a discrimination complaint made by a black employee. His boss reportedly told the manager that he would "fire her black ass." When the manager pointed out that company policy protected her from dismissal, the senior executive reportedly said, "I guess we treat niggers differently down here."[92] In addition, a *New York Times* report noted, "Scores of Texaco's nonwhite employees contend in the court papers that they were subjected to racially hostile behavior but did not report the infractions for fear of losing their jobs."[93] Court documents also showed that among the 873 highest-paid executives at the company there were just six black executives. A Department of Labor audit of a controller division at the company found employees of color got less desirable job evaluations and were promoted much more slowly than whites.[94]

In 1996 the EEOC found that Texaco had discriminated against black employees in promotions. The company eventually agreed to a $176 million settlement with its black employees, the largest award ever in a class-action discrimination lawsuit. Still, the lead plaintiff, Bari-Ellen Roberts, has written of Texaco's top executive, "He claimed that the bigoted acts that led to our suit were aberrations, not the product of a corporate climate of racism. I believe the evidence we gathered in our suit proved otherwise."[95]

Texaco is of course not unique. One veteran consultant who works with corporations on diversity issues, Michele Synegal, has reported little change in corporate racial climates in her recent experience. From observations of corporate clients, she has estimated that among minority managers and employees, depending on the workplace, 18 to 36 percent report blatant discrimination, such as a denial of promotion, and 40 to 49 percent cite other discrimination such as lack of mentoring and exclusion from networks. Some 30 to 50 percent of the black employees encounter racist jokes and slurs at work.[96]

Racial Barriers in Business   In recent years many mainstream analysts have suggested that the solution to employment problems for black workers is "black capitalism," the development of more business enterprises in the so-called free market system. However, this naive approach ignores a number of important factors. Not only are most business arenas more or less dominated by large corporations, to the detriment of many small businesses, but there are also the numerous racial barriers created by top corporate executives and lower level managers, as we saw above.

Building a successful business requires access to the necessary resources. Unjust impoverishment in the distant past continues as unjust impoverishment for many generations. Melvin Oliver and Thomas Shapiro have shown how difficult it has been for African Americans to build up much family wealth because of centuries of far-reaching legal and de facto segregation. Until the late 1960s various forms of government-sanctioned discrimination and segregation not only kept black Americans out of business sectors serving communities outside black areas, but also thereby kept their descendants from inheriting or generating the resources and wealth necessary to develop a proportionate share of business in the U.S. economy later on, under conditions of desegregation. Until recently, African Americans were forced by blatant discrimination and segregation into an economic detour away from more lucrative consumer markets.[97]

Today, how well black businesspeople succeed in business depends substantially on their business costs, some of which are linked directly to the past discrimination they or their predecessors have suffered. Not only are members of an oppressed group likely to have less education or fewer skills because of past and present discrimination, but they often lack access to the important social networks or to the business knowledge necessary to compete effectively with privileged whites. An average black businessperson will not have the same resources, experiences, and opportunities of her or his white competitors. Comparing a black (B) and a white (W) businessperson, Martin Katz has emphasized the cost structure of discrimination: "Financial advantage — and hence disadvantage — is transferable across generations. If B's heirs and W's heirs each inherit their mothers' businesses, they will likely face cost curves similar to those of their parents. B's daughter will thus face a higher cost curve than W's daughter. . . . Cost structure analysis thus suggests that discrimination is likely to result in racial cost disparities which can persist long after the discrimination has ceased."[98] With a less-developed or more segregated work or business history, because of past or present racism, black businesspeople will have more trouble making the current business venture successful. For example, even unprejudiced white lenders—and many are *not* unprejudiced—will be less willing to loan to those entrepreneurs with fewer resources or a less-developed work or business history. Even the abolition of some types of discrimination, which was attempted through the 1960s civil rights movement, cannot restructure the resource and business inheritances that favor whites. In addition, there are other racial barriers to starting a business. These include ongoing housing and insurance discrimination limiting the ability of black families to build up the substantial housing equities often used to start or expand small businesses.

If a black entrepreneur manages to start a business, he or she is likely to face other racial hurdles. One review of many research studies of contractors' access to business contracts found that black contractors and other contractors of color face problems getting government contracts and that, if they get contracts, they face sabotage at their work sites. They often endure racist comments in carrying out their business contracts, and they may also face racial barriers in securing financing for their business.[99] Another research report examined several thousand black and white businesses with similar characteristics and discovered that the black firms averaged smaller loans than the white firms. Another survey of black firms in Texas found that a third of those reporting discrimination had experienced it in trying to get business loans.[100] Discrimination by banks can bring serious financial difficulties, while fair treatment enhances the possibility of success. Timothy Bates has found that black businesses that somehow get loans comparable to those of white peers do *not* have a higher failure rate than white firms.[101]

Breaking into white business networks is a serious problem for many black firms. Most business sectors have critical networks of interrelated white businesses, what are often termed "good old boy" networks. This common term is interesting in itself, for it shows that many whites recognize this major nonmeritocratic way in which the vested interests of whites are commonly protected and extended. One study of 340 contractors of color in several cities found that they faced certain barriers to doing business because most white contractors already had "a group of favorite subcontractors with whom they have become accustomed to working."[102] Another study found that the private sector enterprises owned by people of color are only half as likely to sell to other firms (to business clients) as similar white-owned firms, even when controls for size, age, and type of industry are included. The reason for this lies in the fact that "entrenched networks, not firm capacity differences, are at the root of these differentials in market access."[103]

Thus, black entrepreneurs and other entrepreneurs of color commonly have trouble breaking into entrenched business networks. Without good access to such networks it is hard to get a fair share of business contracts, in both the private and the public sectors. One Urban Institute report examined fifty-eight disparity studies for major state and city governments and found that the share that black construction, goods, and services firms received of state/local government contract dollars was much less than expected based on the black percentage of all firms — indeed, about half of what might be expected.[104] Doing business is a daily struggle for most black businesspeople, especially those operating in historically white markets. The latter are situated in a business world mostly not of their own making, one with recurring racist hurdles they must overcome if they are to stay in business. "Black capitalism" is certainly no answer to systemic racism.

Racial Barriers in Education

Resegregation of the Public Schools   Residential segregation usually insures public school segregation, and public school segregation encourages residential segregation. Moreover, desegregation in one area can encourage desegregation in the other. One research study found that the extent of housing desegregation in cities of similar size and racial mix is directly related to school desegregation. Those with school desegregation plans covering only central cities had less housing desegregation than those that desegregated the public schools in both central cities and suburban areas.[105]

In the 1960s and early 1970s, much federal government action was directed at school desegregation. However, since the 1980s the federal government, including the federal courts, has allowed or encouraged resegregation of public school systems. Several Supreme Court decisions (for example, *Freeman v. Pitts* in 1992) have permitted the gradual dismantling of school desegregation plans.[106] One major study by Harvard University researchers examined trends in school segregation from the 1968–1969 school year to the 1996–1997 school year.[107] They found that as federal judges have backed away from enforcing desegregation plans, the public schools have resegregated, with children of color being an increasing proportion of those enrolled. Many school districts are phasing out their school desegregation efforts, both in the North and in the South. Over the last few decades many white parents have moved their children to private or suburban schools, while the number and proportion of children of color have continued to grow in the more or less segregated central city areas. In 1972 the Supreme Court issued a ruling approving busing for implementing school desegregation programs. About that time, 64 percent of black students were in public schools where the majority

of the students were not white. By the 1996–1997 school year this figure had actually *increased* to about 69 percent. In an earlier study of similar data, Harvard
researchers concluded that the nation is moving backwards, saying, "We may be
deciding to bet the future of the country once more on separate but equal. There
is no evidence that separate but equal today works any better than it did a century
ago."[108]

This segregation is not accidental. Many white parents and politicians work
hard to keep their residential areas and schools as white as possible. Racial steering is one way to maintain segregation in school districts. One recent report on
New York City schools found widespread steering. Trained testers, posing as parents, were sent to 28 elementary schools in half the city's school districts. Of the
99 visits made by parent testers, 50 were by whites and 49 by people of color. The
white parent testers were able to speak with an educator, such as the principal or
assistant principal, much more often than their black and Latino counterparts.
Whites were two-and-one-half times more likely to get a school tour than were
people of color, and whites were, on the average, given much more information.
The school staff members were more likely to mention programs for gifted children to white testers than to the black and Latino testers. The report describes
these actions as institutional racism that is rooted in conscious prejudices, malign
neglect by officials, and a lack of representation in decision making by the working-class and minority families served by the schools.[109]

Barriers at Colleges and Universities   Discrimination, blatant and subtle, is commonplace at most stages of education at historically white universities. For example, subtle discrimination persists in the screening measures used for admissions
at both the undergraduate and graduate levels. How merit is measured, such as by
standardized tests, has largely been determined by white educators. Historically,
most college entrance tests and related screening devices have been designed by
whites from upper-middle-class backgrounds. Indeed, some of the leading social
scientists of the 1910s and 1920s who helped to develop the forerunners or early
versions of today's college entrance tests, such as Princeton University's Carl
Brigham, were overt racists. By means of psychometric testing they sought to
demonstrate the intellectual superiority of the "Nordic race" over other racial
groups.

Paper-and-pencil college entrance tests have long been designed to measure
the things that white middle-class people know or do well. For example, college
entrance tests have used questions about such things as toboggans and polo, items
that are more familiar to middle- and upper-class whites than to most working-
class people or people of color. In addition, most tests are written in the variant of
the English language most accessible to white middle-class people and are biased
in favor of certain ways of thinking, such as linear, rationalistic thinking.[110] White
middle-class youth do better than many others on such tests because they tend to

be in families with substantial economic and cultural resources (for example, computers and libraries), resources often linked to the unjust enrichment of their ancestors under slavery or segregation. These white middle-class students also tend to have a better precollege education, which gives them an edge not only in scoring well on entrance tests and completing college degree programs but also in competing for jobs and other societal rewards later on in life.

If they get past the college entrance barriers, black students commonly confront a range of discriminatory barriers on college campuses. Research at historically white colleges consistently finds that campus cultures are hostile or alienating for students of color. One study surveyed 54 white students and 109 students of color at a California campus and found that the students of color were more alienated than the white students, with black and Latino students reporting the most isolation and alienation from the campus culture. Another study of black and white students at a Midwestern campus found that black students were more alienated and dropped out more often than white students.[111] Discrimination by whites on and off campus is a recurring problem. One recent study questioned 153 black faculty, staff, and students at a major university; nearly all reported facing some racial discrimination in the last year.[112]

One 1990s study conducted focus-group interviews with black students at a major university on their experiences with white students, professors, administrators, and campus police officers. Most black students reported serious discrimination on or near campus. Negative encounters with white students included being called "nigger" on or near campus, encountering racist graffiti, dealing with whites who left the room just because a black student walked in, various other defensive reactions by white students, white students assuming blacks were athletes or affirmative action students, and whites rudely backing out of new friendships. Black students also reported differential treatment by faculty members, including often being treated as the spokesperson for the race, being graded down for writing on African American topics, and being subjected to subtle racist joking. The students also reported hasty treatment by academic advisors who gave more time to white students, a lack of interest by some key administrators in black students, racial biases in some curricula and courses, fewer campus activities for black students than for whites, overpolicing of black student events, and weak efforts at black student retention. Many students had considered dropping out of this university because of the negative racial climate. They, and some parents of students who were interviewed as well, reported a recurring and "agonizing" dilemma for black students: to stay in this university and endure the hostile treatment ,or drop out and go to a historically black college that would be much more supportive, but also likely to have more limited academic resources.

Surveys at numerous other colleges and universities have found black students facing a similar array of racial barriers.[113] In recent years many historically white colleges and universities have reported problems such as racist graffiti scrawled on dorm doors and in various other places on campus. These include Harvard University, Yale University Law School, Swarthmore College, the University of Colorado at Denver, the University of Wisconsin at River Falls, Antioch University, the University of West Virginia, Central Missouri State University, the Southern College of Technology, Ohio's Miami University, and Heidelberg College. Racist flyers were reportedly posted or handed out at Indiana University, the University of Northern Colorado, and the University of California Law School. Racist effigies were reported at the University of Minnesota, and racist cartoons were published in Princeton University's campus newspaper. Incidents involving antiblack threats, including "nigger" epithets, were reported at several other institutions.[114]

Campus cultures at historically white institutions are strongly white-oriented and generally resistant to major changes. The overwhelming majority of white trustees, administrators, advisors, faculty members, and students have shown little desire to remake their campuses in order to truly integrate black interests, history, and concerns into the center of campus life and culture.

Racial Discrimination in Public Places

The Ecology of Oppression   Racial oppression has a distinctive spatial dimension, and its character can vary as a black person travels from the private home site to more public spaces. In one study that interviewed a large number of middle-class black Americans, a professor at a major university noted the stress that comes from dealing with whites in public places:

> If I'm in those areas that are fairly protected, within gatherings of my own group, other African Americans, or if I'm in the university where my status as a professor mediates against the way I might be perceived, mediates against the hostile perception, then it's fairly comfortable. . . . When I divide my life into encounters with the outside world, and of course that's ninety percent of my life, it's fairly consistently unpleasant at those sites where there's nothing that mediates between my race and what I have to do. For example, if I'm in a grocery store, if I'm in my car, which is a 1970 Chevrolet, a real old ugly car, all those things—being in a grocery store in casual clothes, or being in the car—sort of advertises something that doesn't have anything to do with my status as far as people I run into are concerned.[115]

The increase in unpleasant encounters that comes as this professor moves from her home into public arenas such as stores is attributed to the absence of mediating factors such as whites knowing that she is a professor. Much antiblack discrimination occurs outside social contexts where there are family or friends or symbols of status that may reduce the likelihood of discrimination. On the way to work or school there can be unpleasant contacts with white police officers, white clerks who will not touch your hand, white teenagers at a traffic light, or white customers in stores who are rude. These racist practices are not limited to one setting but rather take place across many public arenas.

Discrimination in Public Places   Psychological researchers have staged situations of possible discrimination in public places, and have discovered that white bystanders will often not respond to a black person's call for help in a staged emergency situation. In contrast, whites are much more likely to respond to calls for help from a white person.[116] One study found that when a black woman drops a bag of groceries in a public setting, a white person is less likely to help her than to help a white woman who has the same mishap.[117] The racial identity of the person needing help strongly affects white responses. Overt dislike of black people is one likely reason. One analyst has suggested yet another possible reason for the white reactions: The more whites see of black people suffering, such as in the media, the more they come to see that condition as normal, and the less sympathy they have for blacks in difficulty.[118]

In a recent Gallup survey asking black respondents about discrimination in various settings in the preceding month, retail shopping was the area in which the largest percentage (30 percent) of the sample reported racial mistreatment. Indeed, 45 percent of the young men in this sample reported such discrimination. Twenty-one percent of the sample (and 32 percent of young men) also reported discrimination when dining out. Discrimination in dining includes very poor service that seems racially motivated and often being seated in an undesirable place, such as at the back of the restaurant near the kitchen. Discrimination in retail stores encompasses the extra surveillance often faced by black shoppers and other discrimination by white sales clerks. In this survey, moreover, those black respondents with higher incomes reported encountering more discrimination than those with lower incomes.[119] Leanita McClain, a prize-winning black columnist for the *Chicago Tribune*, once suggested an important difference between contemporary racist practices and the old segregationist practices: "The old racism wouldn't let blacks into some stores; the new racism assumes that any black person, no matter how well dressed, in a store is probably there to steal, not to buy." Undoubtedly drawing on her own experience, she added that the old racism "didn't have to address black people; the new racism is left speechless when a black, approached condescendingly, has an eloquent comeback."[120]

Black customers face discrimination in the buying process. One major Chicago study examined more than 180 buyer-salesperson negotiations at ninety car dealerships. Black and white testers, with similar economic characteristics and bargaining scripts, posed as car buyers. White male testers got much better prices from the salespeople than did white women or black men and women. Compared to the markup given to white men, black men paid twice the markup and black women paid more than three times the markup. The average dealer profit in the final offers to each category of tester was as follows: white men, $362; white women, $504; black men, $783; and black women, $1237. In another study the researchers used thirty-eight testers who bargained for some 400 cars at 242 dealers. Again, black testers were quoted much higher prices that white men, though this time black men were quoted the highest prices.[121] In some cases racist language was used by salespeople, but the researchers concluded that the more serious problem was stereotyping about how much black customers will pay. The cost of this commonplace discrimination is high. Given that black customers pay two to three times the markup offered to white men — if this holds across the nation — then black customers "annually would pay $150 million more for new cars than do white males."[122]

Discrimination has also been found in professional services. Recently, one group of researchers used actors to portray black and white patients with certain coronary disease symptoms. A total of 720 physicians were asked to look at these recorded interviews and other patient data, to assess the probability of coronary artery disease, and to suggest treatment. The researchers found differences in proposed treatment: blacks, and especially black women, were less likely to be recommended for cardiac catheterization, compared to whites with the same dress, occupations, and medical histories.[123] Another recent study reported in the *New England Journal of Medicine* found that black patients with lung cancer were less likely to receive the best surgical treatment than white patients.[124] The reasons for these patterns of differential medical treatment along racial lines are yet to be delineated, but they may include not only traditional racial stereotypes but also specific stereotypes shared by some white medical practitioners, such as the notion that black patients who get special or expensive treatments are not as likely as whites to take proper care of themselves after treatment. The explanation for differences in surgery may also include the reluctance on the part of some black patients to trust the recommendations of white physicians. More research remains to be done, but there is no reason to expect that the racism of the larger society does not extend into the medical professions.

Conclusion   Being black in U.S. society means always having to be prepared for antiblack actions by whites — in most places and at most times of the day, week, month, or year. Being black means living with racial oppression from cradle to grave. Until whites quit thinking and acting in racist ways — and thereby maintaining their racial privilege — the system of racial oppression will persist.

In a June 1963 address to the nation President John F. Kennedy explained why he had called out the Alabama National Guard — against the wishes of the governor of Alabama, George Wallace — in order to enforce a federal court order allowing two black students to enroll at the University of Alabama. "This nation was founded by men of many nations and backgrounds," he said. "It was founded on the principle that all men are created equal, and that the rights of every man are diminished when the rights of one man are threatened. . . . One hundred years of delay have passed since President Lincoln freed the slaves, yet their heirs, their grandsons, are not fully free. They are not yet freed from the bonds of injustice; they are not yet freed from social and economic oppression."[125]

After accenting this theme of slavery unwilling to die, Kennedy continued by framing the issue of equality as a moral question that the nation must face. After the speech Kennedy sent to the U.S. Congress proposals that soon became the 1964 Civil Rights Act. This important new law officially prohibited much overt discrimination and abolished legal segregation in employment, schools, federally assisted programs, and public accommodations (see chapter 8). Over the next few years, the 1965 Voting Rights Act and the 1968 Civil Rights Act would prohibit discrimination in voting practices and in housing. However, as we have seen, laws banning discrimination are often weakly enforced, and black Americans still do not have the full and equal opportunities promised in the official rhetoric of the 1960s. Today they are still living under the legacy of slavery and are "not yet freed from social and economic oppression."

six

White Privileges
and Black Burdens
The Continuing Impact
of Oppression

The Reality of White Privilege   White privilege entails the set of benefits and advantages inherited by each generation of those defined as "white" in the social process and structure of U.S. society. The actual privileges and the sense that one is entitled to them are inseparable parts of a greater whole. These white advantages can be material, symbolic, or psychological. They infiltrate and encompass many thousands of interactions and other events played out in an individual American's life over the course of a lifetime.

   The Confidence of Whiteness   Whiteness is so ubiquitous, so habitual, so imbedded that it exists even where and when most whites cannot see it. Stated or unstated, it is a fundamental given of this society. White prerogatives stem from the fact that society has, from the beginning, been structured in terms of white gains and white-group interests. Once this system was put into place in the seventeenth century, white privileges soon came to be sensed as usual and natural. The active or passive acceptance of this system as normal has long conferred advantages for whites, even including antiracist whites seeking to eradicate racism. Today, most whites of all political persuasions will say they are opposed to racism, although most continue to overtly or covertly support racist practices and institutions. Indeed, many whites will even say that do not feel powerful or privileged, and they will emphasize that their own family problems are at least as serious as those of black Americans and other people of color.

Still, at some level most whites know they are indeed privileged in racial terms. Today, most whites seem confident that the future will be bright for themselves and their children. One research study interviewed white, black, Asian, and Latino American groups. The researchers found that white adults generally demonstrated a strong confidence in their future economic chances. As a group, they firmly believed that their children would go to college and/or have good employment choices. No such strong assumptions were made by the black, Latino, and Asian American groups—they were not as confident about the future.[1] One of the privileges of whiteness is not having to worry as much about the economic, political, and social futures of oneself or one's family as do the racial others. A substantial majority of whites have a sense of personal and/or family well-being and do not seem to care, or are unaware, that this level of confidence is not available to many other Americans.

Privileging White Interpretations   Most whites have an uncritical habit of mind that accepts the existing racist order with little or no questioning. Recall Joyce King's research on white students, most of whom were unaware of how their own white identities entailed an "uncritical identification with the existing social order."[2] Almost all the students explained racial inequality without connecting it to the larger system of white power and privilege. Indeed, a majority of whites deny that whites as a group have benefited from past or present discrimination (see chapter 4). Most whites internalize whiteness and the rightness of who they are and how they live. They accept the longstanding system of privilege and do not think much, if at all, about it. Not surprisingly, most everyday events confirm their privileges and the status of whiteness. When whites encounter information about persisting inequality across the color line, they usually do not connect that information with their own white privilege.[3]

Individualistic values often incline whites to deny the brutal realities of past and present racism. It is easier to blame racism's victims and their genetic or cultural heritage than to blame white racism. White privilege even embraces the assumption that white interpretations of the social world should be dominant. This can be seen, for example, in white interpretations of the drug and crime problems of black communities in central cities. In the mass media and elsewhere, whites tend to define these conditions in terms of the cultural, family, or moral inferiority of the black inhabitants but rarely care what residents of these areas think about such matters. White privilege also includes an entitlement to decipher a black person's reality and experience. For example, the mother of one newborn reported a white nurse's comment on seeing her infant: "Oh, this one's a militant, a little Black Panther!"[4] The newborn is not only constructed as "black" (the mother was white, the father black), but also downgraded, in this case humorously, in white eyes as an alien and potentially dangerous other. Whites often take it for granted that they are entitled to their interpretation of black conditions without consulting those so interpreted.

Social Transmission of White Privilege   From the beginning the system of racial oppression was designed to bring a range of benefits for white Americans. The society rooted in slavery provided whites with many undeserved social, economic, political, and cultural advantages. Once the framework of unjust impoverishment and enrichment was created under slavery, the white leadership of the new nation, strongly supported by the average white man and woman, set into motion the segregative and discriminatory means for perpetuating this enrichment and impoverishment across the generations. Slavery, and subsequent segregation and contemporary racism, have all provided whites with many advantages. Whites as individuals and as a group have an interest in maintaining the system of oppression. As Frances Lee Ansley has noted, the system of racism ensures whites "greater resources, a wider range of personal choice, more power, and more self-esteem than they would have if they were (1) forced to share the above with people of color, and (2) deprived of the subjective sensation of superiority they enjoy as a result of the societal presence of subordinate non-white others."[5]

Most white Americans underestimate not only the level of their privileges but the degree to which these privileges exist because they have been passed down from their families and ancestors. Consider again the principle of unjust enrichment we discussed in chapter 1. Under law an innocent person who benefits unknowingly from wealth gained illegally or by unjust actions in the past generally cannot, if the ill-gotten gains are discovered and challenged, claim a right to keep them.[6] "If a thief steals so that his children may live in luxury and the law returns his ill-gotten gain to its rightful owner, the children cannot complain that they have been deprived of what they did not own," explains Patricia Williams.[7] A coerced taking of one's possessions by an individual criminal is similar to the coerced taking of one's labor or just due by a slaveholder or other white discriminator.

Unjustly gained advantages have a social inertia. When large groups of whites gained jobs, income, property, status, or wealth unjustly under slavery and segregation, and then passed the advantage or wealth gained to later generations, that did not make the wealth and advantage inherited and enhanced today by their white descendants justly held. Each generation's racist arrangements not only create new opportunities for unjust enrichment but also provide processes of transmission that pass social and economic capital to later generations. For several centuries the system of racial oppression has created severe inequality in life chances between white and black Americans, and the transmission of this inequality remains a critical factor in the continuing reproduction of systemic racism.

Racial Consciousness: Elites and Ordinary Whites   Periodically over the course of American history, white elites have intentionally tried to divide ordinary Americans in order to reduce or eliminate the possibility of social protest. They have worked to divide white and black farmers and workers to prevent effective coalitions. Elite fears of multiracial coalitions in the seventeenth and eighteenth centuries, which were discussed in chapter 1, surfaced again after the Civil War. For a time black and white farmers joined in organizations, such as the Farmers Alliance and the Populist Party, working for their class betterment. During the 1870s and 1880s the Farmers Alliance spread throughout the South and Midwest. Hundreds of thousands of white and black farmers joined in organizations whose goals included regulation of the railroads, banks, and grain combines exploiting the nation's farmers. Many white farmers and workers were also active in other integrated, and often populist, political organizations.[8] However, white elites, fearing successful multiracial coalitions, regularly used violence, intimidation, and aggressive promotion of the racist ideology to convince ordinary whites to separate from their black counterparts.

While there have been periods when some white farmers and workers have joined with their black counterparts, for most of American history the majority of white farmers and workers have been more or less active players in buttressing and maintaining the racist system. From the 1600s to the 1860s most ordinary whites, not just slaveholders, benefitted from the economic development spurred by the slavery complex. Indeed, many of these whites provided the necessary infrastructure servicing the slavery system (see chapter 2). The encompassing structure of slavery conveyed many benefits to the white populace not only by providing general economic expansion for the growing nation but also by limiting the jobs that black men and women could hold to menial and segregated positions and by restricting the places where black Americans could live. As we have seen in earlier chapters, the cities of the North were not much better for those enslaved or for free black workers and their families. From at least the early 1800s, many whites in the urban working and middle classes worked to restrict or reduce job, educational, political, and housing competition from black Americans, as well as other Americans of color—without being urged on by elites.

The majority of white farmers and workers were racist in thought and action, not just because it benefited them materially, but also because they had come to look at the world in broadly racist terms. They came to accept the "public and psychological wage" of whiteness. Historian David Roediger has proposed that the "problem is not just that the white working class is at critical junctures manipulated into racism, but that it comes to think of itself and its interests as white."[9] Accentuation of whiteness appears to be one major way that white workers have dealt with their own fears about the exploitative wage-labor system and difficult working conditions they have encountered under capitalism. Since at least the late eighteenth century white workers and farmers have been much more race conscious than class conscious, a condition facilitating their own class oppression. This was true for the new European immigrants as well as for older white groups. In the mid- to late nineteenth century most of these immigrants, who had not seen themselves initially as "white" but rather as Irish, German, or Swedish, came to view themselves as white Americans (see chapter 2). In the new United States race early became the core stratification reality because it effectively decentered or replaced class oppression in the thinking and practice of most white Americans.

While there are class and other social divisions among whites, when "faced with a serious challenge from people of color, whites would join ranks despite internal rifts. Race is key, not class."[10] Though there have been significant exceptions, most white workers have historically been more likely to join racially with their class oppressors than to join with their brothers and sisters of the same class across the racial line. One likely reason there has been much less class struggle in the United States than in many European countries is because white workers have historically been more interested in struggling against their potential class allies — black workers and other workers of color — than they have been in struggling against their class enemies, the capitalist/employers. As a result, the majority of white workers not only have lost the chance for class solidarity with black workers but also have corrupted their own consciousness of class relations and of themselves as workers under capitalism.

Today, as in the past, those white workers living in modest circumstances may not feel privileged or powerful, especially relative to white elites. They sense the need for significant economic improvements in their lives. However, because of the myths of racism — and their own false consciousness — most seem unable to see deeply into the real sources of their own class oppression. Their racist ideology likely makes it hard for most of them to understand not only the situation of the racialized others but also their own situation of class oppression. The racial consciousness of most white Americans remains very strong as we move into the twenty-first century.

This does not mean, however, that class oppression is not central to U.S. society, for it too is very much a part of the nation's social fabric. In the United States today, as in the past, racial structure and class structure overlap and interrelate. Being white includes not only a higher racial status no matter what one's class is, but also on the average having a higher class position and greater income and wealth than if one were black. More often than not, a somewhat higher or much higher position in the class system comes with birth into the top rank in the system of racial categorization. In the majority of cases, whiteness is associated with a higher class position than blackness. In a number of ways the systems of racial and class oppression coreproduce each other.

The Many Benefits of Whiteness: A Brief Overview

Privileged Access to Economic Resources   As we have seen in earlier chapters, from at least the mid-1600s to the 1960s the American economy was openly, often imperiously, run as a racist system using black labor and Native American lands to create wealth for white Americans. Historically, white Americans have been the direct beneficiaries of much government assistance intended to create white prosperity and mobility. An array of "affirmative action" programs for whites provided the basis for prosperity and mobility. For example, in the late 1600s several new colonies, including Virginia and Maryland, provided land grants to white settlers, land not available to those enslaved. Moreover, from its passage in 1862 to the early 1900s, the federal government, operating under the Homestead Act, gave away large amounts of federal government (originally Native American) land to white families homesteading western areas. Black Americans were for the most part excluded from access to this land because they were then enslaved (in the 1860s) or, later, because they were still locked into debt peonage in southern agriculture. Violence was also used by white supremacist groups to drive out those black families that did manage to gain some land by their own means. The federal homestead program created many billions of dollars in wealth for white homesteaders and their descendants, to the present day.[11]

Slavery and legal segregation created preferences for whites in access to jobs, education, politics, and housing. The long-term impact of such preferences for ordinary whites accounts for a substantial proportion of the income and wealth differentials between black and white Americans today (see below). Large-scale preferential programs for whites were legitimate and openly implemented for more than three hundred years. Even later white entrants into the United States, such as immigrants from southern and eastern Europe, benefited greatly from the nation's racist laws and informal practices during the late nineteenth and early twentieth centuries. Some conservative scholars have tried to argue that the situation of black Americans is essentially similar to that of white European immigrants. As they see it, white-ethnic immigrants faced some discrimination but still were able to use their opportunities and move into the middle class in a generation or two; they contend that this will work for black Americans if they will reform themselves (and their families) and work harder.[12]

However, this conservative view is naive at best and ignores the major advantages that these white immigrant groups had over the black Americans who were already in the cities into which the immigrants settled. The newcomers were able to move up the socioeconomic ladder because most arrived when the U.S. economy was expanding greatly and jobs were relatively abundant; because many of them had some skills or modest money resources; because most faced far less job and other discrimination than did black urbanites; because they were not excluded from residential areas near their workplaces as black urbanites were; and because cities were increasingly under the control of political machines oriented to these immigrant voters.[13] These European immigrants and their children were able to get into important whites-only unions and to secure better-paying blue-collar or government jobs from which black Americans were usually barred. The newcomers were allowed a job or business niche in which they could develop economically. As a result, the immigrants and their descendants were generally able to do better economically, politically, and residentially than black Americans who had resided in the country for nearly three centuries before these immigrants arrived.

White workers have long tried to keep black workers out of better-paying jobs. Indeed, the first major exclusion of black Americans from a large organization after the abolition of slavery was that imposed by the National Labor Union in 1866. This pattern would persist in U.S. unions, with occasional exceptions, for more than a century.[14] Until the 1960s most unions discriminated more or less openly against black workers, reinforcing the racial division in the labor market and increasing white workers' incomes, at least relative to those of black workers. From the 1880s to the 1960s southern labor organizations, in particular, worked very hard to create rigidly segregated white and black job tracks.[15]

This history of economic privilege is the backdrop for present-day privilege for white workers. In recent years many black workers have confronted significant tracking favoring white workers, as well as discrimination in unionized and other blue-collar workplaces by white workers. In my own research in such workplaces, I have found that the discriminatory practices range from subtle to blatant harassment—such as putting hangman's nooses, hoods, or racist effigies at black workers' job positions—and that management often ignores these actions by whites, at least until the black workers file a lawsuit. White workers in white-collar workplaces often engage in an array of less overt racist behavior, as we saw in chapter 5. By engaging in such hostile antiblack behavior, whites help to maintain their dominance of certain more desirable jobs or job tracks. Black workers are frequently kept in a state of stress that may keep them from performing as well as they might otherwise have done, or that forces them to quit the job, both of which responses can mean more job opportunities or benefits for white workers.[16]

Large-Scale Government Handouts   In the first decades of the twentieth century many other government-controlled resources were given away, or made available on reasonable terms, to the American people. Yet it was almost exclusively white Americans who were given these valuable resources. For example, the Air Commerce Act gave U.S. air routes to new companies, mainly those started by aviators who had been trained during World War I. During that war black Americans were not allowed into the segregated Army Air Corps, and thus had no opportunity to participate in this giveaway of resources that over time were used to generate individual and family wealth. Many other resources and opportunities, such as access to government-controlled mineral resources and the radio and television airwaves, were similarly kept from black taxpayers, especially in the critical decades of the early twentieth century, by means of overt discrimination.[17]

Similarly, during the 1930s, federal New Deal programs provided differential access to important governmental resources. As we noted in chapter 2, many key programs heavily favored white Americans. One of the most important subsidy programs was provided by the Federal Housing Administration (FHA). FHA loan insurance and related programs—later buttressed by veteran's programs—enabled millions of white families to buy homes. As a result, many of these families accumulated enough home equity to use for startup capital for small businesses or for funding advanced education for their children and grandchildren. For many years the FHA worked with the white-dominated real estate industry and white homeowners to make sure that black Americans not only got less housing assistance than whites but also had to reside in rigidly segregated communities. Other 1930s' New Deal programs provided much aid to white farmers, bankers, and business executives, enabling them to survive the Great Depression and, soon thereafter, to thrive during World War II and the postwar years. In addition to direct assistance programs, the growing government contracting programs after 1940 made contracts available more or less exclusively to white businesses, whereas firms owned by Americans of color were not allowed significant access to these contracts until the 1970s.[18]

In the decades just before and after World War II many government programs helped white builders, contractors, and other businesspeople to get a start and/or to thrive. These included privileged access to building permits, licenses, and government franchises.[19] These and other multibillion-dollar government aid programs have helped to built up prosperity and wealth for white businesses now over several generations. This pattern of government favoritism for white firms laid the framework for doing business in most counties and cities to the present day. Even some Supreme Court cases knocking down remedial programs for discrimination, such as *City of Richmond v. J.A. Croson Co.* (1989), have cited data in passing indicating that white firms get an extremely disproportionate share of government contracting business in cities with large black populations.[20] Similarly, we noted in chapter 5 some data from a number of research studies that indicate that whites still dominate most business networks and get a much greater share of construction, goods, and services contracts from state and local governments than one might expect based on the white percentage of all firms. Once again, we see a continuing pattern of undeserved enrichment for white Americans and unjust disadvantage for black Americans.

Cultural, Legal, and Political Advantages   Whites have profited not only economically but also educationally, politically, legally, and aesthetically from systemic racism. For example, white Americans have, on the whole, had much greater access to good educational programs than have black Americans for several centuries. Until the 1960s, most U.S. colleges and universities—except for the historically black colleges—were either all-white or nearly so. Whites had privileged access to this critical type of cultural and networking capital over many generations. Today, white students' access to good college programs is still greater than for black students—and unencumbered by the racist barriers black students currently face. Moreover, for most of the years since public elementary and secondary schools were first created in significant numbers in the nineteenth century, they have been overtly segregated along racial lines. The period of active school desegregation—from about 1970 to about 1990—was relatively brief, and increasing racial segregation seems to be the current trend (see chapter 5). On the whole, all-white or mostly white public schools have had better educational environments and facilities than schools predominantly composed of students of color. At all levels of education, the average white child has had substantial advantages over the average black child. Once a family's children have access to good educational capital, they are more likely to be successful in securing good jobs and housing, and they are thus more likely to pass along major economic and social capital benefits to their descendants.

Generally speaking, much of contemporary American culture is still shaped by the white population's European heritage and background. White views and values, especially those of early Anglo-Protestant groups, have been determinative in much of North American development from the beginning. From the 1600s forward, whiteness has been the normative standard for much of what is valued in society. Established rules and patterns are created by and tend to work in the interest of whites, particularly those at the helm of major institutions. There are numerous examples of this normative whiteness or Europeanness. For example, the dominant language in the United States has long been English, with the most privileged variant and accent being that of middle-class whites. Those Americans not from Europe, including the many Africans forced into the new nation, have had to adopt the language of the dominant group. In addition, the core legal system is rooted substantially in the English legal system, and the nation's capitalistic economy is heavily European in origin and continuing economic values. Indeed, many people still call the privileged individualistic value system the "Protestant ethic."

In addition, the U.S. political system was originally crafted using European (often English) political ideas about such matters as representation, republicanism, branches of government, and limited democracy. Today, the U.S. political system often does little to implement real democracy in everyday operations at state, local, and federal government levels. This can be seen most clearly, perhaps, in the many ways the political structure allows those with money—especially well-off white men—to corrupt and control its most important aspects and institutions. Whites as a group benefit handsomely from this white control of a theoretically democratic political system.

In some recent analyses of U.S. society, there is a tendency to play down this white-European dominance in favor of a melting-pot perspective that sees the central U.S. culture as a grand mixture with substantial input from diverse immigrant groups over several centuries, including Africans and other immigrants of color. However, apart from a few matters such as popular entertainment, music, certain sports, and, to some degree, religion, most of North American culture is still heavily determined or shaped by white, Anglo-European values, practices, and arrangements.

Controlling U.S. Institutions: White Men at the Top   Not only have whites dominated the economic, political, legal, and educational values of this society, they have also been in firm control of the key roles and top positions in all major institutions for nearly four centuries. In earlier chapters we have seen how this dominance was established, and then transmitted over generations. Today, all major institutions remain white-normed and white-framed in their internal sociocultural structures, and white individuals, most especially white men, are generally in command at and near the top.

Today, white men make up about 39 percent of the adult population. Yet, after several decades of affirmative action, the overwhelming majority of those who run most major political, economic, educational, and legal-justice organizations are *still* white men. Recent research shows that there is a concrete ceiling that blocks black Americans, other Americans of color, and white women from the higher-level positions in the society. White men control almost every major U.S. institution—from most Fortune 1000 companies and elite universities, to the presidency, the military, and federal and state legislatures. In most of these sectors they make up 95 to 100 percent of those in the top positions. One 1980s analysis of the 7,314 most powerful positions in major economic, political, and educational organizations found only 20 black men and women, and 318 other (mostly white) women, altogether less than five percent of the total.[21]

More recent studies have shown a similar dominance of major institutions by the white male minority. According to one mid-1990s *Newsweek* report, white men were then dominant in the political sphere, holding 77 percent of House and Senate seats and 92 percent of the state governorships. In the corporate world even positions below the very top were held mostly by white men. White men were dominant in the mass media, holding 90 percent of newspaper editor positions and 77 percent of TV news director positions.[22] Most higher-level executives in other business sectors are also white men. According to a recent report of the federal Glass Ceiling Commission, about 95 percent of the holders of corporate positions at the level of vice president and above are white men.[23] Perhaps the clearest evidence of the corporate world's failure to promote meritorious black employees is the fact that in 1998 not a single one of the Fortune 1000 companies had a black executive as its head. As we move into the twenty-first century, these patterns of white male dominance persist.

In recent years much ado has been made about so-called "reverse discrimination." Many white men believe that discrimination against blacks and other people of color has declined dramatically and that whites, especially white men, are now major victims of discrimination. While some white men do occasionally lose a few opportunities for advancement because of the modest remedial programs—usually to well-qualified white women or people of color—the statistics noted above do not bear out the notion of widespread reverse discrimination. Indeed, the most successful quota program in U.S. history is the one that sees to it that white men continue to dominate very disproportionately the society's powerful institutions and organizations. All the pressures and programs for change put together have so far forced only modest changes in this white-male dominance.

White men also dominate among those with the greatest amounts of wealth. A recent study of the wealthiest four hundred Americans found that almost all were white, and 83 percent were white men. The wealthiest man was then Microsoft's Bill Gates, a billionaire several times over. The inheritance of business and other resources from one generation to the next has been very important in perpetuating the position of most white men at the top of the wealth pyramid. About 56 percent of the wealthiest four hundred Americans had inherited wealth in the millions of dollars from their families, and another 14 percent came from a family with substantial economic resources to be passed along but less than one million dollars. Just 30 percent had inherited no substantial economic resources. Yet even most of these people had inherited substantial cultural resources, such as access to a very good education and social network, that enabled them to move up economically over their lifetimes. The majority of wealthy whites do not now, and did not in the past, pull themselves up by their own bootstraps.[24] Some significant portion of this inherited wealth built up over the generations doubtless originated from the various mechanisms of undeserved enrichment for white Americans during the periods of slavery and legal segregation.

White Women: Second-Class Citizens in White America   Today, only about five percent of those who run major corporations and other major organizations are women—mostly white women—or men of color. While white women are more common than people of color at the top of such organizations, they have not yet penetrated these decision-making heights in anything akin to proportionate numbers. Sex discrimination remains a central aspect of this society, and changes are coming slowly. As we have recounted in earlier chapters, white women have historically played a less central role than white men in creating and maintaining the system of racism. At the time of the founding of this nation, no women were among its framers and founders. While white women were not specifically singled out for gender oppression in the new Constitution, they were seen by the male founders as unequal by nature and in need of male control. The state and federal legal systems made sure that they were second-class citizens—generally under a father's or husband's control. In the colonies—and later in the United States—

white women did have a few more legal rights than black men or women. Constitutionally, white women were covered in the category of "free persons," not in the category termed "all other persons," the founders' euphemism for those enslaved. Thus, there were some limited rights for white women, albeit only those allowed by the white men who made the laws. Until the twentieth century, for example, U.S. law generally protected white women from attacks on their persons and property by strangers, though it usually did little to protect them from violence inflicted by husbands or male relatives. In contrast, as the famous Dred Scott case (1857) made clear, black Americans "had *no rights* which the white man was bound to respect."[25]

From the late 1600s to the 1860s white women in the upper income group sometimes inherited significant resources, including in some cases enslaved African Americans inherited under the mandates of state law.[26] In the subsequent century and a half, many white women at various class levels have directly supervised or benefited from the labor of exploited black slaves, servants, and maids in their homes. Over many generations, most white women have benefited to some degree from the undeserved enrichment of their families through the racist arrangements of slavery, legal segregation, and contemporary racial discrimination. For centuries white women's access to economic and cultural resources, privileges, and opportunities—though significantly restricted by patriarchy and sexism—has on the average been significantly greater than that of black women or men. Still, we should keep in mind that it is white men who have played the most central role, to the present day, in creating, shaping, and maintaining the ongoing system of racism.

The Many Costs of Racial Oppression   Unjust impoverishment and the struggle against everyday racism for black Americans are the other side of the unjust enrichment and enhanced opportunities for white Americans. In earlier discussions we have examined many of the burdens and barriers that constitute racial oppression, particularly the discriminatory barriers in employment, housing, education, law, politics, and public accommodations. For African Americans this recurring and widespread discrimination has many costs and consequences—not only economic costs but also psychological, physical, family, and community costs.

The Many Economic Costs   In recent decades, U.S. government census data have shown the median family income of black families to be consistently in the range of 55 to 61 percent of the median family income of white families. During the late 1980s and into the 1990s this percentage actually declined. In the late 1990s black median household income ($25,351) was still about 60 percent of white median income ($42,439). These data present a clear picture of persisting and substantial inequality across the color line. In addition, today, as in the past, black families face poverty at a much greater rate (26 percent) than white families (8 percent) and an unemployment rate roughly twice that of whites.[27]

Black workers are often the first laid off during economic downturns and the last to be recalled. Coupled with a high unemployment rate is a high underemployment rate. In recent decades this rate has ranged up to one-third or more of black workers in many communities, a much greater figure than for whites; underemployment here includes workers without jobs and those who can only find part-time work or are making very low wages. Moreover, employment conditions for many black Americans, particularly those in lower-paying jobs, have now changed for the worse with increasing automation in many industries. As Sidney Willhelm argues, "lacking any economic usefulness for capitalist America, Blacks are being removed from their relations to the system of production and thus become declassed persons."[28]

One dramatic indicator of generations of white access to the acquisition of material and educational resources can be seen in measures of family net worth. The median net worth of white households ($61,000 in 1995) is more than *eight times* that of black households ($7,400 in 1995). In addition, black families have most of the wealth they do hold in cars and houses, while white families are far more likely than black families to have interest-bearing bank accounts and to hold stock in companies.[29] Even white families with modest incomes — in the $7,500 to $15,000 range — actually have greater wealth (net worth) than black families with incomes in the $45,000 to $60,000 range.[30]

Some of these income and wealth inequality data periodically appear in the mass media, but there is usually no attempt to understand the role of centuries of systemic racism in creating this large-scale inequality. Instead, there is often some argument that somehow black workers and their families are to blame. Whether it is openly or subtly asserted, many mainstream writers and scholars suggest that blacks are not working hard enough, are culturally handicapped, or do not have the intelligence to do better.

Stolen Labor   The real explanation requires a much deeper probing. As we saw in earlier chapters, undeserved impoverishment and advantage began at an early period in American history. Much of the capital and wealth of whites in earlier centuries came directly from the labor of enslaved Africans and African Americans, or from the economic development spurred by the profits from slave plantations. For African Americans the economic costs of slavery included not only the value of the labor expropriated but also the value of lost opportunities to acquire economic and educational resources.

James Marketti has estimated the dollar value of the labor taken from enslaved African Americans from 1790 to 1860 at, depending on the historical assumptions, from at least $0.7 billion to as much as $40 billion (in 1983 dollars). This is what black individuals and their families lost in income because they did not have control of their own labor under slavery. If this stolen wealth is multiplied by a figure taking into account lost interest from then to the present day, the economic loss for black Americans is put at from $2.1 to $4.7 trillion (in 1983 dollars).[31] Extending

Marketti's calculation for the entire period from the beginning of enslavement in the 1600s, and calculating it in terms of year-2000 dollars, would increase the dollar value of the lost wealth to a much higher figure.

After the Civil War the newly freed black Americans faced new economic exploitation and oppression. During the Civil War and Reconstruction periods there were proposals in Congress to give those recently freed some land—the famous "forty acres and a mule"—to begin new lives. Black families never got access to the land promised, and the inequality in agricultural land was a major cause of persisting racial inequalities in the decades after the Civil War. Using violence and terrorism, as well as the law, white southerners actively denied black southerners access to good land, to fair credit arrangements, to political power, and to education and other types of cultural capital.[32]

The costs of segregation for black workers included not only little access to capital over the next four generations—even in the form of small businesses or farms—but also the lower wages stemming from widespread discrimination and exploitation. White planters extracted much profit from the labor of their black tenant farmers and sharecroppers. Because the new exploitation was done under cover of contracts within a "free market" framework, no one seemed responsible for the poverty of the impoverished tenant farmers and sharecroppers except themselves. Under the burden of segregation, the economic losses for black Americans were again high. Some researchers have estimated the costs of the labor market discrimination against black Americans for the years 1929 to 1969 (in 1983 dollars) at $1.6 trillion.[33] Calculating the cost of discrimination for a longer period, from the end of slavery in 1865 to 1968, the end of legal segregation, and putting it into year-2000 dollars would likely increase the cost estimate to much more. Moreover, since the end of official segregation black Americans have suffered additional economic losses. For the year 1979 alone, one estimate of the cost of continuing racial discrimination in employment was put at $123 billion for black workers.[34]

A simple total of the worth of all the black labor stolen by whites through the means of slavery, segregation, and contemporary discrimination is staggering—perhaps six to ten trillion dollars. The sum represents a large portion of the nation's total wealth for the current decade. In addition, this economic cost is only one aspect of the total system of racial subjugation. These monetary figures do not include other major costs—the great pain and suffering thereby inflicted, the physical abuse, or the many early deaths. Consideration of this massive noneconomic damage needs to be figured into the ultimate social cost accounting of systemic racism.

Some Economic Consequences of Blocked Access   In order to build successful families and provide for their children, parents need access to significant economic, educational, and other social resources. Opportunities are greatly truncated for those who are targeted by racism. Exclusion from even one major opportunity to secure resources can have both immediate and long-term consequences for the families involved. Stephen DeCanio has developed an economic model that suggests that African Americans who had no property because of slavery and who were emancipated without the promised forty acres—without significant arable land—were as a group fated to endure major long-term economic disparity with whites even if they had experienced favorable employment conditions, which they did not. The initial gap in land access "would have produced by itself most of the gap in income between blacks and white Americans throughout the late nineteenth and early twentieth centuries."[35] This racial disparity has passed along to many subsequent generations, to the present day. The long-term impact of the initial racial disparity in agricultural resources would, as David Swinton has noted, "prevent attainment of racial equality even if current discrimination ended and blacks and whites had identical tastes and preferences."[36]

Not only were black families substantially excluded from homestead lands by law or white violence, they were forced into segregated schools, workplaces, and residential areas. Legal segregation in the South and de facto segregation in the North generally kept black families from generating the resources and wealth necessary to compete effectively with whites over many lifetimes.

Take, for example, the attempt to create a small business. Compare a black person and a white person trying to set up new businesses today. Often such entrepreneurs must draw on family savings, such as a house equity, or borrow from relatives and local banks. The black entrepreneur is less likely than a white entrepreneur to have significant personal or family resources to draw upon because his or her family has been unable to build up resources due to generations of systemic racism. In addition, a black entrepreneur is more likely to face discrimination in getting bank loans today. Discrimination in the past can seriously multiply the costs of doing business today. (Recall the discussion of lending and other business discrimination in chapter 5). Once white families garner some economic resources, they may invest those assets and profit from what might be called the "money value of time." Having resources, often unjustly gained, over some period of time often allows for the further enhancement of family resources. In the past, however, the black businessperson's parents and grandparents likely faced harsh segregation, which cut down sharply on what they could earn, save, and pass on to later generations.

There are other effects from this heritage of racism. Even if the black entrepreneur's predecessors had been able to start a business, they would likely have been limited to black customers and would have been located in a black community. Such a business is likely to have had no name recognition outside the black community. Earlier discrimination and segregation reduce business visibility, especially with nonblack customers, and the effects commonly persist into later generations of business operation. This is not a problem confronting most white businesses. The lack of capital or name recognition stemming from past discrimination means that today the black business may well have much more trouble than an otherwise comparable white firm in getting customers and employees. The removal of legal segregation does not get rid of its lasting impact.[37]

Today there is relatively little monetary inheritance across the generations for most black families, regardless of their social status. The majority of those in the black middle class are first generation, so they have not had the time to accumulate significant assets for two or more generations like the majority of white middle-class families. For families with some assets the major source is usually an equity built up from home purchases over a few generations. Historically, the majority of whites have gotten some material advantages in terms of the transmission of material assets in the form of homes, savings, land, securities, or small businesses. Centuries of discrimination in employment and housing mean that today black families are less likely to own their homes than whites (47 percent for blacks versus 69 percent for whites), and this is true for middle-class as well as working-class black Americans. Discriminatory practices in home sales and insurance have long limited the ability of black Americans to build up the housing equities that can be used to start a business or help the next generation get a better education.[38] Some research also indicates that the current white-black differential in wealth is *not* the result of differences in savings rates. It exists because black individuals generally inherit little or nothing from their families, and inheritance is the major source of wealth transmission in the United States.[39]

Interestingly, in recent public opinion polls whites often say that black Americans are now roughly equal with them, as though whites do not see the many costs of racism laid on black Americans (see chapter 4). However, at some level most whites seem to be aware that being black in America involves major personal, family, and economic costs. For example, political scientist Andrew Hacker reports on asking white college students how much they would seek in compensation if they were suddenly changed from white to black. Most white students indicated that "it would not be out of place to ask for $50 million, or $1 million for each coming black year."[40]

Some Cultural Costs   From the first years of the colonial period to the present day, African Americans have taken much strength from their social and cultural heritage, one strongly rooted in extended families and friendship networks. The knowledge carried in these networks includes positive values and perspectives on life, as well as portraits of role models that buttress identity and self-respect. Black Americans have had to be like experienced anthropologists and know white society well in order to survive or thrive; they have had to be experts on how to respond to the hostile actions of the dominant group. Black American culture did not arise freely on its own but under conditions of oppressive slavery, segregation, and modern racism. It thus has important elements of cultural resistance. While this culture has many strengths, and undoubtedly draws on its African heritage, it also reflects the past and present exclusion of black Americans from the many privileges and resources available to whites, as well as the forced assimilation into Anglo-American ways often pressed on black Americans. Reflecting on earlier centuries, legal scholar Patricia Williams has concluded that the black slave experience "was that of lost languages, cultures, tribal ties, kinship bonds, and even of the power to procreate in the image of oneself and not that of an alien master."[41] Because of this and the impact of later segregation, full cultural decolonization is a major step yet to be taken for most Americans of African descent—a key argument made by many Afrocentric analysts.

In recent years some analysts have tried to counter arguments that racism is still systemic in the United States with the contention that the nation now has a "rainbow culture." The suggestion is that many whites accept aspects of black culture, such as much of the music (for example, jazz and rap) and other entertainment that has emerged out of black communities. However, whites in decision-making positions, such as the whites at the head of media corporations, generally control the way in which black music and entertainment elements move into the white-dominated society and culture. As Ellis Cashmore has put it, whites have converted much of black culture "into a commodity, usually in the interests of white-owned corporations" and "blacks have been permitted to excel in entertainment only on the condition that they conform to whites' images of blacks." Whites can feel good by deploring past discrimination and accepting black achievements in areas such as music, entertainment, and sports. "Aspects of the black experience can be integrated into the mainstream and, with the advent of the mass media, consumed without even going near black people," Cashmore tells us. "Hit a button and summon the sounds and images of the ghetto."[42] This apparently respectful acknowledgment by whites of black cultural achievements usually conceals, just below the surface, old stereotypes of black Americans as entertaining, odd, and marginal to the mainstream of U.S. society and culture.

In addition, the absorption of a few elements of a subordinated culture into the dominant culture does not mean much if there is little or no change in the fundamental aspects of the dominant culture and society, such as in its legal values and practices, its discriminatory ways of employment, and its discriminatory political and business practices. Under the regime of racism African Americans are still pressured, even today, to assimilate and adapt in a more or less one-way fashion to the dominant culture and institutions.

The Psychological Impact   In several recent studies many black respondents have indicated in one way or another that they feel like "outsiders" in the United States.[43] The omnipresent reality of modern racism generates this feeling. "Race" is constructed not just in white minds, but in the ways whites still regularly and routinely interact with blacks across this society. When a black person enters an organization where whites are present in large numbers or walks down a street where whites are commonplace, race is seen and created in those specific places by recurring white animosities, images, proclivities, and actions. Whites, in an ongoing, lifelong series of interactions, determine who is "black" and how that blackness is treated. This, in turn, affects how black women and men see themselves. In interactions with whites, blacks are often excluded from full human recognition, from important social positions, and from significant societal rewards.

Recurring discrimination can bring a significant psychological toll. For instance, few whites reflect on the impact of the defensive actions they often take when they are near black men. As we mentioned earlier, frequently when a black man is near, white women will tightly clutch their purses and white women and men will take such defensive actions as getting out of elevators, crossing the street, or locking car doors. If such actions come to whites' attention, they tend to view them as only "minimal slights."[44] Yet these actions can have a negative and lasting impact, for the targeted black man will feel like an outcast or alien. At a minimum, every black person has to develop strategies to counter this psychological warfare by whites.

The psychologist William James once concluded that humans inflict no more "fiendish punishment" on each other than social marginalization.[45] Modern social science has documented the negative, often severe, effects that social marginalization and dehumanization have on the physical and emotional health of human beings.[46] Racist oppression inflicts a type of marginalization and dehumanization on its victims. Under slavery, segregation, and contemporary racism, recurring discrimination and degradation have brought onerous psychological health and physical health burdens to many black Americans. Indeed, many black Americans today suffer from something like the post-traumatic stress syndrome—with its pain, depression, and anxiety—that has been documented for military veterans of some U.S. wars.

Recurring Challenges to Self-Confidence and Identity   The impact of racism includes a broad range of psychological reactions—from anxiety and worry to depression, anger, and rage. In interviews with a large number of black Americans, I and my colleagues have found that many speak poignantly and in detail about the impact of blatant and subtle discrimination on the self-esteem and self-confidence not only of themselves but also of friends and relatives. Many are especially concerned about the negative impact on the youth in their communities.[47]

Recent sociopsychological research has examined the impact of racist stereotypes on the performance of students. In pioneering studies by Claude Steele and his associates, black and white students were given skills tests similar to the Graduate Record Examination (GRE). When this examination was presented to black students as a test of their "intellectual ability," they did less well on the tests than white students of comparable ability. However, when the test was presented to the black students without the suggestion that it was a type of intelligence test-ing, they performed at a level similar to that of the white students. Steele describes this situation as one of "stereotype threat," a condition where commonplace soci-etal stereotypes come to the front of the black students' minds. Stereotype threat can distract and create anxiety and self-consciousness that hurts test performance.[48] If black students come to think that they are not as intelligent as whites, they may not perform as well—especially under time pressure—as otherwise comparable white students. The researchers found that stereotype threat was the most dam-aging to the performance of black students who strongly identify with the area of performance concerned. It was the confident students more so than the less confident who were likely to be affected by the implied stereotype. As Steele men-tions, "This is a threat that in the short run can depress their intellectual perfor-mance and, over the long run, undermine the identity itself, a predicament of seri-ous consequence."[49]

These findings point to a more general problem. The United States is still a society where the lack-of-intelligence stereotype is regularly pressed on black Americans in schools and through the mass media, such as in the discussion of black-white "IQ" differentials that reappears every few years. Spoken or written stereotypes, when repeated enough times, can have a negative impact, perhaps reducing a person's effort to achieve certain important personal or family goals. From cradle to grave, whites force black Americans to live out their lives under a constant bombardment of stereotype threats and to create a repertoire of psyche-saving measures to counter them.

Marxist and feminist analyses have suggested how those who are oppressed sometimes help to create or reproduce their own oppression.[50] Caught in the vise of an oppressive society, those who are subjugated often internalize the negative views and stereotypes of their own group, an internalizing that can lead to low self-esteem and self-hatred. Over time, many who are racially colonized come to accept, to some degree, the racist rationalizations put out by the colonizers. In order to survive or thrive, a black person must constantly battle not only the every-day discrimination of whites but also the racist imagery and questioning routinely placed in her or his own mind by the racist system.

The Reaction of Rage Psychiatrists William Grier and Price Cobbs examined the extent to which the anger and rage of black Americans are created by the per-vasiveness and complexities of racial discrimination. Drawing on clinical inter-views, they concluded that successful psychological counseling with black Americans must deal directly with the omnipresent discrimination they endure. From years of counseling they have concluded that blacks "bear all they can and, if required, bear even more. But if they are black in present-day America they have been asked to shoulder too much. They have had all they can stand. They will be harried no more. Turning from their tormentors, they are filled with rage."[51] Today, anger and rage over everyday racism is commonplace among black Americans. Overtly expressed or silent, this rage can lead to inner turmoil, emotional withdrawal, or serious physical problems.

The seriousness of black anger over discrimination is made clear in the following comments from an interview with a retired black professor. Replying to a question about the level of his anger (on a scale from one to ten) toward white racism, he answered, "Ten! I think that there are many blacks whose anger is at that level. Mine has had time to grow over the years more and more and more until now I feel that my grasp on handling myself is tenuous. I think that now I would strike out to the point of killing, and not think anything about it. I really wouldn't care. Like many blacks you get tired, and you don't know which straw would break the camel's back."[52] In his interview he makes it clear that he gets most angry from observing the discrimination that white men, women, and children constantly inflict on black young people.

Psychological rage can build to a high level. One black man, Colin Ferguson, shot six people and injured numerous others on a New York commuter train. His attorneys wanted to use black rage as a partial explanation for the multiple killings. They wanted to argue in court that Ferguson's preexisting mental problems were made worse by the recurring racism and consequent anger he faced as a black man. (Ferguson fired his attorneys and did not use this defense.) Numerous white commentators rejected the proposed rage defense as absurd or radical. Conversely, when Bernard Goetz, a white man, was tried in New York for shooting four black teenagers who smiled at him and "asked" for five dollars, his attorney used a rage-and-fear defense, arguing that Goetz was fearful of the teenagers because of previous muggings he had endured. His attorney demonized the black teenagers, using such terms as "vultures" and "savages," and a predominantly white jury acquitted Goetz. Few whites saw this rage-and-fear defense as problematic.[53]

The Lifetime Energy Loss   Psychologists Alexander Thomas and Samuel Sillen have pointed out that to survive everyday racism a black person has to view every white person as "a potential enemy unless he personally finds out differently."[54] Black Americans of all ages and statuses are thus forced into a vigilant, cautious, and defensive orientation as they deal with potentially dangerous whites throughout their lives. By virtue of an accident of birth, they must expend an enormous amount of energy defending themselves and their families from the assaults of blatant and subtle racism on a more or less daily basis.

The energy thus drained from blacks can have major benefits for whites even beyond the immediate benefits of discrimination. Over their lifetimes whites have a major energy advantage in competing with blacks, for they do not waste large amounts of time dealing with the impositions of antiwhite discrimination. Moreover, as a consequence of the huge energy waste, black men, women, and children may not be able to achieve what they might otherwise have achieved;

they may not have enough energy left to develop to their full human potential. This energy drain may also mean they do not have as much energy to put into their families, organizations, and communities as they might otherwise have had. In this way the impact on an individual has major societal consequences.

The Negative Impact on Physical Health   The stress, anger, and rage created by everyday racism can generate serious physical health consequences. When asked in interview studies about the costs of the discrimination they face, black respondents cite a broad range of problems—from hypertension and stress diabetes to stress-related heart and stomach conditions. One recent research study examined stress and blood pressure for more than four thousand black Americans. Those reporting substantial discrimination tended to have higher blood pressure than those who reported less discrimination.[55] One study that I and my colleagues recently conducted involved focus group interviews with a number of middle-class African Americans. Several participants in our focus groups gave details on how high blood pressure and other health problems were linked, at least in part, to discrimination. One nurse in the Midwest commented on her body's reactions to a workplace with a hostile racial climate, saying,

> That's when I got high blood pressure. And my doctor. . . . I told him what my reaction, my body's reaction would be when I would go to this place of employment . . . which was a nursing home. When I turned into the driveway I got a major headache. I had this headache eight hours until I walked out that door leaving there. . . . I went to the doctor because the headaches had been so continuously. And he said . . . "You need to find a job because you do not like where you work." And within myself I knew that was true. But also within myself I knew I had to have a job because I had children to take care of. But going through what I was going through wasn't really worth it because I was breaking my own self down . . . it was constant intimidation. Constant racism, but in a subtle way. You know, but enough whereas you were never comfortable. . . . And then I finally ended up on high blood pressure pills because for the longest, I tried to keep low. I tried not to make waves. It didn't work. I hurt me.[56]

Modern racism literally makes people sick. Similarly, other research studies that have conducted in-depth interviews with middle-class black Americans have found that they associate the discrimination they encounter with such physical problems as chronic fatigue, back pain, insomnia, and recurring stomach problems and headaches.

Demographic data on longevity indicate the physical harshness of racism in cold statistical terms. In the United States blacks average significantly shorter lives than whites, a situation probably true for centuries. Thus, historian James Oakes reports that most black slaves died by the age of forty, and other historical studies suggest that on the average white slaveholders lived more than forty years.[57] By the year 1900 the life expectancy for an average black person was still only about thirty-two to thirty-five years, some sixteen years less than that for the average white person.[58] Today, this black/white gap has closed somewhat but is still large. The life expectancy for black Americans is now about sixty-nine years, which compares to about seventy-five to seventy-six years for whites. The system of racism costs the average black American about six to seven years of her or his life. Thus, for many deceased African Americans, everyday racism could be listed on their death certificates as a major cause of death.

A Complex and Accumulating Burden   Thinking in terms of the cumulative impact, sociologist Rodney Coates has described everyday racism as a cage: "To the casual observer, each wire does not appear to be sufficient in and of itself to retain the bird. But when viewed from either within or as a whole we see a finely constructed cage. The problem, from a pedagogical, policy, research, or activist perspective, is that we tend to concentrate on only one wire or phenomenon, removal of which leads to great anticipation that the war has been won. Unfortunately, while even more insidious wires are being constructed, the others are left intact."[59] The cage of racism has many wires.

For any given individual, repeated encounters with white animosity and mistreatment accumulate across many institutional arenas and over long periods of time. As we have suggested previously, the number of such encounters for the average black adult is undoubtedly in the thousands. Moreover, the impact on an individual is usually much greater than what a simple summing of her or his experiences might suggest. The cumulative impact of psychological and physical problems directly or indirectly linked to racism can likely be seen in the large differential in life expectancy noted previously. The steady acid rain of racist encounters with whites can significantly affect not only one's psychological and physical health but also one's general outlook and perspective. Thus, research by Tyrone Forman indicates that African Americans who are locked into traditional "black jobs" report a weaker sense of efficacy and less satisfaction with the quality of their lives and health than those African Americans not segregated in such traditional jobs.[60] Of course, most black Americans, even those not in traditional job categories, face recurring discrimination at the hands of whites. A black American's life perspective must of necessity embed a repertoire of responses designed to counter the many discriminatory actions of whites.

For many white commentators, whatever racial discrimination remains in U.S. society is viewed as an individual problem that should be dealt with on an individual basis. However, this view of contemporary racism is way off the mark. The assaults of blatant, covert, and subtle racism have strong effects not only on black individuals but also on their larger social circles, for the reality and pain of discriminatory acts are usually shared with relatives and friends as a way of coping with such inhumanity. Over time the long-term pain and memory of one individual becomes part of the pain and collective memories of larger networks, extended families, and communities. This negative impact requires the expenditure of much individual, family, and community energy to endure the oppression and to develop strategies for fighting back.

The Price Whites Pay for Racism   Writing in a late-1960s Supreme Court decision cited previously, Justice William O. Douglas argued that "the true curse of slavery is not what it did to the black man, but what it has done to the white man. For the existence of the institution produced the notion that the white man was of superior character, intelligence, and morality."[61] Thus white-supremacist thinking entails living a lie, for whites are not superior in character, intelligence, or morality. This self-deception takes a corrupting toll on the souls of white Americans.

The majority of white Americans do not seem to have much empathy for the suffering and pain of those who face racial discrimination. Participation in discrimination, or winking at the practice of discrimination of others, feeds a distancing of the racial other. This distancing in turn feeds further discrimination. Several recent analyses of corporate workplaces have concluded that discrimination by white male employers and managers lies substantially in their inability to deal with any group—be it black or female—that is quite different from themselves. The social inheritance of racial privilege has meant that whites, and especially white men with power, have rarely had to position themselves to relate in egalitarian ways with the outsiders. There is an unconscious failure to extend to the racialized others the same recognition of humanity they enjoy themselves.[62]

Living a Hypocritical Ethic   Traditionally optimistic approaches to racial matters have accented the egalitarian values supposedly held by the majority of white Americans. For example, in the late 1930s and early 1940s Gunnar Myrdal, a Swedish social scientist, and his U.S. colleagues conducted a major study of racial segregation, one funded by the Carnegie Corporation and reported in the influential 1944 book *An American Dilemma*. Representing the small left wing of the ruling class at the time—the majority in the elite then supported segregation and held to the doctrine of biological racism—these progressive researchers argued that white Americans were under the spell of the American creed—the "ideals of the essential dignity of the individual human being, of the fundamental equality of all men, and of certain inalienable rights to freedom, justice, and a fair opportunity."[63] As they saw it, this equality ethic was in great tension with the society's racist practices—thus the phrase "an American dilemma." Myrdal and his associates saw the U.S. racial problem as solvable in principle because it was situated in whites' failure to live up to the American creed of equality. However, as Oliver Cox pointed out in a critical review at the time, these social scientists failed to understand that the problem of racism is *not* at base a problem of ideals but rather of the social, economic, and political interests of whites as a privileged group. The vested interests of whites lie in keeping a system of oppression that works to their advantage, and for most this outweighs commitments to egalitarian values.[64]

Myrdal and his associates were right that the realities of racism keep the nation from realizing the ideals that for centuries whites have proclaimed to be very important: equality, freedom, fairness, and justice. However, today as in the past, the majority of whites have at best a very limited commitment to the equality and justice ideals. They seem to wish these ideals to be implemented for themselves, but not for the the racial others. Most whites do not yet wish to see such principles actually incorporated as the foundation of the society. What is proclaimed is not an equality ethic really guiding the nation but rather a hypocritical or hypothetical ethic designed to deflect a real understanding of oppression and inequality.

Suffering for the System   Some of the price that the system of racism has demanded from whites can be calculated in lives. For example, the slavery system not only cost millions of African and African American lives over the course of its bloody existence, but it also took some white lives. Being a white overseer on slave plantations was often a dangerous job, as those enslaved sometimes lashed out at or killed their immediate oppressors. Slaveholders sometimes lost their lives as well, or their plantation houses and fields were burned to the ground by those they enslaved. The Civil War, the "war over slavery," took 620,000 lives on both sides, more than all other U.S. wars taken together. Nearly two in every one hundred Americans were killed. Many more were injured.[65] Black soldiers died in significant numbers fighting against slavery and for the Union, but most of those killed and maimed were ordinary white farmers and workers.

Moreover, white farmers and workers who have accepted the psychological wage of white superiority are much less likely to organize effectively with Americans of color. For at least two centuries, this lack of united organization has meant less desirable working and living conditions for ordinary Americans, including many white Americans. We have previously discussed how elites broke up a promising interracial movement of farmers by convincing white farmers they were racially superior. The same tactics have historically been used in keeping unions segregated.

Today, the impact of this historical segregation can still be seen in continuing divisions between white workers and workers of color. In various areas of the nation many white workers are still reluctant to organize aggressively with black workers and other workers of color. Even more important perhaps is the fact that many white workers still do not have a strong class consciousness and a well-developed class ideology that would enable them to better understand their own economic difficulties. As we move into the twenty-first century, racial consciousness is still dominant for the majority of white workers. When white workers, openly or half-consciously viewing themselves as racially superior, have refused to organize with workers of color against employers, they have often received less in the way of wage and workplace improvements than they might otherwise have secured.

Before and after the Civil War, ordinary whites paid a political price for structural racism. In creating an undemocratic society where barbaric violence against black Americans was enshrined in the laws, such as the fugitive slave laws, or legitimated by informal practice, such as brutal lynchings, whites lost some liberty as well. This was perhaps most true for those southern states with large numbers of enslaved men, women, and children—where the system of social control for enslaved blacks spilled over into greater political inequality for less powerful whites there than in the North. In these states the dominant political arrangements, for whites as well as blacks, were authoritarian—with elite-dominated, one-party political systems being the rule. For the most part, ordinary white farmers and workers had little say in the undemocratic political system. Moreover, the autocratic elites dominating local and state governments were little interested in providing adequate (not to mention, first-rate) social-welfare institutions, such as public health programs, public schools, and public colleges, for ordinary whites or blacks.

Today, southern states still reflect this racist heritage in critical ways. As a group, these states not only have larger proportions of poverty-stricken citizens but also generally weaker public schools and colleges, public health programs, and other important public programs providing for the general welfare of their citizens than do the northern states. This inferiority in public services affects the white, black, and other citizens of these states in significant ways.[66] The weak public sector is one of the continuing legacies of the authoritarian eras of slavery and segregation—and of the openly racist, one-party governments in place in most southern states until the 1970s. In addition, the political conservatism characteristic of the majority of southern white voters is in part a lingering consequence of the southern racial past (see chapter 8). And the South has provided a modest share of the nation's intellectual and scientific leaders and innovators—one striking consequence of its historically weaker public educational systems.

The Costs of White Isolation   Today white and black Americans are still largely segregated in terms of residence, a de facto segregation largely created and maintained by whites. As we have seen, this segregation has had severe consequences for black Americans, limiting access to jobs and services. It has also had some negative consequences for whites, who have fled the central cities and moved to ever more distant suburbs, often for racist reasons. In the process white families have paid a price in terms of higher housing costs, long-distance commuting, pollution from automobiles, and the social problems associated with metropolitan growth and central city decline. Thus growth is costly in terms of infrastructural costs— for transportation, water, and sewage systems—that increase greatly with sprawling and leapfrogging exurban development. Moreover, when the general economic health of central cities declines significantly, this can have a significantly negative impact on inner-ring white suburbs, which often lose jobs and businesses.

In this way some white suburbanites pay a price for the multigenerational exclusion of black Americans from good jobs and integrated residential areas.

Whites also pay for racism in elevated levels of fear and ignorance. Recall the Chicago study of two adjacent suburbs, one white and one black. Whites there were found to reside in an isolated bubble where they were generally able to live out their lives with few experiences that enabled them to get to know black Chicagoans; they were fearful of their black counterparts because they had had few contacts with them. Such social isolation is serious because it means that whites with greater privileges and power do not have the experience necessary to view other Americans with accuracy. Most do not understand, nor do they wish to understand, the reality and experiences of black Americans or other Americans of color. Given this lack of understanding, it is easy for whites to see black Americans as quite different from themselves. Gary Orfield has noted that whites who grow up in suburban enclaves will have "no skills in relating to or communicating with minorities."[67] In the future, as the nation becomes more diverse and multiracial, this orientation will become a major disadvantage for social and political interaction. In addition, such white isolation will be ever more of a handicap as the United States becomes more involved in international trade and diplomacy in a world where the leadership is becoming much more diverse and where non-European nations are becoming ever more powerful economically and politically.

Denying the Multiracial Reality   There is a deep secret about the nature of the so-called "whites" that few so named wish to confront. The secret is that many "whites" are *black*, and that most "blacks" are *white*; that is, many white and black Americans have *both* European and African ancestry. Indeed, many black Americans have as much European ancestry as they do African ancestry. One major source of this heritage is the many thousands of instances of white men raping black women during centuries of slavery and segregation. If one reverses the infamous one-drop-of-blood rule, which has long categorized any American with a little African ancestry as "black," then those with *any* European ancestry should by the same rule be "white." Sally Hemings, Thomas Jefferson's enslaved servant, was at least three-quarters European in ancestry. It is likely that many of her descendants have passed as white. In addition, many of her descendants who are taken as black have white cousins, in parallel lines stemming ultimately from Jefferson's and his wife's parents (see chapter 2). At least three-quarters of African Americans, it has been estimated, have at least one European ancestor. By an inverted one-drop-of-blood rule they are indeed "white."[68]

Estimates are that about 5 to 50 percent of white Americans have at least a little African or African American ancestry gained over fifteen or so generations.[69] Something closer to the lower figure seems most likely, and the proportion doubtless varies by area. In addition to those whites whose ancestors were African but who were able to pass into the white community, there were some European immigrants who came to the United States with some African ancestry—especially immigrants from southern areas of Spain and Portugal and other parts of southern Europe. Whites with some African ancestry have included prominent Americans. Among them is Jacqueline Kennedy Onassis, who has been celebrated in the media as a paramount symbol of white womanhood. Another is the actor Humphrey Bogart, who is often treated as a paramount example of white masculinity.[70] There are numerous other examples. Two recent books and a documentary by white researchers have shown that many prominent white families in the South have some black ancestors and relatives.[71]

However, many white families do not recognize, or have intentionally rejected, their black ancestors and contemporary black relatives. The aforementioned researchers report that some whites with whom they talked denied strongly the cross-racial linkages of their ancestors. Once again, collective forgetting and denying is a crucial part of the way in which whites have resolved the internal tension between the values of social justice and the reality of racist oppression, including that tension in their own kinship networks.

Once the fact that most black Americans have some European ancestry and many white Americans have some African ancestry is made clear, one can perceive how deep the pathology of racism is for white Americans. Systemic racism inclines whites to see what is *not* there—white racial purity—and to not see what *is* there—white multiraciality. This failure to see what is there afflicts not only whites with black ancestry but also many other whites. Examples of the latter include the white historians and other intellectuals who long denied Thomas Jefferson's multiracial descendants because they believed Jefferson was "too moral" to have transgressed the racial-sexual boundary.

One can push the argument about the African linkages of white Americans farther back into human history. Archaeological research indicates that the earliest members of *Homo sapiens* evolved in Africa. Thus, if one goes back far enough, *all people* now living have African ancestors; all living humans are not only Africans but distant cousins. Yet this point about African origins and ancestry is rarely discerned by white Americans. It would appear that by hating and attacking blacks, those who see themselves as white are thereby hating and attacking themselves, their own kin, their own family tree. Denial of the African origins and of a common humanity is ultimately a type of self-hatred. As Lewis Gordon has observed, "To accept racism to the grave is to capitulate to others' dehumanization and one's own. . . . Lurking within such an attitude is the total elimination of the social world. It is a consciousness that seeks the dissolution of the framework of being contacted by others. It is a consciousness that truly accepts the dictum 'Hell is other people.'"[72]

Conclusion   The racist reality of the United States remains harsh, brutal, and largely the responsibility of white Americans. As we have seen, systemic racism has had, and currently has, profound human consequences. This is even recognized by international agencies. A recent United Nations report calculated a Human Development Index (HDI). The HDI is an evaluation of quality of life and incorporates data on education, income, and life expectancy for various countries and for subgroups within these countries. For all countries and groups examined, U.S. whites ranked first in overall quality of life. In contrast, black Americans ranked only thirty-first in the list of all groups and countries, next to people from the islands of Trinidad and Tobago. The quality of life for black Americans as a group remains relatively low, and that of white Americans quite high, by international standards.[73] Today, black families average about 60 percent of what white families earn and survive on about 12 percent of the wealth of average white families. As individuals, they can expect to live six to seven years shorter than whites.

Even these damning data tell only part of the story. To these statistics must be added centuries of uncounted pain, suffering, psychological damage, and rage over injustice. Only by adding all these factors together can one assess accurately the long-term impact of slavery, segregation, and continuing racism. The total cost of nearly four centuries of systemic racism has been extraordinarily high—one likely reason the majority of white Americans spend much effort in denying the real causes and sources of black inequality.

While whites pay some price for the ancient system of racism, that price pales when put up against that paid by black Americans. Black Americans—and many other Americans of color—typically pay a direct, overt, heavy, immediately painful, and accumulating price for racism, while white Americans pay a more indirect, usually unseen, and long-term price.[74] Moreover, most whites get major advantages and privileges from the operation of systemic racism that much more than offset these costs.

seven

Systemic Racism
Other Americans of Color

In recent years some representatives and researchers from Latino, Asian, and Native American groups have criticized what they see as a dominant "binary black-white paradigm" in the contemporary United States. From their vantage point this binary paradigm is pervasive in the mass media, government agencies, and academic research.

For example, Angela Oh, an Asian American member of the presidential Advisory Board on Race in the late 1990s, called on policy makers to get beyond the black-white paradigm to a broader view of U.S. racial relations. Similarly, social scientist Yolanda Flores-Niemann has suggested that the prevailing black-white paradigm is misleading, that "the color of America is rapidly changing, and reality is masked by the assumption that issues dealing with racial minorities are a question of black and white."[1] Latino legal scholar Juan Perea has argued vigorously that the black-white paradigm assumes "race in America consists, either exclusively or primarily, of only two constituent racial groups, the Black and the White." In his view much literature on racial issues "comprehends only the study of White racism against Blacks as the legitimate scope of racism."[2]

Many who adopt this viewpoint view the "black-white paradigm" as too limiting and argue that it should be abandoned because each group has its own distinctive experiences with oppression and discrimination. These scholars and writers often portray the society as a buzzing confusion of racial-ethnic groups and experiences and emphasize differences and divergences among various groups. Much of the critical focus targets what is viewed as excessive attention to white and black Americans in the mass media, in government, and in academia, rather than the underlying system of white racism.

However, a deep understanding of the racial situations of nonblack, non-European groups require digging deeply into U.S. history to examine the systemic racism built into the foundation of the new nation by European entrepreneurs and colonists in the seventeenth and eighteenth centuries, as they enslaved Africans and killed off or drove away Native Americans. By the middle of the seventeenth century those enslaved were viewed by whites, and their legal system, as chattel property—a category that by the 1820s was composed almost entirely of black Americans.[3] This cruel white-on-black oppression was soon well-institutionalized and rationalized in a racist ideology, and has lasted now for nearly four centuries.

Thus, white-on-black oppression is much more than a "black-white paradigm," conceptual framework, media emphasis, or dialogue about race. It is a comprehensive system of exploitation and oppression originally designed by white Americans for black Americans, a system of racism that for centuries has penetrated every major area of American society and thus shaped the lives of every American, black and nonblack. Elaborating on their racist practices, the white founders of the nation made it ever clearer by the early 1700s that they wished to make this nation as white and homogenous as possible. Even liberal white leaders, such as Benjamin Franklin, spoke of maximizing the "lovely white" population and keeping it from being "stained" by too many "blacks and tawneys."[4] The ideal was white homogeneity, but a core economic and social reality was white-on-black oppression.

From the beginning a key aspect of the foundation of the United States, and of the colonies earlier, has been a system of racism centered substantially in white-on-black oppression. This long-standing structure of racism has been extended and tailored for each new non-European group brought into the sphere of white domination. Thus, U.S. society is not a multiplicity of disconnected racisms directed at peoples of color. Instead, this U.S. society has a central white-supremacist core initially developed in the minds, ideologies, practices, and institutions of those calling themselves "whites" for destroying the indigenous societies and for exploiting African American labor. This structure of racialized domination was later extended and adapted by the descendants of the founders for the oppression of other non-European groups such as Asian and Latino Americans. The critics are justified in criticizing the social sciences, media, and government agencies for not researching or discussing more centrally the racially oppressed situations of Asian and Latino Americans. These and other non-European groups are becoming ever more important to the racial-ethnic mix of the United States, and they do

suffer greatly from the white-racist system. However, one must also accent a critical point too often missed by critics of the so-called binary paragidm: That white
elites and the white public have long evaluated, reacted to, and dominated later
non-European entrants coming into the nation from within a previously established and highly imbedded system of antiblack racism.

The Foundation: Systemic Racism

The Scope of White-on-Black Oppression   Let us review briefly key aspects of the
broad system of white-on-black oppression. The whites who crafted the foundation of systemic racism were most concerned with the "black race within our
bosom," to use James Madison's phrase. Thus, African Americans were the only
group brought in large numbers to North America in chains. They were the only
group explicitly singled out several times in the U.S. Constitution for coercive control and violent subordination. They were the only group incorporated into the
economic and social center of the new society as chattel property from the first
century of colonial development. They were placed in a position at the economic
center because their labor was used to create the prosperity of the new white-
dominated nation. They were the only group viewed by the legal system as having no rights whatsoever, as the 1857 Dred Scott decision made clear.

White-on-black oppression extended well beyond the economy. It destroyed
cultures, families, and heritages. Thus, during slavery and later segregation many
black women were sexually assaulted by white men. The children that resulted
from these sexual attacks — and most of their descendants — were classified as
black under the racist rule of descent. African Americans are the largest racial or
ethnic group in North American history to involuntarily lose substantial control
over their own procreation — the largest group whose physical makeup was
significantly determined over time by the coercive control and sexual assaults of
white men. No group has lost so much of its home country ties and cultural heritage (see chapter 6). In a pioneering analysis Michael Omi and Howard Winant
have argued that the U.S. social system has seen multiple and overlapping "racial
formations" that have evolved historically.[5] While this is an important insight,
these multiple racial formations are not all of equal significance in the past or
present history of U.S. society. The system of antiblack racism is older, deeper,
and more central, while other racist arrangements are generally webbed to it or
have been shaped by it.

Timing and Size   The time of entry, size, distribution, and economic impor-
tance of non-European groups have made a difference in the character of their
racist incorporation by whites into the society. Note the extent, scale, and location
of the oppression of Africans and African Americans over several centuries. Because
of their early centrality to the American economic system, African Americans have
been more at the core of the white-dominated society than smaller or more region-

alized groups. Today, as in the past, sizeable numbers of African Americans are found in more areas of the nation than any other non-European group. Later non-European immigrants, including most Asians and Latinos, have been integrated later and selectively into the U.S. economy and polity—and in fewer places geographically.

Viewed historically, black Americans have been oppressed much longer by whites than any other group except Native Americans. Over nearly four centuries whites have routinely stolen much of the value of black labor under slavery, segregation, and contemporary racism. Moreover, the extremely large number of black Americans who were, and are, oppressed underscores the central significance of white-on-black oppression. Between 1619 and 1865 approximately six to seven million black Americans lived under conditions of slavery in North America.[6] Moreover, between 1619 and the year 2000 a total of perhaps sixty to seventy million blacks have lived in North America—and thus have had their labor taken and their lives burdened and truncated by slavery, segregation, and contemporary racism. This rough estimate is larger than for any other group that has suffered racial discrimination at the hands of white Americans.[7]

Another sign of the centrality of white-on-black oppression is the high level of white effort and energy put into maintaining antiblack racism. From the first decades of European colonialism, black Americans have been at the core of the racist system because they are the group whose subjugation has been given the greatest attention by whites. Whites have devoted enormous amounts of energy to oppressing African Americans—initially for labor reasons and later for a range of economic, social, and ideological reasons. Indeed, in the Civil War many thousands of southern whites gave their lives, at least in part, to maintain the enslavement of African Americans. In contrast, whites on the whole have put much less time and physical and mental energy into exploiting and oppressing groups such as Asian and Latino Americans, if only because the latter have been in the United States in large numbers for much shorter periods of time.[8]

Antiblack racism has been reproduced now for several centuries. This reality can be seen not only in the social, economic, and cultural resources passed along generations of white families but also in white dominance of the economic, legal, educational, and political arrangements that imbed white interests. Moreover, once the system of racism was established, substantial individual and collective resistance by black Americans forced whites to put even more effort into maintaining and periodically reframing white-on-black oppression. As some scholars see it, "One of the reasons why black people are so integral a part of American civilization is because black people have raised a lot of hell."[9]

African Americans were central to the two largest and most successful antiracist movements in U.S. history—that of the abolitionists from the 1830s to the 1860s, and that of the civil rights demonstrators in the 1950s and 1960s. The oppression of African Americans was crucial to the development of the nation's bloodiest war, and the course of that Civil War was affected by the participation of thousands of formerly enslaved black men as Union soldiers. From the first century to the most recent year, moreover, white-on-black oppression and black resistance to it have regularly shaped the trajectory of local and national politics in fundamental ways. Since at least 1800 white-black relations have been central to many government hearings, reports, laws, and court decisions, and there have been many private conferences dealing with this matter as well.

For the first two hundred years of colonial development, the only other non-European groups of significant concern to most European Americans were the Native American societies, which were generally seen as enemies to be destroyed or driven far from white borders. Until the 1870s they often rimmed the western boundaries of white expansion on the continent. Recall from chapter 2 that over several centuries numerous Native American societies were able to confront whites on their own turf and to draw on strong indigenous resources. Whites were intent on the destruction or displacement of the indigenous societies by whatever means were necessary. In the 1830s no less a figure than President Andrew Jackson led the expulsion of most of the remaining Native Americans from the eastern states, and by the 1870s Native Americans had lost the ability to make treaties as separate nations. They were usually forced into isolated reservations, where they have periodically been targets of private and government intervention intending to steal more land or other resources, destroy community solidarity, or force acculturation to white culture.[10]

While they have been the recurring targets of extreme brutality and genocide, Native Americans have not played as a central role in the *internal* socioracial reality of the colonies or the United States as have African Americans. Native American labor never became integral to the booming eighteenth and nineteenth century economy of the new white-controlled nation, nor were Native Americans integrated as a group into the new nation's core socioeconomic institutions. Still, the ideological notions of white supremacy and superiority over those viewed as "inferior" peoples were early honed by white colonizers in regard to both Native Americans and African Americans. Native Americans were seen as people who were not making proper use of the land, and thus as available targets for whites' theft of the land. Whites viewed Native Americans as uncivilized "savages" to be driven away or killed. Some significant attention was given to rationalizing this theft in racist terms by leading European and European American theologians and other intellectuals, as well as by the white public. Nonetheless, whites have historically put much more effort into developing a broad-ranging and persisting antiblack ideology.

Rationalizing White-on-Black Oppression   As we saw in chapters 3 and 4, a thorough racist ideology with its associated prejudices and stereotypes targeting black

Americans was created at an early stage in North American history and then was elaborated on in subsequent centuries. By the last decades of the eighteenth century and the early decades of the nineteenth century most whites—from southern slaveholders to northern liberals—agreed on a white-supremacist ideology with two key features: (1) white Europeans have a God-given right to exploit the labor of Africans and African Americans; and (2) the savage and un-Christian "black race" is far inferior to the civilized and Christian "white race." This ideology was not just tacked onto the nation's new institutions; it was an intimate part of the nation's foundation. Since the late eighteenth century whites have developed and extensively utilized this ideology, including those in corner taverns and members of the U.S. Supreme Court. For the first two-and-a-half centuries, numerous laws, including state and federal court decisions, used this ideology in insuring the subordination of black Americans. Moreover, from George Washington in the 1790s to Richard Nixon in the 1970s most U.S. presidents openly expressed antiblack views or took significant antiblack actions based on covertly held stereotyped views.[11]

Since the eighteenth century most racist discussions by whites inside and outside the halls of power have centered on white-black issues. Over this period white popular commentators, scholars, and politicians—those who dominate most public discussions of racial matters—have written many thousands of articles and books trying to rationalize slavery, segregation, and contemporary discrimination. The overwhelming majority of articles and books articulating a racist ideology in North America have focused centrally, if not exclusively, on rationalizing the subordination of black Americans.

While the literature of white extremist groups such as the Ku Klux Klan, today as in the past, does sometimes attack Native Americans, Asian Americans, and Latino Americans—often as "mud peoples" who are viewed as racial "mongrels" and thus inferior—such racist attacks tend to be far less common than those against black Americans (and in some circles Jewish Americans). When verbal attacks on these nonblack groups are made, they are usually brief or tacked onto more extensive attacks on black Americans.[12] Indeed, taking into account all racist authors, few have done books focusing on those nonblack groups. In the last few years several writers have developed book-length, racist arguments against immigrants of color, but even in this period the overwhelming majority of racist books and articles have still focused on black Americans.

Perhaps the most widely circulated of recent analyses defending the ideas of racial inferiority and superiority in intelligence, Richard Herrnstein and Charles Murray's *The Bell Curve*, is striking in its insistent focus on the centrality and inferiority of black Americans in this regard.[13] This foundation-funded book does discuss the intelligence levels of immigrants, Latinos, and Asian Americans, but those discussions are not extensive and are not as central to the book's main arguments.

Even with this focus on African Americans, whites regularly extend the ideology of white superiority to other Americans of color, including Native Americans, Latinos, and Asian Americans. As we will see in detail below, the hostile actions generated by this ideology periodically move well beyond verbal attacks—to the stark reality that can be seen in the large number of hate crimes targeting Americans in all these groups over recent decades.

White Identity and Emotions   During the first century of development a sense of white identity was brought about both in regard to the Native Americans on the borders of white territory and in regard to African Americans within the midst of the white colonists. By the late 1700s, however, this sense of whiteness was increasingly asserted mostly in terms of white views of an undesirable blackness. This orientation has persisted. For more than two centuries now, many whites have viewed the nation in mostly white-on-black terms. Judging from field interviews that my associates and I have done with whites in recent years, the racialized other most central to white identity and thinking—and the only such group that seems to obsess a large number of whites—is black Americans.[14] This research and other interview studies of whites suggest that the racist socialization of whites in regard to Americans of color other than blacks is much less systematic and basic to white identity, emotions, thought, and practices. Interviewing in the racially diverse state of California, researcher Ruth Frankenberg recently found that white women there accorded a hypervisibility to black Americans and a "relative invisibility to Asian Americans and Native Americans; Latinos are also relatively less visible than African Americans in discursive terms."[15] White women often singled out Asian Americans and Latinos as less different from whites than blacks are. Several studies have now shown that white women and men have more developed and detailed views of black Americans than of other groups.

The antiblack orientation is much more than cognitive. As we saw in earlier chapters, strong emotions, such as fear and loathing, and visual images often undergird the antiblack attitudes of many whites. The racist emotions of these whites seem much weaker in regard to other Americans of color. For example, whites seem to be much less likely to go into defensive maneuvers when an Asian or Latino man is nearby than when a black man is nearby. Whites are also less emotional about interracial marriage when it does not involve whites and blacks (see below).

Implementing the Racist Continuum   The developed and imbedded system of oppression originally created for African Americans has influenced the way whites have reacted to, oppressed, or accepted other people of color. Since the 1850s, one by one, most other non-European groups have been recruited by whites as cheap labor. Yet other immigrants have come as political refugees. Most have originated in societies linked to overseas military operations or imperialism on the part of the United States. Examples of this are China, Japan, and the Philippines in the nineteenth century and Korea, Taiwan, Vietnam, and Cuba in the twentieth. These non-European immigrants and their descendants have frequently been judged and evaluated by whites from within the framework of the white-on-black oppression and ideology already set in place.

Each new immigrant group is usually placed, principally by the dominant whites, somewhere on a *white-to-black status continuum*, the commonplace measuring stick of social acceptability. This socioracial continuum has long been imbedded in white minds, writings, and practices, as well as in the developing consciousness of many in the new immigrant groups. Generally speaking, the racist continuum runs from white to black, from "civilized" whites to "uncivilized" blacks, from high intelligence to low intelligence, from privilege and desirability to lack of privilege and undesirability. From at least the seventeenth century on, blackness was conceptualized as the opposite of whiteness and Europeanness. Lewis Gordon has suggested that "[o]ne is black the extent to which one is most distant from white. And one is white the extent to which one is most distant from black. . . . Blackness functions as the prime racial signifier."[16] Central to U.S. society is a comprehensive white-superiority conceptual paradigm imbedded in an underlying structural reality. "White" and "black" are socially constructed categories riveted to a white-dominated structure of oppression, and it is those with the greatest power—white Americans—who control who gets placed where in the continuum's categories. This longstanding continuum accents physical characteristics and color coding in which European features and cultural norms are privileged.

New non-European groups are customarily placed somewhere along this continuum in relation to white emotions, racist thought, and discriminatory practice. On occasion, some Americans of color are placed toward the privileged white end of the racial spectrum. In the old apartheid system of South Africa some Asians were officially categorized as "honorary whites" because the white government needed Asian investors. In the U.S. case some Latinos and Asian Americans have from time to time been classified as "honorary whites" or "near whites" for somewhat similar reasons, such as in white-led, anti-affirmative-action efforts where Asian Americans are praised as being the equals of whites who supposedly need no affirmative action. Moreover, Frank Wu has accented the opposite phenomenon in which some people of color are defined as "constructive blacks," as being near or at the black end of the racist continuum.[17] We will see several examples of this process of black or near-black definition in later discussions of Latino and Asian Americans. Moreover, at some points in history some Latino, Asian, and Native American groups may be moved to intermediate positions on the racist continuum—again principally by white elites and for white purposes.

Of course, all racially defined groups do not share the same fate or have the same experiences. As we saw earlier, the treatment of Americans of color has varied according to their time of entry, size, culture, physical characteristics, and wealth. In the case of Asian and Latino groups, as we will see below, whites added a new dimension to the placement equation, that of "foreignness." Yet in every case it is the *dominant white group* that has set the major terms for their incorporation and interpretation. For instance, one important study of early California history shows that Mexican, Asian, Native, and African American groups did not develop in exactly the same way in California history, yet each was shaped by the preexisting framework of white supremacy, the central organizing principle of U.S. society that was brought there by white migrants from the East. Those migrating to the West carried the system of U.S. racism with them—in their heads, hearts, practices, and institutions. They brought a well-developed ideology rationalizing black subordination and applied these ideas, often with new embellishments, to other groups seen as intellectually or culturally inferior. Thus, in 1848 the California area's first English-language newspaper put it bluntly: "We desire only a white population in California."[18]

For later groups of non-European immigrants, whites' racist attitudes and practices targeting them were tailored to the particular conditions of these entrants. These groups have been shaped dramatically in this tailoring process. When, for instance, Asian American or Latino groups have become important for whites seeking their labor, whites have often ranked and categorized them along the light-to-dark, and close/not close to European-American culture, continua. Often the lighter a group is, and the more Anglicized it seems to whites, the better it will be treated and viewed. Thus, if light-skinned Cuban Americans are defined by whites as "near to white," they will have a different experience than darker-skinned immigrants of color, including darker Latinos like most Mexican Americans, whom many whites will place toward the "black end" of the socioracial continuum.

The Importance of Becoming White: European Immigrants   After the large-scale, forcible importation of Africans, the next large group of non-Protestant workers to come to the newly created United States were the Irish Catholics. Beginning in the 1830s, millions of these Irish immigrants found work in a growing number of industrial enterprises. As we saw in chapter 3, at first they were seen by native-born white Protestants as an undesirable Irish "race." However, within a generation or two, and thanks to aggressive efforts by many in the elites, Irish Catholics came to be seen, and to see themselves, as part of a superior "white race." As David Roediger has noted, "the emphasis on a common whiteness smoothed over divisions in the Democratic ranks within mainly northern cities by emphasizing that immigrants from Europe, and particularly from Ireland, were white and thus unequivocally entitled to equal rights."[19] Similarly, when large groups of workers from southern and eastern Europe were recruited for the rapidly industrializing U.S. economy in the last decades of the nineteenth century and the first decades of the twentieth century, they too were initially seen by native-born whites as unassimilable "inferior races." Still, these European immigrants often came with a little money, cultural capital, or political capital, resources generally unavailable to black Americans.

Within a generation most of these European immigrant groups were able to establish themselves as at the "white end" of the socioracial continuum, and they too participated in driving black workers out of jobs, labor organizations, and residential areas. Without exception, each new group of European immigrants has accepted the psychological wage of whiteness and rejected class solidarity with black workers. Even Jewish Americans, the European immigrant group suffering extreme hostility from gentile whites, worked hard to become white, often changing their names and undergoing cosmetic surgery to assimilate. In her probing analysis of how Jewish Americans gradually and intentionally became white, Karen Brodkin has shown how they often bought into preexisting white Protestant values and orientations as part of this process of becoming white.[20]

Significantly, for more than a century now the descendants of the Irish immigrants, as well as the southern and eastern European immigrants, have cited their predecessors' experience in playing down the racism still faced by African Americans. A typical argument asserts that all immigrants have suffered from discrimination and abuse in the past, and are thus not greatly different from black Americans in this regard. Speaking to black leaders at a meeting in the 1960s, Attorney General Robert Kennedy argued that "other Americans also had to endure periods of oppression." He pointed out that his grandfather was an immigrant who had suffered anti-Catholic discrimination. However, author James Baldwin pointed out to Kennedy the major flaw in this argument: "Your grandfather came as an immigrant from Ireland and your brother is President of the United States. Generations before your family came as immigrants my ancestors came to this country in chains, as slaves. We are still required to supplicate and beg you for justice and decency."[21]

Some Later Entrants into the Racist System: The Chinese and the Mexicans   By the early decades of the nineteenth century white adventurers and entrepreneurs were moving rapidly into the western areas of the North American continent. As a result of this expansion, more non-European groups were brought into the white sphere. The racist system developed for black Americans was often extended to Asian, Native American, and Mexican groups as whites took over western areas. Each set of relations between European Americans and a non-European group has historical specificity, and this means different experiences and, often, distinctive long-term outcomes. Historical circumstances, particularly the timing and mode of entry into the sphere of white domination and the group's size and resources, can mean a significant difference in experiences with whites. Let us examine briefly the experiences of selected non-European immigrant groups in the United States. I will focus here mainly on the experiences of those from China and Mexico.

Chinese Immigrants   In the 1850s Commodore Matthew Perry sailed U.S. warships into Tokyo Bay, and by this show of military might soon forced a treaty granting trading rights with Japan to the United States. By the late nineteenth century the United States was involved in major imperialistic pursuits in Asia and around the globe. In this process many overseas areas came under U.S. control or influence. U.S. and European missionaries and business people moved across the world, invading numerous Asian nations; Western incursions disrupted Asian economies and sometimes stimulated out-migration. For example, in the mid-nineteenth century various enterprises in Hawaii and on the Pacific Coast were seeking low-wage workers. U.S. labor recruiters secured some two hundred thousand Chinese workers between 1848 and 1882 to work on the railroads, in the mines, and in personal service jobs. Laborers were brought into western states and, in smaller numbers, into other regions. The Chinese were sought as workers who would work at low wages and set a model of hard work for other groups.[22]

When Chinese labor was imported in the 1850s, whites across the nation already had in place a well-developed system of antiblack racism. This white supremacist system was adapted, embellished, and expanded to encompass these new immigrants of color. Anti-Chinese images and stereotypes took root not only in the views of white elites seeking to justify their exploitation of Chinese laborers but also in the views of the white workers who faced competition from these immigrant workers.

As Ronald Takaki has pointed out, at an early point in time the Chinese immigrants were often associated "with blacks in the racial imagination of white society."[23] They were "Africanized" and grouped with blacks, with both groups being seen as dangerous to the health of U.S. politics and society by whites thinking in white supremacist terms. Even into the late 1920s, the U.S. Supreme Court upheld state laws placing Chinese Americans in racially segregated black (not white) schools. Early on the *San Francisco Chronicle* compared Chinese workers to black slaves: "When the coolie arrives here he is as rigidly under the control of the contractor who brought him as an African slave was under his master in South Carolina or Louisiana."[24] The new immigrants were seen as a subservient class of workers with few civil rights.

Over several decades many whites came to view the Chinese as another threat to white racial purity. In 1880, for example, the California legislature passed a law prohibiting whites from marrying a "negro, mulatto, or Mongolian." ("Mulatto" referred to someone with black and white ancestors, "Mongolian" meant Asian.) Earlier, in 1854, the California Supreme Court had overturned a lower court's ruling convicting a white man of murder on the basis of testimony by Chinese

Americans. A California law declaring that "no black or mulatto person, or Indian, shall be permitted to give evidence" against a white person was said by this court to include the Chinese because they fell under the term "black person." The court explicitly said that "black" includes "all races other than Caucasian."[25] Moreover, in areas of the southern United States, where some Chinese laborers were also imported, they were initially assigned a black or near-black position, although they were sometimes allowed in certain business situations, especially when their numbers were small, to operate as a middle group between whites and blacks.[26] Any variations from the white-on-black system of oppression were controlled by powerful whites.

In the 1840s, many thousands of white workers and adventurers began to migrate to California. Chinese and other Asian workers were often intentionally used by white employers to displace the more demanding (in terms of wages) white workers. With increasing competition between white and Chinese laborers came the adaptation and application by these whites of negative stereotypes, images, and epithets already used to defame black Americans. In the white mind there seems to be a "shelf" of long-standing racist images and stereotypes, which can be taken off as needed and employed to explain and interpret difficult social conditions, such as job losses and economic downturns. Like black Americans, Chinese immigrants were often called "niggers" or similar epithets and described in vicious racist imagery as childlike, immoral, and savage. The physical appearance of the Chinese was viewed by whites as only slightly different from that of African Americans. In cartoons and caricatures Chinese Americans were often portrayed as having what were thought of as African features such as darker skin and big lips.[27] Once again, whites portrayed themselves as the physically superior, aesthetically incomparable, and highly civilized group. Instead of working to build organizational alliances with Asian-American workers against the exploitative practices of white employers, white workers again persisted in their commitment to a strong racial consciousness and the psychological wage of whiteness. Indeed, white unions led in much of the growing anti-Asian agitation.

Like other leading newspapers, the *New York Times* compared "millions of degraded negroes in the South" with a similar "flood-tide of Chinese . . . with all the social vices."[28] The nation's mass media soon spread the racist imagery of an unassimilable "flood" of Asian immigrants—a theme still common in anti-Asian sentiment today. This white fear of being overwhelmed by those who are not white and who do not fit into white culture is an old theme that began in late-eighteenth-century antiblack racism—in, for example, the intellectualized racism of Thomas Jefferson (see chapter 3).

Over time whites did distinguish the Chinese immigrants more clearly from African Americans. While both groups were often seen as lazy, devious, or criminal, the Chinese were additionally stereotyped as culturally alien and undesirable immigrants. A racist immigration law excluding "undesirable" Chinese immigrants was passed in 1882 by the U.S. Congress. It was not until World War II, when China was a military ally, that Chinese immigrants—and then only 105 immigrants a year—were again allowed to come into the United States legally. In the intervening decades the majority of the nation's white leaders, as well as the white public, viewed Chinese Americans not as Americans but rather as an alien and excludable "race." For example, in 1896, even as he defended some rights for blacks as the lone dissenter in the *Plessy v. Ferguson* case, Supreme Court Justice John Marshall Harlan added this negative comment on Chinese Americans: "There is a race so different from our own that we do not permit those belonging to it to become citizens of the United States. Persons belonging to it are, with few exceptions, absolutely excluded from our country. I allude to the Chinese race."[29]

At the end of the nineteenth century the view of the white leadership, including its most liberal members, was that Asian Americans should not be citizens and should mostly be excluded. This dimension of foreignness is an amplification of earlier views of all immigrants as alien and foreign. While some earlier white immigrants, such as the French in the early 1800s, were initially seen as dangerous and alien by native-born Americans and legislation was crafted against them, it was only with the immigration of significant numbers of Asians and Mexicans that whites developed and amplified the dimension of their racist ideology to include the dimension of the foreignness of certain peoples of color. Sociologist Claire Jean Kim has argued that Asian immigrants have often been triangulated between whites and blacks, with a negative evaluation on the two axes of superior/inferior and insider/foreigner.[30] It would seem that initially the white view of Chinese immigrants gave some stress to their similarity to African Americans in status and inferiority, but over time this dimension decreased in importance as the aspect of foreignness was given more emphasis.

The established system of white supremacy, with its ingrained coding of racist thought and practice in all institutions, was once again extended and adapted, this time for Chinese Americans. As Gary Okihiro has put it, "insofar as Asians and Africans share a subordinate position to the master class, yellow is a shade of black, and black, a shade of yellow." The two groups are kindred peoples "forged in the fire of white supremacy."[31]

Other Asian Immigrants   After the Chinese were excluded, there was a division within the white community regarding the possibility of more Asian immigration. Needing labor, some West Coast employers pressed hard for new workers from other Asian countries. Soon, modest numbers of Japanese and Filipino workers were imported to fill low-wage jobs in Hawaii and certain areas of the West Coast. However, many whites—including some powerful members of the elite—were opposed to the presence of new immigrants, usually on racist grounds.

Initially, the Japanese and Filipino immigrants had to endure white supremacist attacks that characterized them, much like African and Chinese Americans, as unintelligent, physically ugly, lazy, or unmanageable.[32] In chorus with many white supremacists of his day, James Phelan, U.S. senator from California, went so far as to claim hysterically that Japanese immigrants were a major threat to the "future of the white race, American institutions, and Western civilization."[33] Aspects of the antiblack imagery were gradually given less attention than the foreign character of these Asian immigrants. Like the Chinese immigrants, the Japanese also faced the antiforeign stereotypes portraying them as unassimilable and threatening to the future of the "white race." Eventually opposition to Japanese immigration led to the infamous "Gentleman's Agreement" between the United States and Japan, whereby under U.S. government pressure the Japanese government agreed to cut off most immigration to the United States. Similarly, the modest numbers of Filipino immigrants permitted in the 1900 to 1930 period were cut sharply to just fifty a year by the 1930s. White supremacist thinking regularly interfered with the labor needs of many West Coast employers.

In the late nineteenth and early twentieth centuries, some whites were even opposed to overseas imperialism by the United States in Asia and Latin America because they feared such involvement would bring more immigrants of "inferior" or "mixed" blood into the American mix. However, white supremacist thought also took other turns. Some white supremacists lauded U.S. and European imperialism because it meant that whites brought some measure of "civilization" to, as they said, their "little brown brothers" overseas.[34] Many whites, especially in the elites, shared the sentiments in Rudyard Kipling's poem of the time: "Take up the White Man's burden / Send forth the best ye breed." Superior whites had a missionary obligation to civilize the world's peoples. Indeed, this latter view won out. When the United States defeated Spain in the Spanish-American War of the 1890s, both the Philippines and Cuba became major colonies in the growing U.S. empire.

Realizing that classification as near black on the white-to-black continuum means consignment by whites to extreme racial oppression, Asian immigrants and their descendants have often tried, in a variety of ways, to break out of this white-determined classification. The Naturalization Act of 1790 had explicitly limited the privilege of naturalized citizenship to "white" immigrants. This designation of white was created in opposition to black, and for some decades being non-European meant being classified politically and legally as more or less black in the minds of whites in power, as we saw in the aforementioned California court case. Moreover, between 1878 and the 1920s numerous U.S. courts were forced to examine applications for naturalization from members of several Asian groups. In one important 1878 case, *In re Ah Yup*, a federal district judge decided that a Chinese American could not become a naturalized citizen because he was *not white*.[35] This decision explicitly cited the classification of races by Johann Blumenbach in arguing that the meaning of "white person" was generally agreed upon (see chapter 3). Consistently, these court cases decided that those who were partially or totally Asian were not white and were ineligible for citizenship. The judges made clear that being white meant not having any known African or other non-European ancestry.[36] Significantly, the racist criterion for U.S. citizenship was not altered until the World War II period, and it was completely eliminated only in the 1952 Immigration and Nationality Act.

The Incorporation of Mexican Immigrants   The first Mexican residents of the United States did not immigrate, but were brought into the United States by violent conquest during the Texas rebellion and Mexican-American War of the 1830s and 1840s. Mexicans were thereby incorporated into the ever-expanding U.S. empire by whites determined to spread European dominance across the continent. Significantly, many whites who invaded northern Mexico in the early decades of the nineteenth century were from the slaveholding South, and some of these brought with them enslaved African Americans. Not surprisingly, these white intruders opposed the Mexican government's attempt to abolish slavery in northern Mexico.

Whites who migrated to southwestern areas carried the system of U.S. racism in their minds, propensities, and practices. Not surprisingly, they applied their white supremacist, antiblack ideology to Mexicans and Mexican Americans, who were seen as intellectually, physically, morally, and culturally inferior. Indeed, at the time of Anglo-American settlement of Texas and California a significant number of Mexicans, including those in some leading families, had African ancestry. (The Spanish conquerors of Mexico had early brought in enslaved Africans.) This multiracial heritage undoubtedly fueled early racist reactions to Mexicans on the part of whites immigrating to these area.[37] Whites often called Mexicans "niggers" or epithets with similar meaning and treated Mexicans in the same racist terms that they did black and Native Americans. Stephen F. Austin, a white adventurer who founded new communities in Texas, viewed Mexicans as a "mongrel Spanish-Indian and negro race."[38] Moreover, in the congressional debate over annexing Mexico, a leading U.S. senator, John C. Calhoun, opposed such government annexation. The United States, he asserted, had never "incorporated into the Union any but the Caucasian race. . . . Ours is a government of the white man. . . . in the whole history of man . . . there is no instance whatever of any civilized colored race, of any shade, being found equal to the establishment and maintenance of free government."[39] Most whites had no trouble moving from malevolent conceptualizations of the "black race" to similarly venomous views of other "colored races." Typically, the two concepts blended together in white minds.

By the early 1900s, however, agricultural and industrial expansion, some of it associated with World War I, created a demand for low-wage labor in the Southwest. Employers there moved to secure more immigrant workers from Mexico; large numbers were recruited for U.S. farms and factories, often with federal government assistance. After a decline in Mexican importation during the Great Depression, during World War II employers again sought Mexican workers for low-wage jobs in agriculture. Periodically since World War II, some white employers and their allies in government have sought Mexican workers to do low-wage agricultural and manufacturing jobs, especially but not only in the Southwest, although other business and political groups have agitated against such immigration. By bringing in large numbers of Mexican workers, U.S. employers have gradually changed the racial and ethnic landscape of the United States.

Like black Americans, Mexican Americans have been the targets of white supremacist thought and action. Indeed, the first extensive discrimination targeting Latinos in the United States was aimed at Mexican Americans, and it began in the middle of the nineteenth century. During and after the Mexican-American War, many Mexican families lost their lands by force or chicanery to the white Anglo newcomers. In New Mexico alone, at least two million acres of privately owned land were lost between 1854 and 1930.[40] Those who lost their lands often became landless laborers or sharecroppers on land formerly owned by Mexicans or Mexican Americans—in some cases land that had been owned by their ancestors.

In the century after the Mexican-American War there was little official racial segregation in the Southwest, but much informal discrimination targeted Mexican Americans, especially those who were dark skinned and of substantial African or Native American ancestry. In numerous towns and cities Mexican Americans faced blatant discrimination and overt segregation in employment, housing, schools, and public accommodations. This blatant discrimination lasted well into the 1960s—with some instances continuing to the present day. As Joan Moore explained in a 1970s book, "for decades the Texas Rangers terrorized the Mexican Americans of the Rio Grande Valley, and even today, although they are reduced in numbers, *los rinches* are still used to 'handle' Mexicans."[41] In the Sunbelt states this informal discrimination was a logical extension of, and often patterned on, that developed by whites for black Americans, but whites added new embellishments—such as hostility to the Spanish language—to their racist thinking and discriminatory practices. For decades Mexican children, to take just one important example, were punished for speaking Spanish in public schools and their names were Anglicized.[42]

In 1897 a federal court ruled that a Mexican American petitioner could become a naturalized citizen only because of special treaty agreements with Mexico. The white judge declared that if a "strict scientific classification of the anthropologist should be adopted, he would probably not be classed as white."[43] Periodically, other Latinos have also faced this type of racist categorization by white Americans. For example, in the last census of Cuba conducted by the Spanish colonial government before the U.S. conquest of the island, the Mexican and Chinese residents there were listed as "white." However, in the 1907 U.S. census, after the U.S. takeover, both groups were listed as "colored."[44] Racial classification is often a matter of state action. Well into the middle of the twentieth century prominent whites, including some in state legislatures and the U.S. Congress, openly described Mexican Americans in negative terms as mixed-race "mongrels" or inferior coloreds — often with specific reference to their Spanish, Native American, and African "blood."[45] In contrast to the white imaging and treatment of Asian immigrants, in the case of Mexican Americans whites have given much more attention to this "mixed blood." Until relatively recently in U.S. history, most whites have viewed mixed-ancestry people like most Mexican Americans as not white, and many doubtless still do. Once again, we observe the operation of the socioracial continuum so well imbedded in white minds and practices.

Anti-Mexican prejudices and rationalizations of discrimination developed among white workers as well as among elites. The situation was comparable to that of Asian immigrant workers. Because of competition with Mexican workers — especially after the large-scale immigration beginning in the 1910s — white workers and union organizations often participated in verbal and physical attacks on Mexican immigrants. There were occasional lynchings of Mexican Americans.

In some ways Mexican Americans have been able to fight racial discrimination better than black Americans, in part because it has usually been more informal and in part because as a group Mexican Americans have somewhat greater resources, including the resource of being close to their home country. (This closeness to home can also have the negative consequence of charges of not being fully "American.") Mexican, other Latino, and Asian immigrants who have come to the United States over the last century or so have usually had the ability, if they wish, to maintain a strong identity with and link to the home country. These ties have provided family and moral support, and sometimes monetary aid, in the face of racist barriers established by whites. For these immigrants and their descendants the home ties have generally not been destroyed by centuries of oppression, as they have been for most black Americans. In addition, from the 1850s to the 1920s Mexicans on both sides of the border had a history of armed struggles against whites, struggles that have inspired later generations to fight openly anti-Mexican discrimination. Given these social resources, Mexican Americans were even able to gain modest political power in some areas of the Southwest at an early point in time.[46]

When Chinese, other Asian, and Mexican immigrants were brought into the United States by employers seeking to exploit their labor, most whites automatically placed them in a status much inferior to that of native-born whites. They were initially categorized at or near the black end of the white-to-black continuum. This placement has not meant that Mexican Americans or other Americans of color have shared exactly the same treatment from whites as black Americans, but it has shown that whites, especially white elites, set the terms for each group's incorporation into U.S. society, for their level of economic and political development, and for the character and degree of the racial oppression they face.

Intermediate Placement Status   From the first stages of the development of systemic racism in the seventeenth and eighteenth centuries, black Americans were placed at the bottom of the hierarchy in the new society, with the only other non-European groups—the Native American societies—usually being destroyed or forced beyond what whites determined was their territory. As new non-European groups entered the nation from the 1840s to the early 1900s, they were initially placed near the black end of the racist continuum in white thought, imagery, and practice. Over time, whites have moved some of these groups to an intermediate position on the white-to-black continuum.

Placement in Intermediate Status   Some Americans with ancestral roots in Asia, or Latin America have been able to alter their racialized status within the white-dominated society, but only because whites have come to see them as "better" in racial, physical, or cultural terms than African Americans. Writing in the 1940s, sociologist Oliver Cox emphasized the determinative importance of this white ranking, saying "Whenever there are two or more races in the same racial situation with whites, the whites will implicitly or explicitly influence the relationship between these subordinate races. . . . The race against whom the whites are least prejudiced tends to become second in rank, while the race that they despise most will ordinarily be at the bottom."[47] Certain lighter-skinned, more white-looking, more acculturated—always as defined by whites—subgroups among Asian and Latino Americans have sometimes been viewed by whites as more acceptable than darker-skinned, less white-looking, less assimilated members of these same umbrella groups. At various places and times in U.S. history, some Asian and Latino Americans have been accepted by whites in an intermediate status, especially if they are only a small part of a local population or if this intermediate placement is of benefit to whites in some way. For example, in the early decades of Anglo-American settlement in the Southwest a modest number of lighter-skinned Mexican Americans in south Texas, New Mexico, and California, especially those in families with land and money, were treated more or less as "honorary whites."[48] In addition, after World War II, Japanese Americans, including some who had been in the U.S. concentration camps in western states, were more likely to be hired than black Americans in a number of the better-paying job categories in California. Their educational attainments were one reason, but so was their placement by whites in an intermediate status on the racist continuum.

More recently, certain groups among Latino Americans, such as lighter-skinned, middle-class Cuban Americans and South Americans, and certain groups among Asian Americans, such as middle-class Indian, Chinese, and Japanese

Americans, have frequently been accepted as closer to the white than the black end of the racist continuum. However, this near-white placement is not ordinarily extended to the majorities of the largest Latino groups—Mexican Americans and Puerto Ricans.

Whites make much use of placement in the intermediate status in order to keep the racist system flexible but intact. For example, when white commentators and analysts write or say positive things about the success of certain Asian or Latino American groups, they usually single out those who are lighter skinned and white acting. They point to the achievements of groups like middle-class Japanese Americans, Asian-Indian Americans, or Cuban Americans to suggest that Asian and Latino Americans are working harder and assimilating better to the core culture than black Americans.[49] Whites often cite some in these groups as examples of achievement without a need for affirmative action. In this way the racist system is protected and reproduced, as one group is placed or played off against another to white advantage.

Since the 1960s certain Asian American groups, such as Japanese Americans, have periodically been cited by opinion makers as "model minorities." Whites, especially the elites, again determine how a group is to be viewed. At earlier points in U.S. history, most Asian Americans were typed negatively as blacks or near blacks, but now certain groups within that umbrella category are publicly constructed as nearer to white. Somehow, their "nonwhiteness" and their foreignness are not as much of a problem in the white mind as they once were. Not surprisingly, the stereotyped "model minority" image was originally created by white politicians and commentators seeking to condemn black Americans for their aggressive protests against discrimination in the 1960s. Certain Asian Americans were then, and are now, said to be moving rapidly up the socioeconomic ladder unhindered by racial discrimination and without the recurring and irritating mass protests of black Americans. Today, as in the past, Asian Americans are said to be models of success because of their commitment to the "Protestant work ethic" and other values of importance to the white commentators.

Nonetheless, this model minority stereotype is linked to the current racist ideology. It not only misrepresents the condition of Asian Americans—many of whom are poor and most of whom still suffer discrimination by whites—but it also creates resentment among non-Asian Americans of color because it is widely used to assert that the United States is now a just and egalitarian society. The ability of whites to control the placement of peoples of color on the white-to-black continuum and to define their position in the society is yet another valuable tool for the reproduction of systemic racism over time.

The Position of Immigrants and Their Children   Until the increased immigration that began in the late 1960s, there were relatively modest numbers of Asian and Latino Americans in the United States. Today, majorities in all major Asian

American groups, except for Japanese Americans, are immigrants, and the majorities in all major Latino groups are immigrants or their children. These groups tend to be heavily concentrated in certain areas of the country— in states on the West Coast, in a few other states like Texas and Florida, and in a few large metropolitan areas like New York City and Chicago. There also seems to be more regional variation in whites' racist attitudes directed at Asian and Latino immigrant groups than in the racist antagonism directed against black Americans, who confront serious antiblack prejudice and discrimination virtually everywhere. In areas of the country where there are relatively few Asian or Latino Americans, whites tend to be less prejudiced and to worry less about Asian and Latin American immigration. Nationally, the image of the threatening foreigners today is not strong. Indeed, recent national opinion polls reveal that most whites do not see Asian and Latino immigration as a major U.S. problem.[50]

In states with substantial numbers of recent Asian and Latino immigrants, such as Texas and California, the Asian and Latino American communities are much larger and more important in interracial relations than in other regions. There immigrants of color have periodically been targeted in aggressively racist terms by whites. The foreignness imagery is often strong. Thus, in these areas whites have shown much greater antagonism toward the Spanish language and bilingual programs. The Proposition 187 campaign in California in the 1990s succeeded in the attempt to restrict government services to undocumented immigrants, while the Proposition 209 campaign successfully implemented a law eliminating affirmative action programs for college students of color. Both campaigns involved many whites who were concerned about the non-European origins of growing numbers of immigrants and their children.

Significantly, this opposition to immigrants of color has been more muted than it would have been just two decades earlier. Indeed, whites have even framed their opposition to immigration and affirmative action in the language of civil rights. The black-led civil rights movement of the 1960s forced passage of civil rights laws and brought some changes in the racial climate. Recent Asian and Latino immigrants and their children have benefited to some degree from this change in climate. They have not had to face the extremely blatant discrimination and official segregation imposed on some Americans of color, especially black Americans, in the recent past.

Gradually Blending In?   Numerous social commentators and scholars see the children and grandchildren of the recent Asian and Latino immigrants, as well as the descendants of earlier immigrants in these groups, as gradually blending into the dominant white group. Sociologist Nathan Glazer has described Asian and Latino Americans as today becoming less different from whites in residence, income, and attitudes. As he sees it, eventually the "two nations" making up the United States will "become the black and the others."[51] Similarly, political scientist Andrew Hacker has argued that Asian and Latino American groups should be viewed as intermediate groups that "have been allowed to put a visible distance between themselves and black Americans. Put most simply, none of the presumptions of inferiority associated with Africa and slavery are imposed on these other ethnicities."[52] As he sees it, second and later generations of these groups are gradually merging into the white category through assimilation into the middle class and by means of white recognition of their achievements. Other white commentators have gone so far as to argue that Mexican Americans are already viewed as whites and thus no longer need the protection of antidiscrimination and affirmative action programs. Clearly, there is a certain lack of candor in much discussion of Latinos and Asian Americans blending into the white group. Many white commentators seem to accent this potential because it enables them to distance themselves—and the white-oriented society—farther from black Americans, who are still, explicitly or implicitly, viewed as the most problematical group. The blending arguments would be far more convincing if the white authors showed a deeper interest in the cultures of, and acceptance of, Latino and Asian Americans.[53]

One sign of the partial acceptance of Latino and Asian Americans as intermediate groups may be seen in white attitudes toward intermarriage. In one National Opinion Research Center (NORC) survey two-thirds of white respondents said that they would be opposed to a close relative marrying a black person, compared to just under half being opposed to a relative marrying a Hispanic or Asian American.[54] It appears that a majority of whites now see white-Asian and white-Latino marriages in their family as more or less acceptable—or at least they are willing to say that to a pollster.

Intermarriages are in fact growing in number, particularly in these latter two categories. According to a U.S. Census report, 77 percent of all intermarriages are now between whites and groups other than blacks.[55] Even for the white-Asian and white-Latino marriages, one must be careful not to overestimate their significance for broad societal change. Intermarriage is often seen as an important measure of group assimilation to the dominant white society and a signal of dramatic change toward a more multiracial and multiethnic society. In reality, however, the intermarriage trend is an ambiguous measure of such assimilation. Most intermarriages may represent two people relating to one other for reasons that do not indicate mutual adaptation between their two groups. For example, historically many white-Asian marriages have been between white men and Asian war brides from areas where the U.S. government was involved militarily.[56] These relationships account for a significant number of current intermarriages in the United States. There is also a growing international trade in Asian and Latino brides for white men. In these cases the patterns of intermarriage disproportionately reflect the interests and choices of individuals, including white men who are seeking "traditionally submissive" mates, rather than a mutual adaptation between two different racial groups.[57] Moreover, we do not yet have substantial data on how multiracial families and their children are treated by their relatives and neighbors, particularly by those who are white. Scattered anecdotal evidence suggests white-black families are often not treated well by their white relatives and neighbors. It remains to be seen if the interracial marriages mark a major societal change toward a truly integrated and congenial multiracial society.

Who Is White Today?   Today, those white analysts who are hostile toward, or critical of, Asian and Latino immigrants tend to accent certain groups within these umbrella categories, such as Southeast Asians (Vietnamese) and Mexican Americans, respectively. The latter groups, it seems, look and act less like middle-class whites, at least as seen by whites. In this manner anti-immigration analysts and activists pick and choose among the groups in these umbrella Asian and Latino categories to suit their own ideological purposes. As these latter groups have grown in number, intense opposition has emerged from some segments of white America. We noted previously *Forbes* editor Peter Brimelow's assertion that the American nation "has always had a specific ethnic core. And that core has been white."[58] Brimelow seems particularly worried about the large numbers of immigrants of color entering the United States. Less strident views making the same point on the deteriorating "white core" can now be found in such prestigious journals as *Foreign Affairs*.[59]

Moreover, being categorized as nearer the white than the black end of the racist continuum does not mean that a group or person is viewed as being fully white. According to some survey research most whites do not see the larger groups of Latino and Asian Americans as white. Giving questionnaires to students over an eight-year period, one sociologist asked mostly white groups of Canadian students to assess which nationalities in a list were "white" people. Most students consistently evaluated all Latin Americans in the list—Mexicans, Cubans, Chileans, and Argentines—as not white. In addition, all Asian nationalities in the list— Chinese, Japanese, Vietnamese—were consistently viewed as not white.[60] These findings likely apply to the views of whites in the United States as well. Note too that these students had no trouble placing these groups on a racial-color continuum, which is still central to much white thinking. And it would appear that people across the globe are categorized by North American whites in terms of this color continuum. From the still dominant white viewpoint the world is to be sorted out along a racist continuum—with whites at one end and blacks at the other, and other groups placed somewhere in between.

Moreover, two recent surveys have found that the majority of Latino Americans do not see themselves as white. In a 1997 Houston area survey, the majority of Hispanic respondents, including 64 percent of those born in the United States, said that they did not think Hispanics were members of the "white race." And in a recent census survey in Houston, just over half the Latino residents there indicated that they were not white.[61] It seems likely that surveys of Asian Americans would find similar statements from the majority that they too do not see themselves as white. Having an intermediate status on the racial spectrum does not mean that one is seen, or sees oneself, as fully white.

Continuing Discrimination Today   An intermediate status on the white-to-black continuum also does not mean equality in rights, perquisites, and privileges with whites. Today, there is still much stereotyping and discrimination—including violently racist attacks—directed at intermediate groups, with the most attacks seemingly being directed at their darker-skinned members. We can briefly sketch the contours of this serious discrimination.

A number of research studies show that many Asian Americans are moving into the mainstream of the economy and into suburban neighborhoods, yet they still face much overt discrimination.[62] Many Asian Americans—including managers, administrators, and professionals who have secured jobs in historically white institutions—report ingrained patterns of anti-Asian discrimination in the workplace and the larger society. While discrimination is reported at all levels, it is the best educated who in several studies report the most discrimination in the workplace, and it is they who are also the most active in Asian American organizations and in organizational efforts aimed at social change. In field interviews these Asian American workers recount a variety of types of discrimination, including the "glass ceiling" that keeps most from moving up to higher-level positions in many business settings.[63] There is discrimination in other areas as well, including public accomodations and policing. For example, in one late 1990s incident a number of Asian American students were excluded from service at a Syracuse, New York, restaurant, then beaten by whites as they left. U.S. Civil Rights Commission studies have reported that in many communities white-controlled police agencies are reluctant to offer adequate police protection to Asian Americans, including protection against racially motivated crimes.[64] Moreover, one recent study of the redevelopment of a shopping center in Monterey Park, California, showed how a white minority there forced the redevelopment project to be done their way. "Rather than reflecting the city's current and future position as a major node for Asian-themed businesses, the shopping center was remodeled to provide a place where whites could shop and 'feel at home.'"[65]

Today, Latinos also report much stereotyping and discrimination. In the mid-1990s California whites, many of whom were fearful of non-European immigrants, voted in the majority for ballot propositions designed to abolish government services for immigrants, eradicate government affirmative action, and reduce bilingual programs in schools, producing major consequences for the lives of Latinos and Asian Americans. White politicians and voters elsewhere in western states have pressed for similar restrictions. Employment discrimination, while less common than for African Americans, is also frequent. One Los Angeles study found

that Latino workers reported much workplace discrimination, with the better educated reporting the most.[66] In addition, white hostility to the Spanish language
faced by early Latino residents of the Southwest persists today—in the "English
only" movement, in white opposition to bilingual education, and in the
widespread mocking of the Spanish language and Latino cultures. Recall Jane
Hill's research (chapter 4) on the mock Spanish used by whites in the mass media
and many other settings. She shows that many whites use a wide array of made-up
Spanish phrases such as "el cheapo," "hasta banana," and "hasta la vista, baby",
language that explicitly or implicitly mocks Latinos. This ridicule reveals an underlying stereotyping of Latinos, especially Mexican Americans, and their culture.
Here we see another assertion of white cultural superiority.

In addition, white attacks on Latinos and Asian Americans often take the form
of racially motivated hate crimes, some of which are violent. For example, one
report for Orange County in California reported 169 hate crimes there in just 1998,
a number up from the previous year. While blacks were the most frequent targets,
both Latino and Asian Americans were singled out for a variety of hate crimes.
Today, across the nation, hundreds of racially motivated crimes against Latinos
and Asian Americans are reported each year, with many others going unreported.
These hate crimes have ranged from racist graffiti making threats of violence—
often painted on homes or businesses or circulated on the Internet—to violent
attacks, such as the racially motivated killing of a Vietnamese American student
in California.[67]

Other Costs of Intermediate Status   Those Latino and Asian Americans placed
into an intermediate or near-white status, or who seek that status for themselves,
endure various costs from trying to be white. One such cost is self-deception. The
model minority stereotype has been more or less accepted by some Asian
Americans, particularly youth growing up in predominantly white suburbs. These
young Asian Americans come to think of themselves and their group in terms of
the white-crafted model-minority imagery, probably because it appears to to be
positive.[68] These youth do not yet understand the ideological purpose for which
this imagery was created by whites, and they do not yet comprehend the full reality of anti-Asian discrimination. However, as these young people move beyond
their restricted friendship groups and school settings into the larger society, such
as white-dominated employment settings, they will doubtless learn that whites still
target Asian Americans for stereotyping and discrimination, which will prevent
them from achieving the status suggested by the model-minority stereotype.

Many Latinos and Asian Americans have felt pressured to give up their real
identities in order to be as white as they can be. For example, in a recent documentary Janice Tanaka has shown the negative impact of pressures for assimilation to white ways. In interviews with third-generation Japanese American parents
she found that their second-generation parents, the Nisei, most of whom had been

interned as youth (and American citizens) in barbed-wire internment camps by fearful and racist U.S. government officials during World War II, were greatly affected by that incarceration. After the war the Nisei put great pressure on themselves and their children to conform to white norms and patterns, probably in hope of keeping that racist outrage from happening again. Yet the effects of this conformity to whiteness on them and their children have often been negative, with significant numbers facing great personal distress, painful self-blame, physical or mental illness, or alcoholism and drug addiction. Some have committed suicide as a result of pressures ultimately grounded in white racism.[69] Today, there is often much pressure on Asian American youth to assimilate to whiteness that comes from the media and peer groups, especially in white majority suburbs, as well as from parents or other relatives. Let me draw on a pilot interview I have recently conducted. One Asian American college senior and honors student, a second generation Filipino American, recently explained the broad impact of racism, saying, "Honestly, I think the way a lot of us [Asian Americans] think about racism is that we don't. I mean, even though it's . . . something I've thought about a lot, it's still even for me a hard topic to think about. Because it's hard to see, when you don't discuss it often. . . . To me, racial oppression's like a silent killer." As this woman sees it, many Asian Americans suppress their consciousness of the silent killer. She also commented on how the pressures work in her social networks:

> And for me, for Filipinos. . . . When the kids are born, they check out the nose—it's good if it's pointy, narrow, not too wide—the skin tone—my mom worried that people would say stuff about my sister because she was slightly darker-complected when she was born. I was brought up to think that being called mestizo was this huge compliment. Being called mestizo was like being told "you look more Spanish, that's good, that's beautiful." The idea of "pure" Filipino had negative connotations. "Pure" Filipino means having a non-Spanish, non-Chinese last name, wider nose, darker skin, mountain, backwards. . . . We grew up thinking white—white is good, not oppressive—if anything, civilizing, educating. Learning about racism is hard to internalize; it's hard to think about, hard to be really convinced that it's going on. Everything in society goes against the idea that there's any racism going on. Without the kind of collective memory that blacks have that informs them of their past, their cultural pride—it's easy to get sucked into a white mentality.[70]

This perceptive student has interviewed Filipino Americans in her own field research. She draws on that research and her own experience to describe the ways in which many Asian Americans have been significantly shaped by the system of racism and its white-to-black continuum. However, not all Asian Americans feel these pressures from their family networks. Indeed, some research indicates that many immigrant parents, such as those in the Chinese and Vietnamese immigrant communities, often press their children to remain close to traditional values and to socialize within their own Asian-American groups. These parents struggle, often unsuccessfully, to keep their children from succumbing to the intense pressures from outside sources, such as the media and peer groups, to assimilate to whiteness.[71]

Sociologist Nestor Rodriguez has noted a parallel phenomenon of whiteness pressures among Latinos. Some of the latter, especially those up the income ladder, "share this experience, and some do it in a state of denial, that is, they deny the reality of anti-Latino bias, discrimination and prejudices around them. And they push their children into an Anglo-like existence."[72] While much more research on this assimilation is needed, among many Asian and Latino Americans it appears that the pressure to look, dress, talk, and act as white as possible increases personal or family stress and reduces their recognition of the racism that surrounds them. This is yet one more destructive consequence of the underlying system of white racism.

In addition, first-generation Asian and Latino immigrants, particularly those in modest economic circumstances, often find themselves in a different position than groups residing in the United States for several generations. Most recent immigrants of color seem to view other problems they face as having a higher priority, at least for the time being, than discrimination by whites. They worry greatly about finding shelter and jobs, learning the language and local laws, keeping authorities from deporting them, and sending money to families back home. Rodriguez has noted that "they are aware that discrimination exists, but many first-generation migrants see it initially as the cost of being an immigrant and maybe not as disadvantageous as being back home in absolute poverty. They don't usually make good participants of civil rights groups, unless they are dealing with immigrant-related issues or labor issues—then they can organize effectively."[73]

Resisting Oppression   With time in the United States, however, later generations frequently become more willing to organize and take on the discrimination they encounter from white Americans. In spite of the pressures to assimilate to whiteness, many Asian and Latino Americans, like the student above, resist the racism that oppresses them. For example, during the 1990s anti-affirmative action drive in California, like the aforementioned Proposition 209 campaign, many Asian and Latino American students worked with black students against this conservative effort. They were clearly willing to be seen as students of color, and they were joined in this effort by many older Asian and Latino Americans. In spite of the assimilationist pressures, or the trials of being first-generation Americans, many Asian and Latino Americans do not deny the reality of white racism but openly organize against it in community and national organizations.

Since the 1960s many Asian and Latino Americans have joined in group-pride or panethnic organizations as a countering response to racism. Among Mexican Americans group-pride movements like the La Raza Unida Party and the Brown Berets have pressed for an end to discrimination and accented a perspective sometimes called "Chicanismo." Periodically, groups like the National Council of La Raza have brought together a diverse group of Latinos to work on panethnic issues such as increasing positive representations of Latinos in the media and developing political coalitions. Similarly, pan-Asian groups have aggressively asserted Asian American interests and concerns. They have pressed for an end to anti-Asian hate crimes, better police protection for Asian communities, a rejection of racist terms like "Oriental" in the press, and effective political organization. In New York and several West Coast cities activists have created important pan-Asian political and university organizations.[74]

Hostility among Subordinated Groups: Links to White Racism   Systemic racism affects everyone caught in its web. It is the social context for relations between all Americans, those defined as white and those defined as nonwhite. Intermediate groups often come to stereotype or attack those below them on the racial ladder, who may in turn retaliate, and these internecine attacks reinforce the racist system set in place by and for whites. Historically, whites have encouraged groups below them on the status ladder to stereotype and disparage each other. Stereotypes and prejudices in one racially subordinated group that target those in other subordinated groups are not independent of the larger context of systemic racism. Many negative racial images carried in subordinated communities exist because of the age-old racist ideology originally created by whites to rationalize white-on-black oppression. All groups of color assimilate many of the attitudes of the dominant society. As the black legal scholar Charles Lawrence has put it, "we use the white man's words to demean ourselves and to disassociate ourselves from our sisters and brothers. And then we turn this self-hate on other racial groups who share with us the ignominy of not being white."[75] Many other scholars of color have also noted the ways in which oppression is internalized when people of color adopt racist attitudes toward themselves and others.

The white supremacist system intentionally fosters hostility between groups of color. When those higher on the white racist ladder express racist views about those lower, this helps preserve the systemic racism that benefits whites the most. By asserting that one's own group, though subordinated, is still better than those considered lower, members of an in-between group underwrite the racist ladder of privilege. Intergroup stereotyping and hostility among communities of color are very useful for whites who can play down the significance of their own racist thinking and practice. Whites can assert that "everyone is prejudiced."

As we saw in chapters 3 and 4, racist attitudes and images are central to the operation of systemic racism. What most Americans know about racial and ethnic matters beyond their own experience is what they are taught by those who control major avenues of socialization, such as the movies, music videos, television, radio, and print media that circulate racist images not only in the United States but across the globe. When these stereotyped images and accompanying discriminatory propensities are brought by Asian, Latino, and other immigrants to the United States, they can become the basis for intergroup conflict. These attitudes and practices are not independent, but generated by the now global white-racist order. Much negativity between groups of color reflects the foundation of systemic racism. As Lawrence has expressed it, "when a Vietnamese family is driven out of its home in a project by African-American youth, that is white supremacy. When a Korean store owner shoots an African-American teenager in the back of the head, that is white supremacy. When 33 percent of Latinos agree with the statement, 'Even if given a chance, [African-Americans] aren't capable of getting ahead,' that is white supremacy."[76]

Positioning one's own group closer to whites can involve the articulation of strongly antiblack attitudes and participation in antiblack discrimination. We have seen this historically in the actions of later European immigrants desperately seeking to be defined as white. Similarly, in recent years some Latino American leaders have tried to reposition their group, as Roberto Suro puts it, "on the racial spectrum so that they ended up closer to the side of privilege and whiteness than to the side of color and minority-group status."[77] These leaders and those persuaded by them attempt to reposition themselves by parroting antiblack stereotypes and creating positive stereotypes for their own group, such as an accent on a strong work ethic. Suro notes, "Sometimes implicitly, sometimes explicitly, Latinos endorse one of the most basic tenets of American racism by suggesting that blacks remain at the low end of society as a result of their own failings and inferiority, rather than as a result of circumstances."[78] Similarly, one 1990s survey of Chinese, Korean, and Japanese Americans found that these groups held more negative views of black (and Latino) Americans than even white Americans held. Many of the Asian American respondents viewed black (and Latino) Americans as lazy and lacking in-born ability. Although many of these Asian American respondents had been in the United States for only a generation or so, they had already accepted the pervasive antiblack attitudes propagated by whites for more than fourteen generations.[79]

Many Asian Americans and Latinos make choices in the direction of whiteness for reasons that are similar to those of the white workers who historically have made similar choices. Many seek the privileges of whiteness in preference to a strong multiracial alliance with black Americans. Still, there is much tension in Latino and Asian American communities over such issues. As we will see in chapter 8, many Latinos and Asian Americans are joining with black Americans to press for the elimination of systemic racism.

Even within the groups often placed by whites in an intermediate position, the white racist system can create divisions. As we noted above, recent immigrants from Asia and Latin America have triggered renewed hostility directed by some whites not only at the immigrants but also at the larger Asian and Latino communities. Because of this negative white reaction, some native-born Asian and Latino Americans have themselves expressed resentment toward new immigrants from Asia and Latin America. Similarly, some Latino organizations have been critical of, and opposed the continuing immigration of, undocumented Mexicans because the latter have been used by white employers to frustrate the unionization of native-born Latino workers.[80] Such internal group divisions make it more difficult to create group alliances to fight the larger problem of white racism facing all in these communities.

Conclusion   For nearly four centuries those whose stolen labor has been central to the development of prosperity and wealth for white Americans — black Americans — are those who have most required control, segregation, and discrimination. As a group, black Americans are the most American in blended ancestry and are among the most American in the amount of time (nearly four centuries) spent working to build the prosperity of the new nation, yet they are also among the *least* American historically in terms of their rights, privileges, and opportunities. The oppression endured by black Americans is much more than a mental construction in white heads. Their oppressive reality is one that has been economically, physically, socially, and ideologically constructed.

Social science research on torture has found that people can endure much if there appears to be some hope of escape from such severe conditions, but torture is much harder to endure when it has gone on for some time and those tortured feel there is no hope of escaping. Drawing on this insight, one can perhaps understand why African Americans often have a different sense of how burdensome, omnipresent, and imbedded is the system of racist oppression than do other Americans, including many other Americans of color. Today as in the past, black Americans must operate with collective memories of many generations of racist oppression with its well-developed antiblack ideology. As a group they have an amplified culture of resistance that has enabled them to endure and counter this racist torture for centuries. Fifteen generations of oppression create a deep, critical, and nuanced perspective that may be different from that developed over one or two generations of racial discrimination. As we have seen, the majorities in most Asian and Latino American groups are recent immigrants and their children. Some researchers suggest that compared with native-born black Americans many of these immigrants are less aware of or downplay the discrimination they face, in part because they are trying to establish an economic toehold and in part because they compare their current situation with that of the home country, and by this latter standard the United States often looks good.

However, it seems likely that as the next U.S.–born generations of Latinos and Asian Americans come of political age the barriers and pain of systemic racism will be attacked more openly, and many more will likely come to share the views of black Americans about organizing to bring major changes in the racist system. Historically, in the organized pursuit of civil rights and equality in the United States black Americans have usually led the way. Since at least the early 1900s they have forced the passage of all major civil rights laws and the majority of the pivotal executive orders and court decisions protecting or extending antidiscrimination efforts. Latinos, Native Americans, and Asian Americans have been able to make some use of these civil rights mechanisms to fight discrimination against their own groups, and this will likely continue in the future.

African, Asian, Latino, and Native Americans all have a history of white oppression and of attempts to liberate themselves from that oppression. These groups have all had to struggle hard for human dignity and equality. Since various forms of racist oppression have often drawn heavily on the white supremacist framework created for black Americans, most forms of white-racist attitudes and practices directed against these various groups reproduce or reinforce each another. Moreover, as we have seen, the character of the racism faced by a group can vary depending on its timing of entry into the nation, its region of entry, its size, its cultural characteristics, or its physical characteristics. In earlier periods whites usually placed new Asian or Latino groups near the black end of the racist continuum and targeted them for racial exploitation and oppression. Later in the process of group interaction, some groups within these broad umbrella categories — especially the better educated and lighter-skinned — have been moved by whites to an intermediate position or one closer to the white end of the racist white-to-black continuum. The purpose of this placement is often to destroy coalitions between peoples of color, and to thereby protect the system of white privilege.

In the last few decades, this intermediation process seems to have increased in importance, perhaps because the nation is becoming less white in its demographic composition. Taking a panoramic view of this society, one might even speak of the "Brazilianization" of the United States. Like other Latin American countries, Brazil's racialization process has distinguished mulatto (black and white ancestry) and mestizo (white and Native American ancestry) groups that lie in a middle status somewhere between those Brazilians mostly of African ancestry and those of mostly European ancestry. The groups in the middle are socially more acceptable to whites than are Afro-Brazilians, who suffer intense racist stereotyping and discrimination. Possibly, a fully developed tripartite Brazilian pattern — with its clearly recognized and named intermediate groups providing a social buffer between whites and blacks — may be the future for the United States. Because of the apparently privileged position of the intermediate groups, white Brazilians have long proclaimed their nation to be one not infected by racism. And those in the intermediate groups tend to be antagonistic to Afro-Brazilians at the bottom of the racial ladder. Not surprisingly, many North American whites have lately taken a similar position, citing the mobility and advancements of certain groups in the Asian-American and Latino communities, and their in-between and economically enhanced status, as evidence that the United States has become a democracy no longer infected by racism. Many whites in Brazil and the United States have adopted a similar color-blind position where they claim, falsely as we have seen, that there is no longer a problem of racism in either nation.[81]

eight

Antiracist Strategies and Solutions

The liberal wing of the white elite has an inordinate fondness for setting up commissions to study matters of racism in the United States. Over the last century at least a dozen major federal government commissions have looked into problems of racial discrimination or racism. For example, in 1997 President Bill Clinton set up a seven-member advisory board to start a "national conversation on race." The advisory board heard much important testimony about racial and ethnic discrimination across the nation. Its final report, *One America in the 21st Century*, incorporated important findings on racial stereotyping and discrimination but concluded with mostly modest solutions. The report did not provide an integrated analysis of how and why institutional racism still pervades the society, nor did it call for major restructuring of institutions to get rid of racism.[1] Most important, no serious congressional or presidential action was taken to implement the report's more significant recommendations, such as increasing enforcement of the civil rights laws.

Today, U.S. society remains a racist system. It was founded as such, and no large-scale action has ever been taken to rebuild this system of racism from the foundation up. From the first decades European colonists incorporated land theft and slavery into the political-economic structure of the new nation. After the Civil War slavery was replaced by the near slavery of legal segregation in the South, while some legal and much de facto segregation continued in the North. These institutional arrangements were designed to keep antiblack oppression firmly in place. Periodically, the racist structure has been altered, particularly in the 1860s when slavery was abolished and in the 1960s when legal segregation was replaced by the current system of more informal racial oppression. Other Americans of color have been incorporated into U.S. society by whites operating from within this well-established white supremacist framework. The American house of racism has been remodeled somewhat over time—generally in response to protests from the oppressed—but its formidable foundation remains firmly in place.

What is the likelihood of societal change on the scale required to replace this racist foundation? On this point, there is some pessimism among leading American intellectuals. For some time, African American analysts have pointed to the great difficulty of bringing large-scale changes in the system of racism. In the 1940s sociologist Oliver C. Cox noted that "because the racial system in the United States is determined largely by the interests of a powerful political class, no spectacular advance in the status of Negroes could be expected."[2] More recently, Derrick Bell has contended that "[b]lack people will never gain full equality in this country. Even those herculean efforts we hail as successful will produce no more than temporary 'peaks of progress,' short-lived victories that slide into irrelevance as racial patterns adapt in ways that maintain white dominance."[3]

Nonetheless, the racist patterns and arrangements of U.S. society do regularly generate open resistance and organized opposition. These patterns have been altered to some degree by antiracist movements in the past, and they can conceivably be changed again. Historically, other societies have experienced large-scale revolutions. Future domination of U.S. society by whites is not automatic. Viewed over the long term, no hierarchical system is permanent, and such a configuration must be constantly buttressed and diligently reinforced by its main beneficiaries. If we think dialectically and discern the social contradictions lying deep beneath the surface of this society, we see that the racist system has created the seeds of its eventual destruction. Thus, this system is legitimated by widely proclaimed ideals of equality and democratic participation, ideals that have provided it with some respect internally and internationally. While the equality ideals have been used to gloss over persisting racial inequalities, they have also been adopted as bywords for movements of the oppressed. The ideals of equality and democracy are taken very seriously by black Americans and other Americans of color and have regularly spurred them to protest oppression. The honed-by-struggle ideals of equality, justice, and civil rights are critical tenets of the antiracist theory that has emerged over centuries of protest, and they are periodically implemented in antiracist strategies. They have served as a rallying point and have increased solidarity. The situation of long-term racist oppression has pressed black Americans—and, sometimes, other Americans of color—to unite for their own survival and, periodically, for large-scale protest.

The Demographic Challenge to White Domination   Until major crises in this society occur, most whites are unlikely to see the need for large-scale egalitarian reforms. They are too constrained by their own privileges and conforming minds, by their social biographies, to see the need for radical structural change. Still, at certain times in human history new social options appear. What complexity theory calls "cascading bifurcations" can mean great societal instability and possibly a new social order.[4]

The Coming White Minority   Current demographic trends are creating and amplifying societal contradictions that could eventually lead to a major social transformation, including the reduction or destruction of white domination over Americans of color. As we begin a new millenium, Americans of European descent are a decreasing proportion of the U.S. and world populations. Whites constitute less than half the population of four of the nation's largest cities—New York, Los Angeles, Chicago, and Houston. They are less than half the population in the state of Hawaii, as well as in southern sections of Florida, Texas, and California. Demographers estimate that if current trends continue whites will be a minority in California and Texas by about 2010. By the middle of the twenty-first century, whites will be a minority of the U.S. population if birth rates and immigration trends continue near current levels.[5]

Over the next few decades this demographic shift will likely bring great pressures for social, economic, and political change. For example, by the 2030s a majority of the students in the nation's public school system will probably be black, Asian, Latino, and Native American. They and their parents will doubtless strive for greater representation in the operation, staffing, and curricula of presently white-dominated school systems. In addition, by the mid-2050s demographers predict that a majority of U.S. workers will be from these same groups, while the retired population will be majority white. One has to wonder whether these workers will raise questions about having to support elderly whites (for example, by paying into Social Security) who have long maintained a racist society. As voting majorities change from majority white, there will likely be changes in jury composition, operation of the criminal justice system, and the composition and priorities of many state, local, and national legislative bodies. Where voting majorities change, we will probably see far fewer white politicians opposing affirmative action or pressing for laws restricting Asian and Latin American immigrants. These transformations will, of course, only take place if whites have not reacted to the demographic trend with large-scale political repression.[6]

Negative White Responses and Reactions?   Pressures for change do not necessarily mean a complete overthrow of existing power arrangements and social hierarchies. Even with changes like getting the vote and greater participation in the jury system, over the last century or two the white working class and white women have taken only modest power away from the white male elites. Today, those in the white working class are still substantially manipulated by elite action—such as by well-funded political and commercial advertising—and they must partici-pate politically through undemocratic mechanisms such as the wealth-corrupted political party system.[7] Whether black Americans and other Americans of color become substantially more powerful economically and politically depends on sev-eral factors, including the strength of their social and political coalitions and the potency of countering measures taken by white elites and the white public.

Whites may respond to a new minority status with the old means of political and social repression. They may try to set up by force a racial apartheid system like that in the old South Africa, where the white minority used police and military forces to subordinate the majority-black population. In the United States we see some evidence of a renewed apartheid in the growing balkanization of residential patterns: since at least the 1970s many whites have moved away from large cities with growing populations of black, Asian, and Latino Americans to whiter subur-ban and exurban areas or into guarded-gated communities in those cities. In one interview study a white Californian stated that his ideal home would be on twenty acres, surrounded by a moat filled with alligators.[8] One recent research study found that most U.S. counties with substantial population growth from domestic (inter-nal) migration had little growth in the overseas immigrant population—and thus are becoming whiter and older. Most of the seventy large counties with significant growth in immigrants had low net numbers of domestic migrants.[9] They are thus becoming less white and younger. As detailed in chapter 5, U.S. society is still seg-regated, a society where most white citizens and most citizens of color live largely separate lives at school and in neighborhoods. The workforce continues to be sub-stantially divided along racial lines, with many workers of color in special job niches or at the bottom with low wages or facing chronic unemployment.

We also see some political separation or segregation by whites. Ralph Reed, a Republican Party leader, recently reviewed the past and future of his party, can-didly commenting that "you're going to see a new Republican Party that is still pri-marily white and that is fiscally and morally conservative, but that also is attempt-ing to project an image of racial tolerance and moderation."[10] Established political leaders like Reed suggest that they want to keep the party predominantly white, while trying to look tolerant. Clearly, an antiracist vision of the party would have strongly rejected the party's recent racist strategies (see below) and instead accented aggressive recruitment of a racial-ethnic diversity of voters representative of the general population.[11]

Over the last few decades the Republican Party, which dominated the U.S. Congress in the 1990s, has moved away from the once sought-after black voters. Today, the party is antagonistic to key issues of concern to black Americans and garners relatively few black votes. Beginning with the 1964 presidential campaign, the Republican Party intentionally abandoned black voters and strongly targeted the interests of white voters. While the party lost nationwide in 1964, this prowhite strategy captured five southern states. Reinvigorated by Richard Nixon in the late 1960s, the prowhite strategy captured more white voters, especially in the South, and helped to bring Nixon to the White House. Kevin Phillips, a key Republican strategist, argued that Republicans did not need "urban Negroes" to win major victories.[12]

This strategy was again used successfully by the party in the Ronald Reagan and George Bush campaigns of the 1980s. In chapter 4 we noted the 1988 Bush presidential campaign, which in one advertising effort used the scary image of a black rapist to try to discredit the views of the Democratic Party candidate and attract white voters. The party would not have run such a biased ad (no white rapists were shown, for example) if it had been concerned with winning black voters. Since the late 1960s many working-class and middle-class whites, particularly in the South, have moved away from the party of Franklin D. Roosevelt into the Republican Party, substantially over racial issues. Not surprisingly, since the 1980s the Republican Party has been overwhelmingly white in the composition of its presidential conventions and has rejected aggressive government programs aimed at reducing discrimination or greatly strengthening civil rights laws.

Recently, some conservative Republican officials—including Senate Majority leader Trent Lott, Representative Bob Barr (Georgia), Mississippi Governor Kirk Fordice, and dozens of state and local politicians in several states—have given speeches to or maintained political ties to certain racist-right organizations such as the Council of Conservative Citizens (CCC). The CCC has chapters in twenty-two states and twenty thousand subscribers to its publication, *Citizens Informer*, which has published articles attacking mixed marriages and the Martin Luther King holiday and celebrated nineteenth-century racist thinkers like the Count de Gobineau.[13]

Some human rights activists have underscored the troubling growth of a renewed and broad-based *white nationalism*, which is increasingly linking conservative white politicians and openly white-supremacist groups. Leonard Zeskind, a leading human rights activist, has pointed out that these individuals and groups unite around the "notion of this country as Anglo-American, a white country. That idea is being put forward in a very mainstream way and that has not happened successfully since at least before World War II."[14] There are now many extremist groups, including older groups like the Klan and a variety of neo-Nazi groups and armed militias. Nationally, the number exceeded 540 by the late 1990s. At that time, there were at least 254 U.S. Internet sites disseminating extreme racist diatribes.[15] As the nation becomes less white, a substantial period of increased unemployment could trigger a large-scale increase in this racist-right extremism.

Black Resistance to Racist Oppression   In the United States the system of racism has developed within a framework of constant protests from its targets. Many whites have traditionally viewed black Americans as unwilling to help themselves, but this is a myth. For centuries black religious, civic, and civil rights organizations have not only engaged in self-help community projects but also have striven to improve the nation's general welfare by regularly pressing forward on the goals of equality and social justice. Black Americans have not quietly accepted their oppression as hapless victims. They have fought back, like most oppressed peoples historically. They protest, survive, and even thrive in spite of the racist subjugation they endure. Black Americans have taken much strength from the heritage transmitted through extended families and other social networks. The knowledge carried there includes positive values and perspectives on life. Living in a society with a dominant white-European culture has forced black Americans, as well as other Americans of color, to become bicultural. They have had to know white society well and become experts on how to respond to antiblack actions. As we discussed in chapter 6, this expertise includes learned strategies of protest against oppression passed across the generations.[16] The culture of African Americans stems partly from the heritage that Africans brought with them, and partly from centuries of experience with systemic racism in North America.

Historically and in the present, a small group of black conservatives have argued that blacks as individuals should exercise their free will to achieve, whatever the racial odds.[17] They, and most liberal whites as well, hope that individuals can overcome oppression working by themselves. In contrast, the progressive wing of black leadership—by far the overwhelming majority of that leadership—accents not only working individually to overcome racism but also organizing collectively and actively against it.

A comprehensive theory of racist oppression should recognize the impact of the resistance strategies developed by black Americans on the type and character of the arrangements in the system of racism. Out of their experience with everyday racism has come an individual and collective consciousness that periodically leads to protests, petitions, and large-scale revolts. To this stage in U.S. history, significant alterations in systemic racism have only come when black Americans and their allies, including other Americans of color, have organized and battled for change. U.S. society has usually moved backward when that pressure ebbs.

Past and Present Patterns of Resistance   Black resistance began in the earliest days of slavery. Those enslaved responded in many ways—ranging from passive acquiescence, to flight on a large scale, to attacks on slaveholders and their property, to insurrections. Slave revolts and conspiracies to revolt averaged one per year over the first 250 years of slavery in North America.[18] Moreover, in the early decades of the nineteenth century black and white abolitionists held many protest meetings and demonstrations against slavery and created increasingly militant antislavery organizations—thereby helping to bring about the abolition of slavery. As Merton Dillon has noted, the growing abolitionism "was stimulated—and justified—by the slave unrest for which rebels and swelling numbers of runaways supplied tangible evidence."[19]

Black Americans engaged in extensive political and community organizing during the postwar Reconstruction period of the late 1860s and 1870s. The Reconstruction South was perhaps the closest the United States has come to multiracial political democracy—with large numbers of black men (but still no women) in many areas voting and participating in politics. The new state constitutional conventions and legislatures included many black delegates, and twenty-two black men served in the U.S. House and Senate during that period. Whites and blacks worked together to bring much progressive change and democracy to southern politics. Yet this experiment in democracy was soon repressed by the terrorist actions of thousands of whites led by the southern gentry and working through such white terrorist organizations as the Ku Klux Klan.

A new civil rights movement was born in the early 1900s, taking the form first of the Niagara movement and then of the National Association for the Advancement of Colored People (NAACP). After decades of legal efforts and political organizing by the NAACP and other organizations laid the groundwork, there was a spurt in civil rights protests from the 1940s to the 1970s, with black men, women, and children participating in protests for freedom and equality. There were local and national protests within the framework of the growing civil rights organizations, and there were many protests organized at the local level by smaller groups of working-class black Americans.[20] In the 1950s one successful strategy was the economic boycott. This included the important boycott that targeted segregated buses in Montgomery, Alabama, and brought Rosa Parks, the seamstress who refused to be segregated on a bus, and Dr. Martin Luther King, Jr., who was asked to lead the movement, to national attention as leaders of the reinvigorated civil rights movement.

Soon thereafter came many sit-ins, freedom rides, and other demonstrations by black Americans challenging legal segregation in the South and informal segregation in the North. New organizations oriented toward greater political and economic power for black Americans included the Student Nonviolent Coordinating Committee (SNCC), the Congress of Racial Equality (CORE), and the Black Panthers. Often rooted in a strong base of black churches, civic clubs, and civil rights organizations, this activism provided money and mobilized people, which enabled regional and national civil rights organizations to achieve successes in dismantling racial segregation. One of the lessons added to the book of antiracist strategies by this movement was the well-honed idea that the destruction of the racist system would require more than speeches and traditional electoral politics. Nonviolent civil disobedience was a key strategy that black Americans developed for dealing with official and informal racism. Dr. King and other black leaders became the critical American theorists of the idea that significant change only comes from creative social disruptions, especially those carried out by strong indigenous organizations.[21]

Successes and Limitations   Many victories came out of this 1950s and 1960s civil rights movement, including the passage of major laws prohibiting discrimination in such areas as employment, voting, and housing. The 1964 Civil Rights Act, perhaps the most important of a number of such acts, prohibited discrimination in many areas. Title I set down protections for voting in state and federal elections. Title II asserted, "All persons shall be entitled to the full and equal enjoyment of the goods, services, facilities, privileges, advantages, and accommodations of any place of public accommodation . . . without discrimination or segregation on the ground of race, color, religion, or national origin." Title III required the desegregation of all public facilities operated by local or state governments. Title IV authorized federal action to encourage and facilitate the desegregation of public schools, and Title VI prohibited discrimination in programs receiving federal assistance. Title VII prohibited discrimination in employment. It became illegal for an employer (1) to "refuse to hire or to discharge any individual or otherwise discriminate against any individual with respect to his compensation, terms, conditions, or privileges of employment, because of such individual's race, color, religion, sex, or national origin"; or (2) to "limit, segregate or classify his employees in any way which would deprive or tend to deprive any individual of employment opportunities or otherwise adversely affect his status as an employee, because of such individual's race, color, religion, sex, or national origin."[22] Title VIII required the collection of registration and voting statistics. The civil rights movement had forced the passage of one of the most strongly worded antidiscrimination laws ever established in any nation.

Pressures building from the civil rights movement also prodded federal courts to act against certain extreme manifestations of structural racism. The Supreme Court was often a force for progressive change away from patterns of segregation from the mid-1950s Brown decision, which began the process of dismantling school desegregation, to the early 1970s Griggs decision, which began an effort to reduce covert discrimination in employment.[23] The Brown case was part of an NAACP strategy to dismantle legal segregation and marked a temporary turn by that court to significantly redressing some grievances of black Americans.

However, civil rights laws and desegregation decisions have been overwhelmed by the massiveness of racial discrimination. As we discussed previously, these laws were crafted by the liberal wing of the white elite—mostly in the face of grass roots protests in the period from 1954 to 1972—with only modest concern for the group interests of African Americans. The laws were never intended to uproot systemic racism. While they have gotten rid of legal segregation, they are for the most part ineffective in regard to much informal discrimination and segregation. Each year now there are millions upon millions of instances of racial discrimination perpetrated by whites against black Americans and other Americans of color. Most are *not* countered by effective enforcement of local, state, and federal civil rights laws. Across the nation local, state, and federal agencies with civil rights responsibilities have neither the resources nor staff to vigorously enforce antidiscrimination laws. State agencies like the New York Division of Human Rights and federal agencies such as the Equal Employment Opportunity Commission typically have such a large backlog of cases that most victims of discrimination cannot achieve timely remedies. All local, state, and federal agencies dealing with discrimination complaints process fewer than perhaps one hundred thousand or so cases each year, and most of these are resolved with little in the way of serious penalties for discriminators (see chapter 5).

As they have been enforced—or, more accurately, weakly enforced—over several decades, the civil rights laws often contribute to the persistence of racial discrimination by making it more difficult to file a successful complaint against a white discriminator.[24] The procedures are usually lengthy and bureaucratic. Moreover, by providing a strong rhetoric of rights and equal opportunity, these laws allow white Americans to assume that the problem of serious racial discrimination has largely been solved. Unquestionably, a first step in a renewed antiracist strategy for dismantling systemic racism would be an aggressive program of enforcing the civil rights laws passed in the 1960s.

Community Control as Strategy   Between the 1970s and the 1990s the civil rights movement declined in public protests and visibility. One reason was the apparent achievement of key civil rights goals. For a time, the civil rights laws, court decisions, and government affirmative action efforts suggested a societal commitment to change. Another reason was the hiring or cooptation of many black leaders in corporations and government agencies. Yet another was government repression of more radical change-oriented groups such as the organized police campaign against the Black Panthers, who were calling for an end to police brutality and an increase in black control over black communities. Historically, it appears that the more the pressure builds from below, the more action the white elite takes to repress or reduce that pressure.

Government-sponsored civil rights progress came to a standstill, even backtracked, in the 1980s to 1990s when enforcement of the civil rights laws and implementation of affirmative action programs were significantly cut back under the conservative presidential administrations of Ronald Reagan and George Bush. Yet, even in the difficult period since the 1980s, black organizations have periodically responded with public demonstrations for expanded civil rights and other social programs in Washington, D.C., and several other cities. Since the 1980s there have been numerous local protests against racism, as well as a few national demonstrations, such as the 1995 Million Man March in Washington, D.C., a march accenting the need for black solidarity and community development. There have also been numerous efforts to organize black workers against exploitative employers and to organize against the waste dumps and other environmental hazards often located in or near black communities.[25]

Dissatisfaction with stalled progress or backtracking on the commitment to societal desegregation has periodically led black activists, organizers, and intellectuals to press for separatist and cultural-nationalist strategies. During the 1920s and 1930s, for example, there was a new outpouring of novels, music, dance, and other arts celebrating African American traditions, values, and interests — a movement called the Harlem Renaissance. Coupled with this cultural renaissance was an accent on fostering more black businesses and community institutions. Beginning with Marcus Garvey's Universal Negro Improvement Association (UNIA) in the 1920s, and continuing with the Nation of Islam since the 1940s, a significant number of black Americans have rejected societal integration as the major goal for black Americans and instead accented a community control or separatist strategy. Sometimes, this strategy has been coupled with a call for compensation for racist oppression. Thus, in 1994 the Nation of Islam petitioned the United Nations to investigate the provision of reparations to black Americans and to intervene in pressing for such compensation under the umbrella of international law.[26]

Periodically since the 1960s many black Americans have shown a major interest in separatist or community control strategies. A *New York Times* reporter, Isabel Wilkerson, interviewed several dozen middle class black Americans in Los Angeles after a major riot there in the 1990s. She found them to be angry over police brutality against blacks and other racism issues. As a group, those in the middle class were becoming increasingly committed to the idea of buying from black businesses and to greater black community solidarity and separation from whites.[27] Moreover, in a major policy-oriented book, *Integration or Separation?* the leading legal scholar Roy Brooks has documented the defects and drawbacks of the racial integration strategy as often practiced. Brooks argues that black Americans should keep the traditional integration strategy in their arsenal but couple it with community-focused strategies that have long been necessary for their long-term economic, physical, and psychological well-being.[28] In his view a mix of strategies is essential to future progress.

Working in the tradition of Garvey, Malcolm X, and W. E. B. Du Bois, numerous black scholars and community leaders have reiterated the importance of African values and traditional perspectives for black Americans. They reject myths of European cultural superiority and call for African Americans, as anthropologist Marimba Ani puts it, to refocus their "energies toward the recreation of cultural alternatives informed by ancestral visions of a future that celebrates Africanness."[29] In their view revolution begins not with open warfare but with a counterhegemony of ideas created by the oppressed.

Some Individual Strategies of Resistance   As the 1960s civil rights movement demonstrated, successful antioppression movements require a shattering of negative racial images in the minds of the oppressed themselves. How to increase this self-consciousness remains an ongoing task for antiracist struggles. Consciousness raising among black Americans, as well as among other Americans, includes self-inquiry into one's own attitudes as well as a parallel dialogue with others. The Algerian revolutionary Frantz Fanon cogently stressed that an "authentic national liberation exists only to the precise degree to which the individual has irreversibly begun his own liberation."[30]

Many black Americans have pioneered in this process of individual liberation, and have developed considerable experiential intelligence. Since I and several other researchers have documented and discussed these individual strategies for dealing with discrimination in detail elsewhere,[31] I will note just one major example here. In a national study of middle-class respondents, a black professional explained her approach to whites, saying, "I know I have very little tolerance for white people who expect me to change my behavior to make them comfortable. They don't change their behavior to make me comfortable. I am who I am. Either they sit with me and work with me respecting that, or you can't sit and work together." After indicating that she does not generally tolerate racist attitudes or remarks, she then adds, "Then there are other people, who are personal friends, who may make a racist statement, and it's really based on their ignorance and their lack of understanding, and I'll take the time to deal with it. There's a young white woman that I work with now, and she's really not worked with a lot of different people of color, and she uses the term, 'you people,' and I bring it to her attention, And she's like, 'oh, oh,' and so it's an education, we're working together. But I don't generally accommodate white people's conflicts."[32] Like most black Americans, she tailors her response to racist attitudes to fit the situation and the person.

Over a lifetime of many experiences with whites, a black American is forced to develop an array of strategies to fight racist attitudes and discriminatory practices. Sometimes black respondents in interview studies speak of withdrawing to fight another day. At other times, they describe open confrontations with white discriminators, with all the costs that frequently entails.[33] As in the above account, they often distinguish among whites, taking time to educate those whites who seem to be open to change. Like many black Americans, the woman quoted here has seen to her own liberation from racist oppression. It is on this individual knowledge and experiential intelligence that black Americans have built their individual and collective responses to everyday racism.

The Equality Ideal: Black Support, White Resistance   From the early 1600s to the present day, the subordination of black Americans has conspicuously contradicted the political ideals enshrined in the Declaration of Independence — the stated emphasis on "all men are created equal" and on the inalienable rights of "life, liberty, and the pursuit of happiness." These grandly stated ideals were certainly radical in their day, and the documents of the American Revolution were banned in many European countries. As white men with property, however, the founders had in mind their own freedom and equality. However, once the genie of freedom was let out of the bottle, many other groups of Americans have pressed for their full inclusion under these great ideals.

White Americans have not been the main carriers of *robust* ideals of freedom and justice. For centuries the strongest commitment to fully implementing the ideals of freedom, justice, and equality has been that of black Americans. From the first decades of the new republic, black leaders have been at the forefront of those strongly articulating these concepts. In most generations black Americans have forced white Americans to confront and deal with the ideals of equality and justice. Perhaps the first great manifesto for full human equality in the history of the United States was the 1829 *Appeal to the Coloured Citizen's of the World* by the young black abolitionist David Walker. In this widely circulated manifesto, Walker quotes the words "all men are created equal" from the Declaration of Independence and then adds, for his white readers, "Compare your own language above, extracted from your Declaration of Independence, with your cruelties and murders inflicted by your cruel and unmerciful fathers and yourselves on our fathers and on us—men who have never given your fathers or you the least provocation! . . . I ask you candidly, was your sufferings [sic] under Great Britain, one hundredth part as cruel and tyrannical as you have rendered ours under you? Some of you, no doubt, believe that we will never throw off your murderous government and 'provide new guards for our future security.'"[34] He then assured his white readers that black Americans would indeed take strong action to achieve freedom, equality, and justice. Walker's manifesto created great fear in the white population, especially among slavery interests who saw it as an incitement to revolution. A bounty was placed on his head by slaveholding interests, and he appears to have been poisoned in June 1830 for his militancy.

After the Civil War black Americans pressed hard to secure greater freedom and equality, especially the right to vote and equal treatment in public accommodations and on juries. In the nineteenth century black leaders like Frederick Douglass and Sojourner Truth forcefully enunciated the ideals of freedom and equality. In the early 1900s, with the new movements for civil rights, a growing number of black leaders spoke out for the implementation of these ideals. In a 1902 lecture to a Quaker group, Anna Julia Cooper, a leading activist for the poor and an early feminist, noted how "dragged against his will over thousands of miles of unknown waters to a strange land among strange peoples, the Negro was transplanted to this continent in order to produce chattels and beasts of burden for a nation 'conceived in liberty and dedicated to the proposition that all men are created equal.'"[35] Elsewhere, she added that black men and women are endowed with the unalienable rights of "Life, Liberty, and the pursuit of Happiness" and thus have a "right to grow up, to develop, to reason and to live" just like other Americans.[36]

During the 1950s and 1960s the nation once again witnessed a reinvigorated movement for freedom and equality for African Americans. The participants in these antiracist movements were greatly influenced by national and international ideals of social justice and equal rights. Just before his assassination, Dr. Martin Luther King, Jr., passionately argued for equality for African Americans. He noted that a major problem was getting whites to understand the meaning of the black struggle for liberty, for there is "not even a common language when the term 'equality' is used. Negro and white have a fundamentally different definition."[37] King added that black Americans "have proceeded from a premise that equality means what it says, and they have taken white Americans at their word when they talked of it as an objective. But most whites in America in 1967, including many persons of goodwill, proceed from a premise that equality is a loose expression for improvement. White America is not even psychologically organized to close the gap—essentially it seeks only to make it less painful and less obvious but in most respects to retain it."[38]

Because of centuries of black pressure, as well as the rise of movements among other people of color since the 1960s, the white public's understanding of equality across the color line has slowly been transformed from the idea of the founders that only white men had a right to liberty and representation to a broader view. Surveys suggest that the white majority now holds to this view: At least in principle, all men and women have a right to legal and political equality, as well as to equal opportunities in employment, housing, and education. However, for the majority this new understanding of equality dates only from the 1960s and 1970s and does *not* mean that most whites wish to see a truly egalitarian social reality or even thorough racial integration.[39] Today, as in the recent past, a majority of whites support equality only if that means some chances for individual improvement, and not the goal of real group equality along political, economic, and social lines. Indeed, according to one national survey just over half of white respondents felt that "equal rights" had been pushed *too far* in the United States.[40] Another survey found that many whites are moving backward to the older view that a racially separate-but-equal society is acceptable if formal equality of opportunity is provided.[41]

In contrast, for almost all black men and women the central goal remains real political, social, and economic equality with whites, including being treated fairly and justly in all institutions. As Ralph Ellison long ago expressed it, the goal is the creation of real democracy in which a black person will be "free to define himself for what he is and, within the large framework of that democracy, for what he desires to be."[42]

Elite Responses to Black Pressures   Since the early 1900s renewal of the black movement for equal rights—and especially since the 1960s civil rights revolution—white Americans, including the white elite, have faced a continuing ideological crisis. They have had to confront a growth of antiracist ideas among black intellectuals and leaders, as well as other Americans who are enemies of racism. Protest against white hegemony includes not only overt confrontation with the dominant group but also development of countering perspective — in the case of black Americans an antiracist perspective generated over a long period of fighting domination. Georg Lukacs once noted that an ideological crisis is "an unfailing sign of decay" that forces the ruling class on the defensive.[43] In addition, the ideological crisis is closely linked to a policy crisis.

The Remedial Strategies of White Liberals   Faced with black pressures for racial desegregation, the liberal wing of the white elite has been willing to accept some meaningful changes, if only to damp down black protests. During the period from the 1940s to the 1960s an accent on modest black assimilation and some antisegregation action was the orientation of the liberal wing of the white elite, though not of that elite as a whole nor of the white population generally. Recall the discussion of the pioneering work of Gunnar Myrdal in chapter 6.[44] Reflecting the new social science of his era, Myrdal argued in *An American Dilemma* that biological racism was discredited and that the extent of antiblack discrimination should be recognized. Myrdal's solution for this discrimination was to call for ethical changes on the part of individual whites, who should eventually come to welcome integration. One of his solutions was to reeducate whites to see that their prejudiced views were against their American ideals. He pressed for the gradual, one-way integration of black Americans in white society: It would be, he believed, "to the advantage of American Negroes as individuals and as a group to become assimilated into American culture, to acquire the traits held in esteem by the dominant white Americans."[45] One-way assimilation, however, does not aim at remaking basic institutions.

By the 1950s the white elite and public were confronted by black protestors willing to risk their lives in the new strategy of civil disobedience. By making some policy concessions to these pressures in the 1950s and 1960s, white liberals probably averted more serious protests and more extensive societal changes. The new civil rights laws did eliminate legal segregation, and affirmative action programs began a gradual process of placing some, often token, numbers of black Americans, other Americans of color, and white women in historically white male workplaces and other institutional settings. However, for the most part white liberals have only sought to eliminate the most egregious forms of discrimination and segregation and to provide some increased opportunities. As we showed in chapter 3, liberal white leaders have been successful in placing the idea of equality of opportunity at the top of the list of remedial solutions for the U.S. "racial problem."

The much criticized affirmative action programs of recent decades were originally created *by white men* in the liberal wing of the business and political elites. Since they were put into effect, initially by white men at the top of corporations, universities, and other organizations, these affirmative action programs have involved modest, often successful efforts to bring some people of color and white women into institutions where they had, historically, been excluded. These remedial programs have the look of going beyond equality of opportunity, but actually they have mostly opened up opportunities to those who are highly qualified. Moreover, even from the viewpoint of most white liberals, these government policies were designed to be temporary measures designed to get the opportunity game to work for Americans of color. In recent years most critics of affirmative action seem to have forgotten, or wish to conceal, the fact that the idea called affirmative action was originally created by liberal white male politicians and officials as a limited, and often paternalistic, response to pressures from black and other protesters seeking change in the turbulent 1960s. Not surprisingly given its origin, virtually no affirmative action program has seriously challenged white male domination of historically white and male institutions.

The Conservative Advance   The liberals in the white elite have been in retreat most of the time since the conservative resurgence of the late 1970s. We examined the ideological shift to a conservative approach on racial matters in chapter 3. This ideological shift, with its denial of significant racism, its assertions of white innocence, and its romanticizing of the past was accompanied by actions that moved the nation away from its course of modest attempts at racial change. The conservative wing of the white elite has grown in power since the 1970s. In recent decades conservative white politicians have been elected at all levels of government. Conservative and neoconservative intellectuals have served increasingly as experts, advisors, and speechwriters for leading politicians in the local, state, and federal governments. They have helped in getting conservative politicians elected and in preparing legislation, and they have participated actively in manipulating the views and inclinations of the general public by serving as op-ed writers in newspapers, appearing as experts on news programs and talk shows, and writing best-selling books.[46]

They have worked hard to legitimate conservative political strategies with arguments about the alleged failure of various governmental programs, including affirmative action. Recall the extensive development of conservative theories about black Americans, which we examined in chapter 3. In addition to developing notions of the black "underclass" and black inferiority in "IQ," some white conservatives have engaged in open attacks on the stronger versions of the American ideal of equality. For example, Irving Kristol, a leading white intellectual, wrote that too many Americans prize equality over liberty and that this "egalitarianism . . . will, if permitted to gather momentum, surely destroy the liberal society."[47] Similarly, the influential social scientist Daniel Bell fears that democratic populism has a desire for "wholesale egalitarianism" that unfortunately insists "on complete leveling." He contends that fairness is not the goal of egalitarians, but rather their goal is to get rid of the idea of merit and achievement.[48] Recall too *The*

Bell Curve by Richard Herrnstein and Charles Murray. In addition to arguing for white superiority and black inferiority in intelligence, they go farther to question the idea of human equality. In their view social inequality is inevitable, necessary, and good. [49]

As part of this conservative resurgence, white men in power in governments and businesses have cut back or ended many antidiscrimination programs. The concern for racial, ethnic, and gender diversity is now more rhetoric than reality in many, if not most institutions. For example, most U.S. companies now do little significant training of their white and other employees for interracial cooperation and management. One recent study found that a minority—less than one-fifth—of human resource specialists in large companies reported that diversity training was provided to employees in most jobs.[50] Most affirmative action programs were originally intended to alter the racist system only in modest ways and usually for a short period of time, and often with an eye to preserving the underlying reality of white (or white male) privilege. In recent years conservative whites have moved aggressively to weaken or destroy even this moderate level of remedial action against racial and gender discrimination. Since the 1970s they have filed numerous lawsuits, including those that have resulted in anti-affirmative action Supreme Court decisions, such as the Croson decision (see chapter 5). In that and similar cases, a conservative Supreme Court rejected the well-documented argument that general societal discrimination is the context and shaper of individual instances of discrimination, arguing instead that the rights created by the Fourteenth Amendment are for individuals and cannot be used to destroy institutionalized racism. Since the 1980s, a string of cases from a conservative court have treated white interests in keeping white status and privilege as more important than the interests of black Americans in eradicating the current reality of systemic racism. Such governmental action clearly reflects the racial and class interests of whites in the present system of white privilege. Ironically, by drawing on the civil rights laws, whites, especially white men, have recently claimed the status of victims of discrimination. Using oxymoronic terms like *reverse discrimination*, whites have successfully pushed aside the central issue of the systemic racism still routinely oppressing Americans of color. As Cheryl Harris has noted, white identity is treated as no different from "any other group identity when, at its core, whiteness is based on racial subordination."[51]

As we saw in earlier chapters, preferential treatment for whites has long been legitimate in the United States. It is action to remedy discrimination against African Americans and other people of color that has been controversial. In an important dissenting opinion in the 1978 Bakke decision, the liberal Supreme Court justice Harry Blackmun chided his conservative colleagues for forgetting that racism is still present; he argued that the Constitution as amended does allow recognition of societal discrimination and direct remedial action: "In order to get beyond racism, we must first take account of race . . . and in order to treat some persons equally, we must treat them differently. We cannot . . . let the Equal Protection Clause perpetuate racial supremacy."[52]

A Liberal Program that Brought Significant Change   In the conservative resurgence since the 1980s many analysts have routinely attacked government programs that were developed as part of the white liberal response to the civil rights movement, including affirmative action programs, programs to provide education, and programs creating job opportunities. Supposedly, these liberal programs did not bring the major societal changes promised, so they should be cataloged as failures and thus abandoned.

However, this conservative attack ignores the one program of remedial action against discrimination that did bring substantial changes in a major U.S. organization. Presumably, this is because this program challenges many conservative assumptions and arguments. The showpiece of the liberal strategy of job desegregation can be seen in the U.S. Army. Today the army, which has about half of all black personnel in the military, is the most desegregated large institution in U.S. society. In the late 1990s black Americans made up about 11 percent of all officers, a figure much higher than that for executives in almost all large corporations or that for professors at almost all historically white colleges and universities. The 7,500 black officers there constitute the largest group of black executives in any historically white organization in the entire history of the United States. African Americans also make up one-third or more of the sergeant ranks in the army, a proportion much higher than that for comparable supervisors in most other workplaces. In addition, surveys indicate that black personnel generally see intergroup relations as better in the army than in the larger society, which is one reason that many reenlist.[53]

How was this desegregation of an organization with a very long history of institutional racism accomplished? One explanation lies in the fact that the U.S. Army is an authoritarian organization that punishes overt prejudice and blatant discrimination engaged in by white personnel and that often rewards white and other officers who work for desegregation in meaningful ways. The army has widely attended courses for personnel on racial, ethnic, and gender issues, and diversity in units is often taken into account in personnel decisions. To meet the problem of enlistees without the skills necessary to move up the ranks—a common problem for civilian employers as well—the army has developed the strongest array of compensatory education programs in the nation. Rather than lower its standards, the army has set up major programs to bring skills to the levels necessary for satisfactory performance and promotion. According to Charles Moskos and John Butler, "One program brings young people up to enlistment standards, while another raises enlisted soldiers to NCO standards. A third brings black undergraduates to officer-commissioning standards, and a fourth raises high school graduates to West

Point-admission standards."[54] At any one time in recent years, some 100,000 personnel have been enrolled in 150 education centers. These programs are usually well-crafted and remarkably brief (typically three to eight weeks), and they have generally been successful in providing many black personnel and other personnel of color with the skills necessary to meet entrance and promotion standards. Given this real opportunity, black Americans have excelled in the job structure of a historically white institution with a long tradition of segregation. There are also spinoff effects from the army and other similar military desegregation programs. For example, the most residentially integrated towns and cities in the United States are generally those near military bases. In these areas white-black differentials in health, such as in the infant mortality rate, often disappear because black military families there have more adequate housing and health services than many black families in the civilian sector.

The desegregation of the army demonstrates that the conservative view of government intervention as useless in dealing with discrimination is wrongheaded. The army programs demonstrate that much more can be done to reduce discrimination in the civilian sector, even without a complete restructuring of U.S. society. In the enforcement of antidiscrimination laws and the desegregation of operations, army leaders and ordinary personnel have accomplished far more than white executives and managers in other government agencies, in large corporations and most other businesses, or in most unions. Once the changes were well underway, they developed a critical mass of black personnel in the army, which in turn has fueled further changes. Developing a critical mass that can perpetuate changes is essential to this type of antiracist strategy. However, much remains to be done. The recent Armed Forces Equal Opportunity Survey shows there is still much subtle and covert discrimination, and some blatant discrimination, in all the military branches. For example, three-quarters of black military personnel, across all branches, reported racially offensive encounters with other personnel in the last twelve months, including such things as racist jokes, racial comments or stares, and exclusion from social activities. Yet a substantial proportion of the black military personnel—from 34 to 46 percent depending on the question—felt that freedom from hate crimes, racial harassment, and general discrimination was greater in the military than in the civilian sector. Very small percentages (3 to 7 percent) evaluated the civilian sector as better, with the rest evaluating the two sectors as similar.[55] Thus, in spite of these continuing problems, the 1964 Civil Rights Act has been implemented much more effectively in military units than in the larger society.

It is important to note that this significant desegregation of the U.S. Army has not had a corrosive effect on certain other types of oppression, such as that often involved in U.S. military adventures in postcolonial areas overseas. It is not yet clear what spinoff effects this racial desegregation will have on such operations in the future. Historically, the U.S. military has been used to suppress the rights and aspirations of many peoples around the globe. There is great irony in the fact that an organization that has historically suppressed the freedom of people of color in the United States and across the globe also has made the greatest progress in integrating black Americans and other Americans of color within its own ranks. This integration may conceivably, in the long run, have some effects on U.S. military policy in regard to peoples of color overseas.

Whites Taking Action with Others against Racism   One classical study of prejudice, *The Authoritarian Personality* (1950), concluded that the racist views of whites vary with their social milieu: "What people say and, to a lesser degree, what they really think depends very largely upon the climate of opinion in which they are living; but when that climate changes, some individuals adapt themselves more quickly than others."[56] The social context can restrict or encourage the possibility that whites will take action against the system of racism and for a social system that is more humane, egalitarian, and just. Historical conditions and existing social structure set limits on what individuals can do, but they are not all-determining. There is plenty of evidence, as Karl Marx once wrote, that people "make their own history" even if that action is within limiting and restrictive social arrangements. Today, even within a society thoroughly grounded in racism, a significant number of white Americans are working actively to destroy that racism in their own lives and in the larger society.

Individuals Taking Action   In lecture sessions and classes that I have given across the United States, some whites ask, usually in frustration and after they are convinced white racism is still commonplace, "What can I do to bring change? I am only one individual." The answer to this may lie in the old idea that one individual, however lowly her or his status, can topple a system if the action is taken at the right place and at the right time. The example sometimes cited to illustrate the point about individual actions having a larger impact is that of the one-dollar screw poorly installed that causes an engine on an airliner to fail. One person's actions can often make a difference.

In the U.S. case, the history of antiracist action indicates that individual whites often begin the process of becoming activists by working on their own racist attitudes, stereotypes, and proclivities. Such a step is not easy, because it is seldom encouraged within families and other historically white institutions. For most people the approaches to life learned at an early age, from parents, other relatives, and peers, are repeated in everyday actions throughout their lives. Still, the learned approaches reinforcing systemic racism are not part of the natural order of the universe. They are socially and psychologically constructed. With effort they can be unlearned and replaced, by individuals and groups. To get rid of these views takes great effort through a series of steps. A number of effective programs have been created to assist this unlearning process. Psychologist Patricia Devine has noted some critical steps in an unlearning process: "The individual must (a) initially decide to stop the old behavior, (b) remember the resolution, and (c) try repeatedly and decide repeatedly to eliminate the habit before the habit can be eliminated. In addition, the individual must develop a new cognitive (attitudinal and belief) structure that is consistent with the newly determined pattern of responses."[57]

A new cognitive framework will doubtless require a process of education or reeducation in which whites, as individuals and as groups, move toward understanding how the system of racial privilege was created and how they maintain it in everyday life. This reeducation will likely probe deeply into the character and composition of this society, including its extended racist history, and will require purposeful unlearning of the mythology and sincere fictions most whites use to paper over continuing racist realities. Systemic racism has persisted so well because its operation is often concealed and disguised. As we showed in earlier chapters, collective forgetting is central to the way in which most whites have dealt with the history of racism. Most have chosen not to know their history. Typical high school and college textbooks, as Jim Loewen has shown, try to put a pleasant face on U.S. history: "When textbooks make racism invisible in American history, they obstruct our already poor ability to see it in the present."[58] Thus, learning much about the reality of that history, about its brutality and unjust impoverishment for people of color, and its unjust enrichment for whites, may be critical to increasing the number of whites who join in antiracist efforts and movements at the local and national levels. As of now, this educational project is in an early stage.

Thinking and practicing racism requires a breakdown in empathy across the color line. Racism is about the destruction of natural human empathy; it means a lack of recognition of the humanity of the racialized other. Identification across the color line is hard for most whites to make. It involves understandings and emotions. Whites who change in this regard seem to develop through at least three different stages: *sympathy, empathy*, and what might be called *autopathy*. The initial stage, sympathy, is important but limited. It typically involves a willingness to set aside some racist stereotyping and hostility and the development of a friendly if variable interest in what is happening to the racialized other. A considerable number of whites have moved to this position since the 1960s civil rights revolution. Empathy is a much more advanced stage of development in that it requires a developed ability to routinely reject distancing stereotypes and a heightened and sustained capacity to see and feel some of the pain of those in the out-group. For whites, empathy involves the capacity to sense deeply the character of another's torment and to act on that realization. Autopathy is a third stage of white development, which has not as yet been fully analyzed. Discussing this matter with legal scholar Sharon Rush, I have come to this view of the step beyond empathy: This understanding and feeling is one in which a white person has intentionally put herself or himself, if only partially, into the racist world of the oppressed and thereby not only receives racist hostility from other whites but also personally feels some of the pain that comes from being enmeshed in the racist conditions central to the lives of the oppressed others. This case of feeling pain more directly often comes when whites are the close friends, lovers, parents, or other relatives of blacks who are the direct targets of racism. Recent accounts by some white parents of black children reveal the great autopathic pain the former often endure as they deal with the racism faced by the child.[59]

Today the challenge for those seeking to expand the antiracist strategy seems to include the creation of conditions where more whites will have to confront the reality of the pain that their system of racism has caused African Americans and other Americans of color with whom they come into contact. A large-scale educational campaign—one that is candid and blunt about the past and present reality of racist ideas and practices—seems to be required if more than a handful of whites are ever to move into the stages of empathy and autopathy. Beyond that, the building of more personal networks across the color line seems necessary. This idea may seem elementary, yet it is difficult and profound.

Today, many whites seem to wish to claim a friend across the color line. For example, in a 1976 survey one-third of whites said that they or a member of their immediate family had contact socially with a black friend. By the time of a 1998 survey some 42 percent of whites polled now said that they had a black friend they personally felt close to. However, when this latter survey asked white respondents for the first names of their good friends, only 6 percent actually listed a black person as part of their friendship network.[60] It appears that many whites who say they have a close black friend actually do not have one. Building more cross-racial friendships will likely be a difficult task.

A History of Interracial Organization   Antiracist action began in the first centuries of American development. There is a long history of interracial cooperation and organization against racism. Multiracial groups have periodically helped to bring some social changes, as the 1840s–1850s abolitionists and 1950s–1960s civil rights activists demonstrated. Some whites have even given their lives for such antiracist movements. For example, in October 1859, John Brown, a white abolitionist, led a small band of whites and blacks in an attempt to seize weapons at a federal arsenal at Harper's Ferry, with the goal of arming those enslaved. Today, one needed educational step is for all levels of American education to offer courses that discuss the views and actions of white antiracist activists like John Brown. Radical abolitionists constituted one of the first multiracial groups to struggle openly and aggressively against the oppressiveness of systemic racism. Some died as a result. John Brown's lucid comment on his own sentence of death indicates his commitment to racial justice: "Now, if it is deemed necessary that I should forfeit my life for the furtherance of the ends of justice, and mingle my blood further with the blood of my children and with the blood of millions in this slave country whose rights are disregarded by wicked, cruel, and unjust enactments, — I submit, so let it be done!"[61]

Since the antislavery efforts of the Harper's Ferry band in 1859, a long line of whites, blacks, and others of color have worked together, often against enormous opposition, to bring freedom and justice for all Americans. Recall the creation of the NAACP in the early 1900s, an organization seeking to fight racial exclusion. For many years this organization had black and white officials at its head. In addition, the black-led civil rights movement of the 1950s and 1960s had participants from several different racial and ethnic groups, including many whites. In a social system there seem to be only a few high leverage points from which to precipitate lasting changes, and U.S. history suggests that large coalitions of black and non-black Americans working against racism can create such high leverage points.

Antiracist Organizations Today   Over the last several decades, antiracist whites have helped to organize or have joined in a number of grassroots organizations working against U.S. racism. For example, the Institutes for the Healing of Racism hold seminars and dialogues on racism in more than 150 cities. These multiracial groups of Americans work at the local level to heighten awareness of racism, educate local citizens about how racism works and how to fight it, and provide dialogue across local racial and ethnic boundaries. These groups deal openly with racist prejudices and the reality of institutional racism.[62]

Typical of the range of current antiracist organizations are the People's Institute for Survival and Beyond (PI) and Anti-Racist Action (ARA). Located in New Orleans and created by black activists, PI is a community-oriented group that sets up "Undoing Racism" workshops to train people in community and nonprofit organizations. These multiracial workshops, which had trained about twenty thousand people (about half of them white) as of 1999, are designed to help officials in organizations and community activists understand racism and cultural diversity and to show them how they can undo racism in their own lives and in their organizations. Taking a somewhat different tack, the mostly white ARA groups are working aggressively against racism in several dozen cities in the United States and Canada. Originally established to combat neo-Nazi and Klan organizations, ARA groups have developed other antiracist programs. For example, their Copwatch program attempts to reduce police brutality by having members take video recorders into the streets to tape the police in their dealings with citizens of color. While their objectives and timing have varied, several other organizations have also pressed for changes in institutionalized racism across the United States. A sampling of these would include the Dismantling Racism Program of the National Conference (St. Louis), the Anti-Racism Institute of Clergy and Laity Concerned (Chicago), the Northwest Coalition Against Malicious Harassment, the Southern Empowerment Project, and the Committee Against Anti-Asian Violence.[63]

One next step in a broad antiracist strategy for the United States might be to expand the number of these antiracist organizations and to connect them into a national association working against systemic racism. Broad organizations against racial and ethnic oppression seem to be needed, though sustaining them may be difficult. For example, since the 1980s the Reverend Jesse Jackson, the black civil rights leader, has worked with Americans from several different racial and ethnic groups, including whites, to build the Rainbow Coalition. This organization has pressed for key social justice goals: better jobs and government job creation; more aggressive government efforts against racism, sexism, and homophobia; and government efforts to protect the environment. For a decade the organization helped to win some progressive electoral battles in various states and supported Jackson's bid for the presidency. However, after a period of influence in the 1980s and early 1990s, the organization seemed to decline in its national impact by the late 1990s. Today there are numerous other movements organizing Americans of color and white workers against injustice. One example is the New Party, an alliance of labor, community, and environmental coalitions working for social justice goals, including the rights of workers, consumers, and communities to organize without interference; the creation of a sustainable economy and full employment; and "an absolute bar to discrimination based on race, gender, age, country of origin, and sexual orientation."[64] With this social justice agenda, the New Party has won a number of local and state elections across the country. Renewed efforts at coalitions like the Rainbow Coalition and the New Party might be a valuable aspect of a broader antiracist and antioppression strategy.

A New Constitutional Convention: An Idea Whose Time Has Come   In 1787 fifty-five white men met in Philadelphia and wrote a Constitution for what was seen as the first democratic nation. They met at the end of a long revolutionary struggle and articulated their perspective using strong language about human equality and freedom. However, they had a very restricted view of those grand ideas. As we saw in chapter 1, this Constitutional Convention did not include white women, African Americans, or Native Americans, who collectively made up a majority of the population. Nor did it include representation for white men with little or no property. The representatives of less than 10 percent of the population framed a new constitution that has governed, with some amendments, the United States since the late eighteenth century. The document created by these propertied white men reflected their racial, class, and gender interests. While some of these interests encompassed the desires of all Americans to be free of the tyrannies of Europe—such as the constitutional prohibition of aristocratic titles and of a state religion—it took strong protests in the colonies before a Bill of Rights was added.[65]

The 1858 Constitution   Not one of the original Constitutional Convention's delegates saw black Americans as human beings whose views, interests, and perspectives should be seriously considered in the document being created. How then should black Americans, whose ancestors were present in large numbers in the nation but excluded at the convention and whose enslavement was ratified by the Constitution, regard the document? Why should they accept the authority of a constitution their ancestors played no part in making? As I see it, this undemocratic Constitution and its often biased tradition of prowhite interpretation should be replaced, for this tradition has constrained progressive change toward equality and justice for too long. All attempts to change the system of racism since the late 1700s have been constrained by this document and the interpretations of it by the mostly white and male judges and members of Congress holding office since that time. All court decisions on racial discrimination, the amendment abolishing slavery, all civil rights laws, and all civil rights efforts have been made within this biased and constraining framework. The American democratic project yet remains to be accomplished.

Significantly, only one multiracial group of Americans has, to my knowledge, tried to formulate and implement an antiracist constitution and declaration of independence. On May 8, 1858, more than a year before the Harper's Ferry raid, John Brown and his allies, black and white, met in Chatham, Canada, to formulate a new constitution to govern the band of revolutionaries fighting for liberty—a constitution looking forward to a new antiracist nation of the United States. Twelve white Americans and thirty-three black Americans were present at this convention. The preamble to the document they created read as follows:

> Whereas slavery, throughout its entire existence in the United States, is none other than a most barbarous, unprovoked and unjustifiable war of one portion of its citizens upon another portion . . . in utter disregard and violation of those eternal and self-evident truths set forth in our Declaration of Independence: therefore, we, citizens of the United States, and the oppressed people who, by a recent decision of the Supreme Court, are declared to have no rights which the white man is bound to respect, together with all other people degraded by the laws thereof, do, for the time being, ordain and establish ourselves the following provisional constitution and ordinances, the better to protect our persons, property, lives, and liberties, and to govern our actions.[66]

Their declaration of independence further insisted "that the Slaves are, & of right ought to be . . . free."[67] This 1858 constitution and declaration of independence appear to be the only ones in U.S. history to be prepared by representatives of the oppressed black residents of the United States, with their interests substantially in mind.

A New Constitutional Convention   As I see it, it is time to have yet another constitutional convention, one that represents all Americans. The base of the U.S. system must be replaced if systemic racism is to be removed, just as the sinking foundation of a dilapidated building must be replaced. A new convention is required not only to address restitution and rights for oppressed groups but also to ensure that the governing document of the new multiracial democracy is produced by representatives of all the people. The egalitarian and democratic ideas associated with the Bill of Rights and U.S. civil rights laws could well be points for important discussion at this new convention. However, no existing laws should automatically be part of a new constitution because the meaning of these laws usually rests on their interpretation by the current white-male-dominated judiciary.

What would be a more adequate set of starting points in beginning the debate on a constitution for a true multiracial democracy? The new convention might use the United Nation's Universal Declaration of Human Rights and related human rights documents that have expanded that declaration (especially those on women's rights). First ratified in 1948 by the United Nations, the declaration today represents a growing consensus across the globe on what human rights are essential for a healthy society (see below). Without respect for a broad array of basic human rights there can be no democracy. Thus, the official call for the new convention might indicate a grounding of its discussions in a mutual respect for the broad human rights of all Americans and in a mutual respect for the plurality of U.S. cultures and heritages.

Some civil rights scholars and leaders have opposed the idea of a new constitutional convention because they fear the white majority there might roll back existing civil rights protection, that the situation could be made worse. For example, Roy Brooks has criticized an earlier framing of this idea of a new convention because it "would open debate and reconsideration of the existing document, and the consequences could be dire."[68] He fears that in a society where many whites appear to be moving in a more racist direction that a new convention might be dominated by conservative whites and ban such things as free speech and reproductive rights.

These fears are reasonable if the new convention were to be dominated by white male conservatives. However, in my hypothetical scenario the convention would *not* take place unless those who write the new constitution are fully representative of *all* sectors of the current population. No other arrangement will create the necessary conditions for full and open debates on matters of concern to all the people. If the convention were to be held in the early part of the new millennium, this stipulation would mean that white men would be about 36 percent of the delegates, instead of the 100-percent representation they had at the first convention. Indeed, that 36 percent would include a much more diverse array of white men — such as labor union and gay rights activists — than those at the first convention. In addition, more than a quarter of the delegates would be Americans of color, and women would make up a little more than half of the delegates. Moreover, if the convention were to be delayed for a few decades, the majority of delegates might well be people of color.

Prior to calling an official convention those committed to the creation of a diverse and viable democracy might set up a trial constitutional convention to test how such a truly representative convention might be called and how it would operate in dealing with an array of difficult decision-making, human-rights, and related political issues. Indeed, there could be a practice convention in each U.S. region, which might well generate important human rights and other political debates in every area.

A truly representative assembly would insure that, for the first time in U.S. history, the white majority hears much discussion of, and faces pressure to take seriously, the group interests and rights of all Americans of color. This assembly will be diverse enough that many decisions on constitutional provisions will have to be negotiated among contending groups; they will require a consideration of the originally excluded interests of women and Americans of color, as well as of the more recently asserted interests of gay and disabled Americans. As with the first convention, the debates will likely be revealing and educational, not only for delegates but for the nation as a whole. These debates would likely remove the smokescreen disguising the undemocratic reality of U.S. society and show unequivocally how racial, gender, class, and other forms of exploitation operate to the detriment of many Americans. A true democracy is one in which all people are not only represented but also have equitable input into the creation of its laws and political institutions. Moreover, this new constitutional convention is only a first step. A truly democratic constitution becomes the political basis on which to build an array of effective democratic institutions.

For all its possible difficulties, a new constitutional convention seems required not only to guarantee full human rights for previously excluded Americans but also to insure that the new founding document is actually made by the representatives of all Americans. Even if this convention is a failure, and the white majority there creates a more racist system, that would at least mean a more honest and open system of exploitation, one not hiding behind a veneer of equality and colorblindness. Such a convention might be an important part of a reinvigorated antiracist strategy to build a new democratic foundation for the United States. Equally as important to this antiracist strategy is the symbolism of having a truly representative assembly making the nation's constitution. Once those who have never participated in politics see that their representatives have been actively involved in making the founding document, commitment to the new democracy will likely increase. A strongly democratic constitution—with broad citizen participation in its associated institutions and recurring citizen activism on behalf of human rights—seems the only guarantee of liberty and freedom.

Restitution and Reparations   As yet, no major group of white Americans has taken responsibility for the past and continuing negative impact of slavery, segregation, and modern racism on black Americans. For the most part, white leaders and rank-

and-file whites have ignored or rejected proposals for large-scale reparations and compensation for those who have suffered from systemic racism. Indeed, in the late 1990s President Bill Clinton entertained, then rejected, the idea of a formal public apology to African Americans for slavery. Even the suggestion of an apology was attacked by many whites. Once there is a new constitution in place, a comprehensive antiracist strategy would likely require an early addressing of reparations for the damage done by centuries of oppression to African Americans and other Americans of color. Let us consider here the African American case.

Arguments against Restitution and Reparations   Recall how presidential candidate Bob Dole questioned whether white men should have to pay through programs like affirmative action for slavery and discrimination before they were born. Today a majority of white Americans would likely still answer "no." The common reaction would be, "Let bygones be bygones." The unjust enrichment gained by whites over centuries should be forgotten. Such collective forgetting is one way in which whites handle the tension between the values of liberty and justice and the long history of racist oppression. Unquestionably, this distancing of oppression is useful in the construction of a rationalizing ideology. However, there are major problems in the argument that whites should not be accountable for what their ancestors did, as many whites say, "hundreds of years ago." For example, slavery ended less than 140 years ago. Some black Americans are only a couple of generations removed from their enslaved ancestors. Moreover, the near slavery of legal segregation only came to an end in the late 1960s, well within the lifetimes of many Americans alive today.

In the thinking of most white leaders and the white public, the actions of the founders and later political leaders that have benefited whites are given great weight and legitimacy. Such actions include the making of the Constitution and subsequent court decisions interpreting the Constitution in the interest of whites. However, according to the prevailing white view, the racially oppressive actions by the same white founders and later leaders should be forgiven and forgotten by those whose ancestors were victimized by their oppressive actions. Not surprisingly, a majority of whites do not see the earlier structures of oppression like slavery and legal segregation as relevant to present-day racial inequalities. Nonetheless, these whites will insist that black Americans accept the Constitution and laws established by whites as binding on them, even though they had no say in the laws' creation. Richard Delgado has summarized this point well in the form of a comment from a black professor: most whites insist that blacks "owe obligations arising out of that social contract, but no obligation is owed to us arising from the abuse we suffered in connection with it. Ahistorical young conservatives want the benefit of social compliance from blacks with a system that provides young whites with security, schools, and liberty. But they don't want to pay for it by recognizing a debt they owe blacks arising from their forefathers' wrongs."[69]

Another common white argument against restitution and reparations is that societal discrimination against black Americans is too impersonal and amorphous for the development of remedies. In several recent federal court cases, such as the aforementioned Croson case, the majority of judges have accepted the view that, while there may still be some societal discrimination, no one can determine who in particular is responsible and who has benefited. As a result, these judges argue, one cannot expect government officials to take action to redress the continuing societal discrimination. Martin Katz has pointed out the wrongheadedness of the majority opinion in Croson: if injuries from past or present discrimination cannot be remedied, then "whites will be allowed to retain an advantage which they did not earn, and Blacks will continue to lag behind as a result of acts which, although they may not be amenable to documentation, no one denies were performed in contempt of individuality. Racism has made race relevant to productivity. Treating race as if it were irrelevant will not help to make it any less relevant."[70]

The Case for Restitution and Reparations   In the Charter of the Nuremberg Tribunal convened to deal with Nazi war crimes after World War II, "crimes against humanity" were defined as "murder, extermination, enslavement, deportation, and other inhumane acts committed against any civilian population. . . . whether or not in violation of the domestic law of the country where perpetrated."[71] White Europeans and white Americans have a long tradition of such crimes against humanity. The large-scale enslavement and oppression of Africans across the globe for more than four centuries was, and remains, one of the most serious of the "crimes against humanity."

Most whites have benefited from centuries of racist oppression and the transmission of many privileges and substantial amounts of ill-gotten wealth from that oppression to later generations. As we have seen in previous chapters, enslaved Africans and African Americans created much wealth and capital that to a significant degree spurred not only the economic development of the South but also the industrial revolution in the United States and in Europe. "Western production levels were transformed," Ali Mazrui informs us. "But so were Western living standards, life expectancy, population growth, and the globalization of capitalism. How do we measure such repercussions of slavery?"[72] The current prosperity, relatively long life expectancies, and relatively high living standards of whites as a group in the United States, as well as in the West generally, are ultimately rooted in the agony, exploitation, and impoverishment of those who were colonized and enslaved, as well as in the oppression and misery of their descendants. As we have seen throughout this book, white Americans as individuals, families, and communities have done much damage to black Americans. This damage is not just in the past, for black Americans today suffer from the many psychological, economic, political, and social costs of past and present racism.

Recall that in traditional Western law the concept of unjust enrichment

includes not only receiving benefits that justly belong to another but also the obligation to make restitution to victims. Numerous court decisions have provided
remedies measured more by the gain to a defendant than by a plaintiff's loss. The
defendant must give up the unjust enrichment, including gains made from it.[73]
Thus, U.S. law does not allow the children of a thief to benefit from the theft once
that illegal action is known. However, the law on remedies has traditionally ignored
group claims against unjust enrichment, and systemic racism involves injuries to
a large group. An antiracist strategy might well extend the remedies law aggressively to conditions of group discrimination and oppression. Whites whose families have been in North America for a generation or more, which is the majority,
benefit today from the significant racial advantages that their ancestors gained,
often including gains under slavery or segregation. A majority of whites have
benefited from the economic, political, social, and educational discrimination
that favored their ancestors—and still favors themselves today (see chapter 5). As
with individual remedies, group remedies should encompass stopping the unjust
extraction of benefits now and in the future (prospective action) as well as making restitution to the victim group for past actions (retrospective action). Restitution and reparations are inadequate without stopping the processes that distribute,
maintain, and increase the ill-gotten gains for present and future generations.

Interestingly, a few white judges have recognized the principle of large-scale
restitution as relevant to eliminating the effects of past discrimination. In one 1980s
case, *Larry Williams et al. v. City of New Orleans, et al.*, liberal appellate justice
John Wisdom argued in a partially dissenting opinion that the Congress that crafted
the antislavery amendments to the Constitution and a major civil rights act at the
Civil War's end intended to grant the federal government power "to provide for
remedial action aimed at eliminating the present effects of past discrimination
against blacks as a class. Wholly aside from the fourteenth amendment, the thirteenth amendment is an affirmative grant of power to eliminate slavery along with
its 'badges and incidents' and to establish universal civil freedom. The amendment envisions affirmative action aimed at blacks as a race. When a present discriminatory effect upon blacks as a class can be linked with a discriminatory practice against blacks as a race under the slavery system, the present effect may be
eradicated under the auspices of the thirteenth amendment."[74] Given this historical argument, one can understand why many whites wish to break the historical
link to past oppression. Recognition of that linkage creates great pressure for compensation and restitution.

Support for Some Reparations   Most white Americans probably would consider
significant reparations for group-based damages suffered by black Americans to
be a radical and undesirable policy. However, white political leaders, white judges,
and even ordinary whites have on occasion accepted the principle of reparations
for past damages done to other groups. For example, U.S. courts have required

corporations to compensate the deformed children of mothers who in the past took harmful drugs during their pregnancies without knowing of the drug's side effects. The courts have held that such harm done to later generations was foreseeable by the corporate executives in power at that earlier point in time. The argument that those executives are gone or deceased was not allowed to take the corporation off the hook. Harmed children received significant compensation even though the damage became evident only years later.[75] This compensation principle is essentially the same as that asserted by those arguing for reparations for African Americans, whose current conditions often reflect the damage done by many earlier generations of whites.

Significantly, the U.S. government has justifiably been active in efforts to force the German government to make large-scale reparations (about $60 billion) to Jewish and other victims of the Nazi Holocaust, even though no one in the current German leadership that is making the reparations was part of the Nazi government. Occasionally, U.S. leaders have also recognized a reparations principle in regard to discriminatory action taken against U.S. citizens. Belatedly, and after years of resistance, the U.S. government agreed to pay some very modest reparations to Japanese Americans wrongfully interned as "dangerous" in barbed-wire internment camps in the United States during World War II. In 1987 Congress passed a law including a formal apology to Japanese Americans for their oppressive internment, which was undertaken for essentially ra_ist reasons, and providing $1.2 billion in reparations. Significantly, this modest compensation was not made until Japanese Americans had a strong partner in an increasingly powerful Japanese government.

Specific Proposals for Black Reparations   From the earliest days of abolitionist activity in the eighteenth and nineteenth centuries black leaders and their white allies argued that abolition of slavery and citizenship for African Americans were not enough. Some restitution enabling those freed to provide for their families was required. As we discussed in earlier chapters, during and after the Civil War antislavery leaders called for compensation for newly freed African Americans. At an 1865 Republican convention in Pennsylvania, one important congressional leader, Thaddeus Stevens, called for the taking of 400 million acres from former slaveholders. Another leading abolitionist, Senator Charles Sumner (Massachusetts), called for land grants to those recently enslaved. Legal equality was not enough, for that would not eradicate the "large disparities of wealth, status, and power."[76] In 1866 and 1867 reparations legislation was brought to Congress, but it failed. After the southern oligarchy resumed control in the late 1870s, little was heard on the matter of assistance or restitution to those recently freed from slavery. Since the 1960s civil rights movement the idea of reparations has seen a major resurgence. In a 1963 book Dr. Martin Luther King, Jr. called for compensation for the slavery, segregation, and continuing discrimination faced by African Americans.

He recognized the principle of compensation for stolen wages.[77] Recall too the 1994 petition by the Nation of Islam to the United Nations for reparations for antiblack racism.

Over the last few decades scholars and activists have developed several international campaigns for reparations to Africans or African Americans. In mid-1992 a dozen experts were selected by the Organization of African Unity to develop a campaign for African reparations like those provided by the German government to Nazi Holocaust survivors. Moreover, in March 1996 the British House of Lords had a serious debate on the impact of slavery on Africa and Africans, with a few members of that House proposing the idea of reparations to Africa from Britain and other colonial nations. Lord Anthony Gifford eloquently defended the idea that international law requires those who commit crimes against humanity, including enslavement, to make significant reparations to their victims or their descendants. He noted there is no statute of limitations for crimes against humanity, so the still-harmed descendants of earlier victims of oppression deserve reparations. He also offered a concrete procedure, saying, "The claim would be brought on behalf of all Africans, in Africa and in the Diaspora, who suffer the consequences of the crime, through the agency of an appropriate representative body. . . . The claim would be brought against the governments of those countries which promoted and were enriched by the African slave trade and the institution of slavery. . . . The amount of the claim would be assessed by experts in each aspect of life and in each region, affected by the institution of slavery."[78] Such a debate needs now to be held in the U.S. Congress. Indeed, every year since 1989 Congressman John Conyers, Jr. (Michigan) has introduced a bill in Congress to set up a commission to look into the continuing impact of slavery on black Americans and to examine the possibility of reparations for slavery and its lasting impact. A key feature of the commission would be to educate the public, especially the white public, on the racist realities of U.S. history. While Conyers has been unable yet to secure hearings on his bill, he has gotten thirty-one cosponsors and continues to work patiently for a public discussion of reparations. As he had recently commented, some day the "most hidden, important, silent subject we've ever had in this country" will come to the forefront. He added, "what we're trying to do now is just get the debate going to see where it will lead us."[79]

In the case of African Americans, reparations might take several different but interrelated forms. One type of action would be the transfer of an appropriate amount of compensating wealth from white communities to black communities. For instance, the National Coalition of Blacks for Reparations in America (N'COBRA), which is developing a reparations lawsuit, has sought nearly $400 million in reparations—not just individual compensation but provision of programs enabling black communities to prosper over the long term. One way to make some restitution is to provide well-funded and extensive programs, over several generations, at the local and state levels for upgrading the incomes, education, and skills of black Americans as individuals. A similar program could provide government resources to significantly upgrade major public facilities, including public schools, in all black communities. Yet another type of reparations would guarantee representative political participation in all local, state, and national legislatures, so that black Americans could have an appropriate voice in government decisions about their communities. These programs could be critical steps in an antiracist strategy designed to restore African Americans to the place they would have been, had not trillions of dollars worth in wealth been taken from them by means of slavery, segregation, and contemporary discrimination. Even the beginning of reparations would have significance beyond the monetary compensation, for it would constitute a dramatic symbolism, a recognition of the damage done by whites under nearly four centuries of systemic racism.

Building a Real Democracy   It appears that few white Americans have ever envisaged for the United States the possibility of a truly just and egalitarian democracy grounded solidly in respect for human rights. Certainly, the founders did not conceive of such a possibility, even in the long run. Nor did later white leaders such as Presidents Abraham Lincoln, Woodrow Wilson, Franklin D. Roosevelt, and Dwight D. Eisenhower envision that type of democratic future. In my judgment, as the nation and the world change demographically and dramatically in the future, whites everywhere will face ever greater pressures to create and to participate in a new sociopolitical system that is nonracist, just, and egalitarian.

A Standard for Expanded Rights   As another phase in a comprehensive antiracist strategy, Americans might be pressed to think futuristically and rigorously in terms of what an authentic democracy might be like. Americans, especially white Americans, might be pressured to step outside the existing U.S. system, as best they can, to think carefully about an ideal humane society. To evaluate the U.S. system and suggest a replacement, we might begin by drawing on the international rights perspective as described in the Universal Declaration of Human Rights—a perspective that views every person as having a broad range of basic rights by virtue of being human. The idea that basic human rights *transcend* the boundaries and authority of any particular society or government was early articulated by Thomas Jefferson and his fellow revolutionaries. Today, we need to extend this idea well beyond what the founders envisioned. The international perspective on human rights was greatly strengthened by the Nuremberg trials of former members of the Nazi government just after World War II. The trials established the principle that some crimes, "crimes against humanity," are so extreme that they are condemned by principles higher than the norms and laws of any particular nation-state.[80]

The struggle to deal with the Nazi Holocaust, together with ongoing struggles for human rights by people in many countries around the globe—including black

Americans in the United States—led to the Universal Declaration of Human Rights. This important international agreement stipulates in Article 1 that "all human beings are born free and equal in dignity and rights," and in Article 7 that "all are equal before the law and are entitled without any discrimination to equal protection of the law." Article 8 further asserts, "Everyone has the right to an effective remedy . . . for acts violating the fundamental rights," and Article 25 states that these rights extend to everyday life: "Everyone has the right to a standard of living adequate for the health and well-being of himself and his family, including food, clothing, housing." Since 1948 numerous other international covenants on economic, social, and political rights have been signed by most United Nations members, and agencies like the UN Commission on Human Rights have been established to monitor human rights issues globally. The UN International Convention on the Elimination of All Forms of Racial Discrimination (CERD), put in force in 1969, specifically requires governments to make illegal the dissemination of ideas of racial superiority and the operation of organizations set up to promote racial discrimination. This convention, first ratified by some nations in the late 1960s, was ratified by the United States only in 1994. Today CERD commits the U.S. and other governments to "adopt all necessary measures for speedily eliminating racial discrimination in all its forms and manifestations."[81] These agreements provide some legal support for implementation of the human rights principles of the Universal Declaration of Human Rights.

International Pressure for Change   Since its adoption the Universal Declaration of Human Rights has been used in crafting many international treaties and agreements, and many of its major provisions are part of international law. Virtually all international documents on human rights at least allude to this declaration. At a 1993 World Conference on Human Rights more than one hundred nations reiterated support for its principles. Court systems in numerous nations have cited the declaration—on occasion in overturning patterns of discrimination. The United States has made less use of the declaration than many other nations. As of 1999, the Declaration had been cited in only 101 of the many U.S. federal court decisions, and then usually in an insignificant footnote. The Declaration has been cited only five times by the U.S. Supreme Court, and *not at all since 1970*. To this point in time, most U.S. courts have been unwilling to take this strong international statement of broad human rights seriously.[82]

Recently, the International Human Rights Law Group (IHRLG) has begun an effort of public advocacy and assistance to U.S. civil rights groups that seeks to show the latter how they can use the language and techniques of international human rights agreements to further the antidiscrimination cause in the United States. This advocacy group is seeking to go beyond traditional civil rights approaches to build broad coalitions and familiarize civil rights groups with knowledge of international human rights laws. They hope that placing continuing racial discrimination in the United States in the international spotlight will pressure the U.S. government to take more action to eradicate discrimination.[83]

The comprehensive human rights perspective expressed in these UN documents draws not only on the progressive human rights traditions of Europeans but also from the human rights insights and perspectives of Native, African, Latino, and Asian Americans, and of other peoples around the globe. These UN agreements strongly affirm that human beings have rights independent of particular governments and press those governments to incorporate basic human rights into their everyday operations. They provide an internationally legitimated standard that can be used to judge and critique systemic racism in the United States. As noted above, they can be the basis for discussion at a new constitutional convention. Implementing this egalitarian standard of human interaction and development by new institutionalized arrangements to effect real democracy would dramatically restructure or eliminate current racist structures and institutions.

Major change away from racist institutions will require much more than one-way integration into existing institutions. Multifaceted integration and adaptation are critical—among European Americans, African Americans, and all other Americans of color. Dr. Martin Luther King, Jr. once spoke of the movement of black Americans to be "creative dissenters who will call our beloved nation to a higher destiny," and not to seek to integrate "into existing values of American society."[84] A new U.S. society will require new human rights commitments, which will perhaps lead to the higher destiny that Dr. King contemplated. Ideally, the new social system would insure equality and justice in practice as well as in principle.

Certain human needs seem universal: the need for self-respect, for substantial control over one's own life, for significant group self-management, and for access to the necessities of material life. In an authentic democracy there would need to be respect for a diversity of individuals, communities, and cultures. In the process of societal change, European Americans would come to view themselves as what Marimba Ani has described as "limited beings with limited powers, existing in a culture among cultures."[85]

Links with Other Antioppression Efforts   Ultimately, a robust democracy is not possible without an elimination of all major types of oppression. Significant destruction of systemic racism is likely to be corrosive of other types of oppression. In this relatively short book, even as I have tried to dig deeply into one major type of social oppression, I have needed to discuss, albeit too briefly, some connections between racial, class, and gender oppression. Numerous scholars have noted the important interconnections between these types of oppression. For instance, Sandra Harding has argued that "We should think of race, class and gender as interlocking; one cannot dislodge one piece without disturbing the others."[86] Not only racist structures, but capitalistic, sexist, homophobic, ageist, and bureaucratic-authoritarian arrangements will have to be dismantled if the lives of individuals and the functioning of their communities are to be democratic and rid of anti-human oppression.

Historically, Marxist analysis has played perhaps the greatest role in generating protest movements against oppression in modern societies. Labor movements, many of them inspired by Marxist analysis, have brought improvements to the lives of workers in capitalist systems. Clearly, all Americans need access to sufficient economic, housing, and other social resources. Labor progressives have long argued that a full-fledged economic democracy is a requisite step in destroying structures of oppression and exploitation.[87] There are strong similarities and cross-cutting linkages between antiracist and class struggles. Ordinary white workers are exploited by the capitalist class and the latter's political and intellectual elites. White workers have little role in how their workplace or the general economy is run. However, as we have seen in earlier chapters, the white elite has worked hard to secure the acceptance of the existing racial and class hierarchies by white workers by offering them the psychological wage of whiteness, and white workers as a group have more privileges and opportunities than black workers.[88] A successful antiracist coalition across the color line will need to deal with white workers' commitments to racist privileges, stereotypes, and practices. Ultimately, many aspects of societal oppression will have to be dealt with, including not only antiblack and other racism among white male and female workers but also sexism among men of color and homophobia among whites and people of color.[89]

Clearly, there are multiple societal oppressions, and no one analysis can adequately deal with all major oppressions. My argument in this book is that systemic racism is a central part of the foundation of U.S. society, and that a deep understanding of racism's history, framing, character, operation, and maintenance is essential both to making sense of this society generally and to destroying racist oppression. Having set this task, by no means do I downplay the importance of analyzing and fighting the other types of social oppression central to U.S. society, including class exploitation, sexism, and homophobia.

Over the last century there has been much conflict between those in one group fighting against a particular type of oppression and those in another group contending against yet another oppression, and so far there has been little joining together in more general antioppression efforts. Yet at the heart of each of these social movements are certain paramount issues that can be accented by those seeking to build successful coalitions now and in the future. Perhaps the most important idea held in common is that of ridding the society of oppressive domination by one group over another, together with the related idea of self-determination to the fullest extent possible for every group. With great effort and new imagination in organizing, perhaps this shared vision of a nation free of all such oppression and domination can be used to build successful coalitions in the future.

Conclusion   Antiracism is more than a theoretical framework organizing, explaining, and interpreting the realities of systemic racism. Antiracism now and in the past has encompassed numerous strategies to eradicate racism. Many researchers have studied racial oppression. The point is to eradicate it.

The eradication of systemic racism requires more than removing inequalities and disparities in existing institutions. Steps in the direction of removing discrimination and inequalities, as we have seen, are important and will improve people's lives. However, the full eradication of racism will eventually require the uprooting and replacement of the existing hierarchy of racialized power. A developed antiracist strategy will eventually go beyond reform of current institutions to the complete elimination of existing systems of racialized power. One analysis of liberation strategies for the United States concluded that "oppressors cannot renounce their power and privilege *within* a racist relationship; they must *abandon* that relationship. . . . there is no historical example of genuine, peaceful abdication of racist supremacy by the whole ruling group."[90] Historically, oppression leads to conflict, and major conflict often leads to significant social change. Most of the progressive developments in human rights in the United States and across the globe have come only after large-scale protests, people's movements, civil disobedience, open conflict, and revolutions. As Paul Lauren has noted, from the "emancipation of slaves after the French Revolution and United States Civil War to the gaining of independence by colonial peoples after World Wars I and II, the cause of human rights invariably has required some drastic upheaval to shift power away from those unwilling to share it voluntarily."[91] Antiracist theorists and activists cannot prove that there will be change again, but they can act on the assumption that it is likely. As Ben Agger has noted about antioppression theory generally, "the future is a risk, a choice, framed by the past, the legacy of which is difficult to overcome. But critical social theorists . . . are certain that the past and present do not neatly extend into the future without any slippage."[92] Human agency is possible in spite of oppressive structures, but it must be regularly supported and regenerated.

Why should whites support major changes in the system of racism? We have described the reasons that most whites resist societal change. Yet, we have also seen reasons for change as well. One is general but essential: whites have a moral obligation to take action, as individuals and as groups, to overturn the system of racism that they and their ancestors have created and make meaningful the clichés of freedom, equality, and justice they often proclaim. Jean-François Lyotard has underscored the deeper standard here: "Thou shalt not kill thy fellow human being: To kill a human being is not to kill an animal of the species Homo Sapiens, but to kill the human community . . . as both capacity and promise. And you also kill it in yourself. To banish the stranger is to banish the community, and you banish yourself from the community thereby."[93] Destroying the racial other means destroying one's own humanity.

If there is no real societal change in the near future, pressures for change will increase dramatically as whites become an ever smaller minority of the population over the course of the twenty-first century. As Abraham Lincoln once predicted, a "house divided against itself cannot stand." At the time, Lincoln's provocative metaphor accented the centrality and contradictions of slavery in U.S. society. We can extend it today to the reality of a nation still divided because of "slavery unwilling to die." The question hanging over white Americans is this: Do white Americans wish to face open racial conflict, even racial war, for themselves, their children, or their grandchildren? During the 1960s urban rebellions numerous black leaders and a few white leaders pointed out that without social justice there can be *no* public order. This is still the long-term reality in the United States. Without social justice the nation will never achieve a democratic social order.

Black Americans remain at the center of the U.S. system of racial oppression, and their antiracist consciousness has perhaps the greatest potential for continuing challenges to the racist order. They have developed large-scale social change movements a few times in U.S. history, and smaller-scale movements many other times, and there will doubtless be more such movements in due course. While large-scale liberation movements have come and gone, strong efforts against racism have never disappeared. As a group, black Americans have not retreated to an enervating pessimism but have slowly pressed onward. They continue to join religious, civic, and civil rights organizations working to eradicate racism, to get civil rights laws enforced, and to secure better living conditions for themselves and for all Americans. Historically, this nation has seen periods when black Americans have changed what their "rulers perceive to be in their own best interests. The destabilizing effects of protest and resistance can alter the cost-benefit calculus so that change favorable to blacks actually comes to be in the interest of dominant forces."[94] This was true during the abolitionist period from the 1830s to the 1860s and again during the civil rights movement and black rioting of the period from the 1950s to the early 1970s. Perhaps it can be so again.

The efforts of black Americans to free themselves from oppression have often stimulated other Americans of color to do the same. Inspired by black efforts or acting on their own, the latter have often reacted strongly to the variations of white oppression that specifically target them. Today, there are numerous antiracist and civil rights groups in the United States, including the American Indian Movement, the Mexican American Legal Defense and Education Fund, the Puerto Rican Legal Defense Fund, the Japanese American Citizens League, the Asian American Legal Defense Fund, and the Organization of Chinese Americans. These and similar groups are working now for change in patterns of racial oppression. To take just one example, today Native American activists are organizing protest movements and fighting legal battles to force the federal government to honor its hundreds of legal treaties. Today these groups are joined by an array of other organizations pressing for social justice, including women's organizations and gay and lesbian organizations. One major challenge today is to build united coalitions against the many types of established oppression.

The world around the United States is slowly but dramatically changing. A number of contradictions have emerged out of the global racist order originally created by the various colonial adventures of European nations. This imperialism created social and political structures that, then as now, have imbedded racist images, norms, and ideologies of subordination. International relations, global markets, global financial institutions, and multinational corporations are all racialized, with white European perspectives and agents often at their core. For centuries these Eurocentric institutions have been globalizing, dominant, and resistant to change. Today, however, there is much ferment against various types of oppression across the globe. Over the next century neither the United States nor the world is likely to stay the same. It seems likely that over the next century many groups and nations will move farther out from under the dominance of white Americans and Europeans. People everywhere are organizing for change. In recent years we have seen strong antiracism movements in South Africa and Brazil, and renewed labor movements in South Africa, Brazil, China, and Nigeria.

Today, people of African descent remain the globe's largest racially oppressed group, a group now resident in many countries. In the 1980s and 1990s we saw a systemically racist society, the Republic of South Africa, move from white to black political control and begin to change the rest of its social and economic structure of racism (apartheid) with relatively little bloodshed. Few social analysts predicted such a sea change, and even though South Africa faces many serious challenges before it attains full economic and political democracy, it has already changed faster and more substantially than any Western commentator or analyst had predicted. The possibility of a global democratic order rid of racism remains only a dream, but the South African revolution shows that it is a powerful dream. More changes in the world's racist system will likely come as the human spirit conquers the continuing realities of oppression, however daunting they may be. The chair of the Special United Nations Committee against Apartheid has recently expressed this hope: the "world can never be governed by force, never by fear, never by power. In the end what governs is the spirit and what conquers is the mind."[95]

Introduction

1   Kevin Johnson, "ACLU Campaign Yields Race Bias Suit," *USA Today*, May 19, 1999, 4A; "ACLU Report Blasts Racial Profiling," *Boston Globe*, June 3, 1999, A15.

2   Paul M. Sniderman and Thomas Piazza, *The Scar of Race* (Cambridge, MA: Harvard University Press, 1993), pp. 5, 175; Dinesh D'Souza, *The End of Racism: Principles for a Multiracial Society* (New York: Free Press, 1995), pp. 70–87.

3   Everett C. Ladd, "Moving to an America beyond Race," *The Public Perspective* 7 (February/March 1996): 36.

4   John H. Bunzel, "Words that Smear, Like 'Racism,' Provoke Polarization," *San Francisco Chronicle*, July 26, 1998, D7.

5   C. L. R. James, *American Civilization*, ed. Anna Grimshaw and Keith Hart (Cambridge, MA: Blackwell, 1993), p. 201.

6   James Madison, quoted in Michael P. Rogin, *Fathers and Children: Andrew Jackson and the Subjugation of the American Indian* (New York: Knopf, 1975), p. 319.

Chapter One

1   National Archives and Records Administration, *Framers of the Constitution* (Washington, DC: National Archives Trust Fund Board, 1986).

2   Max Farrand, ed., *Records of the Federal Convention of 1787*, vol.1 (New Haven, CT: Yale University, 1911), p. 486.

3   Herbert Aptheker, *Early Years of the Republic: From the End of the Revolution to the First Administration of Washington (1783–1793)* (New York: International Publishers, 1976), pp. 74–95.

4   Ibid., p. 57.

5   Ibid., p. 55.

6   William Lee Miller, *Arguing about Slavery: The Great Battle in the United States Congress* (New York: Knopf, 1996), p. 21.

7   Farrand, *Records*, volume 1, 587. See also

William M. Wiecek, *The Sources of Antislavery Constitutionalism in America, 1760–1848* (Ithaca, NY: Cornell University Press, 1977), p. 15.

8   James Madison, Alexander Hamilton, and John Jay, *The Federalist Papers*, ed. Isaac Kramnick (New York: Viking Penguin, 1987). This quote is from number 54.

9   James Madison, quoted in Michael P. Rogin, *Fathers and Children: Andrew Jackson and the Subjugation of the American Indian* (New York: Knopf, 1975), p. 319. See also Paul Jennings, "A Colored Man's Reminiscences of James Madison," *White House History* 1 (1983): 46–51.

10   W. E. B. Du Bois, *The Suppression of the African Slave Trade to the United States of America, 1638–1870* (New York: Schocken Books, 1969), pp. 54–62.

11   Donald Robinson, *Slavery in the Structure of American Politics* (New York: Norton, 1979), p. 71.

12   Robert A. Rutland, ed., *The Papers of George Mason: 1725–1792*, vol. 3 (Chapel Hill: University of North Carolina Press, 1970), pp. 965–66.

13   Paul Finkelman, "Slavery and the Constitutional Convention," in *Beyond Confederation: Origins of the Constitution and American National Identity*, eds. Richard Beeman, Stephen Botein, and Edward C. Carter (Chapel Hill: University of North Carolina Press, 1987), p. 225.

14   Paul Finkelman, *Slavery and the Founders: Race and Liberty in the Age of Jefferson* (Armonk, NY: M. E. Sharpe, 1996), p. 23.

15   James Madison, *The Debates in the Federal Convention of 1787 which Framed the Constitution of the United States of America*, vol. 2, eds. Gaillard Hunt and James B. Scott (Buffalo, NY: Prometheus Books, 1987), p. 481.

16   Aptheker, *Early Years of the Republic*, p. 93.

17   Donald E. Lively, *The Constitution and Race* (New York: Praeger, 1992), pp. 4–5. Lively

draws in part on the work of William M.
Wiecek.

18   F. Nwabueze Okoye, "Chattel Slavery as the
     Nightmare of the American Revolutionaries,"
     William and Mary Quarterly 37 (January 1980):
     28.

19   Okoye, "Chattel Slavery as the Nightmare of
     the American Revolutionaries," p. 13.

20   John Dickinson, *Letters from a Farmer in Penn-
     sylvania to the Inhabitants of the British
     Colonies* (Philadelphia, 1768), p. 38, as quoted
     in Okoye, "Chattel Slavery as the Nightmare of
     the American Revolutionaries," p. 3; emphasis
     in the original.

21   Benjamin B. Ringer, *"We the People" and Oth-
     ers* (New York: Tavistock, 1983), pp. 130–31.

22   Both quotes are from William Lloyd Garrison,
     "A Compact with Hell," in the *United States
     Constitution*, ed. Bertell Ollman and Jonathan
     Birnbaum (New York: New York University
     Press, 1990), p. 96.

23   There is no general book on slaveholding
     among these elites. I draw on several sources,
     especially Dennis Cauchon, "For Founding
     Fathers, Slave Ownership Common; Practice
     Went Unquestioned by Many Admired Histori-
     cal Figures," *USA Today*, March 9, 1998, 8A.

24   Herbert Aptheker, *The Unfolding Drama: Stud-
     ies in U.S. History*, ed. Bettina Aptheker (New
     York: International Publishers, 1978), p. 100.

25   William M. Wiecek, "The Origins of the Law
     of Slavery in British North America," *Cardozo
     Law Review* 17 (May 1996): 1791.

26   Aptheker, *Early Years of the Republic*, p. 93.

27   W. E. B. Du Bois, *The World and Africa* (New
     York: International Publishers, 1965 [1946]), p.
     23.

28   Frederick Douglass, "The Color Line," *North
     American Review* (June 1881), as excerpted in
     Jones et ux. v. Alfred H. Mayer Co., 392 U.S.
     409, 446–47 (1968); emphasis added.

29   W. E. B. Du Bois, *Darkwater* (1920), as
     reprinted in *The Oxford W. E. B. Du Bois
     Reader*, ed. Eric J. Sundquist (New York:
     Oxford, 1996), p. 504.

30   Oliver C. Cox, *Caste, Class, and Race* (Garden
     City, NY: Doubleday, 1948), p. 344.

31   Kwame Ture [Stokely Carmichael] and
     Charles V. Hamilton, *Black Power: The Politics
     of Liberation in America* (New York: Vintage,
     1967). See also Robert L. Allen, *Black Awaken-
     ing in Capitalist America: An Analytic History*
     (Garden City, NY: Anchor Books, 1970).

32   See Bob Blauner, *Racial Oppression in Amer-
     ica* (New York: Harper and Row, 1972).

33   Du Bois, *The World and Africa*, p. 37.

34   See Theodore Cross, *The Black Power Impera-
     tive: Racial Inequality and the Politics of Nonvi-
     olence* (New York: Faulkner, 1984), p. 510;
     Patricia Williams, *The Alchemy of Race and

     Rights* (Cambridge, MA: Harvard University
     Press, 1991), p. 101; Ian Ayres and Fredrick E.
     Vars, "When Does Private Discrimination Jus-
     tify Public Affirmative Action?" *Columbia Law
     Review* 98 (November 1998): 1598–1610; and
     Richard Delgado, *The Coming Race War?*
     (New York: New York University Press, 1996),
     pp. 104–105.

35   James A. Ballentine, *Ballentine's Law Dictio-
     nary*, 3rd ed., ed. William S. Anderson, (San
     Francisco: Bancroft-Whiteney, 1969), p. 1320.

36   Philomena Essed, *Understanding Everyday
     Racism* (Newbury Park, CA: Sage, 1991), p. 37.

37   I draw here on Karl Marx, *Economic and Philo-
     sophical Manuscripts* (Moscow: Progress Pub-
     lishers, 1959); and Bertell Ollman, *Alienation:
     Marx's Conception of Man in Capitalist Soci-
     ety*, 2nd ed. (Cambridge: Cambridge Univer-
     sity Press, 1976).

38   Catharine A. MacKinnon, *Toward a Feminist
     Theory of the State* (Cambridge, MA: Harvard
     University Press, 1989).

39   I am influenced here by MacKinnon, *Toward a
     Feminist Theory of the State*, p. 4.

40   See Melvin M. Leiman, *The Political Economy
     of Racism: A History* (London: Pluto Press,
     1993).

41   William Julius Wilson, *The Declining Signifi-
     cance of Race: Blacks and Changing American
     Institutions* (Chicago: University of Chicago
     Press, 1978); William Julius Wilson, *When
     Work Disappears: The World of the New Urban
     Poor* (New York: Alfred A. Knopf, 1996).

42   See Wilson, *The Declining Significance of
     Race*; and Jim Sleeper, *The Closest of
     Strangers: Liberalism and the Politics of Race in
     New York* (New York: Norton, 1990).

43   Michael Omi and Howard Winant, *Racial For-
     mation in the United States: From the 1960s to
     the 1990s*, 2nd ed. (New York: Routledge,
     1994), p. 48.

44   Robert Miles, *Racism* (London: Routledge,
     1989).

45   Jorge Klor de Alva, Earl Shorris, and Cornel
     West, "Our Next Race Question: The Uneasi-
     ness between Blacks and Latinos," in *Critical
     White Studies: Looking Behind the Mirror*, eds.
     Richard Delgado and Jean Stefancic,
     (Philadelphia: Temple University Press, 1997),
     p. 485.

46   Dole comments on "Meet the Press," NBC
     Television, February 5, 1995; Hyde is quoted in
     Kevin Merida, "Did Freedom Alone Pay a
     Nation's Debt," *The Washington Post*, Novem-
     ber 23, 1999, p. C1.

47   I am indebted to Sidney Willhelm for help in
     clarifying this point.

48   Iris Young, *Justice and the Politics of Difference*
     (Princeton, NJ: Princeton University Press,
     1990), p. 52.

49 *Jones et ux. v. Alfred H. Mayer Co.*, 392 U.S. 409, 445 (1968).

50 See Karl Marx, *Capital*, vol. 1 (New York: Vintage Books, 1977), p. 717. I am indebted to Nestor Rodriguez for pointing out the parallel to Marx.

51 Edward Ball, *Slaves in the Family* (New York: Ballantine Books, 1999), p. 14.

52 Martin J. Katz, "The Economics of Discrimination: The Three Fallacies of Croson," *Yale Law Journal* 100 (January 1991): 1041–44.

53 Frantz Fanon, *Black Skin, White Masks* (New York: Grove Press, 1967), p. 116. See also William W. Hansen, *A Frantz Fanon Study Guide* (New York: Grove Press, 1996), p. 6.

54 Joe R. Feagin, Kevin Early, and Karyn D. McKinney, "The Many Costs of Discrimination," unpublished paper, University of Florida, 1999.

55 Race is not mentioned in the Bible. This story appeared later in the Talmud, from which Christian tradition borrowed.

56 W. E. B. Du Bois, *Black Reconstruction in America 1860–1880* (New York: Atheneum, 1992 [1935]), p. 700.

57 Theodore Allen, *The Invention of the White Race: Racial Oppression and Social Control* (London: Verso, 1994), pp. 19–21.

58 Ibid., p. 143.

59 Du Bois, *Black Reconstruction in America 1860–1880*, p. 27.

60 Louise Michele Newman, *White Women's Rights: The Racial Origins of Feminism in the United States* (New York: Oxford University Press, 1999), pp. 179–85. See also bell hooks, *Feminist Theory: From Margin to Center* (Boston: South End Press, 1984), pp. 6–51.

61 Charles W. Mills, *The Racial Contract* (Ithaca, NY: Cornell University Press, 1997), p. 138.

62 Oliver C. Cox, *Elements and Social Dynamics* (Detroit: Wayne University Press, 1976), p. 22.

63 Du Bois, *Darkwater* (1920), as reprinted in *The Oxford W. E. B. Du Bois Reader*, pp. 497–98.

64 See Ronald T. Takaki, *Iron Cages: Race and Culture in 19th Century America* (New York: Oxford University Press, 1990), pp. 4–15.

65 Benjamin Franklin, *Observations Concerning the Increase of Mankind, Peopling of Countries, Etc.* (1751), as quoted in *Benjamin Franklin: A Biography in His Own Words*, ed. Thomas Fleming (New York: Harper and Row, 1972), pp. 105–106. I have altered this excerpt to include modern capitalization.

66 Robert S. Feldman, *Social Psychology* (Englewood Cliffs, NJ: Prentice-Hall, 1995), p. 94.

67 Cox, *Caste, Class, and Race*, p. xxxi.

68 Ibid., p. 393.

69 Michel Foucault, *Discipline and Punish: The Birth of the Prison*, trans. Alan Sheridan. (New York: Vintage Books, 1978 [1975]), p. 27.

Chapter Two

1 United Nations, "Convention on the Prevention and Punishment of Genocide," *The United Nations and Human Rights, 1945–1995* (New York: United Nations Department of Public Information, 1995), p. 151.

2 Charles W. Mills, *The Racial Contract* (Ithaca, NY: Cornell University Press, 1997), pp. 98, 155; David E. Stannard, *The American Holocaust: Columbus and the Conquest of the New World* (New York: Oxford University Press, 1992).

3 William T. Hagan, *American Indians* (Chicago: University of Chicago Press, 1961), p. 14. The discussion of these wars is taken from pp. 12–15. An earlier, much less developed version of this discussion, as well as that in a few later paragraphs of this chapter, appears in Joe R. Feagin and Clairece B. Feagin, *Racial and Ethnic Relations*, 6th ed. (Upper Saddle River, NJ: Prentice-Hall, 1999), chapters 7 and 8.

4 Michael P. Rogin, *Fathers and Children: Andrew Jackson and the Subjugation of the American Indian* (New York: Knopf, 1975), p. 319.

5 Winthrop D. Jordan, *White over Black: American Attitudes toward the Negro, 1550–1812* (Chapel Hill: University of North Carolina Press, 1968), pp. 239–41.

6 Benjamin B. Ringer, *"We the People" and Others* (New York: Tavistock, 1983), pp. 134–38.

7 *Dred Scott v. John F. A. Sandford*, 60 U.S. 393, 403–404 (1857).

8 Ibid., 408.

9 Ringer, *"We the People" and Others*, p. 36.

10 Robin Blackburn, *The Making of New World Slavery: From the Baroque to the Modern, 1492–1800* (London: Verso, 1997), p. 10.

11 A. Leon Higginbotham, Jr., *Shades of Freedom: Racial Politics and the Presumptions of the American Legal Process* (New York: Oxford University Press, 1996), pp. 14–51.

12 Forrest G. Wood, *The Arrogance of Faith: Christianity and Race in America from the Colonial Era to the Twentieth Century* (New York: Knopf, 1990), p. xviii.

13 Higginbotham, *Shades of Freedom*, p. xxiii; Lawrence M. Friedman, *A History of American Law* (New York: Simon and Schuster, 1973), pp. 72–76, 192–200; Herbert Aptheker, *American Negro Slave Revolts* (New York: International Publishers, 1943), pp. 53–78.

14 Thomas Jefferson, quoted in Peter M. Bergman, *The Chronological History of the Negro in America* (New York: Harper & Row, 1969), p. 52.

15 Eric Williams, *Capitalism and Slavery* (Chapel Hill: University of North Carolina Press, 1994 [1944]), pp. 106–21.

16   Blackburn, *The Making of New World Slavery*, p. 19; Herbert Aptheker, *The Colonial Era* (New York: International Publishers, 1959), pp. 18–39.

17   Ronald Segal, *The Black Diaspora* (New York: Farrar, Straus and Giroux, 1995), pp. 58–59.

18   Kenneth S. Greenberg, *Honor and Slavery* (Princeton, NJ: Princeton University Press, 1996).

19   Peter J. Parish, *Slavery: History and Historians* (New York: Harper and Row, 1989), p. 129; see also pp. 126–32.

20   Elizabeth Fox-Genovese, *Within the Plantation Household: Black and White Women of the Old South* (Chapel Hill: University of North Carolina Press, 1988), p. 24.

21   See Kenneth Stampp, *The Peculiar Institution: Slavery in the Ante-Bellum South* (New York: Vintage Books, 1956); and Robert W. Roel and Stanley Engerman, *Time on the Cross: The Economics of American Negro Slavery* (Boston: Little, Brown, 1974). For a summary of the scholars and their views, see Fox-Genovese, *Within the Plantation Household*, pp.56–86.

22   Lorenzo J. Greene, *The Negro in Colonial New England* (New York: Atheneum, 1969), pp. 56–69. This quote is on pp. 68–69.

23   Ronald Bailey, "The Other Side of Slavery," *Agricultural History* 68 (Spring 1994): 36.

24   James W. Loewen, *Lies My Teacher Told Me: Everything Your American History Textbook Got Wrong* (New York: The New Press, 1995), p. 135.

25   A. Leon Higginbotham, Jr., *In the Matter of Color* (New York: Oxford University Press, 1978), pp. 63–70, 144–49. An earlier discussion of some data in this section appeared in Joe R. Feagin, "Slavery Unwilling to Die: The Background of Black Oppression in the 1980s," *Journal of Black Studies* 17 (December 1986): 173–200.

26   Ringer, *"We the People" and Others*, p. 533.

27   John R. McKivigan, "The Northern Churches and the Moral Problem of Slavery," in *The Meaning of Slavery in the North*, eds. David Roediger and Martin H. Blatt (New York: Garland, 1998), pp. 77–94.

28   Olaudah Equiano, "The Interesting Narrative of the Life of Olaudah Equiano," in *Afro-American History*, ed. Thomas R. Frazier (New York: Harcourt, Brace & World, 1970), pp. 18–20.

29   William Wells Brown, *From Fugitive Slave to Free Man*, ed. William L. Andrews (New York: Mentor Books, 1993), p. 30.

30   See T. Lindsay Baker and Julie P. Baker, eds., *The WPA Oklahoma Slave Narratives* (Norman: University of Oklahoma Press, 1996).

31   See Patricia Morton, introduction to *Discovering the Women in Slavery*, ed. Patricia Morton (Athens: University of Georgia Press, 1996), pp. 7–8.

32   Patricia J. Williams, *The Alchemy of Race and Rights* (Cambridge, MA: Harvard University Press, 1991), pp. 154–56.

33   Melton A. McLaurin, *Celia: A Slave* (Athens: University of Georgia Press, 1991); see also Harriet A. Jacobs, *Incidents in the Life of a Slave Girl*, ed. Jean Fagan Yellin (Cambridge, MA: Harvard University Press, 1987).

34   The three-quarters-white Hemings was the half-sister of Jefferson's deceased wife. Jerry Fresia, *Toward an American Revolution: Exposing the Constitution and Other Illusions* (Boston: South End, 1988), pp. 1–2; Dinitia Smith and Nicholas Wade, "DNA Evidence Links Thomas Jefferson to Slave's Offspring," *Gainesville Sun*, November 1, 1998, 4A.

35   James Parton, quoted in Paul Finkelman, *Slavery and the Founders: Race and Liberty in the Age of Jefferson* (Armonk, NY: M. E. Sharpe, 1996), p. 143.

36   Jordan, *White over Black*, p. 153

37   The lower estimates come from Philip D. Curtin, *The African Slave Trade: A Census* (University of Wisconsin Press, 1968). The higher and probably more accurate figures are calculated in Joseph E. Inikori, ed., *Forced Migration* (New York: Africana Publishing, 1982), pp. 19–33; and S. E. Anderson, *The Black Holocaust* (New York: Writers and Readers Press, 1995), pp. 156–58.

38   See Dinesh D'Souza, *The End of Racism: Principles for a Multiracial Society* (New York: Free Press, 1995), pp. 70–87.

39   I am partially indebted here to an interpretation of the literature suggested to me by Holly Hanson. See also John Thornton, *Africa and Africans in the Making of the Atlantic World, 1400–1680* (New York: Cambridge University Press, 1992), pp. 5–9; and Molefi Kete Asante, "The Wonders of Africa," post to Discussion List for African American Studies (H-Afro-Am), November, 1999.

40   Stanley M. Elkins, *A Problem in American Institutional and Intellectual Life* (New York: Grosset and Dunlap, 1963), pp. 96–97. This was true as well of the slave trade between sub-Saharan Africa and certain Islamic countries.

41   W. E. B. Du Bois, *Darkwater* (1920), as reprinted in *The Oxford W. E. B. Du Bois Reader*, ed. Eric J. Sundquist (New York: Oxford, 1996), p. 504.

42   W. E. B. Du Bois, *Black Reconstruction in America 1860–1880* (New York: Atheneum, 1992 [1935]), p. 10.

43   John Willinsky, *Learning to Divide the World: Education at Empire's End* (Minneapolis: University of Minnesota Press, 1998), p. 191.

44   Rafael Tammariello, "The Slave Trade," *Las Vegas Review-Journal*, February 8, 1998, 1E.

45   J. H. Parry and P. M. Sherlock, *A Short History of the West Indies*, 3rd ed. (New York: St. Mar-

tin's Press, 1971), p. 110–11. I am influenced here by William M. Wiecek, *The Sources of Antislavery Constitutionalism in America, 1760–1848* (Ithaca, NY: Cornell University Press, 1977), pp. 15–16.

46   William M. Wiecek, "The Origins of the Law of Slavery in British North America," *Cardozo Law Review* 17 (May, 1996): 1739.

47   Williams, *Capitalism and Slavery*, pp. 98–107; Douglass C. North, *The Economic Growth of the United States, 1790–1860* (Englewood Cliffs, NJ: Prentice-Hall, 1961), pp. 38–45; Bailey, "The Other Side of Slavery," p. 40; Blackburn, *The Making of New World Slavery*, chapter 12.

48   Anderson, *The Black Holocaust*, p. 19.

49   Barbara L. Solow and Stanley L. Engerman, "British Capitalism and Caribbean Slavery: The Legacy of Eric Williams: An Introduction," in *British Capitalism and Caribbean Slavery: The Legacy of Eric Williams* (Cambridge: Cambridge University Press, 1987), pp. 8–9.

50   Wilson E. Williams, *Africa and the Rise of Capitalism* (New York: AMS Press, 1975 [1938]), pp. 23–25.

51   Williams, *Capitalism and Slavery*, pp. 93–95, 102–107.

52   See the documentary *The Art of Darkness*, written by David Dabydeen and directed by David Maloney, Central Production, 1986. I am indebted to Joseph Rahme for suggesting this point.

53   Du Bois, *Black Reconstruction*, p. 15.

54   Williams, *Capitalism and Slavery*, p. 52.

55   Solow and Engerman, "British Capitalism and Caribbean Slavery," p. 4.

56   Ibid., pp. 5–7; Ronald Bailey, "'Those Valuable People, the Africans,'" in *The Meaning of Slavery in the North*, eds. Roediger and Blatt, p. 11.

57   See Fred Bateman and Thomas Weiss, *A Deplorable Scarcity: The Failure of Industrialization in the Slave Economy* (Chapel Hill: University of North Carolina Press, 1981); and Stanley Lebergott, *The Americans: An Economic Record* (New York: Norton, 1984).

58   Robert S. Browne, "Achieving Parity through Reparations," in *The Wealth of Races: The Present Value of Benefits from Past Injustices*, ed. Richard F. America (New York: Greenwood Press, 1990), pp. 201–202.

59   North, *The Economic Growth of the United States, 1790–1860*, p. 63.

60   Ibid., p. 68.

61   Ronald T. Takaki, *Iron Cages: Race and Culture in 19th-Century America* (New York: Oxford University Press, 1990), p. 78.

62   Bailey, "'Those Valuable People, the Africans,'" in *The Meaning of Slavery in the North*, eds. Roediger and Blatt, p. 14.

63   Ibid., p. 19.

64   North, *The Economic Growth of the United States, 1790–1860*, p. 41; Takaki, *Iron Cages*, p. 77.

65   Browne, "Achieving Parity through Reparations," p. 201.

66   Segal, *The Black Diaspora*, pp. 56–58.

67   North, *The Economic Growth of the United States, 1790–1860*, p. 122.

68   Ali A. Mazrui, "Who Should Pay for Slavery? Reparations to Africa," *World Press Review* 8 (August 1993): 22.

69   Anderson, *The Black Holocaust*, p. 20.

70   Herbert Aptheker, *The Unfolding Drama: Studies in U.S. History*, ed. Bettina Aptheker (New York: International Publishers, 1978), p. 84. Slavery was profitable for most slaveholders, and the cost of maintaining a slave laborer was low. See Segal, *The Black Diaspora*, p. 58.

71   Fritz Hirschfeld, *George Washington and Slavery: A Documentary Portrayal* (Columbia: University of Missouri Press, 1997), p. 49. See also pp. 16, 37.

72   Hirschfeld, *George Washington and Slavery*, p. 236.

73   Ibid., pp. 68–69.

74   Takaki, *Iron Cages*, pp. 43–54.

75   Derrick Bell, "White Supremacy in America: Its Legal Legacy, Its Economic Costs," in *Critical White Studies: Looking Behind the Mirror*, eds. Richard Delgado and Jean Stefancic (Philadelphia: Temple University Press, 1997), p. 596.

76   Edmund S. Morgan, *American Slavery, American Freedom: The Ordeal of Virginia* (New York: Norton, 1975), p. 5.

77   Jack Niemonen, "The Role of the State in the Sociology of Racial and Ethnic Relations: Some Theoretical Considerations," *Free Inquiry in Creative Sociology* 23 (May 1995): 28.

78   *Merriam-Webster's Collegiate Dictionary*, 10th ed. (Springfield, MA: Merriam-Webster, 1993), p. 901.

79   William Lee Miller, *Arguing about Slavery: The Great Battle in the United States Congress*, (New York: Knopf, 1996), p. 13.

80   Loewen, *Lies My Teacher Told Me*, pp. 143–46.

81   Aptheker, *The Unfolding Drama*, p. 83.

82   Herbert Aptheker, unpublished lectures on American History, Minneapolis, University of Minnesota, 1984. I draw here on tapes of the lectures.

83   John Hope Franklin, *From Slavery to Freedom*, 4th ed. (New York: Knopf, 1984), pp. 250–53.

84   Stetson Kennedy, *After Appomattox: How the South Won the War* (Gainesville: University Press of Florida, 1995), p. 3. See also Cedric J. Robinson, *Black Movements in America* (New York: Routledge, 1997), pp. 86–88.

85   Kennedy, *After Appomattox*, pp. 3–4.

86   *Civil Rights Cases*, 109 U.S., 62–63, (1883).

87   John W. Cell, *The Highest State of White*

Supremacy: The Origins of Segregation in South Africa and the American South (Cambridge: Cambridge University Press, 1982), pp. 168–70.

88   *Plessy v. Ferguson*, 163 U.S. 537, 552–53 (1896).

89   Ibid., 563.

90   Richard Wright, *Black Boy* (New York: Harper-Collins, 1993 [1944–1945]), p. 231.

91   Trudier Harris, *Exorcising Blackness: Historical and Literary Lynching and Burning Rituals* (Bloomington: Indiana University Press, 1984), p. 7.

92   The quotes are from Nedra Tyre, "You All are a Bunch of Nigger Lovers," in *Red Wine First* (New York: Simon and Schuster, 1947), pp. 120–22, as quoted in Harris, *Exorcising Blackness*, p. 10.

93   Sidney Willhelm, personal communication with the author, July 1998; Melvin L. Oliver and Thomas M. Shapiro, *Black Wealth/White Wealth: A New Perspective on Racial Equality* (New York: Routledge, 1995), pp. 14–15.

94   Oliver and Shapiro, *Black Wealth, White Wealth*, p. 14.

95   Du Bois, *Black Reconstruction*, p. 602.

96   Pete Daniel, *The Shadow of Slavery: Peonage in the South, 1901–1969* (Urbana: University of Illinois Press, 1972), p. ix.

97   Ibid., p. ix; Feagin, "Slavery Unwilling to Die," pp. 173–200.

98   John Egerton, *Speak Now against the Day: The Generation before the Civil Rights Movement in the South* (Chapel Hill: University of North Carolina Press, 1994), pp. 29–30.

99   Ringer, *"We the People" and Others*, p. 535. I draw in part in the next few paragraphs on Feagin, "Slavery Unwilling to Die," pp. 173–200.

100   Bob Blauner, *Racial Oppression in America* (New York: Harper and Row, 1972), p. 64.

101   Arthur I. Waskow, *From Race Riot to Sit-In, 1919 and the 1960s* (Garden City, NY: Doubleday, 1966), pp. 209–40.

102   David Chalmers, *Hooded Americanism: The History of the Ku Klux Klan* (Durham, NC: Duke University Press, 1987 [1965]), pp. 200–50.

103   Gunnar Myrdal, *An American Dilemma*, vol. 1 (New York: McGraw-Hill, 1964 [1944]), p. 240.

104   Harvard Sitkoff, *A New Deal for Blacks: The Emergence of Civil Rights as a National Issue* (New York: Oxford, 1978), pp. 37–38.

105   C. G. Wye, "The New Deal and the Negro Community," *Journal of American History* 59 (December 1972): 630–40; Nancy J. Weiss, *Farewell to the Party of Lincoln: Black Politics in the Age of FDR* (Princeton, NJ: Princeton University Press, 1983), p. 119.

106   William H. Harris, *The Harder We Run: Black Workers Since the Civil War* (New York: Oxford University Press, 1982), pp. 124–31.

107   Harris, *The Harder We Run*, p. 131.

108   Sidney M. Willhelm, *Who Needs the Negro?* (Cambridge, MA: Schenkman, 1970); and Sidney M. Willhelm, *Black in a White America* (Cambridge, MA: Schenkman, 1983).

109   I draw in part here on Sidney Willhelm's presentation to my seminar at Syracuse University, June 10, 1998, as well as on several letters from Willhelm.

110   *Jones et ux. v. Alfred H. Mayer Co.*, 392 U.S. 409, 442–43 (1968).

111   Ibid., 446–47.

Chapter Three

1   W. E. B. Du Bois, *Dusk of Dawn: An Essay Toward an Autobiography of a Race Concept* (New Brunswick, NJ: Transaction Books, 1984 [1940]), p. 144.

2   Teun A. van Dijk, *Elite Discourse and Racism* (Newbury Park, CA: Sage, 1993), pp. 40–41; Karl Mannheim, *Ideology and Utopia* (London: Routledge and Kegan Paul, 1936), p. 52.

3   Karl Marx and Friederich Engels, *The German Ideology*, ed. R. Pascal (New York: International Publishers, 1947), p. 39.

4   Kenneth O'Reilly, *Nixon's Piano: Presidents and Racial Politics from Washington to Clinton* (New York: Free Press, 1995), p. 11.

5   Jan N. Pieterse, *White on Black: Images of Africa and Blacks in Western Popular Culture* (New Haven, CT: Yale University Press, 1992), p. 24.

6   Frank Snowden, *Color Prejudice* (Cambridge, MA: Harvard University Press, 1983), pp. 3–4, 107–108; St. Clair Drake, *Black Folk Here and There*, vol.1 (Los Angeles: UCLA Center for Afro-American Studies, 1987), p. xxiii.

7   Pieterse, *White on Black*, p. 24.

8   Ibid., pp. 28–29.

9   Oliver C. Cox, *Caste, Class, and Race* (Garden City, NY: Doubleday, 1948), pp. 331–34. See also Joe R. Feagin and Clairece B. Feagin, *Racial and Ethnic Relations*, 6th ed. (Upper Saddle River, NJ: Prentice-Hall, 1999), chapter 14.

10   Ronald T. Takaki, *Iron Cages: Race and Culture in 19th Century America* (Oxford: Oxford University Press, 1990), pp. 11–14.

11   Marimba Ani, *Yurugu: An African-Centered Critique of European Cultural Thought and Behavior* (Trenton, NJ: Africa World Press, 1994), pp. 482–84; Edward W. Said, *Orientalism* (New York: Vintage Books, 1979), pp. 6–7.

12   See Ani, *Yurugu*, p. 348.

13   Takaki, *Iron Cages*, pp. 12–14.

14   James Fenimore Cooper, *The Last of the Mohicans* (1826), as quoted in Emily Morison Beck, ed., *John Bartlett's Familiar Quotations*, 15th ed. (Boston: Little Brown, 1980), p. 463.

15   Winthrop D. Jordan, *White over Black: Ameri-*

can Attitudes Toward the Negro, 1550–1812 (Chapel Hill: University of North Carolina Press, 1968), pp. 18–19.

16   Quoted in A. Leon Higginbotham, Jr., *Shades of Freedom: Racial Politics and the Presumptions of the American Legal Process* (New York: Oxford University Press, 1996), p. 119.

17   Michael Banton, *Racial and Ethnic Competition* (Cambridge: Cambridge University Press, 1983), pp. 37–38.

18   Jordan, *White over Black*, p. 12.

19   James Oakes, *The Ruling Race* (New York: Vintage Books, 1982), p. 3.

20   Jordan, *White over Black*, p. 96. See also pp. 94–96.

21   Manning Marable, *Black American Politics* (London: New Left Books, 1985), p. 5.

22   Higginbotham, *Shades of Freedom*, p. 11.

23   Tomás Almaguer, *Racial Fault Lines* (Berkeley and Los Angeles: University of California Press, 1994), p. 28.

24   Takaki, *Iron Cages*, pp. 30–34.

25   Edmund S. Morgan, *American Slavery, American Freedom: The Ordeal of Virginia* (New York: Norton, 1975), pp. 3–20.

26   William M. Wiecek, "The Origins of the Law of Slavery in British North America," *Cardozo Law Review* 17 (May 1996): 1777.

27   See Frances Lee Ansley, "Stirring the Ashes: Race, Class and the Future of Civil Rights Scholarship," *Cornell Law Review* 74 (September, 1989): 993.

28   Samuel Hopkins, quoted in Jordan, *White over Black*, p. 276; emphasis added.

29   John Willinsky, *Learning to Divide the World: Education at Empire's End* (Minneapolis: University of Minnesota Press, 1998).

30   Du Bois, *Dusk of Dawn*, p. 6.

31   A. Leon Higginbotham, Jr., and Barbara K. Kopytoff, "Racial Purity and Interracial Sex in the Law of Colonial and Antebellum Virginia," *Georgetown Law Journal* 77 (August 1989): 1671.

32   Benjamin Franklin, quoted in Takaki, *Iron Cages*, p. 50.

33   Claude-Anne Lopez and Eugenia W. Herbert, *The Private Franklin: The Man and His Family* (New York: Norton, 1975), pp. 194–95.

34   George Frederickson, *The Black Image in the White Mind* (Hanover, NH: Wesleyan University Press, 1971), p. 282.

35   Joel Kovel, *White Racism: A Psychohistory*, rev. ed. (New York: Columbia University Press, 1984), pp. xli–xlvii.

36   Cox, *Caste, Class, and Race*, p. 332.

37   See Lewis R. Gordon, *Her Majesty's Other Children: Sketches of Racism from a Neocolonial Age* (Lanham, MD: Rowman & Littlefield, 1997), p. 55.

38   Frantz Fanon, *The Wretched of the Earth* (New York: Grove Press, 1963), p. 32.

39   Audrey Smedley, *Race in North America* (Boulder, CO: Westview Press, 1993), p. 303.

40   Pieterse, *White on Black*, p. 41.

41   Thomas Jefferson, *Notes on the State of Virginia*, ed. Frank Shuffelton (New York: Penguin, 1999 [1785]), p. 145.

42   Ibid., pp. 147–48.

43   Benjamin Schwarz, "What Jefferson Helps Explain," *Atlantic Monthly*, March 1997, n.p. This is quoted from the website http://www.theatlantic.com.

44   Paul Finkelman, *Slavery and the Founders: Race and Liberty in the Age of Jefferson* (Armonk, NY: M. E. Sharpe, 1996), p. 148.

45   Immanuel Kant, *Gesammelte Schiften*, as quoted in Emmanuel C. Eze, "The Color of Reason: The Idea of 'Race' in Kant's Anthropology," in *Postcolonial African Philosophy: A Critical Reader*, ed. Emmanuel C. Eze (London: Blackwell, 1997), p. 130.

46   Ibid., p. 118.

47   Ibid.

48   William H. Tucker, *The Science and Politics of Racial Research* (Urbana: University of Illinois Press, 1994), p. 8.

49   Ibid., p. 9; Ivan Hannaford, *Race: The History of an Idea in the West* (Baltimore: Johns Hopkins University Press, 1996), pp. 205–207.

50   Smedley, *Race in North America*, p. 26.

51   "Negroes," *Encyclopedia Brittanica* (1978), quoted in Paul G. Lauren, *Power And Prejudice: The Politics and Diplomacy of Racial Discrimination* (Boulder, CO: Westview Press, 1988), p. 21.

52   Fredrickson, *The Black Image in the White Mind*, p. 48.

53   Pieterse, *White on Black*, p. 34.

54   Ibid., p. 60.

55   Arthur de Gobineau, *Selected Political Writings*, ed. M. D. Biddiss (New York: Harper & Row, 1970), p. 136.

56   Allan Chase, *The Legacy of Malthus: The Social Costs of the New Scientific Racism* (New York: Knopf, 1977), p. 91.

57   Tucker, *The Science and Politics of Racial Research*, p. 23. See also Chase, *The Legacy of Malthus*, p. 94.

58   *Dred Scott v. John F. A. Sandford*, 60 U.S. 393, 407–408 (1857).

59   Abraham Lincoln, "The Sixth Joint Debate at Quincy, October 13, 1858," in *The Lincoln-Douglas Debates: The First Complete, Unexpurgated Text*, ed. Harold Holzer (New York: HarperCollins, 1993), p. 283.

60   Andrew Johnson, quoted in Ani, *Yurugu*, p. 299.

61   James Brooks, quoted in Tucker, *The Science and Politics of Racial Research*, p. 25.

62   *Plessy v. Ferguson*, 163 U.S. 537, 560 (1896).

63   Ian F. Haney Lopez, *White By Law: The Legal*

Construction of Race (New York: New York University Press, 1996), pp. 1–7, 203–27.

64 Charles Darwin, quoted in Frederickson, *The Black Image in the White Mind*, p. 230.

65 See Joe R. Feagin, *Subordinating the Poor: Welfare and American Beliefs* (Englewood Cliffs, NJ: Prentice-Hall, 1975), pp. 35–36.

66 See Frederick L. Hoffman, "Vital Statistics of the Negro," *Arena* 5 (April 1892): 542, cited in Frederickson, *The Black Image in the White Mind*, pp. 250–51.

67 M. G. Delaney, cited in Stephen Jay Gould, *Hen's Teeth and Horse's Toes* (New York: Norton, 1983), pp. 21–22.

68 John Higham, *Strangers in the Land* (New York: Atheneum, 1963), pp. 96–152.

69 Tucker, *The Science and Politics of Racial Research*, p. 35.

70 Carl C. Brigham, *A Study of American Intelligence* (Princeton, NJ: Princeton University Press, 1923), pp. 124–25, 177–210.

71 Madison Grant, *The Passing of the Great Race* (New York: Charles Scribner's Sons, 1916).

72 Lothrop Stoddard, *The Rising Tide of Color: Against White World-Supremacy* (New York: Scribner's, 1920), p. 3.

73 Tucker, *The Science and Politics of Racial Research*, p. 93.

74 See Theodore Cross, *Black Power Imperative: Racial Inequality and the Politics of Nonviolence* (New York: Faulkner, 1984), p. 157.

75 Magnus Hirschfeld, *Racism*, trans. and ed. by Eden and Cedar Paul (London: V. Gollancz, 1938). The book was published in German in 1933.

76 Warren G. Harding and Calvin Coolidge, each quoted in Tucker, *The Science and Politics of Racial Research*, p. 93.

77 Rudyard Kipling, "The White Man's Burden," in *Rudyard Kipling's Verse: Inclusive Edition 1885–1926* (New York: Doubleday, Doran and Co., 1929), p. 373–74.

78 Cox, *Caste, Class, and Race*, pp. 575–76, 578.

79 Theodore W. Allen, *The Invention of the White Race* (New York: Verso, 1994), pp. 21–50, 184.

80 David R. Roediger, *The Wages of Whiteness: Race and the Making of the American Working Class* (London: Verso, 1991), p. 127.

81 David K. Shipler, "Blacks in the Newsroom," *Columbia Journalism Review*, May/June 1998, pp. 26–29; Robert M. Entman et al., *Mass Media and Reconciliation: A Report to the Advisory Board and Staff, The President's Initiative on Race* (Washington, DC, 1998).

82 Edward Herman, "The Propaganda Model Revisited," *Monthly Review* 48 (July 1996): 115.

83 Sidney Blumenthal, *The Rise of the Counter-Establishment* (New York: Times Books, 1986), pp. 4–11, 133–70; Peter Steinfels, *The Neoconservatives: The Men Who Are Changing Amer-*

ica's Politics (New York: Touchstone, 1979), pp. 214–77.

84 Franklin D. Gilliam Jr., and Shanto Iyengar, "Prime Suspects: the Effects of Local News on the Viewing Public," University of California at Los Angeles, unpublished paper, n.d.

85 Richard Cohen, "Ignorant, Apathetic and Smug," *Washington Post*, February 2, 1996, A19.

86 See the summary in Bobbie Harville, "History: Knowledge Is Lacking; Americans' Understanding of the Country's History Is Thin, a New Survey Reveals," *Dayton Daily News*, July 14, 1996, 15A.

87 James W. Loewen, *Lies My Teacher Told Me: Everything Your American History Textbook Got Wrong* (New York: The New Press, 1995).

88 Lerone Bennett, *Confrontation: Black and White* (Baltimore: Penguin, 1965), pp 187–88.

89 John H. Franklin, *From Slavery to Freedom*, 4th ed. (New York: Knopf, 1974), p. 421.

90 Derrick Bell, "*Brown v. Board of Education* and the Interest Convergence Dilemma," *Harvard Law Review* 93 (1980): 518.

91 *Brown v. Board of Education of Topeka*, 347 U.S. 483 (1954).

92 Thomas Ferguson and Joel Rodgers, *Right Turn: The Decline of the Democrats and the Future of American Politics* (New York: Hill and Wang, 1986), pp. 55–56.

93 Samuel P. Huntington, "The Erosion of American National Interests," *Foreign Affairs* (September/October 1997): 28.

94 *Report of the National Advisory Commission on Civil Disorders* (Washington, DC: U.S. Government Printing Office, 1968), pp. 1, 5.

95 Ferguson and Rodgers, *Right Turn*, pp. 65–66.

96 *City of Richmond, Virginia v. J. A. Croson Co.*, 488 U.S. 469 (1989).

97 See, for example, *Adarand Constructors, Inc. v. Pena*, 515 U.S. 200 (1995).

98 Larry T. Reynolds, *Reflexive Sociology: Working Papers in Self-Critical Analysis* (Rockport, TX: Rockport Institute Press, 1999), pp. 141–45.

99 Arthur R. Jensen, "How Much Can We Boost IQ and Scholastic Achievement?" *Harvard Educational Review* 39 (1969): 1–123. See also Feagin and Feagin, *Racial and Ethnic Relations*, pp. 243–44.

100 See Jean Stefancic and Richard Delgado, *No Mercy: How Conservative Think Tanks and Foundations Changed America's Social Agenda* (Philadelphia: Temple University Press, 1996), p. 34.

101 Daniel P. Moynihan, *The Negro Family: The Case for National Action* (Washington, DC: U.S. Government Printing Office, 1965), p. 5.

102 Nathan Glazer, *Affirmative Discrimination: Ethnic Inequality and Public Policy* (New York: Basic Books, 1975), pp. 71–72.

103 Ken Auletta, *The Underclass* (New York: Random House, 1982).

104 Ellen K. Coughlin, "Worsening Plight of the Underclass Catches Attention," *Chronicle of Higher Education*, March 1988, A5. See also Joe R. Feagin and Leslie Inniss, "The Black Underclass Ideology in Race Relations Analysis," *Social Justice* 16 (Winter 1989): 12–34.

105 Sidney Willhelm, *Who Needs the Negro?* (Cambridge, MA: Schenkman, 1970), p. 250.

106 Anthony Farley, "The Black Body as Fetish Object," *Oregon Law Review* 76 (Fall 1997): 522–26.

107 See Rhonda Levine, "The Souls of Elite White Men: White Racial Identity and the Logic of Thinking on Race," paper presented at annual meeting, Hawaiian Sociological Association, February 14, 1998.

108 "Black and White in America," *Newsweek*, March 7, 1988, 19.

109 Van Dijk, *Elite Discourse and Racism*, p. 8.

110 Hernan Vera and Andrew Gordon, "Sincere Fictions of the White Self in the American Cinema: 1915–1998," unpublished paper, University of Florida, 1998.

111 Cedric J. Robinson, *Black Movements in America* (New York: Routledge, 1997), p. 12.

112 Vera and Gordon, "Sincere Fictions of the White Self in the American Cinema: 1915–1998," n.p.

113 Dinesh D'Souza, *The End of Racism: Principles for a Multiracial Society* (New York: Free Press, 1995), p. 113.

114 William Henry III, *In Defense of Elitism* (New York: Doubleday, 1994).

115 The government brochure is titled "South Carolina: Smiling Faces, Beautiful Places," n.d.

116 Jacqueline Soteropoulos, "Skeptics Put Cops on Trial: The American Public Isn't Giving Government or Police Officers the Blind Trust It Once Did," *Tampa Tribune*, April 17, 1995, A1. I draw here on Nick Mrozinske, "Derivational Thinking and Racism," unpublished research paper, University of Florida, fall, 1998.

117 The search algorithm did not allow searches for the word "whites" alone, because this picks up the surnames of individuals in the Lexis/Nexis database.

118 Mrozinske, "Derivational Thinking and Racism."

119 Edward Ball, *Slaves in the Family* (New York: Ballantine Books, 1999), p. 13.

120 See Levine, "The Souls of Elite White Men: White Racial Identity and the Logic of Thinking on Race."

121 Patrick Buchanan, quoted in Clarence Page, "U.S. Media Should Stop Abetting Intolerance," *Toronto Star*, December 27, 1991, A27.

122 Patrick Buchanan, quoted in John Dillin, "Immigration Joins List of '92 Issues," *Christian Science Monitor*, December 17, 1991, 6.

123 Peter Brimelow, *Alien Nation: Common Sense about America's Immigration Disaster* (New York: Random House, 1995), pp. 10, 59.

124 Arthur Schlesinger, Jr., *The Disuniting of America: Reflections on a Multicultural Society* (New York: Norton, 1991), pp. 13, 124–25.

125 Huntington, "The Erosion of American National Interests," p. 28.

126 Frank Furedi, *The Silent War: Imperialism and the Changing Perception of Race* (New Brunswick, NJ: Rutgers University Press, 1998), p. 1.

127 George Lakoff and M. Johnson, *Metaphors We Live By* (Chicago: University of Chicago Press, 1980), p. 158.

Chapter 4

1 Derrick Z. Jackson, "Unspoken During Race Talk," *Boston Globe*, December 5, 1997, A27.

2 See Teun A. van Dijk, *Discourse, Racism and Ideology* (La Laguna, Spain: RCEI Ediciones, 1996), p. 49.

3 Herbert Blumer, "Race Prejudice as a Sense of Group Position." *Pacific Sociological Review* 1 (Spring 1958): 3–7.

4 Gordon Allport, *The Nature of Prejudice*, abridged ed. (New York: Anchor Books, 1958), p. 10. See also van Dijk, *Discourse, Racism and Ideology*, p. 50.

5 David R. Roediger, *The Wages of Whiteness: Race and the Making of the American Working Class* (London: Verso, 1991), pp. 96–121.

6 Survey results are cited in Richard Morin, "Unconventional Wisdom; New Facts and Hot Stats from the Social Sciences," *Washington Post*, April 6, 1997), C5.

7 William Brink and Louis Harris, *The Negro Revolution in America* (New York: Simon and Schuster, 1964), pp. 140–43.

8 William Brink and Louis Harris, *Black and White* (New York: Simon and Schuster, 1966), pp. 109, 136.

9 Howard Schuman, Charlotte Steeh, and Lawrence Bobo, *Racial Attitudes in America: Trends and Interpretations* (Cambridge, MA: Harvard University Press, 1985), pp. 71–162. Other studies show a reduction in antiblack prejudice, depending on the questions. See Herbert H. Hyman and Paul B. Sheatsley, "Attitudes toward Desegregation," *Scientific American* 211 (July 1964): 16–22; and Glenn Firebaugh and K. E. Davis, "Trends in Antiblack Prejudice, 1972–1984: Region and Cohort Effects," *American Journal of Sociology* 94 (1988): 251–72.

10 See Dinesh D'Souza, *The End of Racism: Principles for a Multiracial Society* (New York: Free Press, 1995).

11 Anti-Defamation League, *Highlights from an Anti-Defamation League Survey on Racial Attitudes in America* (New York: ADL, 1993), pp. 8–25.

12   See Paul M. Sniderman and Thomas Piazza, *The Scar of Race* (Cambridge, MA: Harvard University Press, 1993), pp. 41–45.

13   General Social Survey, National Opinion Research Center, Chicago, Illinois, 1994. Tabulation is by the author. These items were asked of all respondents on Ballot C.

14   See John F. Dovidio et al., "Stereotyping, Prejudice, and Discrimination: Another Look," in *Stereotypes and Stereotyping*, eds. C. Neil Macrae, Miles Hewstone, and Charles Stangor (New York: Guilford, 1995), pp. 276–319.

15   Eduardo Bonilla-Silva and Tyrone A. Forman, "'I Am Not A Racist But . . . ' : Mapping White College Students' Racial Ideology in the U.S.A.," *Discourse and Society*, 11 (2000): 51–86.

16   I am indebted to Christiana Otto for helpful discussions on this point; see also Joe R. Feagin and Hernan Vera, *White Racism: The Basics* (New York: Routledge, 1995).

17   General Social Survey, National Opinion Research Center, Chicago, Illinois, 1994.

18   Sut Jhally and Justin Lewis, *Enlightened Racism* (Boulder, CO: Westview Press, 1992), p. 95. See also pp. 96–110.

19   See Thomas F. Pettigrew, "The Ultimate Attribution Error: Extending Allport's Cognitive Analysis of Prejudice," *Personality and Social Psychology Bulletin* 5 (1979): 461–76. I draw here on the summary of research in Robert S. Feldman, *Social Psychology* (Englewood Cliffs, NJ: Prentice-Hall, 1995), pp. 91–92.

20   Patricia Hill Collins, *Black Feminist Thought: Knowledge, Consciousness, and the Politics of Empowerment* (Boston: Unwin Hyman, 1990), p. 67. I draw here on Yanick St. Jean and Joe R. Feagin, *Double Burden: Black Women and Everyday Racism* (Armonk, NY: M. E. Sharpe, 1998), chapters 3–4.

21   See Jan N. Pieterse, *White on Black: Images of Africa and Blacks in Western Popular Culture* (New Haven: Yale University Press, 1992).

22   Maureen Dowd, "Americans Like G.O.P. Agenda But Split on How to Reach Goals," *New York Times*, December 15, 1994, A1, A24.

23   See Joe R. Feagin, *Subordinating the Poor: Welfare and American Beliefs* (Englewood Cliffs, NJ: Prentice-Hall, 1975). For current data, see Farai Chideya, *Don't Believe the Hype: Fighting Cultural Misinformation about African Americans* (New York: Plume, 1995), p. 37.

24   Cited in Jackson, "Unspoken During Race Talk," A27.

25   See Joe R. Feagin and Melvin P. Sikes, *Living With Racism: The Black Middle-Class Experience* (Boston: Beacon Press, 1994).

26   Diane Roberts, *The Myth of Aunt Jemima: Representations of Race and Region* (New York: Routledge, 1994), p. 5.

27   St. Jean and Feagin, *Double Burden*, pp. 90–91; on the history, see Iris M. Young, *Justice and the Politics of Difference* (Princeton, NJ: Princeton University Press, 1990), p. 128.

28   See Mark Warr, "Dangerous Situations: Social Context and Fear of Victimization," *Social Forces*, 68 (1990): 905–906.

29   Earl Warren, quoted in Theodore Cross, *Black Power Imperative: Racial Inequality and the Politics of Nonviolence* (New York: Faulkner, 1984), pp. 157–58.

30   D'Souza, *The End of Racism*, pp. 245–72.

31   U.S. Department of Justice, *Criminal Victimization in the United States, 1991* (Washington DC: U.S. Government Printing Office, 1992), p. 61.

32   Feagin and Vera, *White Racism*, p. 159.

33   P. R. Klite, R. A. Bardwell, and J. Salzman, "Local TV News: Getting Away with Murder," *Press/Politics* 2 (1997): 102–12.

34   Franklin D. Gilliam Jr., and Shanto Iyengar, "Prime Suspects: the Effects of Local News on the Viewing Public," unpublished research paper, University of California (Los Angeles), n.d.

35   Robert M. Entman, "Violence on Television: News and 'Reality' Programming in Chicago," *Report for the Chicago Council on Urban Affairs*, May 9, 1994.

36   See Daniel Romer, Kathleen H. Jamieson, and Nicole J. de Coteau, "The Treatment of Persons of Color in Local Television News," *Communication Research* 25 (June 1998): 286–90.

37   Gilliam and Iyengar, "Prime Suspects," p. 17.

38   See Feagin and Vera, *White Racism*, pp. 114–24.

39   Ron Paul, quoted in Daniel Kurtzman, "The Lone Ranger," *Jewish Monthly*, November/December, 1997, 36.

40   Robert B. Hill et al., *Research on the African American Family: A Holistic Perspective* (Westport, CT: Auburn House, 1993); see the summary of Hill's work in James Bock, "Sociologist Touts Strengths of Black Families; He Lists Work Ethic, Kin Support Network, Religious Foundation," *Baltimore Sun*, July 7, 1997, 2B.

41   "African Americans and the Criminal Justice System," *The Legal Intelligencer*, February 5, 1996, 8.

42   James A. Rada, "Color Blind-Sided: Racial Bias in Network Television's Coverage of Professional Football Games," *Howard Journal of Communications* 7 (July–September 1996): 234–36.

43   Tom Steiger, personal communication with the author September, 1992; Priscilla Labovitz, "Just the Facts," *New York Times*, March 25, 1996, A2.

44   Charles A. Gallagher, "Living in Color: Perceptions of Racial Group Size," unpublished research paper, Georgia State University, 1999.

45 Tim Cox, "Rights Groups Cautious about 'Odd Couple' Appearances," United Press International, November 22, 1988.

46 Kenneth O'Reilly, *Nixon's Piano: Presidents and Racial Politics from Washington to Clinton* (New York: Free Press, 1995), pp. 6–7.

47 Both examples are from http://novusordo.com, as cited in Margaret Ronkin and Helen E. Karn, "Mock Ebonics: Linguistic Racism in Parodies of Ebonics on the Internet," *Journal of Sociolinguistics* 3 (August 1999): 360–80.

48 Bonnie Henry, "What Will I Do With $21 Mil?" *Arizona Daily Star*, January 19, 1997, J1.

49 Jane H. Hill, "Mock Spanish: A Site for the Indexical Reproduction of Racism in American English," unpublished research paper, University of Arizona, 1995; Jane H. Hill, "Junk Spanish, Anglo Identity, and the Forces of Desire," paper presented at Symposium on "Hispanic Language and Social Identity," Albuquerque, NM, February 10–12, 1994.

50 Rosina Lippi-Green, *English with an Accent* (New York: Routledge, 1997), p. 201.

51 I draw here from *Merriam-Webster's Collegiate Dictionary*, 10th ed. (Springfield, MA: Merriam Webster, 1993), pp. 118, 1348; and Robert B. Moore, "Racist Stereotyping in the English Language," in *Racism and Sexism: An Integrated Study*, ed. Paula S. Rothenberg (New York: St. Martin's Press, 1988), pp. 270–71.

52 Thomas Greenfield, as quoted in Moore, "Racist Stereotyping in the English Language," p. 273.

53 Joanna Russ, *How to Suppress Women's Writing* (Austin: University of Texas Press, 1983), pp. 17–25. I am indebted to Nick Mrozinske for suggesting this point.

54 Toni Morrison, *Playing in the Dark: Whiteness and the Literary Imagination* (New York: Vintage Books, 1992), pp. 63–65.

55 No name was given. The spelling and punctuation are per the original letter; it was signed in capitals.

56 Terrel Bell, *The Thirteenth Man: A Reagan Cabinet Memoir* (New York: Free Press, 1988), pp. 103–105.

57 "Baseball Committee Formed to Investigate Racist, Ethnic Remarks Made by Cincinnati Reds Owner," *The Ethnic NewsWatch*, December 9, 1992, 1.

58 James R. Kluegel and Eliot R. Smith, *Beliefs about Inequality* (New York: Aldine de Gruyter, 1986), pp. 186–87.

59 Ibid., p. 190.

60 General Social Survey, National Opinion Research Center, Chicago, Illinois, 1990.

61 Matthew P. Smith, "Bridging the Gulf Between Blacks & Whites," *Pittsburgh Post-Gazette*, April 7, 1996, A1.

62 Robert J. Blendon et al., "The Public and the President's Commission on Race," *The Public Perspective*, February, 1998, 66.

63 Scot Lehigh, "Conflicting views of Massachusetts; Poll Shows a Sharp Racial Divide over the State of Equality," *Boston Globe*, June 14, 1998, B1.

64 See Joe R. Feagin and Clairece B. Feagin, *Racial and Ethnic Relations*, 6th ed. (Upper Saddle River, NJ: Prentice-Hall, 1999), pp. 254–62.

65 Feagin and Vera, *White Racism*, pp. 160–61.

66 Jerome M. Culp, Jr., "Water Buffalo and Diversity: Naming Names and Reclaiming the Racial Discourse," *Connecticut Law Review* 26 (Fall 1993): 209.

67 Richard Delgado, *The Coming Race War?* (New York: New York University Press, 1996), p. 12.

68 Patricia G. Devine, "Stereotypes and Prejudice: Their Automatic and Controlled Components," *Journal of Personality and Social Psychology* 56 (1989): 15–16. I draw on the summary of Devine's work in Feldman, *Social Psychology*, p. 97.

69 David Wellman, *Portraits of White Racism* (Cambridge: Cambridge University Press, 1977), p. 42.

70 David O. Sears, "Symbolic Racism," in *Eliminating Racism*, eds. Phyllis A. Katz and Dalmas A. Taylor (New York: Plenum, 1988), pp. 55–58; and Lawrence Bobo, "Group Conflict, Prejudice, and the Paradox of Contemporary Racial Attitudes," in *Eliminating Racism*, eds. Katz and Taylor, pp. 99–101; and Michael Hughes, "Symbolic Racism, Old-Fashioned Racism, and Whites' Opposition to Affirmative Action," in *Racial Attitudes in the 1990s: Continuity and Change*, eds. Steven A. Tuch and Jack K. Martin (Westport, CT: Praeger, 1997), p. 73–74.

71 Lawrence Bobo, James R. Kluegel, and Ryan A. Smith, "Laissez-Faire Racism: The Crystallization of a Kinder, Gentler, Antiblack Ideology," in *Racial Attitudes in the 1990s: Continuity and Change*, eds. Steven A. Tuch and Jack K. Martin (Westport, CT: Praeger, 1997), pp. 25, 39. They draw on the survey data in Schuman, Steeh, and Bobo, *Racial Attitudes in America: Trends and Interpretations.*

72 Sidney Verba and Gary R. Orren, *Equality in America: The View from the Top* (Cambridge, MA: Harvard University Press, 1985), p. 63.

73 Everett C. Ladd, "Rethinking the Sixties." *The American Enterprise*, May/June 1995, 102.

74 Blendon et al., "The Public and the President's Commission on Race," p. 66.

75 Lehigh, "Conflicting views of Massachusetts; Poll Shows a Sharp Racial Divide over the State of Equality," B1.

76 Smith, "Bridging the Gulf Between Blacks & Whites," p. A1.

77   Robert M. Entman, "Manufacturing Discord: Media in the Affirmative Action Debate," *Press/Politics* 2 (1997): 36.

78   Blendon et al., "The Public and the President's Commission on Race," p. 66.

79   Ruth Frankenberg, *White Women, Race Matters* (Minneapolis: University of Minnesota Press, 1993), pp 228–29.

80   Joyce E. King, "Dysconscious Racism: Ideology, Identity, and the Miseducation of Teachers," *Journal of Negro Education* 60 (1991): 138.

81   Survey results cited in Blendon et al., "The Public and the President's Commission on Race," p. 66.

82   Marimba Ani, *Yurugu: An African-Centered Critique of European Cultural Thought and Behavior* (Trenton, NJ: Africa World Press, 1994), p. 294.

83   See Theodor W. Adorno et al., *The Authoritarian Personality* (New York: Harper, 1950), pp. 248–79; Thomas F. Pettigrew, *Racially Separate or Together?* (New York: McGraw-Hill, 1971), pp. 131–35; and Robin M. Williams, Jr., *Strangers Next Door* (Englewood Cliffs, NJ: Prentice-Hall, 1964), pp. 110–13.

84   John Briggs and F. David Peat, *Turbulent Mirror: An Illustrated Guide to Chaos Theory and the Science of Wholeness* (New York: Harper & Row, 1990), p. 154.

85   Feldman, *Social Psychology*, p. 399.

86   The 1999 source is http://db.cbs.com/prd1.

87   Feagin and Vera, *White Racism*, p. 149.

88   General Social Survey, National Opinion Research Center, Chicago, Illinois, 1990.

89   Jean Piaget, *The Moral Judgment of the Child* (Glencoe, IL: The Free Press, 1932).

90   Debra Van Ausdale and Joe R. Feagin, "Using Racial and Ethnic Concepts: The Critical Case of Very Young Children," *American Sociological Review* 61 (October 1996): 779–93.

91   Isabel Wilkerson, "The Tallest Fence: Feelings on Race in a White Neighborhood," *New York Times*, June 21, 1992, section 1, p. 18.

92   Feldman, *Social Psychology*, p. 90; Jim Sidanius, Felicia Pratto, and Lawrence Bobo, "Racism, Conservatism, Affirmative Action, and Intellectual Sophistication," *Journal of Personality and Social Psychology* 70 (1996): 487.

93   Dovidio et al., "Stereotyping, Prejudice, and Discrimination: Another Look," pp. 276–319.

94   Faye Crosby, Stephanie Bromley, and Leonard Saxe, "Recent Unobtrusive Studies of Black and White Discrimination and Prejudice," *Psychological Bulletin* 87 (1980): 546–63.

95   Russell H. Fazio et al., "Variability in Automatic Activation as an Unobtrusive Measure of Racial Attitudes: A Bona Fide Pipeline?" *Journal of Personality and Social Psychology* 69 (1995): 1025–26.

96   Bridget C. Dunton and Russell H. Fazio, "An Individual Difference Measure of Motivation to Control Prejudiced Reactions," *Personality and Social Psychology Bulletin*, in press.

97   Richard J. Barnet and John Cavanagh, *Global Dreams: Imperial Corporations and the New World Order* (New York: Touchstone, 1994), p. 138. I draw here from Joe R. Feagin and Pinar Batur-Vanderlippe, "The Globalization of Racism and Antiracism: France, South Africa and the United States," unpublished manuscript, University of Florida, 1996.

98   Hsiao-Chuan Hsia, "Imported Racism and Indigenous Biases: the Impacts of the U.S. Media on Taiwanese Images of African Americans," paper presented at the annual meeting of American Sociological Association, August 5–9, 1994, Los Angeles.

99   Nestor Rodriguez, personal communication with the author, March 1996.

100   Yolanda Flores-Niemann, Tatcho Mindiola, and Nestor Rodriguez, "U.S.–Born and Foreign-Born Latinas' Perceptions of Black/Brown Relations: Implications for Future Inter-Group Relations," unpublished research paper, University of Houston, 1997, pp. 12–13.

Chapter Five

1   See Gordon Allport, *The Nature of Prejudice*, abridged ed. (New York: Anchor Books, 1958).

2   See Kwame Ture [Stokeley Carmichael] and Charles Hamilton, *Black Power* (New York: Random House, 1967).

3   Philomena Essed, *Understanding Everyday Racism* (Newbury Park, CA: Sage, 1991), p. 50.

4   United Nations, "Convention on the Prevention and Punishment of Genocide," in *The United Nations and Human Rights, 1945–1995* (New York: United Nations Department of Public Information, 1995), pp. 219–25.

5   See Robert S. Feldman, *Social Psychology* (Englewood Cliffs, NJ: Prentice-Hall, 1995), p. 364.

6   Essed, *Understanding Everyday Racism*, p. 50.

7   Joe R. Feagin and Melvin P. Sikes, *Living With Racism: The Black Middle-Class Experience* (Boston: Beacon Press, 1994), p. 54.

8   John O. Calmore, "To Make Wrong Right: The Necessary and Proper Aspirations of Fair Housing," in *The State of Black America 1989* (New York: National Urban League, 1989), p. 89.

9   See Feagin and Sikes, *Living With Racism*; Joe R. Feagin, Hernan Vera, and Nikitah Imani, *The Agony of Education: Black Students at White Colleges and Universities* (New York: Routledge, 1996); and Yanick St. Jean and Joe R. Feagin, *Double Burden: Black Women and Everyday Racism* (New York: M. E. Sharpe, 1998).

10   Nancy Krieger and Stephen Sidney, "Racial Discrimination and Blood Pressure," *American*

Journal of Public Health 86 (1996): 1370–78.

11 Tyrone Forman, David R. Williams, and James S. Jackson, "Race, Place, and Discrimination," in *Perspectives on Social Problems*, ed. Carol Brooks Gardner (Stamford, CT: JAI Press, 1997), pp. 231–61; Gallup Organization, *Black/White Relations in the United States* (Princeton, NJ: Gallup Organization, 1997), pp. 29–30, 108–10.

12 Lee Sigelman and Susan Welch, *Black Americans' Views of Racial Inequality: The Dream Deferred* (Cambridge: Cambridge University Press, 1991), p. 59.

13 Frank R. Parker, *Black Votes Count* (Chapel Hill: University of North Carolina Press, 1990); Chandler Davison and Bernard Grofman, eds., *The Quiet Revolution in the South: The Impact of the Voting Rights Act 1965–1990* (Princeton, NJ: Princeton University Press, 1994).

14 See David Garrow, "Lani Guinier," *The Progressive*, September 1993, 28; and Lani Guinier, *The Tyranny of the Majority: Fundamental Fairness and Representation Democracy* (New York: Free Press, 1994), pp. 14–21.

15 *City of Richmond, Virginia v. J.A. Croson Co.*, 488 U.S. 469 (1989).

16 Michel Rosenfeld, "Decoding Richmond: Affirmative Action and the Elusive Meaning of Constitutional Equality," *Michigan Law Review* 87 (June 1989): 1762.

17 *City of Richmond, Virginia v. J.A. Croson Co.*, 488 U.S. 469, 503 (1989).

18 Martin J. Katz, "The Economics of Discrimination: The Three Fallacies of Croson," *Yale Law Journal* 100 (January 1991): 1044.

19 *City of Richmond, Virginia v. J.A. Croson Co.*, 488 U.S. 469, 552–53 (1989).

20 Jerome McCristal Culp Jr., "Understanding the Racial Discourse of Justice Rehnquist," *Rutgers Law Journal* 25 (Spring, 1994): 604.

21 See Matthew P. Smith, "Bridging the Gulf Between Blacks & Whites," *Pittsburgh Post-Gazette*, April 7, 1996, A1.

22 Gunnar Myrdal, *An American Dilemma*, vol. I (New York: McGraw-Hill, 1964 [1944]); Joe R. Feagin and Harlan Hahn, *Ghetto Revolts* (New York: Macmillan, 1973).

23 A. E. Bessent and L. Tayler, "Police Brutality: Is It No Problem?" *Newsday*, June 2, 1991, 5.

24 Cathleen Decker, "Most Rank Police High in L.A. and Orange Counties," *Los Angeles Times*, February 13, 1990, A1. See also Kim Lersch and Joe R. Feagin, "Violent Police-Citizen Encounters: An Analysis of Major Newspaper Accounts," *Critical Sociology* 22 (1996): 29–49.

25 Gallup, *Black/White Relations in the United States*, pp. 29–30, 108–10.

26 Lersch and Feagin, "Violent Police-Citizen Encounters: An Analysis of Major Newspaper Accounts," pp. 29–49.

27 James Bovard, "Drug-Courier Profiles: Forget Warrants—Police Can Stop and Search Almost Anyone," *Playboy*, November, 1994, 46.

28 Michael R. Cogan, "The Drug Enforcement Agency's Use of Drug Courier Profiles: One Size Fits All," *Catholic University Law Review* 41 (1992): 943–46.

29 Sonya Ross, "Clinton Targets Racial Profiling," *San Diego Union-Tribune*, June 10, 1999, A2.

30 Ibid.

31 Ian Ayres and Joel Waldfogel, "A Market Test for Race Discrimination in Bail Setting," *Stanford Law Review* 46 (May 1994): 993.

32 Ibid., p. 994.

33 David L. Lewis, "Bias in Drug Sentences," *The National Law Journal* (February 5, 1996): A19.

34 Eric Schlosser, "The Prison-Industrial Complex," *Atlantic Monthly*, December 1998, 34–35.

35 Amnesty International, *United States of America: Rights for All* (London: Amnesty International Publications, 1998), pp. 3, 109–10; Susan Estrich, *Real Rape* (Cambridge, MA: Harvard University Press, 1987), p. 107.

36 Amnesty International, *United States of America: Rights for All*, p. 110.

37 Roger Boesche, "How White People Riot: Quietly, at the Ballot Box," *Baltimore Sun*, October 15, 1995, 3F.

38 See Feagin and Hahn, *Ghetto Revolts*, pp. 78–81.

39 "Hate Crime Violence," *The Race Relations Reporter*, August 15, 1994, 2.

40 Thomas Fields-Meyer et al., "One Deadly Night: Deep in the Woods of East Texas, James Byrd Died a Terrible Death, Leaving a Town and a Nation in Shock," *People*, June 29, 1998, 46.

41 Howard Chua-Eoan and Hilary Hylton-Austin, "Beneath The Surface; A 'New South' Town is Haunted by 'Deep South' Ghosts—And a Fresh, Ugly Murder," *Time*, June 22, 1998, 34.

42 This article is dissected in Les Payne, "Exploitation and Dismissal of a Victim," *Newsday*, June 21, 1998, B6.

43 Connie Chung and Barbara Walters, "Roy Smith's America," ABC News "20/20" transcript, July 6, 1998; Joanne Ostrow, "Racism Hits Home on '20/20,'" *Denver Post*, March 19, 1998, E1.

44 Klanwatch Project, *False Patriots: The Threat of Antigovernment Extremists* (Montgomery, AL: Southern Poverty Law Center, 1996), p.3.

45 Ibid., pp. 37–38.

46 Ibid., p. 5.

47 Douglas S. Massey and Nancy A. Denton, "Trends in Segregation of Blacks, Hispanics and Asians, 1970–1980," *American Sociological Review* 52 (1987): 802–25; Douglas S. Massey and Nancy A. Denton, *American Apartheid:*

Segregation and the Making of the Underclass (Cambridge, MA: Harvard University Press, 1993), pp. 221–23.

48　See Joe R. Feagin and Clairece B. Feagin, *Racial and Ethnic Relations*, 6th ed. (Upper Saddle River, NJ: Prentice-Hall, 1999), chapter 8. An earlier version of some of these arguments appeared in Joe R. Feagin, "Excluding Blacks and Others from Housing: The Foundation of White Racism," *Cityscape* 4 (1999): 79–91.

49　*Jones et ux. v. Alfred H. Mayer Co.*, 392 U.S. 409, 441–43 (1968).

50　Ibid., 444 (1968).

51　Ibid., 445 (1968).

52　Massey and Denton, *American Apartheid*, pp. 92–94; Farai Chideya, *The Color of Our Future* (New York: William Morrow, 1999), p. 132.

53　Margery Austin Turner, Raymond J. Struyk, and John Yinger, *Housing Discrimination Study: Synthesis* (Washington, DC: U.S. Government Printing Office, 1991), pp. ii–viii.

54　See Fair Housing Council of Fresno County, "Audit Uncovers Blatant Discrimination against Hispanics, African Americans and Families with Children in Fresno County," press release, Fresno, California, October 6, 1997; Central Alabama Fair Housing Center, "Discrimination in the Rental Housing Market: A Study of Montgomery, Alabama, 1995–1996," January 13, 1996; Fair Housing Action Center, Inc., "Greater New Orleans Rental Audit," New Orleans, Louisiana, 1996; and San Antonio Fair Housing Council, "San Antonio Metropolitan Area Rental Audit 1997," San Antonio, Texas, 1997. See also Fair Housing Council of Greater Washington, as reported in Caroline E. Mayer, "Minorities Said to Face Bias in House Hunting; Study Finds Blacks, Hispanics Treated Worse," *Washington Post*, April 9, 1997, C9.

55　I draw here on the summary in "The Multi-City Study of Urban Inequality," Russell Sage Foundation Newsletter, fall, 1999, p. 2. See also John Yinger, "Housing Discrimination is Still Worth Worrying About," *Housing Policy Debate* 9, no. 4 (1998): 899–900.

56　Shanna L. Smith and Cathy Clous, "Documenting Discrimination by Homeowners Insurance Companies through Testing," in *Insurance Redlining: Disinvestment, Reinvestment, and the Evolving Role of Financial Institutions*, ed. Gregory D. Squires (Washington, DC: Urban Institute Press, 1997), pp. 106–17.

57　Office of Thrift Supervision, *Report on Loan Discrimination* (Washington, DC: Department of the Treasury, 1989), p. 2; Paulette Thomas, "Federal Data Detail Pervasive Racial Gap in Mortgage Lending," *Wall Street Journal*, March 31, 1992, 1; Joe R. Feagin, "A House is

not a Home: White Racism and U.S. Housing Practices," in *Residential Apartheid: The American Legacy*, ed. Robert Bullard (Los Angeles: UCLA Center for Afro-American Studies, 1994), pp. 17–48.

58　John Goering and Ron Wienk, "An Overview," in *Mortgage Lending, Racial Discrimination, and Federal Policy*, eds. John Goering and Ron Wienk (Washington, DC: Urban Institute Press, 1996), pp. 16–19; Yinger, "Housing Discrimination is Still Worth Worrying About," p. 913.

59　James S. Byrne, "Lenders Set Plans To Eliminate Unintentional Discrimination; More Bad Numbers Expected," *American Banker-Bond Buyer* 2 (September 21, 1992): 1.

60　James Bates, "Obstacle Course," *Los Angeles Times*, September 6, 1992, A27.

61　Yinger, "Housing Discrimination is Still Worth Worrying About," pp. 901–902.

62　Gregory D. Squires, personal communication with the author, 1998.

63　Sunwoong Kim and Gregory D. Squires, "The Color of Money and the People who Lent It," *Journal of Housing Research* 9 (1998): 271–84.

64　"Dallas Officials Twice as Likely to Raze Black Homes," *Houston Chronicle*, September 14, 1998, 14A.

65　See Joe R. Feagin and Robert Parker, *Building American Cities* (Englewood Cliffs, NJ: Prentice-Hall, 1990), chapter 5. See also Norman Nager, "Continuities of Urban Policy on the Poor," in *Back to the City*, eds. Shirley B. Laska and Daphne Spain (New York: Pergamon Press, 1980), p. 240.

66　Shanna L. Smith, National Fair Housing Alliance, personal communication with the author, June 9, 1997.

67　I draw here on Feagin and Parker, *Building American Cities*, chapter 8.

68　William J. Wilson, *Power, Racism and Privilege* (New York: Free Press, 1973), pp. 189–90.

69　Derrick Bell, "Property Rights in Whiteness— Their Legal Legacy, Their Economic Costs," in *Critical Race Theory: The Cutting Edge*, ed. Richard Delgado (Philadelphia: Temple University Press, 1995), p. 75.

70　Lawrence Bobo and Susan A. Suh, "Surveying Racial Discrimination: Analyses from a Multiethnic Labor Market."

71　Gallup, *Black/White Relations in the United States*, pp. 29–30, 108–10.

72　Alfred W. Blumrosen et al., *Employment Discrimination against Women and Minorities in Georgia* (Newark, NJ: Rutgers University S. I. Newhouse Center for Law and Justice, 1999).

73　This research is summarized in Pamela Mendels, "Up for Evaluation; Is Affirmative Action Still Working After 30 Years on the Job?" *Newsday*, June 13, 1995, 6.

74 Marc Bendick, Jr., Mary Lou Egan, and Suzanne Lofhjelm, *The Documentation and Evaluation of Anti-Discrimination Training in the United States* (Geneva: International Labour Office, 1998), p. 8; Marc Bendick Jr., *Discrimination against Racial/Ethnic Minorities in the United States: Empirical Findings from Situation Testing* (Geneva: International Labor Office, 1996), pp. 17–21. See also H. Cross et al., "Employer Hiring Practices: Differential Treatment of Hispanic and Anglo Job Seekers," Urban Institute Report 90, no. 4 (1990).

75 Bendick, *Discrimination against Racial/Ethnic Minorities in the United States*, pp. 22–23.

76 I draw here on "The Multi-City Study of Urban Inequality," pp. 1–3, and on an attached supplement.

77 Ibid., p. 3; see also William J. Wilson, *When Work Disappears: The World of the New Urban Poor* (New York: Knopf, 1996), pp. 136–38.

78 Bendick, *Discrimination against Racial/Ethnic Minorities in the United States*, p. 24.

79 Lawrence Bobo et al., "Work Orientation, Job Discrimination, and Ethnicity: A Focus Group Perspective," in *Research in the Sociology of Work*, eds. Richard L. Simpson and Ida H. Simpson (Stamford, CT: JAI Press, 1995), pp. 81–82. The quote is on p. 82.

80 Lawrence Bobo and Susan A. Suh, "Surveying Racial Discrimination: Analyses from a Multi-ethnic Labor Market," unpublished research report, Department of Sociology, University of California at Los Angeles, August 1, 1995.

81 Pam Lambert et al., "What's Wrong with This Picture? Exclusion of Minorities Has Been Way of Life in Hollywood," *People*, March 18, 1996, 42.

82 Sharon Collins, "Blacks on the Bubble: The Vulnerability of Black Executives in White Corporations," *Sociological Quarterly* 34 (August 1993): 429–47.

83 Jacquelyn Scarville et al., *Armed Forces Equal Opportunity Survey* (Arlington, VA: Defense Manpower Data Center, 1999), pp. 46–78; Office of the Under Secretary of Defense Personnel and Readiness, *Career Progression of Minority and Women Officers* (Washington, DC: Department of Defense, 1999), pp. 83–85.

84 Lawrence M Kahn, "The Effects of Race on Professional Football Players' Compensation," *Industrial and Labor Relations Review* 45 (January 1992): 295–310; Lawrence M. Kahn and Peter D. Sherer, "Racial Differences in Professional Basketball Players' Compensation," *Journal of Labor Economics* 6 (January 1988): 40–61.

85 Willhelm, *Black in a White America*, p. 345.

86 Bendick, Egan, and Lofhjelm, *The Documentation and Evaluation of Anti-Discrimination*

Training in the United States*, pp. 8–9; Bendick, *Discrimination against Racial/Ethnic Minorities in the United States*, p. 20; Craig Zwerling and Hilary Silver, "Race and Job Dismissals in a Federal Bureaucracy," *American Sociological Review* 57 (October 1992): 651–60.

87 Scarville et al., *Armed Forces Equal Opportunity Survey*, pp. 46–78.

88 Bendick, Egan, and Lofhjelm, *The Documentation and Evaluation of Anti-Discrimination Training in the United States*, p. 9.

89 *The Race Relations Reporter*, December 15, 1996, 1.

90 Kurt Eichenwald, "Texaco Executives, On Tape, Discussed Impeding a Bias Suit," *New York Times*, November 4, 1996, A1.

91 Bari-Ellen Roberts, *Roberts v. Texaco: A True Story of Race and Corporate America* (New York: Avon Books, 1998), pp. 1, 283.

92 Kurt Eichenwald, "The Two Faces Of Texaco," *New York Times*, November 10, 1996, section 3, p. 1.

93 Ibid.

94 Ibid.

95 Roberts, *Roberts v. Texaco*, p. 283.

96 Ellen Neuborne, "March of Time Yields Little Progress for Many Blacks," *USA Today*, November 25, 1996, 3B.

97 Melvin L. Oliver and Thomas M. Shapiro, *Black Wealth/White Wealth: A New Perspective on Racial Equality* (New York: Routledge, 1995), pp. 36–50.

98 Katz, "The Economics of Discrimination," p. 1044.

99 Maria Enchautegui et al., *Do Minority-Owned Businesses Get a Fair Share of Government Contracts?* (Washington, D C: Urban Institute Press, 1996), p. 51.

100 Timothy Bates, "Commercial Bank Financing of Black and White Small Business Startups," *Quarterly Review of Economics and Business* 31 (1991): 64–80; Carmen Grown and Timothy Bates, "Commercial Bank Lending Practices and the Development of Black Owned Construction Companies," *Journal of Urban Affairs* 14 (1992): 25–41; National Economic Research Associates, *The State of Texas Disparity Study* (Cambridge, MA: National Economic Research Associates, 1994), pp. 139–41.

101 Bates, "Commercial Bank Financing of Black and White Small Business Startups," pp. 64–80.

102 Robert W. Glover, *Minority Enterprise in Construction* (New York: Praeger, 1977), p. 65. See also Carmenza Gallo, "The Construction Industry in New York City: Immigrant and Black Entrepreneurs," working paper, Conservation of Human Resources Project, Columbia University, 1983.

103 Timothy Bates, *Strategies for the Black Worker:*

Preparing for the 21st Century (Washington, DC: Joint Center for Political and Economic Studies, 1997).

104   See Enchautegui et al., *Do Minority-Owned Businesses Get a Fair Share of Government Contracts?*

105   Diana Pearce, "Breaking Down Barriers: New Evidence on the Impact of Metropolitan School Desegregation on Housing Patterns," research report, School of Law, Catholic University, 1980, pp. 48–53.

106   *Freeman v. Pitts*, 503 U.S. 467 (1992).

107   Gary Orfield and John T. Yun, *Resegregation in American Schools* (Cambridge, MA: Harvard University Civil Rights Project, 1999).

108   Quoted in Peter Applebome, "Schools See Reemergence Of 'Separate but Equal,'" *New York Times*, April 8, 1997, A10.

109   New York ACORN Schools Office, *Secret Apartheid: A Report on Racial Discrimination against Black and Latino Parents and Children in the New York City Public Schools* (New York: ACORN, 1996).

110   See Richard Delgado, *The Coming Race War?* (New York: New York University Press, 1996), p. 71.

111   Chalsa M. Loo and Garry Rolison, "Alienation of Ethnic Minority Students at a Predominantly White University," *Journal of Higher Education* 57 (January/February 1986): 64–67; Hoi K. Suen, "Alienation and Attrition of Black College Students on a Predominantly White Campus," *Journal of College Student Personnel* 24 (March, 1983): 117–21.

112   Hope Landrine and Elizabeth A. Klonoff, "The Schedule of Racist Events: A Measure of Racial Discrimination and a Study of its Negative Physical and Mental Health Consequences," *Journal of Black Psychology* 22, no. 2 (1996): 144–68.

113   See Feagin, Vera, and Imani, *The Agony of Education*. On other universities see Urban Affairs Programs, *The Graduate School Climate at MSU: Perceptions of Three Diverse Racial/Ethnic Groups* (East Lansing: Michigan State University Office of the Provost, 1995); and Cynthia A. Villis, Stephen Parker, and Robert P. Gordon, *Institutionalizing Cultural Diversity: Assessment, Year One* (San Diego, CA: University of San Diego, 1993).

114   Feagin, Vera, and Imani, *The Agony of Education*, pp. 60–61. The data are from 1993–1995 issues of *The Race Relations Reporter*.

115   Feagin and Sikes, *Living With Racism*, pp. 20–21.

116   John F. Dovidio, "The Subtlety of Racism," *Training and Development*, April 1993, 51–55.

117   Faye Crosby et al., "Recent Unobtrusive Studies of Black and White Discrimination and

Prejudice: A Literature Review," *Psychological Bulletin* 87 (1980): 546.

118   Delgado, *The Coming Race War?*, p. 17.

119   Gallup, *Black/White Relations in the United States*, pp. 29–30, 108–10.

120   Leanita McClain, "The Insidious New Racism," in *A Foot in Each World*, ed. Clarence Page (Evanston, IL: Northwestern University Press, 1986), pp. 20–21.

121   Ian Ayres, "Fair Driving: Gender and Race Discrimination in Retail Car Negotiations," *Harvard Law Review* 104 (February 1991): 820, 829–30.

122   Ibid., p. 824.

123   Kevin A. Schulman et al., "The Effect of Race and Sex on Physicians' Recommendations for Cardiac Catherization," *New England Journal of Medicine* (February 25, 1999): 618–26; Peter B. Bach et al., "Racial Differences in the Treatment of Early-Stage Lung Cancer," *New England Journal of Medicine* (October 14, 1999): 1198–1205.

124   Benjamin B. Ringer, *"We the People" and Others* (New York: Tavistock, 1983), p. 327.

Chapter Six

1   Lawrence Bobo et al., "Work Orientation, Job Discrimination, and Ethnicity: A Focus Group Perspective," in *Research in the Sociology of Work*, eds. Richard L. Simpson and Ida H. Simpson (Stamford, CT: JAI Press, 1995), p. 81.

2   Joyce E. King, "Dysconscious Racism: Ideology, Identity, and the Miseducation of Teachers," *Journal of Negro Education* 60 (1991): 135.

3   I am indebted to Nancy DiTomaso for comments on this point.

4   Jane Lazarre, *Beyond the Whiteness of Whiteness* (Durham, NC: Duke University Press, 1996), p. 41.

5   Frances Lee Ansley, "Stirring the Ashes: Race, Class and the Future of Civil Rights Scholarship," *Cornell Law Review* 74 (September 1989): 1035.

6   See, for example, Theodore Cross, *The Black Power Imperative: Racial Inequality and the Politics of Nonviolence* (New York: Faulkner, 1984), p. 510.

7   Patricia J. Williams, *The Alchemy of Race and Rights* (Cambridge, MA: Harvard University Press, 1991), p. 101.

8   Joe R. Feagin and Clairece B. Feagin, *Social Problems: A Critical Power-Conflict Perspective*, 4th ed. (Englewood Cliffs, NJ: Prentice-Hall, 1994), p. 425.

9   David R. Roediger, *The Wages of Whiteness: Race and the Making of the American Working Class* (London: Verso, 1991), p. 12.

10   Ansley, "Stirring the Ashes: Race, Class and the Future of Civil Rights Scholarship," p. 1035.

11 Kenneth W. Smallwood, "The Folklore of Preferential Treatment," unpublished manuscript, Southfield, Michigan, 1985; Cross, *The Black Power Imperative*, pp. 515–18.

12 Irving Kristol, "The Negro Today Is Like the Immigrant of Yesterday," *New York Times Magazine*, September 11, 1966, 50–51, 124–42.

13 Theodore Hershberg et al., "A Tale of Three Cities: Blacks, Immigrants, and Opportunity in Philadelphia: 1850–1880, 1930, 1970," in *Philadelphia*, ed. Theodore Hershberg (New York: Oxford University Press, 1981), pp. 462–64.

14 Herbert Hill, "The Racial Practices of Organized Labor — The Age of Gompers and After," in *Employment, Race and Poverty*, eds. Arthur M. Ross and Herbert Hill (New York: Harcourt, Brace & World, 1967), p. 365.

15 Stanley B. Greenberg, *Race and State in Capitalist Development* (New Haven, CT: Yale University Press, 1980), p. 349.

16 See Joe R. Feagin and Melvin P. Sikes, *Living With Racism: The Black Middle Class Experience* (Boston: Beacon Press, 1994); and Joe R. Feagin, Kevin Early, and Karyn D. McKinney, "The Many Costs of Discrimination: The Case of Middle-Class Americans," unpublished paper, University of Florida, 1999.

17 For details see Cross, *The Black Power Imperative*, pp. 515–18; and Melvin L. Oliver and Thomas M. Shapiro, *Black Wealth/White Wealth: A New Perspective on Racial Inequality* (New York: Routledge, 1995), pp. 36–45.

18 Harvard Sitkoff, *A New Deal for Blacks* (New York: Oxford University Press, 1978); Joe R. Feagin, "Slavery Unwilling to Die: The Background of Black Oppression in the 1980s," *Journal of Black Studies* 17 (December 1986): 173–200.

19 See Cross, *The Black Power Imperative*, p. 515.

20 *City of Richmond, Virginia v. J. A. Croson Co.*, 488 U.S. 469 (1989).

21 Thomas Dye, *Who's Running America?* 4th ed. (Englewood Cliffs, NJ: Prentice-Hall, 1986), pp. 190–205.

22 David Gates, "White Male Paranoia," *Newsweek*, March 29, 1993, 48.

23 "Federal Panel Reveals That Most Top Jobs Are Still Held By White Men," *Jet*, April 3, 1995, 24.

24 United for a Fair Economy, "Born on Third Base: The Sources of Wealth of the Forbes 400," n.d., this is taken from the website http://www.stw.org.

25 *Dred Scott v. John F. A. Sandford*, 60 U.S. 393, 407 (1857); emphasis added.

26 Mary Beth Norton, *Liberty's Daughters* (Boston: Little, Brown, 1980); Edmund S. Morgan, *American Slavery, American Freedom: The Ordeal of Virginia* (New York: Norton, 1975), p. 165.

27 United for a Fair Economy, "The Racial Wealth Gap: Left Out of the Boom," Boston, MA, 1999, as listed at http: //www.stw.org/ html/racial_wealth_gap.html; William A. Darity, Jr., and Samuel L. Myers, *Persistent Disparity: Race and Economic Inequality in the United States Since 1945* (Northampton, MA: Edward Elgar, 1998), pp. 7–10.

28 Sidney M. Willhelm, *Black in a White America* (Cambridge, MA: Schenkman, 1983), p. 346.

29 United for a Fair Economy, "The Racial Wealth Gap"; U.S. Bureau of the Census, *Household Wealth and Asset Ownership: 1991*, Current Population Reports P70–34 (Washington, DC: U.S. Government Printing Office, 1994), pp. xiii–xiv.

30 Rhonda V. Magee, "The Master's Tools, from the Bottom Up: Responses to African-American Reparations Theory in Mainstream and Outsider Remedies Discourse," *Virginia Law Review* 79 (May 1993): 863.

31 James Marketti, "Estimated Present Value of Income Diverted during Slavery," in *The Wealth of Races: The Present Value of Benefits from Past Injustices*, ed. Richard F. America (New York: Greenwood, 1990), p. 118.

32 See Roger L. Ransom and Richard Sutch, "Growth and Welfare in the American South in the Nineteenth Century," in *Market Institutions and Economic Progress in the New South 1865–1900*, eds. Gary Walton and James Shepherd (New York: Academic Press, 1981), pp. 150–51.

33 David H. Swinton, "Racial Inequality and Reparations," in *The Wealth of Races*, ed. America, p. 156.

34 William A. Darity, Jr., "Forty Acres and a Mule: Placing the Price Tag on Oppression," in *The Wealth of Races*, ed. America, p. 11. Total estimates of the debt due to African Americans have been put at $10–24 trillion by Richard America and Jack White. See Kevin Merida, "Did Freedom Alone Pay a Nation's Debt," *The Washington Post*, November 23, 1999, p. C1.

35 Stephen J. DeCanio, "Accumulation and Discrimination in the Postbellum South," in *Market Institutions and Economic Progress in the New South 1865–1900*, eds. Walton and Shepherd, p. 105; see also pp. 103–25.

36 Swinton, "Racial Equality and Reparations," p. 157.

37 Martin J. Katz, "The Economics of Discrimination: The Three Fallacies of Croson," *Yale Law Journal* 100 (January 1991): 1041–45.

38 Oliver and Shapiro, *Black Wealth/White Wealth*, pp. 36–50; United for a Fair Economy, "The Racial Wealth Gap."

39   Darity and Myers, *Persistent Disparity*, pp. 150–52.

40   Andrew Hacker, *Two Nations: Black and White, Separate, Hostile, Unequal* (New York: Scribner's, 1992), pp. 31–32.

41   Patricia J. Williams, "Alchemical Notes: Reconstructing Ideals from Deconstructed Rights." *Harvard Civil Rights and Civil Liberties Review* 22 (1987): 415.

42   Ellis Cashmore, *The Black Culture Industry* (New York: Routledge, 1997), pp. 1, 3.

43   See Feagin and Sikes, *Living With Racism: The Black Middle Class Experience*.

44   See Judith Lichtenberg, "Racism in the Head, Racism in the World," *Philosophy and Public Policy* 12 (Spring/Summer 1992): 4.

45   William James, *The Principles of Psychology* (New York: Dover, 1950 [1890]). See also Robert H. Lauer and Warren H. Handel, *Social Psychology: The Theory and Application of Symbolic Interactionism* (Boston: Houghton-Mifflin, 1977), p. 42.

46   See John J. Macionis, *Sociology*, 5th ed. (Englewood Cliffs, NJ: Prentice-Hall, 1995), pp. 125–28.

47   Feagin and Sikes, *Living With Racism*, chapters 3 and 7; Yanick St. Jean and Joe R. Feagin, *Double Burden: Black Women and Everyday Racism* (Armonk, NY: M. E. Sharpe, 1998).

48   Claude M. Steele and Joshua Aronson, "Stereotype Threat and the Intellectual Test Performance of African Americans," *Journal of Personality and Social Psychology* 69 (1995): 797–811.

49   Claude M. Steele, "A Threat in the Air: How Stereotypes Shape Intellectual Identity and Performance," *American Psychologist*, June 1997, 627.

50   Antonio Gramsci, *Letters from Prison: Antonio Gramsci*, ed. Lynne Lawner (New York: Harper Colophon, 1975 [1932]); Catharine A. MacKinnon, *Toward a Feminist Theory of the State* (Cambridge, MA: Harvard University Press, 1989), p. 8.

51   William H. Grier and Price M. Cobbs, *Black Rage* (New York: Basic Books, 1968), p. 4. See also Price M. Cobbs, "Critical Perspectives on the Psychology of Race," in *The State of Black America: 1988*, ed. Janet Dewart (New York: National Urban League, 1988), pp. 61–70.

52   Feagin and Sikes, *Living With Racism*, p. 294.

53   Patricia J. Falk, "Novel Theories of Criminal Defense Based upon the Toxicity of the Social Environment: Urban Psychosis, Television Intoxication, and Black Rage," *North Carolina Law Review* 74 (March 1996): 750–53; Jody David Armour, *Negrophobia and Reasonable Racism: the Hidden Costs of Being Black in America* (New York: New York University Press, 1997), p. 5.

54   Alexander Thomas and Samuel Sillen, *The Theory and Application of Symbolic Interactionism* (Boston: Houghton-Mifflin, 1977), p. 54.

55   This study by Nancy Krieger is summarized in Amanda Husted, "Discrimination Can Pose Health Risk for Blacks and Homosexuals," *Atlanta Journal and Constitution*, November 1, 1994, D22. Those who reported no discrimination had blood pressure as high as those who reported much discrimination, which Krieger interprets to mean that the former are underreporting. See also Nancy Krieger, "Embodying Inequality: A Review of Concepts, Measures, and Methods for Studying Health Consequences of Discrimination," *International Journal of Health Services* 29 (1999): 295–352.

56   Feagin, Early, and McKinney, "The Many Costs of Discrimination: The Case of Middle-Class African Americans."

57   See James Oakes, *The Ruling Race: A History of American Slaveholders* (New York: Vintage Books, 1983); and Kenneth M. Stampp, *The Peculiar Institution: Slavery in the Ante-Bellum South*, (New York: Vintage Books, 1956), pp. 318–21.

58   Thomas F. Pettigrew, *A Profile of the Negro American* (Princeton, NJ: Van Nostrand, 1964), p. 99.

59   Rodney Coates, personal communication with the author, November 9, 1995. For a similar image of sexism, see Marilyn Frye, *The Politics of Reality* (Freedom, CA: Crossing Press, 1983), p. 4.

60   Tyrone A. Forman, "The Social Psychological Costs of Racial Segmentation: A Study of African Americans' Well-Being," unpublished research paper, University of Michigan, 1999, p. 24.

61   Concurring opinion in *Jones et ux. v. Alfred H. Mayer Co.*, 392 U.S. 409, 445 (1968).

62   Marc Bendick, Jr., *Discrimination against Racial/Ethnic Minorities in the United States: Empirical Findings from Situation Testing* (Geneva: International Labour Office, 1996), p. 23; John O. Calmore, "To Make Wrong Right: The Necessary and Proper Aspirations of Fair Housing," in *The State of Black America 1989* (New York: National Urban League, 1989), p. 89.

63   Gunnar Myrdal, *An American Dilemma*, vol. 1 (New York: McGraw-Hill, 1964 [1944]), p. 4.

64   See Oliver C. Cox, *Caste, Class, and Race: A Study in Social Dynamics* (New York: Doubleday, 1948), p. 531; and Marimba Ani, *Yurugu: An African-Centered Critique of European Cultural Thought and Behavior* (Trenton, NJ: Africa World Press, 1994).

65   William Lee Miller, *Arguing about Slavery: The Great Battle in the United States Congress* (New York: Knopf, 1996), p. 10.

66   For example, the South has the fewest school-based health clinics. See James W. Button, Barbara A. Rienzo, and Ken Wald, "Politics and School Health Reform: Factors Influencing the Success of School-Based Health Care," unpublished research paper, University of Florida, 1999.

67   Quoted in George J. Church, "The Boom Towns," *Time*, June 15, 1987, 17. This section draws on discussions between the author and Gregory D. Squires.

68   F. James Davis, *Who is Black?* (University Park: Pennsylvania State University Press, 1991), pp. 21–22.

69   Davis, *Who is Black?*, p. 22; Shirlee Taylor Haizlip, "Are There Any Truly Black (or White) Americans?" *Los Angeles Times*, February 20, 1994, M3.

70   See Mario de Valdes y Cocom, "Secret Daughter: The Blurred Racial Lines of Famous Families," January, 1999. This is on the Internet at http://www.pbs.org/wgbh/pages/Frontline/shows/secret/famous.

71   Edward Ball, *Slaves in the Family* (New York: Ballantine Books, 1999); Henry Wiencek, *The Hairstons: An American Family in Black and White* (New York: St. Martin's Press, 1999); Mackey Alston's documentary film is *Family Name*, 1998.

72   Lewis R. Gordon, *Bad Faith and Antiblack Racism* (Atlantic Highlands, NJ: Humanities Press, 1995), pp. 183–84. I am indebted here to comments from Bernice McNair Barnett and Hernan Vera.

73   The report is summarized in Carole Collins, "U.N. Report on Minorities: U.S. Not Measuring Up," *National Catholic Reporter*, June 18, 1993, 9.

74   See Joe R. Feagin and Hernan Vera, *White Racism: The Basics* (New York: Routledge, 1995), p. 2.

Chapter Seven

1   Yolanda Flores-Niemann, "Social Ecological Contexts of Prejudice between Hispanics and Blacks," in *Race, Ethnicity, and Nationality in the United States: Toward the Twenty-First Century*, ed. Paul Wong (Boulder, CO: Westview Press, 1999), p. 170.

2   Juan F. Perea, "The Black/White Binary Paradigm of Race: The 'Normal Science' of American Racial Thought," *California Law Review* 85 (October 1997): 1219–21.

3   In the 1600s and early 1700s a number of Native Americans were enslaved in a few colonies like South Carolina.

4   Benjamin Franklin, *Observations Concerning the Increase of Mankind, Peopling of Countries, Etc.* (1751), as quoted in *Benjamin Franklin: A Biography in His Own Words*, ed. Thomas

Fleming (New York: Harper and Row, 1972), pp. 105–106.

5   Michael Omi and Howard Winant, *Racial Formation in the United States* (New York: Routledge, 1986).

6   This estimate assumes a birth rate of about forty live births per thousand persons under slavery for the period. Estimating this birth rate for the varying black population over the period—the black population grew from about a half million in 1776 to about 4.2 million in 1865—one gets about six million births as a conservative estimate. The actual figure may have been larger. I am indebted to Doug Deal for helping me estimate the six million figure.

7   I base this rough calculation on estimates of the crude birth rate for each year in this entire period.

8   See Ellis Cose, *Color-Blind: Seeing Beyond Race in a Race-Obsessed World* (New York: HarperCollins, 1997).

9   Jorge Klor de Alva, Earl Shorris, and Cornel West, "Our Next Race Question: The Uneasiness between Blacks and Latinos," in *Critical White Studies: Looking Behind the Mirror*, eds. Richard Delgado and Jean Stefancic (Philadelphia: Temple University Press, 1997), p. 485.

10   See Vine Deloria, *Custer Died for Your Sins: An Indian Manifesto* (London: Macmillan, 1969), p. 8.

11   See Kenneth O'Reilly, *Nixon's Piano: Presidents and Racial Politics from Washington to Clinton* (New York: Free Press, 1995).

12   Jessie Daniels, *White Lies: Race, Class, Gender, and Sexuality in White Supremacist Discourse* (New York: Routledge, 1997); Jessie Daniels, personal communication with the author, 1999.

13   Richard J. Herrnstein and Charles Murray, *The Bell Curve: Intelligence and Class Structure in American Life* (New York: Free Press, 1994).

14   Joe R. Feagin and Hernan Vera, *White Racism: The Basics* (New York: Routledge, 1995), chapters 7 and 8.

15   Ruth Frankenberg, *White Women, Race Matters* (Minneapolis: University of Minnesota Press, 1993), p. 12.

16   Lewis R. Gordon, *Her Majesty's Other Children: Sketches of Racism from a Neocolonial Age* (Lanham, MD: Rowman and Littlefield, 1997), pp. 5, 53.

17   Frank Wu, "Neither Black nor White: Asian Americans and Affirmative Action," *Boston College Third World Law Journal* 15 (1995): 249–50. See also Janine Young Kim, "Are Asians Black? The Asian-American Civil Rights Agenda and the Contemporary Significance of the Black-White Paradigm," *Yale Law Journal* 108 (June 1999): 2385–2413.

18   Tomás Almaguer, *Racial Fault Lines* (Berkeley

and Los Angeles: University of California
Press, 1994), pp. 7, 210.

19   David R. Roediger, *Towards the Abolition of
Whiteness* (London: Verso, 1994), p. 140.

20   Karen Brodkin, *How The Jews Became White
Folks: And What That Says about Race in
America* (New Brunswick, NJ: Rutgers Univer-
sity Press, 1998), p. 178.

21   Kenneth Clark, *King, Malcolm, Baldwin*
(Hanover, NH: Wesleyan University Press,
1985), p. 15.

22   Joe R. Feagin and Clairece B. Feagin, *Racial
and Ethnic Relations*, 6th ed. (Upper Saddle
River, NJ: Prentice-Hall, 1999), chapter 12.

23   Ronald T. Takaki, *Strangers from a Different
Shore: A History of Asian Americans* (Boston:
Little, Brown, 1989), p. 100. This section also
draws on pp. 99–104.

24   Takaki, *Strangers from a Different Shore*, p. 101;
see also *Gong Lum v. Rice*, 275 U.S. 78, 85
(1927).

25   *People v. Hall*, 4 Cal. 399 (1854). See Takaki,
Strangers from a Different Shore, p. 102; and
Benjamin B. Ringer, *"We the People" and Oth-
ers* (New York: Tavistock, 1983), p. 382.

26   See James W. Loewen, *The Mississippi Chinese: Between Black and White* (Cambridge,
MA: Harvard University Press, 1971), pp. 58–68.

27   Takaki, *Strangers from a Different Shore*, p. 101.

28   Ibid.

29   *Plessy v. Ferguson*, 163 U.S. 537, 561 (1896).

30   Claire Jean Kim, "The Racial Triangulation of
Asian Americans," *Politics and Society* 27
(March 1999): 105–38.

31   Gary Y. Okihiro, *Margins and Mainstreams:
Asians in American History and Culture* (Seat-
tle: University of Washington Press, 1994), p.
34.

32   Miriam Sharma, "Labor Migration and Class
Formation among the Filipinos in Hawaii,
1940–1946," in *Labor Immigration under Capitalism*, eds. Lucie Cheng and Edna Bonacich
(Berkeley and Los Angeles: University of California Press, 1984), pp. 583–93.

33   Edward K. Strong, Jr., *The Second-Generation
Japanese Problem* (Stanford, CA: Stanford University Press, 1934), p. 133.

34   George Frederickson, *The Black Image in the
White Mind* (Hanover, NH: Wesleyan University Press, 1971), p. 305.

35   *In re Ah Yup*, 1 F.cas. 223 (C.C.D.Cal. 1878).

36   Ian F. Haney Lopez, *White By Law: The Legal
Construction of Race* (New York: New York
University Press, 1996), pp. 1–7, 203–27.

37   See Mario de Valdes y Cocom, "Secret Daughter: The Blurred Racial Lines of Famous Families," January, 1999. This is on the internet at
http://www.pbs.org/wgbh/pages/frontline/shows
/secret/famous.

38   James J. Scheurich and Michelle D. Young,

"Coloring Epistemologies: Are Our Research
Epistemologies Racially Biased?" *Educational
Researcher* 26 (May 1997): 7.

39   John C. Calhoun, quoted in Frederickson, *The
Black Image in the White Mind*, p. 136.

40   Abel G. Rubio, *Stolen Heritage* (Austin, TX:
Eakin Press, 1986).

41   Joan Moore, *Mexican Americans*, 2nd ed.
(Englewood Cliffs, NJ: Prentice-Hall, 1976), p.
108.

42   See Feagin and Feagin, *Racial and Ethnic
Relations*, pp. 306–20.

43   Lopez, *White By Law*, p. 61.

44   Allen, *The Invention of the White Race*, p. 27.

45   See Feagin and Feagin, *Racial and Ethnic
Relations*, pp. 300–301.

46   Feagin and Feagin, *Racial and Ethnic Relations*, pp. 304–306; Nestor Rodriguez, personal
communication with the author.

47   Oliver C. Cox, *Caste, Class, and Race: A Study
in Social Dynamics* (New York: Doubleday,
1948), p. 349.

48   Roberto Suro, *Strangers among Us: How
Latino Immigration is Transforming America*
(New York: Knopf, 1998), pp. 81–82.

49   See Dinesh D'Souza, *The End of Racism: Principles for a Multiracial Society* (New York: Free
Press, 1995), p. 300.

50   John Liu, personal communication with the
author.

51   Nathan Glazer, *We Are All Multiculturalists
Now* (Cambridge, MA: Harvard University
Press, 1997), p. 149.

52   Andrew Hacker, *Two Nations: Black and
White, Separate, Hostile, Unequal* (New York:
Scribner's, 1992), p. 16.

53   See Michael Lind, *The Next American Nation:
The New Nationalism and the Fourth American
Revolution* (New York: Free Press, 1995), pp.
115–16. I am indebted here to some comments
on an earlier draft by Claire Jean King.

54   General Social Survey, National Opinion
Research Center, Chicago, Illinois, 1990.

55   Gordon, *Her Majesty's Other Children*, p. 69.

56   Leland Saito, personal communication with
the author, fall, 1998. See also Milton M. Gordon, *Assimilation in American Life* (New York:
Oxford University Press, 1964).

57   See Julie Montgomery, "Cyber Brides: The
Internet and the Asian Commodity," unpublished Master's paper, University of Florida,
1999.

58   Peter Brimelow, *Alien Nation: Common Sense
about America's Immigration Disaster* (New
York: Random House, 1995), pp. 10, 59.

59   See Samuel P. Huntington, "The Erosion of
American National Interests," *Foreign Affairs*
(September/October, 1997): 28.

60   The study was by Doug Daniels. I draw here
on the summary in Maurice Berger, *White*

Lies: Race and the Myths of Whiteness (New York: Farrar, Straus, and Giroux, 1999), pp. 41–42.

61   Tatcho Mindiola, Nestor Rodriguez, and Yolanda Flores-Niemann, "Intergroup Relations between African Americans and Hispanics in Harris County," unpublished research report, Center for Mexican American Studies, University of Houston, 1996; U.S. Bureau of the Census, *1997 Community Survey Profile— Houston City*, 1997; http://www.census.gov.

62   Min Zhou, *Chinatown: The Socioeconomic Potential of an Urban Enclave* (Philadelphia: Temple University Press, 1992); Pyong Gap Min, ed., *Asian Americans: Contemporary Trends and Issues* (Thousand Oaks, CA: Sage, 1995).

63   Lawrence Bobo and Susan A. Suh, "Surveying Racial Discrimination: Analyses from a Multiethnic Labor Market," unpublished research report, Department of Sociology, University of California, Los Angeles, August 1, 1995; Paul Ong, ed., *Economic Diversity: Issues and Policies* (Los Angeles: Leadership Education for Asian Pacifics, 1994); Cliff Cheng, "Are Asian American Employees a Model Minority or Just a Minority?" *Journal of Applied Behavioral Science* 33 (September 1997): 277–90.

64   U.S. Commission on Civil Rights, *Civil Rights Issues Facing Asian Americans in the 1990s* (Washington, DC: U.S. Government Printing Office, 1992).

65   Leland Saito, personal communication with the author, fall, 1998. See Leland Saito, *Race and Politics: Asian Americans, Latinos, and Whites in a Los Angeles Suburb* (Urbana: University of Illinois Press, 1998), pp. 39–54.

66   See Bobo and Suh, "Surveying Racial Discrimination."

67   "Hate Crimes Rise in Orange County," *The Race Relations Reporter*, May 15, 1999, 1; Lena H. Sun, "Anti-Asian American Incidents Rising, Civil Rights Group Says: Organization Executives to Meet with Reno Today," *Washington Post*, September 9, 1997, A2.

68   Leland Saito, personal communication with the author, fall, 1998.

69   "When You're Smiling: The Deadly Legacy of Internment," produced and directed by Janice D. Tanaka, Visual Communications, 1999.

70   Interview by the author, fall, 1998. Used by permission.

71   Karen Pyke, "Vietnamese Parents and their Children: Pressures of Assimilation," unpublished research paper, University of Florida, 1999.

72   Nestor Rodriguez, personal communication.

73   Nestor Rodriguez, e-mail communication, fall 1998.

74   See Yen Lee Espiritu, *Asian American Panethnicity*, (Philadelphia: Temple University Press, 1992).

75   Charles R. Lawrence III, "Race, Multiculturalism, and the Jurisprudence of Transformation," *Stanford Law Review* 47 (May, 1995): 829.

76   Ibid.

77   Suro, *Strangers Among Us*, pp. 251–252.

78   Ibid., p. 254.

79   Tyrone Foreman and Nadia Kim, "Beyond Black and White: Asian Americans' Attitudes toward Blacks and Latinos," unpublished research report, University of Michigan, 1999, pp. 17–23.

80   Saito, *Race and Politics*, p. 59. See also David Gutierrez, *Walls and Mirrors: Mexican Americans, Mexican Immigrants, and the Politics of Ethnicity* (Berkeley: University of California Press, 1995).

81   See Cose, *Color-Blind*.

Chapter Eight

1   Advisory Board on Race, *One America in the 21st Century: Forging a New Future* (Washington, DC: U.S. Government Printing Office, 1998).

2   Oliver C. Cox, *Caste, Class, and Race: A Study in Social Dynamics* (New York: Doubleday, 1948), p. 571.

3   Derrick Bell, *Faces at the Bottom of the Well* (New York: Basic Books, 1992), p. 12; italics omitted.

4   See John Briggs and F. David Peat, *Turbulent Mirror: An Illustrated Guide to Chaos Theory and the Science of Wholeness* (New York: Harper & Row, 1990), p. 177.

5   Steve H. Murdock, *An America Challenged: Population Change and the Future of the United States* (Boulder, CO: Westview Press, 1995), pp. 33–47.

6   See Joe R. Feagin, "The Future of U.S. Society in an Era of Racism, Group Segregation, and Demographic Revolution," in *Sociology for the 21st Century: Continuities and Cutting Edges*, ed. Janet Abu-Lughod (Chicago: University of Chicago Press, 1999).

7   I am indebted to Nancy DiThomaso for helping me sharpen this point.

8   Bill Moyers, *A World of Ideas*, ed. Betty S. Flowers (New York: Doubleday, 1989), p. 283.

9   William H. Frey, "Domestic and Immigrant Migrants: Where Do They Go?" *Current*, January 22, 1997, n.p.

10   Kevin Sack, "South's Embrace of G.O.P. is Near a Turning Point," *New York Times*, March 16, 1998, A1.

11   I am indebted to Chandler Davidson for this point.

12   Kevin Phillips, *The Emerging Republican Majority* (New Rochelle, NY: Arlington House, 1969).

13   Southern Poverty Law Center, "Sharks in the Mainstream," *Intelligence Report*, Winter 1999, 21–26.

14   Leonard Zeskind, "Redefining America: A Longtime Analyst of the Extreme Right Considers Our Situation and the Choices We Face as a Nation," *Intelligence Report*, Spring 1999, 41.

15   Southern Poverty Law Center, "The Year in Hate," *Intelligence Report*, Winter 1999, 7–8.

16   See Bonnie L. Mitchell and Joe R. Feagin, "America's Racial-ethnic Cultures: Opposition within a Mythical Melting Pot," in *Toward the Multicultural University*, eds. Benjamin Bowser, Terry Jones, and Gale Auletta-Young (Westport, CT: Praeger, 1995), pp. 65–86.

17   See Shelby Steele, *The Content of Our Character: A New Vision of Race in America* (New York: St. Martin's Press, 1990).

18   Herbert Aptheker, *American Negro Slave Revolts* (New York: International Publishers, 1952), pp. 162–63.

19   Merton L. Dillon, *Slavery Attacked: Southern Slaves and Their Allies, 1619–1865* (Baton Rouge: Louisiana State University Press, 1990), p. 269.

20   See Robin D. G. Kelley, *Race Rebels: Culture, Politics, and the Black Working Class* (New York: Free Press, 1994).

21   See Aldon Morris, *The Origins of the Civil Rights Movement: Black Communities Organizing for Change* (New York: Free Press, 1984); and Joe R. Feagin and Clairece B. Feagin, *Racial and Ethnic Relations*, 6th ed. (Upper Saddle River, NJ: Prentice-Hall, 1999), chapter 8.

22   I draw quotes from this federal law as reprinted in Benjamin B. Ringer, *"We the People" and Others* (New York: Tavistock, 1983), pp. 311–30.

23   *Brown v. Board of Education of Topeka*, 347 U.S. 483, 493 (1954); *Griggs v. Duke Power Co.*, 401 U.S. 424 (1971).

24   Roy Brooks, *Rethinking the American Race Problem* (Berkeley and Los Angeles: University of California, 1990), p. 105.

25   See, for example, Carol Amoruso, "We ACT for Environmental Justice," *Third Force*, November/December 1997, 18–21.

26   Linda Jones, "Closing the Books on Slavery? African American Groups Seek Reparations on Ancestors' Behalf," *Dallas Morning News*, June 15, 1996, 1C.

27   Isabel Wilkerson, "Middle-Class but Not Feeling Equal, Blacks Reflect on Los Angeles Strife," *New York Times*, May 4, 1993, A20.

28   Roy Brooks, *Integration or Separation? A Strategy for Racial Equality* (Cambridge, MA: Harvard University Press, 1996).

29   Marimba Ani, *Yurugu: An African-Centered Critique of European Cultural Thought and Behavior* (Trenton, NJ: Africa World Press, 1994), p. 570. See also Molefi Kete Asante, *The Afrocentric Idea* (Philadelphia: Temple University Press, 1987).

30   Frantz Fanon, *Toward the African Revolution* (New York: Grove Press, 1967), p. 103.

31   See Joe Feagin and Melvin Sikes, *Living With Racism: The Black Middle-Class Experience* (Boston: Beacon Press, 1994); Yanick St. Jean and Joe R. Feagin, *Double Burden: Black Women and Everyday Racism* (Armonk, NY: M. E. Sharpe, 1998); and Kesho Yvonne Scott, *The Habit of Surviving: Black Women's Strategies for Life* (New Brunswick, NJ: Rutgers University Press, 1991).

32   Feagin and Sikes, *Living With Racism*, pp. 286–87.

33   Ibid.

34   David Walker, *Appeal to the Coloured Citizens of the World*, ed. Charles M. Wiltse (New York: Hill and Wang, 1965), p. 75.

35   Anna Julia Cooper, *The Voice of Anna Julia Cooper*, eds. Charles Lemert and Esme Bhan (Lanham, MD: Rowman and Littlefield, 1998), p. 207.

36   Ibid., p. 212.

37   Martin Luther King, Jr., *Where Do We Go from Here? Chaos or Community* (New York: Bantam Books, 1967), p. 9.

38   Ibid.

39   See Howard Schuman, Charlotte Steeh, and Lawrence Bobo, *Racial Attitudes in America: Trends and Interpretations* (Cambridge, MA: Harvard University Press, 1985), pp. 182–89; and Mary R. Jackman, *The Velvet Glove: Paternalism and Conflict in Gender, Class, and Race Relations* (Berkeley: University of California Press, 1994), pp. 231–41.

40   Cited in Richard L. Berke, "The 1994 Campaign; Survey Finds Voters in U.S. Rootless and Self-Absorbed," *New York Times*, September 21, 1994, A21.

41   See the MTV poll cited in *The Race Relations Reporter*, February 15, 1998, 1.

42   Ralph Ellison, *Shadow and Act* (New York: Random House, 1964), p. 304.

43   Georg Lukacs, *History and Class Consciousness*, trans. Rodney Livingstone (Cambridge, MA: MIT Press, 1971 [1968]), p. 67.

44   Walter A. Jackson, *Gunnar Myrdal and America's Conscience: Social Engineering and Racial Liberalism, 1938–1987* (Chapel Hill: University of North Carolina Pres, 1990), pp. 11–15, 369–70.

45   Gunnar Myrdal, *An American Dilemma*, vol. 2 (New York: McGraw-Hill, 1964), p. 929.

46   Peter Steinfels, *The Neoconservatives: The Men Who Are Changing America's Politics* (New York: Touchstone, 1979), p. 6.

47   Irving Kristol, "Thoughts on Equality and Egalitarianism," in *Income Distribution*, ed. Colin D. Campbell (Washington, DC: American Enterprise Institute, 1977), p. 42.

48   Daniel Bell, *The Coming of Post-Industrial Society* (New York: Basic Books, 1973), p. 453.

49   Richard J. Herrnstein and Charles Murray, *The Bell Curve: Intelligence and Class Structure in American Life* (New York: Free Press, 1994).

50   Marc Bendick Jr., Mary Lou Egan, and Suzanne Lofhjelm, *The Documentation and Evaluation of Anti-Discrimination Training in the United States* (Geneva: International Labour Office, 1998), p. 17.

51   Cheryl I. Harris, "Whiteness as Property," *Harvard Law Review* 106 (June 1993): 1707.

52   *Regents of the University of California v. Bakke*, 438 U.S. 265 (1978).

53   Charles C. Moskos and John S. Butler, *All That We Can Be: Black Leadership and Racial Integration the Army Way* (New York: Basic Books, 1996), pp. 5–8.

54   Ibid., pp. 2, 74.

55   Jacquelyn Scarville et al., *Armed Forces Equal Opportunity Survey* (Arlington, VA: Defense Manpower Data Center, 1999), pp. 46–50, 150–53.

56   Theodor W. Adorno et al., *The Authoritarian Personality* (New York: Harper, 1950), p. 4.

57   Patricia G. Devine, "Stereotypes and Prejudice: Their Automatic and Controlled Components," *Journal of Personality and Social Psychology* 56 (1989): 15.

58   James W. Loewen, *Lies My Teacher Told Me: Everything Your American History Textbook Got Wrong* (New York: The New Press, 1995), p. 163.

59   Sharon Rush prefers the terms "transformative insight" or "transformative love." See Sharon Rush, *Loving Across the Color Line* (Lanham, MD: Rowman and Littlefield, 2000); and Jane Lazarre, *Beyond the Whiteness of Whiteness* (Durham, NC: Duke University Press, 1996).

60   Tom W. Smith, "Measuring Inter-Racial Friendships: Experimental Comparisons," GSS Methodological Report, National Opinion Research Center, University of Chicago, no. 91 (1999).

61   Cedric J. Robinson, *Black Movements in America* (New York: Routledge, 1997), p. 63.

62   See Nathan Rutstein, *Racism: Unraveling the Fear* (Washington, DC: The Global Classroom, 1993), pp. 225–28.

63   Eileen O'Brien, *Whites Doing Antiracism: Discourse, Practice, Emotion and Organizations*, doctoral dissertation, University of Florida, 1999; Michael Omi, "(E)racism: Emergent Practices of Anti-Racist Organizatons," paper presented at American Sociological Association Meetings, San Francisco, CA, August, 1998.

64   *New Party News* (Winter 1999): 10.

65   An earlier version of this argument appears in Joe R. Feagin and Hernan Vera, *White Racism: The Basics* (New York: Routledge, 1995), pp. 188–91.

66   W. E. B. Du Bois, *John Brown* (New York: International Publishers, 1962), pp. 263–64.

67   Ibid., pp 264–265. I use modern spelling here.

68   Brooks, *Integration or Separation*, p. 115.

69   Richard Delgado, *The Coming Race War?* (New York: New York University Press, 1996), p. 108.

70   Martin J. Katz, "The Economics of Discrimination: The Three Fallacies of Croson," *Yale Law Journal* 100 (January 1991): 1052.

71   Lord Anthony Gifford, "The Legal Basis of the Claim for Reparations," paper presented to First Pan-African Congress on Reparations, Abuja, Federal Republic of Nigeria, April 27–29, 1993.

72   Ali A. Mazrui, "Who Should Pay for Slavery? Reparations to Africa," *World Press Review* 8 (August, 1993): 22.

73   Andrew Kull, "Rationalizing Restitution," *California Law Review* 83 (October 1995): 1191–98.

74   *Larry Williams, et al. v. The City Of New Orleans, et al.*, 729 F.2d 1554, 1577 (1984).

75   Delgado, *The Coming Race War?*, p. 103.

76   Rhonda V. Magee, "The Master's Tools, from the Bottom Up: Responses to African-American Reparations Theory in Mainstream and Outsider Remedies Discourse," *Virginia Law Review* 79 (May 1993): 886; Charles Sumner, quoted in Magee, "The Master's Tools, from the Bottom Up," p. 887.

77   Martin Luther King, Jr., *Why We Can't Wait* (New York: Signet Books, 1963).

78   Gifford, "The Legal Basis of the Claim for Reparations."

79   Kevin Merida, "Did Freedom Alone Pay a Nation's Debt," *The Washington Post*, November 23 1999, C1.

80   Gideon Sjoberg et al., "Ethics, Human Rights and Sociological Inquiry: Genocide, Politicide and Other Issues of Organizational Power," *American Sociologist* 26 (Spring 1995): 11–13.

81   United Nations, *The United Nations and Human Rights, 1945–1995* (New York: United Nations Department of Public Information, 1995), pp. 33, 153–55, 219–25.

82   Hurst Hannum, "The Status and Future of the Customary International Law of Human Rights: The Status of the Universal Declaration of Human Rights in National and International Law," *Georgia Journal of International and Comparative Law* 25 (Fall 1995/Winter 1996): 287–320.

83   See International Human Rights Law Group, *Racial Discrimination* (Washington, DC: IHRLG, n.d.).

84   Quoted in Willhelm, *Black in a White America*, p. 352.

85   Ani, *Yurugu*, p. 540.

86   Sandra Harding, "Taking Responsibility for our Own Gender, Race, Class: Transforming Sci-

ence and the Social Studies of Science," *Rethinking Marxism* (Fall 1989): 14.

87   See Melvin M. Leiman, *Political Economy of Racism* (London: Pluto Press, 1993), pp. 7–9, 313.

88   See W. E. B. Du Bois, *Black Reconstruction in America 1860–180* (New York: Atheneum, 1992 [1935]), p. 30.

89   On racial lines in the feminist movement, see Louise Michele Newman, *White Women's Rights: The Racial Origins of Feminism in the United States* (New York: Oxford University Press, 1999), pp. 179–85.

90   Michael Albert et al., *Liberating Theory* (Boston: South End Press, 1986), p. 2.

91   Paul G. Lauren, *Power and Prejudice: The Politics and Diplomacy of Racial Discrimination* (Boulder, CO: Westview Press, 1988), p. 285.

92   Ben Agger, *Critical Social Theories: An Introduction* (Boulder, CO: Westview, 1998), p. 9.

93   Jean-François Lyotard, "The Other's Rights," in *On Human Rights: The Oxford Amnesty Lectures*, eds. Stephen Shute and Susan Hurley (New York: Basic Books, 1993), p. 136.

94   Frances Lee Ansley, "Stirring the Ashes: Race, Class and the Future of Civil Rights Scholarship," *Cornell Law Review* 74 (September 1989): 1002.

95   Quoted in Lauren, *Power And Prejudice*, p. 288.

index of names